# Praise for *Feeling Great*

"BRILLIANT AND POWERFUL!!! This book is pure gold and a breath of fresh air that provides hope and tools to achieve joy and enlightenment. Dr. Burns conveys the message that your suffering as well as your negative thoughts and feelings are not symptoms of mental disorder but instead are the expression of what is most awesome and beautiful about you. Warning: This is not a book in which you just read page after page and expect change in your life. You must do the valuable exercises in order to transform your life radically and rapidly. If you are ready to roll up your sleeves and get to work, this is an outstanding book for you!"

— **Sara Verduzco Shane, LMFT**

"This latest work of Dr. Burns is absolutely groundbreaking! As a therapist in private practice now regularly utilizing these methods, I am witnessing my patients improve in lasting ways, and at a faster rate than ever before! In a delightful twist, applying these tools to my own life has led me to personal enlightenment that I otherwise never expected was possible. Dr. Burns is a genius, and this latest work is a true gift to all."

— **Sarah Lionetti Hester, LMFT**

"Nothing short of amazing! Rapid, effective, drug-free treatment for anxiety and depression has never been so accessible as it is now in Feeling Great. This book actually achieves the ambitious goal of making extremely powerful and effective therapy available, accessible and usable to the general public."

— **Michael D. Greenwald, PhD**, Licensed Clinical Psychologist

"A must for anyone with depression and anxiety. *Feeling Great* describes in plain, clear language how we can all live happier, healthier and more successful lives. Dr. Burns is a visionary in the field of mental health and a genius at helping people overcome depression and anxiety."

— **Matthew May, MD**

"I'm loving *Feeling Great*. It's an amazing book. I would describe it as *Feeling Good* times ten!"

— **Christian Anderson**

"*Feeling Great* is rich with tools to transform feeling; feelings of joy and confidence, no matter your life st.

— **Rhonda Barovsky, LCSW, PsyD**

# Feeling Great

## The Revolutionary New Treatment for Depression and Anxiety

By David D. Burns, MD

*Best-Selling Author of Feeling Good: The New Mood Therapy*

# DISCLAIMER

The ideas and techniques in this book are not intended as a substitution for consultation with a qualified health professional. The names and identifying details of the individuals in this book have been disguised extensively, and any resemblance to any person, living or dead, is purely coincidental.

When I present a vignette (disguised) of someone who is struggling with depression or anxiety, or when I give an example of how a particular technique works, I typically select a positive and encouraging example that shows how that individual recovered. And frequently, I present an example of someone who improved substantially and fairly rapidly. This has the greatest potential for learning and can help create hope, which is essential for healing.

However, you should not take this as a guarantee that the same techniques will be effective for you or for a friend or loved one. We are all unique, and we all respond to different approaches. In addition, while the techniques I describe in this book are powerful, not everyone who reads this book or who seeks professional treatment will experience rapid and dramatic changes.

Some problems that are more severe will require a longer course of treatment. I have never given up on a patient and hope you will never give up on yourself. This philosophy has proven to be tremendously rewarding because a path forward always seems to emerge if you stick with it.

Library of Congress Cataloging-in-Publication Data

Identifiers: LCCN 2020016121 (print) | LCCN 2020016122 (ebook) | ISBN 9781683732884 (hardback) | ISBN 9781683732891 (ebook)
Subjects: LCSH: Depression, Mental—Treatment—Popular works. | Anxiety—Treatment—Popular works. | Cognitive therapy—Popular works.
Classification: LCC RC537 .B873 2020 (print) | LCC RC537 (ebook) | DDC 616.85/27—dc23
LC record available at https://lccn.loc.gov/2020016121
LC ebook record available at https://lccn.loc.gov/2020016122

Published by
Bridge City Books, an imprint of PESI Publishing, Inc.
3839 White Ave
Eau Claire, WI 54703

Cover and interior design: Amy Rubenzer and Bookmasters
Editing: Jenessa Jackson, PhD

ISBN: 9781962305396 (print)
ISBN: 9781962305402 (ePUB)
ISBN: 9781962305419 (ePDF)

Bridge City Books

# Dedication

This book is dedicated to Obie, my best friend and teacher, who I sadly lost during the fall of 2016, and to Rob, my number one fan!

# Table of Contents

Acknowledgments . . . . . . . . . . . . . . . . . . . . . . . . . . . . . . . . . . . . . . . . . . ix

Introduction: Then and Now. . . . . . . . . . . . . . . . . . . . . . . . . . . . . . . . . . . xi

**I. How to Turn Depression and Anxiety into Joy**

1. How Are You Feeling?. . . . . . . . . . . . . . . . . . . . . . . . . . . . . . . . . . . . .3

2. Feeling Great in 15 Minutes—The CliffsNotes Version . . . . . . . . . . . . .15

3. Why Do We Get Stuck in Bad Moods, Relationship Conflicts, or Habits and Addictions? How Can We Get Unstuck?. . . . . . . . . . . . . . . .35

4. Karen's Story: "I'm a Bad Mom.". . . . . . . . . . . . . . . . . . . . . . . . . . . . .59

5. Melanie's Story: "She'll Tell Others Who Will Judge Me!". . . . . . . . . . . .91

6. High-Speed Treatment—Is It Possible? Desirable? Or Just Fool's Gold? . . . 121

7. Mark's Story: "I've Been a Failure as a Father." . . . . . . . . . . . . . . . . . . .127

8. Marilyn's Story: "I've Got Stage 4 Lung Cancer." . . . . . . . . . . . . . . . . .141

9. Sara's Story: "I'm Afraid of Germs!". . . . . . . . . . . . . . . . . . . . . . . . . . .157

10. How to Change the Way You Feel: Part 1—Your Daily MoJo (Daily Mood Journal) . . . . . . . . . . . . . . . . . . . . . . . . . . . . . . . . . . . . .169

11. How to Change the Way You Feel: Part 2—The Great Escape . . . . . . . .201

**II. How to Crush Distorted Thoughts**

12. All-or-Nothing Thinking . . . . . . . . . . . . . . . . . . . . . . . . . . . . . . . . . .209

13. Overgeneralization . . . . . . . . . . . . . . . . . . . . . . . . . . . . . . . . . . . . . . .217

14. Mental Filtering and Discounting the Positive. . . . . . . . . . . . . . . . . . . .227

15. Jumping to Conclusions—Mind Reading. . . . . . . . . . . . . . . . . . . . . . .235

16. Fortune Telling: Part 1—Hopelessness . . . . . . . . . . . . . . . . . . . . . . . . .247

17. Fortune Telling: Part 2—Anxiety . . . . . . . . . . . . . . . . . . . . . . . . . . . . .269

18. Magnification and Minimization . . . . . . . . . . . . . . . . . . . . . . . . . . . . .293

19. Emotional Reasoning . . . . . . . . . . . . . . . . . . . . . . . . . . . . . . . . . . . . .303

20. Should Statements. . . . . . . . . . . . . . . . . . . . . . . . . . . . . . . . . . . . . .315

21. Labeling . . . . . . . . . . . . . . . . . . . . . . . . . . . . . . . . . . . . . . . . . . . .327

22. Self-Blame and Other-Blame. . . . . . . . . . . . . . . . . . . . . . . . . . . . . . .335

### III. The Spiritual/Philosophical Dimension: The Four "Great Deaths" of the Self

23. Do You Have a Self? Do You Need One?. . . . . . . . . . . . . . . . . . . . . . .357

24. Are Some People *More* Worthwhile? Are You One of Them?. . . . . . . . .365

25. Are Some People *Less* Worthwhile? Are You One of Them?. . . . . . . . . .375

26. Let's Be Specific: What Are Your Flaws?. . . . . . . . . . . . . . . . . . . . . . .383

27. How to Join the Grateful Dead! . . . . . . . . . . . . . . . . . . . . . . . . . . . .391

### IV. Relapse Prevention Training

28. How Are You Feeling Now?. . . . . . . . . . . . . . . . . . . . . . . . . . . . . . . .409

29. Feeling Great for Good!. . . . . . . . . . . . . . . . . . . . . . . . . . . . . . . . . . .413

### V. Research Update: Does Science Support TEAM-CBT?

30. TEAM-CBT and the Art of Micro-Neurosurgery:
Special Guest Chapter by Dr. Mark Noble . . . . . . . . . . . . . . . . . . . . .425

31. What Causes Depression and Anxiety?
What's the Best Way to Treat It? . . . . . . . . . . . . . . . . . . . . . . . . . . . .441

### VI. Additional Resources

32. Incredible Free Stuff for You!. . . . . . . . . . . . . . . . . . . . . . . . . . . . . . .469

33. Fifty Ways to Untwist Your Thinking . . . . . . . . . . . . . . . . . . . . . . . . .475

About the Author. . . . . . . . . . . . . . . . . . . . . . . . . . . . . . . . . . . . . . . . . . .501

Index . . . . . . . . . . . . . . . . . . . . . . . . . . . . . . . . . . . . . . . . . . . . . . . . . . .503

# Acknowledgments

I would like to thank many dear colleagues who have helped enormously in the development of TEAM-CBT and in the teaching of my Tuesday evening training group at Stanford, including Jill Levitt, PhD; Matthew May, MD; Helen Yeni-Komshian, MD; and Daniele Levy, PhD.

Thanks also to my esteemed hosts on the weekly *Feeling Good* podcasts, Drs. Fabrice Nye and Rhonda Barovsky. You may already be a fan of our show, which is free. If you are not familiar with it, check it out on my website (www.feelinggood.com), iTunes, YouTube, or my public Facebook page. It can accelerate your learning if you are a therapist, a patient, or simply a member of the general public interested in self-help for depression and anxiety.

I am also grateful to Mike Christensen who has appeared many times on my weekly podcasts. Mike offers TEAM-CBT teletherapy throughout Canada and offers superb online TEAM-CBT classes for mental health professionals throughout the world.

I have *many* fabulous colleagues to thank, including the entire group at the Feeling Good Institute in Mountain View, California, as well as several colleagues who provided invaluable help by providing feedback on portions of this manuscript, including Zane Pierce, Daisy Grewal, John Graham, Marilyn Coffee, and Stephen Pfleiderer.

A special thanks to Drs. Brandon Vance, Mark Noble, and Daniele Levy who went through the entire book and provided helpful feedback. I also want to give a shout-out to Linda Jackson, my publisher at PESI, and Jenessa Jackson, the editor of this book. It has been a joy to work with both of you. I am extremely grateful for your brilliant technical guidance and also for your warmth, positivity, and fantastic TEAM work!

I would also like to thank many individuals who have contributed enormously to this book by giving me permission to share their intensely personal stories. Although I have disguised their identities, their stories are real, and they have helped me bring my message to life in an engaging and inspiring way.

Finally, I would like to thank my beloved wife, Melanie, for her love, support, and patience, and for her incredibly awesome and honest guidance and editing of this book!

# Introduction:
# Then and Now

When we were living in Philadelphia, my wife and I had some carpentry and painting done on our house, which took several weeks. On the last day, Frank, our carpenter, was on his knees at our front door, finishing up the work. As I was walking through the entryway, I noticed that he looked discouraged, so I told Frank that my wife and I had really appreciated the fabulous work he'd done to make our house more beautiful and that we were sad that today was his last day.

Frank thanked me and wondered if he could ask me a question. He said he'd heard that I was some kind of doctor and didn't want to impose. I told him I'd be happy to answer his question if I could. Frank said he was feeling down and wondered if I knew anything about depression or if he needed a medication of some kind.

My heart went out to him because he'd been working so hard and had done such great work for us. I told Frank that depression usually results from the way we think about things and asked if he'd noticed any negative thoughts floating across his mind when he was feeling down. What was he thinking? What was he telling himself?

He said he was thinking about the fact that he was getting old. He was telling himself that his body wouldn't be able to keep up the same pace for much longer, and he was worried that he might not have enough money to support himself and his wife if he retired. He explained that carpentry was all he'd done since graduation from high school. Now that he was in his sixties, it dawned on him that he'd never accomplished anything really meaningful or significant in his life. He looked meek and humble and seemed on the verge of tears. I felt sad for him.

I asked Frank if I could try something that might be helpful called the double standard technique. The basis for this technique is that most of us operate on a double standard. When we're upset or fall short of our goals, we tend to beat up on ourselves with harsh criticisms. But if we were talking to a dear friend with the same exact problem, we'd do so in a far more compassionate, supportive, and realistic way. Once you're aware of this, you can ask yourself if you'd be willing to talk to yourself in the same compassionate way you'd talk to a dear friend. No single method works for everyone, but this one is often effective.

I asked Frank to imagine he was talking to a good friend who was very similar to him, like a long-lost identical twin or a clone. This imaginary friend is also a carpenter who's getting close to retirement, and he's been doing carpentry ever since high school. Then I asked Frank what he'd say to this man, if the man confided that he was also feeling depressed in much the same way Frank was. Would he say this to his friend?:

*Oh, you're getting old, and your body won't be able to keep up anymore. But if you retire, then you'll run out of money and you won't be able to support your wife and family. You've never accomplished anything meaningful during your life either.*

At first, Frank didn't get it. He said that he *would* say that to his friend because it was the truth.

I said, "Okay, I just want to make sure we're on the same page. Let's imagine that I'm your friend. My name is David, but aside from that I'm just like you. I'm also a carpenter, and all the details of my life are the same as yours. In fact, you can imagine that I'm like a long-lost identical twin. Go ahead and say those things to me. Tell me that I'm getting old and my body can't keep up anymore, that my life has been meaningless, and so forth.

Frank looked puzzled and was quiet for about ten or fifteen seconds. Then he said, "Doc, I don't think I could say things like that to a friend."

I asked, "Why not?"

Frank explained that it would be cruel to belittle a friend who you cared about and that those statements didn't sound fair or even valid.

I asked Frank what he would say to David, his friend.

Frank said that he'd say something like this:

*Although you are getting older, you're still capable of doing some really good work. If you cut back a bit, which you deserve, you'll still be quite productive. And gosh, look at the beautiful work you just did on this house. The owners seem thrilled, and the work you did looks great!*

*And besides, even if you decide to retire at some point, you have a decent re-tirement plan, so you and your wife will be fine. Finally, and perhaps most important, think of all the joy you've brought to the people you've worked for during all these years. You've never once had a complaint, you've always done good work at a fair price, and you've never cheated anyone, not even once. That's* definitely *meaningful. You have a lot to be proud of!*

I told Frank that what he just said sounded helpful and asked if it was true. Or was he just saying that to shine me on?

He said it was *absolutely* true.

Then I asked, "So if those statements are true about me, and I'm exactly like you, then would those statements be true about you as well?"

He paused for a moment and then said, "I guess those statements would be true about me too. You're right!"

I explained that the reason he'd been depressed was not that he was get-ting older, but because of the negative way he'd been thinking about things. The harsh messages he'd been giving himself would make anyone unhappy. I asked Frank if he'd be willing to talk to himself the same way he'd talk to a dear friend who was much like him.

Suddenly it was like somebody turned on a light bulb in Frank's brain, and he exclaimed, "Oh, so the problem is just the way I'm thinking? My nega-tive thoughts?"

I said, "Exactly!"

He said, "Wow, I'm feeling so much better! I get it! Thank you, Doc!"

I explained that the type of treatment we'd just done is called cognitive therapy because you learn to change your thoughts, or cognitions. I added that the cool thing was that he'd just completed his "treatment" in about five minutes and wouldn't be needing any pills.

I just LOVE it when that happens—it's one of the greatest thrills of my life. That is why I wrote *Feeling Good: The New Mood Therapy* nearly forty years ago. I wanted to let people know three things:

1. You FEEL the way you THINK. In other words, your negative emo-tions, like depression and anxiety, result from your thoughts and not from the circumstances of your life.

2. The negative thoughts that upset you are nearly always distorted and twisted. They're just not true. Depression and anxiety are the world's oldest cons.

3. When you can change the way you THINK, you can change the way you FEEL.

And here's what's really important: The change can happen rapidly, even if your feelings of depression and anxiety are severe.

A few days ago, I received this fantastic email from a dear colleague, Dr. Robert Schachter:

> *I want to share an experience that almost made me cry. A woman from Nebraska had tracked me down on the internet to treat her mid-20s daughter who was living in New York. She said that she had been profoundly affected by* Feeling Good *shortly after her daughter was born.*
>
> *She went on to say that when her daughter was in preschool, the nursery schoolteacher was fired and had been very distraught. She had liked this woman and felt very bad for her. So she went to her house, but the woman would not come to the door. She then went home and left a copy of* Feeling Good *on the woman's doorstep.*
>
> *Their paths diverged, but sometime later she bumped into her. The woman came up to her and said, "I just want to thank you. I want you to know that you saved my life! My father committed suicide and the day that you came by, I was planning my own suicide. That book saved my life. Thank you." Then my patient's mother said, "God Bless Dr. Burns!"*

I've received tens of thousands of similar testimonials from individuals with depression who have read *Feeling Good*. At first, this was surprising because I had never thought of *Feeling Good* as a self-help book. I was just sharing my excitement about what was then a brand new, drug-free treatment for depression called cognitive behavioral therapy (CBT), pioneered by Drs. Albert Ellis and Aaron Beck. I never anticipated that the book itself might have antidepressant effects all on its own.

The antidepressant effects of *Feeling Good* have since been confirmed in many published studies. For example, Dr. Forrest Scogin from the University of Alabama reported that if you simply hand a copy of this book to individuals seeking treatment for moderate to severe depression, 65% of them will recover or improve substantially within four weeks without any other treatment. In addition, two- and three-year follow-up studies have revealed that these individuals continue to improve on their own without psychotherapy or antidepressant medications.

Many other researchers have since confirmed that the effects of *Feeling Good* "bibliotherapy" (reading therapy) are comparable to the effects of anti-depressant medications or psychotherapy. These findings are exciting because a paperback copy of *Feeling Good* is far cheaper than treatment with drugs or psychotherapy, and there are no side effects!

But what about the other side of the coin? What about the 35% who *didn't* recover or improve after reading *Feeling Good*? Why did they re-main stuck? How did they differ from the people who recovered in four weeks? I thought if I could figure that out, then it might lead to another treatment breakthrough.

After conducting thousands of therapy sessions with individuals strug-gling with severe depression and anxiety, and publishing many research stud-ies to learn why psychotherapy succeeds or fails, I believe I found the answer, and that's why I've written *Feeling Great*.

In contrast to *Feeling Good*, which was all about the cognitive revolution, this book is all about the motivation revolution. It is based on the simple idea that we sometimes get "stuck" in depression and anxiety because we have mixed feelings about recovery. Although we may be suffering and desperately want to change, there may be powerful conflicting forces that keep us stuck. As strange as this might sound, part of you may fight against—or resist—the very change you're yearning for.

This is what Freud called "resistance" way back at the beginning of psycho-analysis. Although most therapists since Freud have given lip service to resis-tance, very few (if any) have explained *why* we resist change or how to solve this problem. And that's where this book comes in: Through a new approach called TEAM-CBT, you can overcome this resistance and achieve recovery quickly.

The TEAM approach evolved from my clinical experience and research on how psychotherapy actually works. It preserves all the best elements of CBT described in my first book, but it works much faster.

Here's what the letters stand for:

**T = Testing:** My colleagues and I test our patients' symptoms at the start and end of every therapy session to find out exactly how much they've improved or failed to improve.

**E = Empathy:** At the start of the session, we listen and try to form a warm, compassionate relationship with each patient without trying to rescue him or her.

**A = Assessment of Resistance:** We bring each patient's resistance to change to conscious awareness and melt it away before trying to help the patient. When the resistance has vanished, the patient is usually super motivated. This allows us to work together as a fantastic TEAM.*

**M = Methods:** We show patients how to rapidly convert feelings of depression and anxiety into joy.

While you're reading, you and I will also work together as a powerful TEAM to blast the negative thoughts that trigger so much pain, such as "I'm not good enough" or "I'm damaged." By working together, we will become a powerful force that can move mountains of pain incredibly rapidly.

Here's how it works: In section I of this book, I will show you how to change the way you're thinking and feeling using all the latest techniques, including how to melt away any resistance keeping you "stuck." In section II, I will show you the most effective way to crush the distorted thoughts that cause depression, anxiety, and anger.

In section III, I will show you how to overcome the belief that you have a "self" that is inferior or simply not good enough and describe the four "Great Deaths" of the self, which correspond to recovery from depression, anxiety, relationship conflicts, and habits and addictions.

We all know that nobody can be happy all the time—there will always be bumps in the road of life for all of us. So, in section IV, I will show how to defeat those relapses quickly so you can continue to feel great once you've recovered!

Finally, in sections V and VI, my brilliant colleague, Dr. Mark Noble, will show you how you can modify the circuits in your own brain using TEAM and why this is so much more effective than antidepressants or traditional talk therapy. I'll also describe some exciting new research on depression and anxiety and provide you with tons of additional free resources.

---

* The A in TEAM used to be described as Agenda Setting, but I've since updated the term to Assessment of Resistance because it more accurately reflects this phase of treatment: melting away the patient's subconscious efforts to resist change.

Although TEAM can provide extraordinarily fast recovery from depression and anxiety, it also involves a change that transcends mere recovery. Many individuals are flooded with feelings of profound joy that they can only describe as a spiritual transformation—one that involves a mind-blowing shift in perspective that I've come to think of as the key to lasting mental health.

At the risk of sounding grandiose, I believe TEAM-CBT represents the biggest treatment advance since the birth of cognitive therapy nearly fifty years ago. And that is why I am so excited to share this book with you.

I wrote this book with two target audiences in mind: therapists who are eager to learn more effective and satisfying treatment methods and individuals who are struggling with depression and anxiety. I hope that these awesome new techniques will help you break out of your own feelings of self-doubt and despair so you, too, can start *Feeling Great* again!

David Burns, MD
Los Altos Hills, California

# Section I

*How to Turn Depression and Anxiety into Joy*

# 1 | How Are You Feeling?

This book is all about changing the way you feel, so let's see how you're feeling right now. Once you've checked off how you feel, put the totals for depression and anxiety in the boxes at the bottom. I'll ask you to take these tests again toward the end of the book so you can compare your scores and see how much you've changed.

## Part 1: Your Moods*

**Instructions:** Use checks (✓) to indicate how you're feeling *right now*.
**Answer all items.**

| Depression | 0—Not at all | 1—Somewhat | 2—Moderately | 3—A lot | 4—Extremely |
|---|---|---|---|---|---|
| 1. Sad or down in the dumps | | | | | |
| 2. Discouraged or hopeless | | | | | |
| 3. Low in self-esteem, inferior, or worthless | | | | | |
| 4. Unmotivated to do things | | | | | |
| 5. Decreased pleasure or satisfaction in life | | | | | |
| Total Items 1 to 5 ➔ | | | | | |

| Anxiety | | | | | |
|---|---|---|---|---|---|
| 1. Anxious | | | | | |
| 2. Frightened | | | | | |
| 3. Worrying about things | | | | | |
| 4. Tense or on edge | | | | | |
| 5. Nervous | | | | | |
| Total Items 1 to 5 ➔ | | | | | |

Are these validated scales or just pop psychology? The American Psychiatric Association claims that only a qualified mental health professional can make psychiatric diagnoses. And in some sense, that's true, mainly because the criteria in the official *Diagnostic and Statistical Manual of Mental Disorders* (DSM-5®) are extremely complicated and convoluted. I prefer to keep things simple.

In terms of what's important—how you really feel inside—scales like the ones you just completed are among the best in the world. Statistical analyses indicate that the tests you just completed are approximately 95% accurate. What do your scores mean? Use the scoring key to find out.

## Scoring Key for Dr. Burns's Depression and Anxiety Scales

| Score | Severity | Meaning |
|-------|----------|---------|
| 0 | No symptoms | That's terrific! You don't seem to have any symptoms at all. |
| 1–2 | Borderline | These scores are normal, but you could use a little tune-up. |
| 3–5 | Mild | Although your scores are not greatly elevated, this is enough depression or anxiety to take the joy out of life. If we work together, we can probably get your scores down to 0, which would be terrific! |
| 6–10 | Moderate | You're feeling quite a bit of depression or anxiety. Although you're not in the severe range, these scores reflect considerable unhappiness. |
| 11–15 | Severe | You have fairly strong feelings of depression or anxiety. That makes me sad, but there's some really good news. The tools in this book can help you transform your negative feelings into joy. |
| 16–20 | Extreme | Scores in this range indicate that your suffering is intense. Friends or family may have trouble grasping how much pain you're in. The good news is that the prognosis for improvement is very positive. In fact, recovery is one of the greatest feelings a human being can have. |

What if your moods change from time to time? That *will* happen. Anxiety tends to fluctuate more than depression. For example, if you're shy, then your anxiety may increase a lot when you're interacting with people at a social gathering or have to give a talk at work. And if you have a phobia, like a fear of heights, flying, spiders, elevators, or storms, then your anxiety will spike when you are exposed to the situation or things you're afraid of.

You can take these tests as often as you'd like if you want to plot them out over time. Doing so is actually a great way to track your progress as you read this book.

Now that we know about your moods, let's see how you're doing in your relationships with other people. Indicate how you're feeling right now on the Anger and Relationship Satisfaction Scales. Remember to add up your scores on each test and put the totals in the boxes at the bottom.

Your feelings about other people can also change quite a bit from time to time, so you can take these tests as often as you like, but make sure that the person you're thinking about on the scale is always the same. Otherwise, your scores may go up and down just because you're thinking about different people.

One final note: You can be angry without being mad at someone you know. For example, you can be angry with yourself, with some irritating event, or with someone you don't even know.

## Part 2: Your Relationships*

**Instructions:** Use checks (✓) to indicate how you're feeling *right now*.
**Answer all items.**

| Anger | 0—Not at all | 1—Somewhat | 2—Moderately | 3—A lot | 4—Extremely |
|---|---|---|---|---|---|
| 1. Frustrated | | | | | |
| 2. Annoyed | | | | | |
| 3. Resentful | | | | | |
| 4. Angry | | | | | |
| 5. Irritated | | | | | |
| Total Items 1 to 5 → | | | | | |

## Relationship Satisfaction Scale*

Think about an important relationship, like your spouse, partner, friend, colleague, or family member. Use checks (✓) to indicate how you feel about this relationship.
**Answer all items.**

| | 0—Very dissatisfied | 1—Moderately dissatisfied | 2—Somewhat dissatisfied | 3—Neutral | 4—Somewhat satisfied | 5—Moderately satisfied | 6—Very satisfied |
|---|---|---|---|---|---|---|---|
| 1. Communication and openness | | | | | | | |
| 2. Resolving conflicts | | | | | | | |
| 3. Degree of affection and caring | | | | | | | |
| 4. Intimacy and closeness | | | | | | | |
| 5. Overall satisfaction | | | | | | | |
| Total Items 1 to 5 → | | | | | | | |

On the next page, you'll see what your scores mean.

---

* Copyright © 1997 by David D. Burns, MD. Revised 2002, 2018.

## Scoring Key for Dr. Burns's Anger and Relationship Satisfaction Scales

| Anger Scale | | Relationship Satisfaction Scale | |
|---|---|---|---|
| Score | Meaning | Score | Meaning |
| 0 | No anger | 0–10 | Extremely dissatisfied |
| 1–2 | A little anger | 11–15 | Very dissatisfied |
| 3–5 | Mild anger | 16–20 | Moderately dissatisfied |
| 6–10 | Moderate anger | 21–25 | Somewhat satisfied |
| 11–15 | Severe anger | 26–28 | Moderately satisfied |
| 16–20 | Extreme anger | 29–30 | Extremely satisfied |

Did you have an elevated anger score and a low relationship satisfaction score? If so, join the club. It's really easy to get ticked off at other people from time to time. I know I do! If you want to develop more loving and satisfying relationships, I'll share some pretty awesome tools with you in this book. However, there's no rule that says you have to try to get along with everyone.

We've covered moods and relationships. How about habits and addictions? Do you have any? Like smoking too much marijuana or drinking or eating too much? Do you have an addiction to internet shopping, video games, your cell phone, or porn? How about an addiction to procrastination?

If so, take my Temptations Test on the next page. As you can see, it asks about cravings and urges to use over the past week. Although it's worded for drugs or alcohol, you can think of binge eating, porn, or anything you're addicted to when you take it.

The reliability of this test is also extremely high, approximately 97%. However, cravings and temptations can change dramatically from time to time. For example, you may wake up in the morning with a bit of a hangover, absolutely determined to cut down on your drinking or to give up drinking entirely. But hours later, when you get home from work, the craving for a drink may overwhelm you again. If you're interested, you can also take my Temptations Test frequently and track the fluctuations in cravings throughout the day or from day to day.

## Part 3: The Temptations Test—
## Your Cravings and Urges to Use*

**Instructions:** Use checks (✓) to indicate how much each statement describes how you have been feeling in the past week, including today.
**Answer all items.**

| | 0—Not at all | 1—Slightly true | 2—Moderately true | 3—Very true | 4—Completely true |
|---|---|---|---|---|---|
| 1. Sometimes I crave drugs or alcohol. | | | | | |
| 2. Sometimes I have the urge to use drugs or alcohol. | | | | | |
| 3. Sometimes I really want to use drugs or alcohol. | | | | | |
| 4. Sometimes it's hard to resist the urge to use drugs or alcohol. | | | | | |
| 5. Sometimes I struggle with the temptation to use drugs or alcohol. | | | | | |
| Total Items 1 to 5 ➜ | | | | | |

What does your score on this test mean? Well, this one is *definitely* a no-brainer. The higher your score, the more tempted you feel, and the more tempted you feel, the more likely it is that you'll give in to the temptation. That's about all there is to it! Nothing fancy.

If your score on the test is 15 or above, then it means your cravings are so high that it's almost a certainty that you give in to them. If you're in treatment, or if you're attending a 12-step program, then you might want to share your scores with your therapist. The scores will provide them with a much clearer picture of what's going on between sessions.

There are just a couple more tests I want to you to take. So far, we've been talking about negatives—gloomy moods, troubled relationships, and bad habits. How about the other side of the coin? Let's find out how *happy* you are.

---

* Copyright © 1997 by David D. Burns, MD. Revised 2002, 2018.

## Part 4: Happiness Test*

**Instructions:** Use checks (✔) to indicate how you're feeling *right now*.
**Answer all items.**

| | 0—Not at all | 1—Somewhat | 2—Moderately | 3—A lot | 4—Extremely |
|---|---|---|---|---|---|
| 1. Happy and joyful | | | | | |
| 2. Hopeful and optimistic | | | | | |
| 3. Worthwhile, high self-esteem | | | | | |
| 4. Motivated, productive | | | | | |
| 5. Pleased and satisfied with life | | | | | |
| **Total Items 1 to 5 ➜** | | | | | |

This test shows how happy you are right now, and it's just the opposite of the Depression Test you took at the start of this chapter. However, getting rid of depression doesn't necessarily mean you're going to feel super happy or fulfilled. That is why the goal of this book isn't just about overcoming negative feelings. It's also about boosting your self-esteem and helping you find joy in life.

In this regard, I'm in agreement with the Dalai Lama, who has said that happiness is the goal of life. I'm not sure it's the only goal, but it is certainly one important goal. At the same time, no one is entitled to be perfectly happy all the time, and I don't even think that would be desirable. Sometimes other kinds of feelings, such as sadness, fear, and even anger, can be perfectly appropriate, and we all know there are bumps in the road for all of us at times.

We'll check your score on the Happiness Test toward the end of the book so we can find out how much your feelings of happiness have increased. But you can take the test as often as you'd like to track changes in these feelings across time.

How do you interpret your scores on the test? You'll find the scoring key on the next page, but it's also a no-brainer—the higher your scores, the happier you are.

---

* Copyright © 1997 by David D. Burns, MD. Revised 2002, 2018.

## Scoring Key for Dr. Burns's Happiness Test

| Score | Happiness Level | Meaning |
|-------|-----------------|---------|
| 0–1 | No happiness | It seems like you're barely having any positive feelings at all right now. That's really sad, but there's some good news—if you want, we can work together and fix that. |
| 2–4 | Minimal happiness | These scores indicate that you have very few positive feelings. There's lots of room for improvement. |
| 3–5 | Some happiness | Your feelings are somewhat positive, which is promising. If we work together, we should be able to make things a lot better. |
| 6–10 | Moderate happiness | You seem to be feeling moderately positive. That's good! I'd love to see your scores increase even more. |
| 11–15 | A lot of happiness | You seem to be feeling very positive and happy, but there's room for feeling even happier. |
| 16–19 | Extreme happiness | Scores in this range are really good. You're feeling extremely positive in at least one of the five areas on the test. Way to go! There's still a little room for feeling even better. |
| 20 | Tremendous happiness | This is fabulous! |

I want my patients' scores, and your scores, to increase as much as possible—hopefully all the way to 20. Would you *like* to feel happier? How much would it be worth to you if I agreed to show you how to break out of bad moods and develop more loving relationships?

As I mentioned in the introduction, roughly 65% individuals with depression who were given a copy of my first book, *Feeling Good*, improved substantially within four weeks without any other treatment. But it wasn't the reading that led to improvement—it was the specific information, tools, and exercises in that book that had the antidepressant effect.

The same has been found in therapy: Patients who do their psychotherapy "homework" between sessions improve significantly, and nearly all those who refuse to do homework fail to improve or simply drop out of treatment.

So if you want to change the way you're thinking and feeling—and you want to feel happier—then you'll also have to do the exercises while you're reading this book. Are you willing to do them? Let's find out! Take the Willingness Test on the next page.

## Part 5: The Willingness Test

Use checks (✓) to indicate how strongly you agree with each of the following statements.
**Answer all items.**

| | 0—Do not agree | 1—Agree slightly | 2—Agree moderately | 3—Agree strongly | 4— Agree completely |
|---|---|---|---|---|---|
| 1. I'm willing to do the written exercises while I read this book. | | | | | |
| 2. I'm willing to do the exercises even if I am not in the mood. | | | | | |
| 3. I'm willing to do them even if I feel hopeless or unmotivated. | | | | | |
| 4. I'm willing to do them even if I feel overwhelmed or tired. | | | | | |
| 5. I'm willing to do them even if they seem difficult at first. | | | | | |

Total Items 1 to 5 ➔

The Willingness Test is not just a pop psychology gimmick. Many published research studies have indicated that scores on this test have powerful causal effects on recovery from depression. As you might imagine, people with high scores recover rapidly, and people with low scores tend to recover much more slowly, if at all.* On the next page, you'll find a scoring key so you can interpret your own scores.

* Burns, D. D., & Nolen-Hoeksema, S. (1991). Coping styles, homework compliance and the effectiveness of cognitive-behavioral therapy. *Journal of Consulting and Clinical Psychology, 59*(2), 305–311.

Burns, D. D., & Spangler, D. (2000). Does psychotherapy homework lead to changes in depression in cognitive behavioral therapy? Or does clinical improvement lead to homework compliance? *Journal of Consulting and Clinical Psychology, 68*(1), 46–59.

Burns, D., Westra, H., Trockel, M., & Fisher, A. (2012). Motivation and changes in depression. *Cognitive Therapy and Research, 37*(2), 368–379.

Burns, D. D. (March/April, 2017). When helping doesn't help. *Psychotherapy Networker, 41*(2),18–27, 60. Retrieved from https://www.psychotherapynetworker.org/blog/details/1160/when-helping-doesnt-help

Reid, A. M., Garner, L. E., van Kirk, N., Gironda, C., Krompinger, J. W., Brennan, B. P., ... Elias, J. A. (2017). How willing are you? Willingness as a predictor of change during treatment of adults with obsessive-compulsive disorder. *Depression and Anxiety, 34*(11), 1057–1064.

## Scoring Key for Dr. Burns's Willingness Test

| Score | Willingness Level | Meaning |
|-------|-------------------|---------|
| 0 | Unwilling | Right now, you don't seem willing to do the written exercises while you read. I totally get it and appreciate the fact that you're reading this! The reading alone could be an important first step to change, but you won't get the full benefit of these powerful tools. |
| 1–5 | Minimally willing | It looks like you're not particularly enthusiastic about doing the written exercises, which is totally understandable. I hope you'll try a few of them, and if you like them, then you may get in the groove and do even more. |
| 6–10 | Somewhat to moderately willing | You are somewhat willing to do the written exercises, but perhaps a bit ambivalent. I appreciate that you're open to the possibility of doing the written exercises. |
| 11–15 | Very willing | You seem to be pretty willing to do the written exercises while you read this book. That will boost your understanding and ability to use these great tools. |
| 16–19 | Extremely willing | Scores in this range are great! You're willing to put forth extra effort to learn how to change the way you think and feel. |
| 20 | Totally willing | This is fabulous! Wow! Kudos! |

Willingness is incredibly important in recovery from depression, anxiety, relationship problems, and habits and addictions. That's why I'm hoping I can persuade you to do the exercises while you read this book. It could make a huge difference in how much you learn and how rapidly you break out of a bad mood.

Getting the "right" answer to the exercises is not terribly important, but putting in the effort can make all the difference in the world. It's the same philosophy Dr. Jill Levitt and I use in our free, weekly standard psychotherapy training seminar for local mental health professionals. In the seminar, we have the philosophy of "joyful failure." That's because we ask the therapists who attend to do challenging exercises designed to highlight their blind spots so they can improve their therapeutic skills. Many of the exercises are difficult, and most therapists fail at first. Sometimes they have to fail several times before they master some new technique.

I want you to adopt the same philosophy. If you give yourself permission to fail—joyfully—while you're reading and doing these exercises, you'll also learn much more rapidly. It's the same as learning how to play the piano. The first time you try, you won't sound very good! But if you stick with it, you'll definitely improve over time. And that can mean a boost in the way you feel for the rest of your life. So if you're willing, take a crack at the exercises and have the courage to fail joyously.

One last point about the written exercises. If you're listening to this book on audio while driving, *don't* try to do the exercises while you're driving. Concentrate on your driving! You can do the written exercises later on when you're safely at home.

That's about it for the testing. Now that we know how you're feeling, let's see what we can do to CHANGE the way you FEEL!

# 2 | Feeling Great in 15 Minutes—The CliffsNotes Version

I have a lot of new and fantastic information to share with you in this book. But if you have a short attention span—or if you're a slow reader, like me, and want the fifteen-minute version of *Feeling Great*—here are the CliffsNotes®. Of course, I want you to dive into the whole book because the information and methods can change your life, but the information in this chapter can at least give you a jump start.

I'll start out with a brief tutorial on how to identify cognitive distortions, followed by an introduction to a remarkably powerful new tool called positive reframing. If you read my first book, *Feeling Good*, then you already learned how to identify cognitive distortions. But this refresher will deepen your understanding and may hopefully inspire you too.

So let's get started.

## WHAT ARE COGNITIVE DISTORTIONS ANYWAY?

What are cognitive distortions and why might you be interested in them? The term *cognitive* may sound pretty intimidating or overly intellectual, but it has a simple meaning. *Cognition* is just a fancy word for a thought. It's the way you think about what's happening. Right now, you're probably having some thoughts about me and what you're reading, and possibly some thoughts about yourself as well. Your thoughts create your feelings every minute of every day.

For example, right now you could be thinking that I'm a con artist or that this will be just another superficial self-help book. If so, you probably feel skeptical, suspicious, or even annoyed.

Or you may be thinking that nothing could possibly help you because your problems are so severe. If so, you probably feel hopeless, discouraged, or demoralized.

Or this may all sound really interesting and exciting to you, and you may be thinking that this book could actually help you. If so, you're probably excited and hopeful.

Do you see what I mean? Everyone reading this book is reading the exact same words, but how they feel about this book can differ greatly. Your feelings result *entirely* from how you're thinking right now. It is your thoughts, and not the circumstances of your life, that create all of your feelings. You FEEL the way you THINK.

Sometimes, though, we think about ourselves and our lives in ways that are pretty illogical and even unfair to ourselves. We make interpretations about what's happening that are twisted and misleading, but we don't realize it. That is what cognitive distortions are: a highly misleading way of thinking about yourself and the world. It's a way of fooling yourself. And when you feel depressed and anxious, you will nearly *always* be fooling yourself. This means that your negative thoughts do not reflect reality. Depression and anxiety are the world's oldest cons.

The following are ten of the most common cognitive distortions:

1. **All-or-Nothing Thinking.** You look at things in absolute, black-or-white categories, as if shades of gray do not exist, and you think of yourself as either a complete success or total failure. This dichotomous way of thinking can make life pretty miserable and make you feel like a zero, or nothing, most of the time. In addition, you can't accurately describe yourself or the world in black-or-white categories. Things are rarely totally horrible or absolutely perfect.

2. **Overgeneralization**. You generalize from some specific flaw, failure, or mistake to your entire self. Or you may generalize the way you feel right now, or some negative experience you've just had, to the future.

   You should suspect overgeneralization whenever your negative thoughts contain global labels (like *bad mom*) or words like *always* or *never*. For example, if you were ever rejected by someone you loved, then you may have told yourself that you were "unlovable" and that you'd be alone forever. In this case, you'd be overgeneralizing the breakup of one relationship to your entire self. You'd also be overgeneralizing from the present to your entire future.

Of course, this distortion isn't limited to matters of the heart. If you've ever failed at something you were trying to accomplish, then you may have thought of yourself as a failure and felt like you'd never be successful. Once again, you're overgeneralizing from some specific failure to your entire self and from this moment to your entire future.

The next two cognitive distortions typically go hand in hand:

3. **Mental Filtering.** You filter out or ignore the positives and focus entirely on the negatives. It's like a drop of ink that discolors the entire beaker of water.

4. **Discounting the Positive.** This is an even more spectacular mental error. You tell yourself that your positive qualities or successes don't count. You convince yourself that you're completely bad, inferior, or worthless.

   For example, if someone compliments you, you may tell yourself, "Oh, she's just saying that to be nice. She doesn't really mean it." Or you may notice what's great about other people—how successful or attractive they are—and overlook their flaws. You may also dwell on your own flaws, thinking you're "too short" or "too tall," and obsess about your appearance, all while insisting your own positive qualities are just "average."

   Even I find myself slipping into these two distortions from time to time. For example, if I'm feeling vulnerable or insecure, and I get a negative or critical comment or email, I'll tend to dwell on it while ignoring a whole host of positive comments from fans filled with praise. It sometimes feels like the criticisms are valid and the positive comments don't really count. Feelings of inferiority nearly always result from mental filtering and discounting the positive.

5. **Jumping to Conclusions.** This is where you jump to painful and upsetting conclusions that aren't really supported by the facts. There are two common versions of this distortion:

   a. **Fortune Telling.** You make arbitrary and disturbing predictions about the future. It's as if you had a crystal ball that only gives you bad news!

**b. Mind Reading.** You jump to conclusions about how others are thinking and feeling without any clear evidence.

Fortune telling can trigger feelings of hopelessness. For example, if you're depressed, then you may tell yourself that things will never change, that your problems can never be solved, and that you'll be depressed forever. These thoughts cause feelings of hopelessness and can sometimes even lead to suicidal urges.

Fortune telling can also trigger feelings of anxiety. For example, if you have anxiety about public speaking, then you might worry that your mind will go blank, that you'll blow it, and that you'll make a total fool of yourself when you get up in front of the audience.

Mind reading also causes social anxiety, especially shyness. For example, when you're at a social gathering, you may tell yourself that other people will see how nervous you are, judge you, and be uninterested in what you have to say. You may also tell yourself that everyone else is confident and relaxed and that no one else ever struggles with insecurities.

6. **Magnification and Minimization.** You exaggerate the negativity in a situation and minimize the positives. I call this the "binocular trick" since magnifying is like looking through a pair of binoculars (which makes everything much bigger), and minimizing is like looking through the opposite end (which makes everything much smaller).

Magnification plays a huge role in anxiety because it causes you to greatly exaggerate danger. Consider the fear of flying. As you know, there's an extraordinarily small probability that you'll die in a commercial air flight. I think you'd have to fly all day every day for about 600 years to be in significant danger. However, people who are afraid of flying massively magnify the actual danger and wrongly believe it's incredibly risky to fly.

Similarly, panic attacks always result from magnification in combination with fortune telling. During a panic attack, you misinterpret normal bodily sensations, like dizziness or tightness in the chest, and become irrationally convinced that something catastrophic is about to happen, such as a massive heart attack, when you're actually magnifying the significance of fairly common and innocuous physical sensations.

Minimization, of course, is the opposite. You tell yourself that something isn't very important—when it is. For example, I just did my "slogging" today, which is my word for super slow jogging. And I only went two miles. I could tell myself that my super slow two-mile "slog" doesn't count because so many other people run a lot farther and faster. But my slogging *does* count, and I'm darn proud of myself for getting out and paying my dues. I've never enjoyed running, but at least I'm getting some fairly decent exercise almost every day.

7. **Emotional Reasoning.** This involves reasoning from the way you feel, such as: "I feel like an idiot, so I must be one" or "I feel hopeless, so things are never going to get better." Or in the case of panic attacks, "I feel like I'm on the verge of a nervous breakdown, so I must be in a lot of danger."

For decades, mental health professionals have urged patients to get in touch with their feelings. But your feelings are not always a reliable guide to reality and can sometimes be incredibly misleading, especially when you feel depressed, anxious, or angry. That's because feelings result from thoughts, and as you're learning, negative thoughts are often distorted. When this is the case, your feelings do not reflect reality any better than the curved mirrors you see in amusement parks that create distorted images of how you look.

8. **Should Statements.** You criticize yourself or other people with *should*s, *shouldn't*s, *must*s, *ought to*s, and *have to*s. There are several types of should statements:

a. **Self-Directed Shoulds** lead to feelings of guilt and inferiority when we don't live up to our self-imposed standards ("I shouldn't have screwed up!").

b. **Other-Directed Shoulds** lead to feelings of anger and frustration when others don't meet our expectations ("He shouldn't feel that way" or "She shouldn't have said that!"). Other-directed shoulds cause conflicts with others, such as marital problems, arguments, and even violence and war.

c. **World-Directed Shoulds** lead to frustration and anger when the world doesn't meet our expectations. For example, I sometimes tell myself that this or that software program *shouldn't* be so dang complicated and hard to learn!

d. **Hidden Shoulds** are not expressed explicitly with terms like *should,* *ought,* or *must,* but they're implied by your negative thoughts and feelings. For example, if you berate yourself whenever you make a mistake, you're essentially telling yourself that you should be perfect and should never goof up.

When you see this distortion in someone else who feels upset, you can probably see how unrealistic it is and how hard that person is being on him- or herself. But when you tell yourself that you shouldn't feel the way you do, that you shouldn't have made that mistake, or that you should be better than you are, it's much harder to see that you're fooling yourself.

9. **Labeling.** Labeling is an extreme form of overgeneralization in which you try to capture the "essence" of yourself or another person with a one-word label. For example, when you make a mistake, you call yourself a "jerk" or "loser" instead of saying, "I made a mistake."

Labeling is very common in political and religious battles. For example, we may label people who disagree with us politically as "lefties" or "righties." Hitler used this type of labeling to achieve power in Germany when he described Jewish people (and others) as "rats" and identified Aryan people as being part of the "superior" race.

Labeling tends to fire up strong negative emotions, like severe depression and intense rage. In addition, it's mean. When you label yourself or another person, it's like taking a jab at someone. It also distracts you from what's important because you use all your energy ruminating about how bad you are instead of pinpointing your error—assuming you've actually made an error—so you can learn from it and grow.

Labeling is also highly irrational. Humans are not objects that can be captured with a single positive or negative label. There's really no such thing as a "jerk" or a "loser"—although plenty of jerky behavior exists. I know that I often do "jerky" things no matter how hard I try to be "good." And if I told you about all the losses I've experienced and things at which I've failed (including just recently), we'd have a pretty long conversation. Does that mean I'm a "loser"?

10. **Self-Blame and Other-Blame.** You find fault in others or your-self instead of solving the problem or identifying the true causes of the problem.

   a. **Self-Blame.** You blame yourself for something you weren't entirely responsible for, or you beat up on yourself because of some mistake you made.

   For example, an attorney blamed himself for losing a case in court, but the evidence against the man he was trying to defend was overwhelming.

   b. **Other-Blame.** You blame others and overlook ways you might have contributed to the conflict.

   For example, a wife complained that her husband was constantly critical of her and said things like "You never listen!" She wanted to know why men were like that.

   I asked her how she typically responded, and she said, "Oh, I just ignore him and say nothing!"

   When you feel depressed or anxious, there's a good chance you're blaming yourself and telling yourself you're no good because of some flaw or failure. When you're angry or not getting along with someone else, the odds are high that you're blaming the other person for the conflict.

You don't need to be diagnosed with depression or anxiety to experience these cognitive distortions. We *all* fall into black holes of insecurity and depression from time to time, including me. I'll give you an example.

After all my workshops, I have the audience members fill out a workshop evaluation. Reading these evaluations can be frightening, and sometimes disturbing, because the participants can be extremely generous in their praise and brutally honest in their critiques. Reading about my flaws and errors is sometimes painful, but it's also a fabulous way to learn and grow.

During a workshop in Cleveland a couple of years ago, I felt like I was doing a poor job. The audience seemed unusually quiet and didn't respond to a couple of my jokes. I also felt I could have done a better job answering some of their questions.

A young man had been hired to drive me to Dayton for another workshop the next day. I sat in the front seat with him and had about 100 workshop evaluations in my hand. I didn't want to look at them because I felt ashamed, but I forced myself to read through them. I even held them at an angle so the driver couldn't see them and find out how bad I was.

The evaluations *were* shocking but not in the direction I had anticipated. The ratings were some of the highest I've ever received. It was hard to believe—and was, of course, a tremendous relief.

In retrospect, I could see that my negative thoughts had contained several cognitive distortions, including:

- **Mental Filtering.** I was thinking about the errors I made and completely ignoring the things I'd said that were effective.
- **Mind Reading.** I was assuming, without any real evidence, that the people in the audience were looking down on me.
- **Emotional Reasoning.** I was reasoning from how I felt. In other words, I *felt* like a failure, so I assumed I really *was* a failure.
- **All-or-Nothing Thinking.** I was evaluating the workshop in black-or-white categories by telling myself that it had been a total flop since everything didn't go perfectly.
- **Hidden Should Statements.** I was also telling myself that I should always hit it out of the park and should never screw up or make mistakes.

I'm not arguing that every time you think you've failed, you're fooling yourself. We all have our share of real failures and setbacks. I know for sure that I do. I've actually had the opposite experience at times as well—workshops that I thought were fantastic when I got slammed in the evaluations. And that can be pretty painful.

What I am saying is that your feelings will result from your thoughts and not from what actually happened. And when you're feeling depressed and anxious, your thoughts will almost always be negative and distorted.

But here's the good news, which I'm repeating:

---

**When you CHANGE the way you THINK, you can CHANGE the way you FEEL.**

---

And this can happen *really fast*. I'll show you how it works and preview some awesome new techniques.

Just last week I worked with a hairstylist named Maria who was struggling with postpartum depression following the birth of her first child. She'd had an extremely difficult delivery that eventually ended up in a caesarean section after two painful and exhausting days of labor. Her recovery was much more painful than expected, and the doctors and nurses had exhibited little compassion or encouragement throughout the whole ordeal. Now that she was finally at home with her daughter, she was struggling with breastfeeding and feeling anxious, inadequate, and overwhelmed.

We are sometimes taught that postpartum depression is a biological disorder, triggered by sudden changes in hormones following childbirth and a lack of sleep. Most doctors treat it with antidepressant medications plus supportive counseling. Although biological and social stresses definitely play a role, postpartum depression and anxiety are always triggered by a host of negative thoughts. And those thoughts are nearly always distorted.

That might sound harsh, and I certainly don't mean to blame anyone (especially mothers!) for how they feel when they're down. In fact, it's quite the opposite: Maria's despair was not the result of some flaw or mental disorder, but was actually a reflection of some really beautiful things about Maria and her core values as mother and as a human being. We'll dive more deeply into that shortly.

I encouraged Maria to fill out a Daily Mood Journal so I could learn more about how she was thinking and feeling. You'll learn more about this tool in chapter 4, but it essentially asks you to describe an upsetting event, to identify and rate your negative emotions, and to record your negative thoughts about the event. Then you indicate how strongly you believe your negative thoughts on a scale from 0 (not at all) to 100 (completely).

Maria described the upsetting event as "Being at home with my newborn and having problems with breastfeeding." She explained that the doctors and nurses had stressed the importance of breastfeeding, but her daughter didn't seem to get it and struggled to latch on. Maria felt like a failure and was thinking of giving up and turning to formula instead.

She circled quite a few negative emotions, which were all intense, as you can see in the following table.

| Emotions | % Now |
|---|---|
| Sad, blue, depressed, down | 70 |
| Anxious, worried | 80 |
| Guilty, remorseful | 90 |
| Inferior, worthless, inadequate, defective | 90 |
| Lonely, unwanted, alone, abandoned | 70 |
| Hopeless, discouraged, pessimistic, despairing | 60 |
| Frustrated, stuck, thwarted, defeated | 70 |
| Angry, mad, resentful, irritated, upset, furious | 80 |

Then she recorded several negative thoughts and indicated how much she believed each one.

| Negative Thoughts | % Now |
|---|---|
| 1. I'm a bad mom for wanting to give up on breastfeeding. | 90 |
| 2. I'm a failure as a mom. | 90 |
| 3. Being home alone with my baby is boring and isolating. Not enjoying this means I'm not cut out to be a mother. | 85 |
| 4. I *should* be feeling happy given how much I wanted a baby. | 100 |
| 5. The next few months are going to be slow and difficult. | 100 |
| 6. We might not be able to manage financially. | 70 |

Now you can see why Maria was struggling with the postpartum blues. Clearly, her negative feelings resulted from her thoughts—from the negative messages she was giving herself. For example, when Maria told herself, "I'm a bad mom," she felt guilty and depressed. When she said, "I *should* be feeling happy," this thought intensified her feelings of failure as a mother. And when she told herself that she and her husband might not be able to manage financially, she felt intense anxiety.

Let's see if Maria's negative thoughts contain any of the ten cognitive distortions. Then we'll see if we can help Maria.

**1. All-or-Nothing Thinking.** Maria strongly preferred breastfeeding because she believed it would offer greater health benefits to her daughter and provide a wonderful chance to bond with her baby. But it just wasn't working, and when she told herself that she was a "bad mom" and a "failure" in response to her troubles with breastfeeding, she was engaging in all-or-nothing thinking.

The world is not made up of two separate groups of "good moms" and "bad moms" but, rather, "real moms." And all real moms (and dads) have flaws *and* strengths.

2. **Overgeneralization.** Maria was overgeneralizing when she concluded that she was a "bad mom" and a "failure" because she and her baby were having trouble with breastfeeding. Being a mom involves vastly more than just breastfeeding, and it seems pretty illogical and unfair for Maria to be so harshly critical of herself just because the breastfeeding wasn't working out.

3. **Mental Filtering.** Maria was engaging in mental filtering by dwelling on the negatives—all the ways she thought she was falling short as a mother—and not giving herself any credit for all the things she was doing right.

4. **Discounting the Positive.** Being a new mother can be incredibly stressful and demanding, and Maria was doing a great job. She was extremely conscientious and loving, and her baby was happy and healthy. But she seemed to think that all of that didn't count.

5. **Jumping to Conclusions.** Maria was jumping to conclusions—specifically fortune telling—when she told herself that she wouldn't be able to manage financially and that the next few months would be slow and difficult.

Although there's definitely some truth in those predictions, since a new baby involves lots of adjustments and hard work, Maria made it sound like she had a future of never-ending isolation, deprivation, and defeat. In reality, Maria and her husband had actually been doing well by budgeting and being careful about money, and Maria's parents, who lived nearby, indicated they would be willing to help out with childcare and finances if money became a problem.

6. **Magnification and Minimization.** Maria was magnifying her so-called "failure" with breastfeeding and minimizing the importance of everything she was doing and sacrificing for her child.

7. **Emotional Reasoning.** Maria *felt* guilty and inadequate, so she concluded she *was* inadequate. But this is very misleading. The reason she felt inadequate was because she had labeled herself as a "bad mom" and a "failure." As we have learned, her emotions did not reflect reality.

8. **Should Statements.** Maria told herself that she *shouldn't* feel depressed and that she *should* feel happy since she and her husband desperately wanted a baby and had tried unsuccessfully for more than two years before she finally became pregnant.

   The problem with these should statements is that they doubled her troubles: Many new mothers struggle and feel discouraged at times, which is common. But by telling herself that she *shouldn't* be upset, she only increased her angst and made herself upset about being upset.

   In addition, childbirth can be incredibly traumatic, and it was especially traumatic for Maria. She struggled to deliver her baby and experienced tremendous pain from the cesarean section. And now that her baby was finally here, things were not going as smoothly as expected.

   She *should* be upset! As my wife puts it, "Babies may have their charming qualities, but they can also be squalling, pooping messes."

9. **Labeling.** When Maria called herself a "bad mom" and a "failure," she was clearly labeling herself.

10. **Self-Blame and Other-Blame.** Maria blamed herself for her daughter's difficulties with breastfeeding, but getting the baby to latch on is a common experience. Her baby's difficulties with breastfeeding were, for the most part, beyond her control.

## POSITIVE REFRAMING

What I've shown you so far—how to identify the distortions in your negative thoughts—is powerful and exciting, but it's not new. What *is* new is this: Your negative thoughts and feelings are not, in fact, the result of what's *wrong* with you (as the American Psychiatric Association would have us believe) but what's *right* with you.

In the DSM-5, various forms of human suffering, such as unhappiness, worrying, or shyness, are transformed into a series of "mental disorders" with names like major depressive disorder, generalized anxiety disorder, and social anxiety disorder. This classification system creates the impression that if you're feeling depressed or anxious, you're defective in some way and need fixing. In fact, your doctor may even tell you that you have a "chemical imbalance" in your brain and that you need medication to try to correct the imbalance.*

But what if Maria's suffering—and your suffering as well—was not the result of what's *wrong* with you but what's *right* with you? What if your depression and anxiety were the expression of what's positive and beautiful about you rather than what's negative and broken about you? Then you could be proud of your negative feelings instead of feeling ashamed of them. That would be quite a switch, wouldn't it?

And here's the really cool thing: The moment you see the positive side of your negative thoughts and feelings, you suddenly won't need them anymore, and your recovery will be just a stone's throw away. In fact, many people recover *really* fast!

How fast? I'm talking minutes, as opposed to months or years of traditional talk therapy or treatment with antidepressant medications.

Does that sound bizarre? It should! If you'd told me such a thing was possible fifteen years ago, I would have laughed at you and called you a con artist. But now I see it all the time. Here's how it works.

At the start of the session, I listened and provided empathy while Maria described how rough the last couple of months had been for her. Although empathy is rarely ever curative, it is important to create trust and bonding. Then I asked Maria if she wanted some help with her negative thoughts and feelings and if this would be a good time to roll up our sleeves and get to work. She said she did want help and was ready to get started.

Next I asked Maria the miracle cure question: If a miracle happened in today's session, what miracle would she be hoping for? She said she wanted her negative thoughts and feelings to disappear so she could enjoy her baby daughter and her role as a new mother without feeling miserable all the time.

---

* In fact, the idea that depression and anxiety result from a "chemical imbalance" has never been proven, and most researchers have abandoned that theory entirely. Scientists do not yet know the cause of any psychiatric disorders, but it seems likely that genetic and experiential factors play a role in how we feel, think, and behave. The great news is that regardless of the as-yet-unknown causes, we now have powerful treatment methods.

I asked her to imagine that we had a magic button and that if she pushed it, all of her negative thoughts and feelings would instantly disappear, with no effort at all, and she'd immediately feel joyous, even euphoric. Would she push the button?

Maria said she'd *definitely* push the button. Almost everyone says that!

I told Maria that I didn't have a magic button, but I did have some awesome tools, and I predicted that if we used them, she'd probably feel a whole lot better by the end of the session and might even feel joyful. But I told her I wasn't so sure it would be a good idea to use those tools.

She was surprised and asked why not. I explained that although her negative thoughts and feelings were certainly creating a lot of pain for her, I suspected there might be some real advantages, or benefits, of thinking and feeling the way she did. I added that her negative thoughts and feelings might also be an expression of her most beautiful and awesome qualities, and that maybe we should take a look at that before we went about trying to change things.

I suggested we could ask the following questions about each negative thought or feeling before she made any decision about pressing the magic button:

1. What are some benefits, or advantages, of this negative thought or feeling? How might it be helping you and your baby?
2. What does this negative thought or feeling show about you and your core values that's positive and awesome?

Together, Maria and I came up with the following list of positives. Sometimes I'd come up with an idea, and sometimes she would add another. When I do this type of positive reframing, it's important that everything on the list is a direct expression of one of the patient's negative thoughts or feelings. This is radically different from the "cheerleading" approach that so many people do, which can be extremely annoying to the person who's depressed or anxious.

### Positives

1. My anxiety motivates me to do the hard work of breast-pumping to make my milk available to my daughter. I don't want her to get sick. I want to give her the best milk. My worries and concerns about nursing show my love for my baby.

2. My anxiety also keeps me vigilant about trying to protect my daughter. I make sure folks have their flu vaccinations before they visit her. I want to protect her and be the best mom I can be.

3. The thought "I'm a bad mom" shows I have high standards and want to do what's best for her. This thought shows I love her tremendously.

4. My depression shows I'm feeling a loss for the many things I enjoyed about my life before having a baby. My sadness shows my passion for the sense of accomplishment I feel every day when I'm at work. Now that I'm on maternity leave, I miss that!

5. When I say, "I'm not enjoying this," it shows that I'm being honest and realistic with myself and how I'm really feeling. There's no rule that says new moms have to enjoy themselves every moment. It's really hard a lot of the time, and I've been through a lot.

6. When I say I should be happier, it shows my commitment to being the best mother I can be. I want my baby to feel secure. I didn't always feel safe, loved, or happy when I was growing up, so I'm super determined to make sure my little girl feels loved and happy.

7. My feelings of guilt and remorse also show my love for her. These feelings motivate me to find out how to be a happier and better mom.

8. My anger shows that I have a sense of justice and fairness. I believe doctors and nurses sometimes need to be reminded that compassion is perhaps their most powerful and important medication.

9. My anger shows that I want to protect my daughter as well. The world can sometimes be pretty harsh and unfair. Maybe I feel a little like a mother lion protecting her cub.

10. My feelings of hopelessness keep my expectations low so I won't be disappointed. I've had so many disappointments and painful experiences along the way. It was incredibly difficult to get pregnant, and the delivery was incredibly painful, complicated, and frightening.

11. Feeling defective motivates me to seek out information by asking other mothers or calling the nursing hotline. That also shows that I'm humble and honest about my defects.

12. My feelings of loneliness show that I care a lot about my relationships with others and that I don't want to be a burden or a strain on them. My loneliness also motivates me to reach out to others.

13. My feelings of discouragement and sadness are reasonable and appropriate since this has been a really hard time for me.

14. When I say we might not be able to manage financially, this shows I want to be responsible and support my baby effectively.

Once we'd listed all the positives we could think of, I asked Maria if she felt the list was realistic. She said the list was absolutely realistic but very surprising since she'd never thought there could be anything positive about how she was thinking and feeling. She'd been thinking that her depression and anxiety meant there was something *wrong* with her and not that there might be something *right* with her.

I asked Maria if she still wanted to press the magic button since all of these positives would go down the drain along with her negative thoughts and feelings. Maria insisted that she still wanted to feel better because her suffering was almost unbearable.

Now she had a dilemma. She wanted to feel better, but she also didn't want to give up all the fabulous things on our list of positives. As her therapist, I also wasn't trying to sell her on the idea of change. Instead, I was doing the opposite. I was trying to persuade her that all of her negative thoughts and feelings showed what was really great about her and that she *shouldn't* give them up.

To help her resolve this dilemma, I asked Maria to imagine that we had a magic dial instead of a magic button and that she could dial down each negative feeling to a more manageable level that would allow her to keep all the benefits of that feeling without feeling so much intense pain. That way, she could feel better without losing all the beautiful things we'd listed about her.

What would she dial each feeling down to, starting with depression? How sad and depressed would she want to feel at the end of our session? What might be an appropriate level of depression given all the horrible things she'd been going through? She said 15% would be plenty of depression, so she recorded this as a goal in the second column of her Daily Mood Journal, as you can see. She also decided to dial her anxiety down from 80% to 20%, so on and so forth.

| Emotions | % Now | % Goal | % After |
|---|---|---|---|
| Sad, blue, depressed, down | 70 | 15 | |
| Anxious, worried | 80 | 20 | |
| Guilty, remorseful | 90 | 20 | |
| Inferior, worthless, inadequate, defective | 90 | 10 | |
| Lonely, unwanted, alone, abandoned | 70 | 15 | |
| Hopeless, discouraged, pessimistic, despairing | 60 | 10 | |
| Frustrated, stuck, thwarted, defeated | 70 | 25 | |
| Angry, mad, resentful, irritated, upset, furious | 80 | 30 | |

When I used the magic dial with Maria, I was actually making a "deal" with her subconscious resistance. If I hadn't done this, she might have fought me and resisted when I tried to help her change the way she was thinking and feeling.

Do you know why? She might resist change because of all the benefits of her depression and anxiety. Taking them away would almost be like taking away a mother's love for her child. No loving mother will let you get away with that.

And that's why people may resist treatment, including you. Because your negative thoughts and feelings can be really helpful and appropriate and because they always reflect your core values as a human being.

Isn't that cool?

By using the magic dial, I put Maria in control and assured her that we would reduce her feelings to the levels she selected and no further. It meant I was working *for* her and that she'd become the boss. I was no longer the "expert" who was trying to fix someone who was "broken."

## THE COGNITIVE "CLICK"

Once we identified the distortions in Maria's thinking and highlighted what was positive and awesome about her negative thoughts and feelings, we were ready to challenge and crush the distorted thoughts that were causing her suffering.

I've developed more than 100 helpful techniques to assist people in challenging and defeating negative thoughts, but one of the easiest is called the double standard technique. If you recall from the introduction, this technique involves imagining how you would talk to a dear friend going through the same exact problem as you.

Using this technique, I asked Maria what she would say to another new mother experiencing the same difficulties as she was. Would she say, "Oh, you're such a bad mom for wanting to give up on breastfeeding?"

Maria immediately responded by saying that she'd *never* say something like that to another mother. When I asked her why not, she said it would be cruel, and it wouldn't be fair or realistic either.

I asked Maria what she would say, and she replied:

*I'd remind her that lots of women have trouble with breastfeeding, that it's not unusual or terrible, and that it's not entirely under her control. I'd also tell her that there's a whole lot more to being a good mother than just breastfeeding.*

I asked Maria if what she was saying was true, and she said it absolutely was.

And here is where the magic happened: I asked Maria if she'd be willing to talk to herself in the same realistic and compassionate way she'd talk to another woman, and she instantly brightened up and got it.

Maria recorded this new positive thought—the one she would have told a dear friend—in her Daily Mood Journal and indicated that she believed this new thought 100%, as you can see on the next page. Then I asked her to re-rate how much she now believed the negative thought, and it suddenly dropped to zero.

That was pretty exciting, so I used the same technique again and asked Maria if she'd tell this other woman that she *should* be feeling happy given how much she wanted a baby. Maria replied:

*Of course not! I'd tell her that wanting a child doesn't mean that there won't be some difficult times and that she's entitled to the same feelings as anybody else!*

| Negative Thoughts | %<br>Now | %<br>After | Distortions | Positive Thoughts | %<br>Belief |
|---|---|---|---|---|---|
| 1. I'm a bad mom for wanting to give up on breastfeeding. | 90 | 0 | All-or-Nothing Thinking, Overgeneralization, Mental Filtering, Discounting the Positives, Magnification, Emotional Reasoning, Should Statements, Labeling, Self-Blame | *Lots* of women have trouble with breastfeeding. It's not unusual or terrible, and it's not entirely under my control. There's a whole lot more to being a good mom than just breastfeeding! | 100 |

At this point, Maria was able to challenge the rest of her negative thoughts just as easily, and her belief in all of them went down to zero or close to zero.

Now, remember that I told you that when you change the way you THINK, you can change the way you FEEL? Did this happen? As you can see in the following table, when Maria re-rated how she was feeling at the end of the session, she met or exceeded her goals in every category.

| Emotions | % Now | % Goal | % After |
|---|---|---|---|
| Sad, blue, depressed, down | 70 | 15 | 5 |
| Anxious, worried | 80 | 20 | 20 |
| Guilty, remorseful | 90 | 20 | 10 |
| Inferior, worthless, inadequate, defective | 90 | 10 | 0 |
| Lonely, unwanted, alone, abandoned | 70 | 15 | 15 |
| Hopeless, discouraged, pessimistic, despairing | 60 | 10 | 10 |
| Frustrated, stuck, thwarted, defeated | 70 | 25 | 20 |
| Angry, mad, resentful, irritated, upset, furious | 80 | 30 | 30 |

You'll notice that she decided to keep her anger slightly elevated at 30%, which was her goal. Maria explained that some anger was justified given the less-than-compassionate treatment she'd received in the hospital at times, as well as the messages that women sometimes receive from society about how they should feel and what they should and shouldn't do.

The entire process took less than an hour and was so joyful. It was wonderful to see her spirits finally soar. In fact, the final part where she challenged her negative thoughts with the double standard technique took less than ten minutes. You *can* change the way you feel, and it *can* happen really fast.

One disclaimer: I've made this process look simple, and sometimes it *is* simple. But sometimes it takes more firepower to crush your own negative thoughts. When you tell yourself that you're a failure or a hopeless loser, these thoughts may seem as obvious and real as the ground you walk on, and you may feel like you've suddenly discovered some awful truth about yourself.

I've been there myself.

But don't lose hope! I've developed a huge number of powerful techniques to help you transform your depression and anxiety into joy. I want your spirits to soar too. I'm excited to teach you all the tricks of the trade as you read this book. Let's work together to change the way you feel too!

# 3 | Why Do We Get Stuck in Bad Moods, Relationship Conflicts, or Habits and Addictions? How Can We Get Unstuck?

Nearly everyone gets down at times, and most of the time, we can pop out of a bad mood fairly quickly. Sometimes, though, bad moods and habits can be incredibly intense and persistent.

For example, I just got an email from a man in India who told me he'd been feeling depressed and hopeless for thirty-two years. He had just started listening to my weekly *Feeling Good* podcasts and was already feeling better.* I loved reading that but felt sad that he had to suffer so long before he found relief.

Some people have had it even worse. One man I recently met told me that he's never even had one happy minute in his entire life. He said he's struggled with feelings of self-hatred, worthlessness, and anger every minute of every day since childhood.

Many experts since Freud have tried to explain why some people have so much trouble overcoming depression and anxiety in spite of therapists' best efforts to help. Freud called this problem "resistance" because he thought many of his patients subconsciously resisted his efforts to help them. If you don't like the term *resistance*, we can call it *stuckness*.

But either way, the question is still the same: Why do we sometimes get stuck in bad moods, conflicts, and habits? And is it possible to get unstuck—quickly—without having to spend years free associating on an analyst's couch?

---

* The *Feeling Good* podcasts are free and you can find them at www.feelinggood.com. If you leave your email in the widget in the upper right-hand corner of any page, you'll receive a link to every blog I publish. The *Feeling Good* podcasts are also available on iTunes, YouTube, and many other outlets.

In my work as a psychiatrist, I've seen many people who seemed to resist recovery. Early in my career, I treated a pharmacist with depression named Melinda who constantly complained about her life, her friends, and the men she was dating. She said they were "losers" but didn't seem interested in using any of the tools I'd developed to overcome her depression or improve her relationships, and she never did any of the psychotherapy homework I assigned.

At the time, it almost seemed like she was more interested in complaining than in recovery. This was frustrating and puzzling since I liked Melinda and was convinced the tools I'd developed would help if she'd just give them a try. Her resistance was painful to witness because she was a beautiful person who had much to offer.

One day I emphasized that completing psychotherapy homework between sessions would be crucial if she wanted to change her life. Melinda bristled and told me if I ever again asked her to do any "goddamn" psychotherapy homework, she'd commit suicide. And she emphasized that she knew exactly how to get the job done: She explained her body would be found in the pharmacy where she worked, with a copy of my book, *Feeling Good*, on her chest and a Post-it note attached that read, "He was my shrink!"

This terrified me, so I pulled back. I told myself that I was pushing too hard and that maybe if I just listened and provided more warmth and support, Melinda would eventually come around. But two years later, Melinda was just as depressed and bitter as the first day she came to see me. I felt sad and knew I was failing her. What was I doing wrong? What was it that I didn't grasp?

Over the years, I've had tons of patients who did their psychotherapy homework and recovered rapidly, and that was (and still is) enormously gratifying. But I've had quite a few patients like Melinda as well. Why were they stuck? Did they *want* to feel depressed, anxious, and angry?

I felt that if I could answer that question, then I might be able to develop faster and vastly more effective ways of helping my patients. But if there was an answer, what was it?

## A STRANGE DREAM

One night, I woke up from a particularly vivid dream. In the dream, I saw a table that listed the two most common causes of therapeutic resistance— *outcome resistance* and *process resistance*—for each of these four targets:

- Depression
- Anxiety
- Relationship problems
- Habits and addictions

The table also made it clear that outcome resistance and process resistance are totally different from each other. But what do these words mean?

Outcome resistance means that you have mixed or even negative feelings about recovery. For example, if you're depressed, you may fight any person or therapist who tries to help you get better. In other words, you don't seem to want a good outcome and may cling to the depression.

Process resistance is quite different from outcome resistance. Process resistance means that although you may want to recover, there is something you'll have to do—but don't want to do—to recover. For example, if you're anxious, you may not want to face your fears because it seems so terrifying. Or if you're depressed, you may not want to do psychotherapy homework between sessions.

The information on the table was illuminating and exciting because it described precisely *why* people get "stuck" in depression, anxiety, troubled relationships, or habits and addictions.

Of course, the dream didn't just come out of the blue, like magic. I'd been thinking about resistance, but not getting anywhere, for some time. My mind often works like this. When I'm stuck on a problem and give up and go to bed, the answer will sometimes come to me in the middle of the night. It's pretty exciting when it happens.

## The Resistance Table

| Target | What Does Recovery Look Like? | Outcome Resistance: Why You Might Resist Recovery | Process Resistance: What's the Price of Recovery? |
|---|---|---|---|
| **Depression** | You experience joy and self-esteem. | You'll have to accept something about yourself or the world that you don't want to accept. | You'll have to do daily psychotherapy homework, and homework is no fun. |
| **Anxiety** | Your fears completely disappear. | Although your anxiety is painful, you may subconsciously believe it protects you from something even worse. | You'll have to face your worst fear, which can be incredibly frightening. |
| **Relationship Problems** | You feel close to the person you've been at odds with. | You want to blame the other person and feel totally convinced that he or she is causing the problem. | To get close to this person, you'll have to stop blaming him or her and examine your own role in the problem, which can be very painful. |
| **Habits and Addictions** | You stop overeating, drinking too much, using drugs, or procrastinating. | Your habit or addiction may be your greatest source of satisfaction. You get an immediate reward when you give in to the urge to binge, get high, or procrastinate. | To recover, you'll have to trade your greatest source of pleasure for discipline and deprivation— and that sucks. |

## DEPRESSION STUCKNESS

When it comes to depression, why do we get stuck? And why do we resist change? As you can see from the resistance table, it's because recovery from depression requires accepting something about ourselves or the world that we may not want to accept. As the Buddha said 2,500 years ago, we suffer because we tell ourselves we *need* certain things to feel happy and fulfilled. For example, we may believe we need some sort of external validation to feel happy, like wealth, success, love, popularity, or fame. Or we may believe it's necessary to achieve perfection or attain a certain level of prestige before happiness can follow.

At the same time, the Buddha also said we can feel completely happy and fulfilled without those things. Yet we fight against this idea because we don't want to accept our flaws or the circumstances of our lives, so we end up feeling depressed, ashamed, or inferior.

Telling yourself that you *need* something to feel happy and fulfilled is a lot like being in a hypnotic trance. That's because you're buying into a message that's actually not true. To be clear, there's nothing wrong with wanting certain things in life, like a baby, a loving partner, money, success, or friends. However, when you elevate a want to a need, you set yourself up for depression.

Many of us, perhaps all of us, have deep-rooted stories about who we think we are, or who we think we should be, and those stories may stand in the way of our happiness.

For example, a Harvard freshman named Biyu went to the student health center because she was profoundly depressed. Biyu was a top high school student in Hong Kong where her father owned a prestigious hardware engineering firm. Biyu was convinced she would be a straight-A student at Harvard, get a PhD in electronic engineering at MIT, and be the president of her father's company one day. But at Harvard, Biyu was struggling just to get B's and C's. She was also having trouble making friends and struggling with feelings of loneliness.

Now let's imagine that you're Biyu's therapist and that you have a magic button on your desk. You tell Biyu that if she pushes it, then she'll be instantly cured of her depression with no effort at all, and she'll walk out of today's therapy session flooded with feelings of joy and self-esteem.

Will Biyu press the magic button? Put your answer here before you continue reading.

|  | (✓) |
|---|---|
| Yes, I think she'll press the magic button. |  |
| No, I don't think she'll want to press it. |  |
| I'm not sure. |  |

Now jot down your ideas about why Biyu might or might not want to press the magic button. Once you've written down some ideas, read on to find out my answer.

---

_____

_____

_____

_____

_____

## My Answer

At first, Biyu probably will say that she wants to press the magic button (almost everyone does!), but once she grasps the implications of doing just that, she may decide that she doesn't want to press it after all. Here's why: The magic button will cause her to feel happy, but it won't change any of the facts in her life. In essence, she'll still be a mediocre student. The only thing that will change is her feelings. She'll feel joy instead of severe depression and inadequacy.

But that means letting go of her "need" to be an academic superstar. To recover today, she'll have to accept and love herself *just as she is*, even though she's not living up to her expectations of who she thinks she should be. Biyu won't want to accept her barely "average" performance because accepting this reality might seem like giving up and betraying her core values. And if this issue with self-acceptance is not addressed, then she may resist your attempts to help her.

To be clear, we're not asking Biyu to give up on attempts to improve her performance in school. We're just asking her to stop criticizing herself and making herself feel miserable. This is called acceptance. But it is very hard to accept yourself when you think you're falling short of who you think you "should" be.

Traditionally, therapists have viewed patient resistance as stemming from something negative about the patient. For example, some therapists believe patients cling to depression because they like to complain (like Melinda) or because they want to get attention (so-called "secondary gain"). Some also think resistant patients are afraid of change or want to indulge in self-pity.

The problem with these formulations is that they pathologize the patient. They are negative and disempowering, and they cast the patient in a bad light, like a whining child. And even more important, they aren't very helpful.

Biyu is not trying to get attention, doesn't complain, and has no desire to feel sorry for herself. She's not afraid of change either. Instead, Biyu's "stuckness" is a result of some of the beautiful and awesome things that her depression says about her. That sort of positive reframe is a startling concept for people who wonder what could possibly be beautiful and awesome about feeling depressed, anxious, hopeless, worthless, or lonely.

Can you see some positive or awesome things that Biyu's depression and anxiety might be saying about her? Things that might explain why she's stuck? Take a moment and jot down a few ideas before you continue reading to find out my answer.

_____

_____

_____

_____

_____

## My Answer

Biyu's depression results from many of her most positive qualities. First, she has high standards, and she's not willing to settle for mediocre performance. Moreover, these high standards have motivated her and worked for her—after all, she was one of the top high school students in Hong Kong.

Second, her depression shows an intense desire to please her parents and remain loyal to her family's values, which place a high priority on hard work and achievement. Third, depression reveals Biyu's integrity and honesty as well: She is able to admit that she's not performing well and that something's not right. When you think about it, those are some pretty amazing qualities.

At the same time, Biyu's depression represents a painful loss for her: the loss of her self-image as someone who always succeeds and excels at any challenge.

This brings us to one of the key insights that has emerged from TEAM-CBT: Is it possible that we sometimes get stuck in depression and resist change not because there is something wrong with us but because there is something right with us? Can we use this insight to reduce therapeutic resistance and vastly accelerate recovery? If so, this could lead to a major breakthrough in the treatment of depression.

Let's assume Biyu has decided she really does want to get over her feelings of depression, inferiority, shame, and hopelessness. What's something that she's going to have to do that she might not want to do?

As you can see on the resistance table, the answer is psychotherapy homework. If you are new to CBT, you may not know what psychotherapy homework is. These are the exercises you do at home between sessions to master the techniques. For example, you may be asked to record your negative thoughts in a Daily Mood Journal and to identify the distortions in them. Or you might be asked to confront something you fear.

The logic of the homework is this: Let's say you went to a tennis coach because you wanted to improve your game. In addition to working with the coach once a week, you'd need to practice between coaching sessions or your tennis game definitely wouldn't improve.

Psychotherapy is no different. My research and clinical experience indicate that homework is the key to recovery. At my clinic, practically every patient who has done at least some consistent psychotherapy homework has improved significantly, and almost every patient who has refused or "forgotten" to do homework has failed to improve. In fact, many of them got worse and eventually dropped out of treatment.

Why would anyone resist doing psychotherapy homework? There are lots of reasons, but the bottom line is that it involves work. It is totally understandable that some people, like Melinda, may just want to come to therapy to vent and get support. Having support is important, but if you want to recover, you need to roll up your sleeves and do a little psychotherapy homework too!

Perhaps you noticed that I've already given you some written homework—like the mood tests in chapter 1 and the questions about Biyu that I previously asked you to complete. Did you complete them? Or did you just skip them and continue reading?

If you skipped them, I don't want you to feel too bad, and I'm not going to scold you. In fact, I'm going to give you a little "homework credit" just for reading this book. But if you do the written exercises while you read, you'll get so much more out of this experience, and you might even enjoy a nice boost in your happiness and self-esteem.

So if you've been struggling with feelings of depression, self-doubt, or inferiority, here is my question: Are you willing to pay the price of change by doing some written exercises while you read? How much is recovery—feelings of joy, self-esteem, and greater intimacy—worth to you?

## ANXIETY STUCKNESS

Now that we've talked about depression, let's move on to anxiety. Why do we get stuck? And why do we resist change?

Anxiety resistance (or "stuckness") is totally different from depression resistance. For anxiety, resistance always results from something called magical thinking. This is the idea that although your anxiety may be painful, you subconsciously believe it protects you or your loved ones from something even worse. You might think about it like this: Anxiety is the price you pay to be safe, to motivate yourself, or to perform at your best.

There are many common types of anxiety, such as:

- Chronic worrying
- Shyness
- Public speaking anxiety
- Test or performance anxiety
- Panic attacks
- Specific phobias (e.g., fear of heights, animals, storms, flying, snakes, spiders)
- Agoraphobia, or the fear of leaving home alone
- Obsessive-compulsive disorder (OCD)
- Post-traumatic stress disorder (PTSD)
- Hypochondriasis

What would successful treatment look like? Your anxiety would suddenly disappear, and you'd feel peaceful, confident, and be completely free of fear, worry, or panic. That sounds good, but is it the outcome you *really* want?

One of the most powerful discoveries I've made is that your negative feelings always say something really good—even great—about you, and they will nearly always help you in important ways too.

Here's an example: A woman named Fran constantly worried all day long. She worried about her children, her husband, and her career. In particular, she constantly worried that her kids would be killed in a drunk-driving accident, despite the fact that they seemed to be very responsible teenagers. She was also worried about her husband's health even though he was in excellent physical shape and had recently completed his first half marathon. Finally, she was anxious about her work as a real estate broker and constantly worried that she might offend a customer or lose her job—in spite of the fact that her sales were excellent and the feedback from customers was always stellar.

Now let's imagine we have another magic button, and if Fran pushes it, she'll be suddenly cured. Her worrying will instantly vanish with no effort at all, and she'll walk out of today's therapy session feeling happy, peaceful, and optimistic about the future. Will she press the magic button?

Put your answer here before you continue reading.

|  | (✓) |
|---|---|
| Yes, I think she'll press the magic button. |  |
| No, I don't think she'll want to press it. |  |
| I'm not sure. |  |

Now jot down your ideas about why Fran might or might not want to press the magic button. Once you've written down some ideas, read on to find out my answer.

_____

_____

_____

_____

_____

## My Answer

Here is what I think: Fran may initially say that she *does* want to press the magic button, but upon some reflection, she is likely to change her mind because she subconsciously believes her worrying keeps her children and husband safe. She also believes anxiety is the price she must pay for a terrific performance in her career.

And it seems to be working! Her children and husband are safe and doing well, and she's doing great at work.

Biyu's depression and Fran's anxiety have something in common: In both cases, their symptoms, as well as their resistance to change, result from something positive, awesome, and beautiful about them. Isn't that cool? Fran's worrying also clearly results from her love for her family and her desire to do her best at work. Therefore, if she resists a therapist or friend who encourages her to stop worrying, it's because she wants to honor her core values and protect her family, not because of some kind of stubbornness or secondary gain.

Magical thinking occurs with every type of anxiety. I've listed several common types of anxiety in the following chart. See if you can figure out why someone with that type of anxiety might not want to press the magic button. Here's a hint: In every case, the person believes that anxiety will protect him or her from danger.

Once you've completed the quiz, you can review the answers at the end of this chapter.

### Magical Thinking Quiz

| Type of Anxiety | Magical Thinking<br>How does this type of anxiety help or protect you? |
|---|---|
| **Performance Anxiety.** You constantly worry that you'll blow it when you take a test, go on a job interview, or perform in public. | |
| **A Phobia.** You're afraid of cats, dogs, spiders, snakes, closed spaces, driving, storms, flying, heights, or elevators. | |
| **OCD.** You wash your hands over and over, compulsively count things, check the locks or stove repeatedly, or arrange things in a particular way. | |
| **PTSD.** You have terrifying flashbacks or upsetting memories about some traumatic event. | |
| **Shyness.** You feel intensely anxious around people, are afraid to ask someone on a date, or feel terrified about giving a talk in front of a group of people. | |
| **Hypochondriasis.** You go to the doctor for every little ache or pain, or for dizziness or some other symptom, but the doctor never finds anything wrong with you. | |

Now let's assume that you *do* want to get over your anxiety despite the magical thinking. What will you have to do (that you probably won't want to do) to overcome your fears? Put your best guess here before you continue reading.

_____

_____

If you remember from the resistance table earlier in this chapter, overcoming any type of anxiety requires confronting the very things you fear the most. You have to *expose* yourself to whatever it is you fear. That process is extremely frightening, and nearly all of us have the powerful urge to avoid intense feelings of fear. This avoidance is powerful and instantaneous because it's the way our brains are built. We are hardwired to avoid anything that feels incredibly dangerous, as it protects us from harm.

I use many techniques in treating anxiety, and if you're my patient, most of them will be fun and interesting for you. But exposure *always* has to be included in the mix. It's no fun, but there's no way around it—and I can vouch for that from my clinical work, as well as from my personal experience. I've had to overcome seventeen different kinds of fears and phobias in my life, starting from when I was a child, so I know what I'm talking about.

For example, when I was in high school, I wanted to be on the stage crew of *Brigadoon*, a play my school was putting on, but it required overcoming my fear of heights since the stage crew had to climb ladders and work near the ceiling to adjust the lights and curtains. My drama teacher, Mr. Krishak, helped me overcome this fear with the very type of exposure techniques I'm talking about. He led me to the theater and put a tall ladder in the middle of the stage, where there was nothing nearby to grab or hold on to. He told me all I had to do was stand on the top of the ladder until my fear disappeared. He reassured me that he'd stand on the floor next to me and wait.

I began climbing the ladder, step by step, and became more and more frightened. When I got to the top, I was terrified. My eyes were almost 18 feet from the floor, since the ladder was 12 feet tall, and I was just over 6 feet tall. I told Mr. Krishak I was in a panic and asked what I should do. Was there something I should say, do, or think about to make my anxiety go away? He shook his head and told me to just stand there until I was cured.

I continued to stand there in terror for about ten more minutes. When I told Mr. Krishak I was still in a panic, he assured me that I was doing great and that I should just stand there a few more minutes until my anxiety went away. A few minutes later, my anxiety suddenly disappeared. I couldn't believe it!

I told him, "Hey, Mr. Krishak, I'm cured now!"

He said, "Great, you can come on down from the ladder now, and you can be on the stage crew of *Brigadoon!*"

I had a blast working on the stage crew. I absolutely loved climbing ladders and adjusting the lights and curtains near the ceiling, and I couldn't even remember why or how I'd been so afraid of heights.

I call that the 200% cure. The 100% cure is when your anxiety entirely disappears. The 200% cure is when you realize that you love doing the very thing you were so afraid of.

As I hope my example illustrates, exposure is vitally important in the treatment of anxiety. It's a must. If you make the courageous decision to face your fears, then the probability of success is tremendously high. But if you refuse to face your fears, the odds of recovery are close to zero. Although you definitely won't *want* to confront your fears and endure the anxiety, that's the price you have to pay if you want to defeat your fears.

In spite of the fact that exposure techniques are incredibly effective, only about 25% or 30% of mental health professionals use these techniques to treat anxiety disorders. This is mind-blowing since exposure is the single most validated psychotherapy technique in the world.

Why do therapists, as well as their patients, resist exposure? I think it's because of a phenomenon I call reverse hypnosis. We all know some mental health professionals use hypnosis as a treatment tool, but you may not realize that patients can also hypnotize their therapists. In this case, patients with anxiety may persuade their therapists that they are too fragile for exposure and that something terrible will happen if they have to confront their fears. Many therapists buy right into that, so they don't use exposure. This mistake can doom the therapy to failure.

Patients can be very forceful and creative when insisting that they cannot, or should not, have to confront their fears. For example, Pedro, a young man from Argentina, emailed me for advice about a problem he was having. He explained that when he was a child, he'd struggled with depression and OCD.

When he was 14 years old, someone gave him a copy of my book, *Feeling Good*, and when he read it, he suddenly recovered.

He was so grateful that he decided to get a doctoral degree when he was older so he could teach everyone in Argentina about cognitive therapy. He followed through on his plan and was now a graduate student seeking a PhD in education.

Pedro explained that his symptoms suddenly returned when he was reading a book by Dr. Albert Ellis, a controversial psychologist who was one of the pioneers of cognitive therapy. In the book, Dr. Ellis claimed that most great spiritual teachers like Jesus were frauds and con artists who didn't really have any "special" knowledge. Dr. Ellis was an atheist and often made strong anti-religious comments in his books and workshops for their shock value.

Dr. Ellis's claim stunned poor Pedro, who was a devout Catholic. He became intensely anxious and started having intrusive fantasies of Jesus having sex with the Virgin Mary in all the positions of the Kama Sutra. He panicked and feared he was losing his mind and turning into a despicable human being. But the more he desperately tried to control these erotic fantasies, the more intense they became.

That's how anxiety works. When you try to control it, it nearly always gets worse.

Pedro asked what he should do. Could I help him?

Before I let you know what I told Pedro, I have a little quiz for you. What will Pedro have to do (that he probably doesn't want to do) to defeat his fears and recover from OCD? Put your ideas here before you continue reading. Don't worry if your ideas seem goofy, just put something down.

_____

_____

_____

_____

_____

## My Answer

I told Pedro he would have to confront his fears using a type of exposure called cognitive flooding. Instead of trying to control his fantasies, he'd have to intentionally fantasize about Jesus having sex with the Virgin Mary until the fantasy no longer made him anxious. This process might take a few minutes or an hour or more. But sooner or later, the fantasy would become boring and uninteresting.

And that's the cure: When you face the very thing you fear, it suddenly loses its power over you.

Do you think Pedro wanted to do this type of exposure? What do you think he said when I suggested this? Put your ideas here before reading on to find out.

_____

_____

_____

_____

_____

What did Pedro say? He told me he couldn't *possibly* do cognitive flooding because it was against his religion and that he would burn in hell if he did it.

That's classic anxiety resistance. Almost anybody who's struggling with any type of anxiety will resist just as strongly as Pedro. The rationale for resisting exposure will vary from patient to patient, but it will nearly always be intense.

I told Pedro I had no idea if using this exposure technique would violate his Catholic faith, but I urged him to check with a priest. I told him I'd also see what I could find out. I asked a Catholic friend who kindly offered to ask several Catholic theologians if it was okay to fantasize about Jesus having sex with the Virgin Mary in all the positions of the Kama Sutra. They agreed to debate the topic and came up with this unanimous conclusion: Cognitive flooding would be okay if the goal was healing and not entertainment.

Armed with this knowledge, I told Pedro that if he was my patient, then cognitive flooding would be a requirement, and it would not be negotiable. I shared what I had learned from the Catholic theologians and explained that exposure was almost certain to be effective and that I simply did not know how to treat him without it.

Pedro was surprised that after just a few minutes of cognitive flooding he became totally bored with his forbidden fantasies and they totally disappeared. Although exposure doesn't always work this fast, the success rate is high. However, the exposure has to be done intentionally, and you have to try to intensify the anxiety rather than trying to control it.

## RELATIONSHIP PROBLEM STUCKNESS

Now we're going to focus on relationship conflicts rather than depression or anxiety. I have a hunch you'll be able to relate to this topic because almost everyone has relationship problems. We all know someone we find annoying, someone we don't like very much, or someone we love but just can't seem to stop arguing or fighting with.

Most therapists assume people who have troubled relationships want more loving and joyous ones, so they naturally jump in and try to "help." But then the therapist runs into a huge wall of resistance and yes-butting from the patient, who complains that he or she has already tried what the therapist suggested or insists that it won't help.

What's this resistance all about? Most people are convinced that human beings want loving, rewarding relationships with others, but is it really true? Let's find out.

I want you to think about someone you really don't like or get along with, now or at any time in your life. Think about someone you resent. Do you have someone in mind? Good. So do I! Now picture what that person does that really turns you off. Maybe he or she:

- Refuses to open up and share feelings.
- Won't even talk to you.
- Pouts and slams doors, all the while insisting he or she isn't angry.
- Gets defensive and never listens.
- Argues and always has to be right.
- Complains and whines but always ignores your good advice.
- Is stubborn and controlling.
- Always has to get his or her way.
- Is self-centered and never takes your needs into account.
- Constantly brags, boasts, and acts superior.
- Is relentlessly critical of you.
- Tries to use you or take advantage of you.

- Makes demands but rarely thanks you or gives you anything in return.
- Is hostile and mean-spirited.
- Lacks compassion and warmth.

Once you can picture that person in your mind's eye, imagine that the magic button is in front of you again. If you press it, the person who you so deeply resent will suddenly become your best friend in the whole world, with no effort whatsoever. Will you press the button?

No? You *don't* want to press the dang button this time? I'm not surprised. That's what more than 95% of people tell me! When I ask this question in my workshops, there's a lot of nervous laughter, and very few people raise their hands. It seems like almost no one wants to press the magic button.

I then tell the audience, "I just offered you a choice between a hostile, troubled, abusive relationship, and a loving, joyous one. What did you choose?" Again, with laughter, they admit that they chose a hostile, troubled, abusive relationship.

And that's why we resist solving relationship problems: Because we usually have mixed feelings, or even strong negative feelings, about getting close to the person we're not getting along with.

I'm not saying this type of relationship resistance is necessarily wrong either. Sometimes it may be wise to keep our distance from certain individuals, and there's no rule that says we have to get along with everybody. All I'm saying is that humans often do not want loving, peaceful, joyous relationships.

The resistance to improving troubled relationships can be intense. You can see this in conflicts between individuals who are angry with each other, as well as conflicts between religious or ethnic groups. The power struggles between competing religious groups in the Middle East have been raging for hundreds or even thousands of years, and there doesn't seem to be a great deal of motivation to resolve these conflicts.

You don't even have to look abroad to see this apparent addiction to conflict and hostility. We can look right here at home and watch the increasingly acrimonious and disturbing political battles between conservatives and liberals.

Now let's assume that you *do* want a better relationship with someone you're not getting along with. It could be a family member, friend, or colleague. What's one thing you're going to have to do (that you probably don't want to do) to get close to that person?

To help you answer this, I have another question for you, and it's a question I also ask at my workshops. Think about the person you aren't getting along with again and answer this question from your heart of hearts: Who, in your opinion, is more to blame for the conflict? You or the other person? And in your opinion, who is the bigger jerk? You or the other person?

Tell me how you *really* feel. I'm not interested in the politically "correct" answer.

At my workshops, the vast majority say, "The other person!" Only a few say that they are to blame.

It's not surprising. Blame is intensely addictive. It makes you feel morally superior, and it makes you feel justified in telling your friends about what a "loser" or "creep" the other person is. In most cases, they'll agree with you and tell you how right you are. And you won't have to do anything to change.

But when you blame others for your relationship problems, the likelihood of recovery is zero. I'm not aware of any techniques powerful enough to help people who blame others for the problems in their relationships.

So if you want to get close to someone you're fighting with, you're going to have to do three things:

1. You'll have to stop blaming him or her for the problem.
2. You'll have to pinpoint your own role in the problem.
3. You'll have to focus all your efforts on changing yourself rather than trying to change the other person.

Those three steps can be very painful, so it's no big surprise that most people resist them. It can be shocking, and even humiliating, to have to look at ourselves and pinpoint what we're doing that provokes and fuels the conflict. It's really hard to let go of the belief that the other person is to blame. But pinpointing our own role in the problem can be liberating and incredibly rewarding because it opens the door to intimacy and trust. To do so, though, you need to allow for the death of your pride and let go of your ego.

I often have to overcome my ego in resolving relationship conflicts. For example, I once treated a woman named Alicia who'd been struggling with severe depression all her life. When she was growing up in New Zealand, she was a victim of incest from her older brothers and sexual abuse from an uncle.

Although Alicia told her parents what was going on, they didn't believe her. After a couple of months, her uncle moved to Sydney, but the abuse from her brothers continued. She felt depressed, humiliated, and enraged.

Alicia initially didn't make much progress in therapy. She seemed to blame everyone else, including me, for the problems in her life. I don't think I ever worked harder for any patient or gave more of myself. But no matter what I said or did, it was never enough.

One day during a session, Alicia looked me in the eye and said, "You know, Dr. Burns, this therapy is worse than the incest and abuse I endured as a child." I couldn't believe my ears. I was outraged. Her comment sounded incredibly ungrateful and mean-spirited. Fortunately, I bit my tongue and managed to hang on to the end of the session without saying much.

That weekend, I was jogging on a local trail and thinking about Alicia, trying to figure out how I could respond to her. I strongly believe in the importance of finding truth in a criticism, but I was stumped and angry, and I couldn't see how there could possibly be any truth in what she had said. Why had she said something so mean-spirited when I'd been trying so hard to help? What could I possibly say?

Out of the blue, it suddenly hit me like lightning, and I was pretty sure I understood what Alicia been trying to tell me.

I realized she might have felt like I had been exploiting her and trying to get her to use my techniques to satisfy myself rather than really listening to her feelings of mistrust, hurt, and anger. In other words, I wasn't providing the support, warmth, and safety she desperately needed. In a way, it really was like the incest and abuse she'd endured as a child since she was once again getting used, only this time the enemy was me. As her therapist, I had not really listened and found her emotional truth. I'd only heard her words that sounded "wrong" and "unfair." But she was right. I had not heard her story or engaged her on a deep level that led to trust.

During our next session, I explained my realization to Alicia. I told her how painful it was for me to see that I'd actually been failing her in the exact way she was claiming and that I felt ashamed and wanted to let her know how badly I felt for letting her down, especially since I had tremendous respect for her. I encouraged her to express all the despair, loneliness, hopelessness, and anger—even the rage—that she'd been feeling. I had let my ego die and said I was ready to listen.

Alicia started sobbing, and all the poison she'd been bottling up for years came spilling out. Our relationship suddenly changed, and we began working together as a team. After a couple of months of hard work, her depression lifted.

Alicia later told me that the moment that changed her life was when I admitted that I'd failed her. She said it helped enormously because someone was finally listening and believing what she was trying to say. It was only when I found truth in her criticisms that therapy became possible.

Being able to find truth in another person's criticism is one of the five secrets of effective communication. You'll learn more about these techniques later in this book, but one of the most important is the disarming technique, which is what I used when working with Alicia. That's where you find genuine truth in a criticism, even if it seems unfair or untrue. When used skillfully, the disarming technique is extremely helpful and sometimes mind-blowing.

The disarming technique is based on the Law of Opposites:

---

### Law of Opposites

When you defend yourself from a criticism that is wrong, unfair, or false, you prove that the criticism is absolutely valid, and the critic becomes even more convinced that the criticism is valid and justified.

This is a paradox.

In contrast, when you find the truth in a criticism that sounds completely unfair, exaggerated, or wrong, you immediately put the lie to rest, and the critic no longer believes the criticism!

☺

This is also a paradox.

---

If used skillfully, the disarming technique can be incredibly effective, but it can be painful to use if you're convinced that the criticism simply isn't true. It's not easy to stop blaming the other person so you can focus on your own role in a problem. But if you're willing to let your ego die, the rewards can be tremendous.

## HABITS AND ADDICTIONS STUCKNESS

This is the final form of resistance that I want to share with you. And I suspect you'll be able to identify with it.

Do you have some kind of habit or addiction that's been bugging you? Most of us do. It could be overeating, smoking, drinking too much, or using too much pot. Or it could be procrastination, excessive internet cruising, or too much cell phone use.

Why is it so hard to break these bad habits? In this case, the resistance to change is really easy to understand. For example, let's say you've slipped into the habit of drinking wine every night. You have the feeling that you may be drinking too much, so I offer you the magic button again. If you simply press the magic button, you'll never take another sip of wine. That's a really fast and simple cure.

Would you press it?

If you love a glass or two of wine every night, I didn't think so. You won't want to press the magic button be-cause a few glasses of wine in the evening may be your favorite thing in the whole world. The wine may be your only comfort after a long and frustrating day. And it may be your go-to treatment for all kinds of negative feelings, like depression, social anxiety, anger, or loneliness.

It's the same for any addiction, such as binging on your favorite food. Press the magic button and you'll instantly and permanently resist the temp-tation to eat a fabulous glazed donut, a warm Cinnabon roll, or whatever snacks and foods tempt you the most. You'll never again give in to the foods that tempt you. Instead, you'll eat small portions of really healthy things, like carrots and celery. Would you press the button?

Heck no! Who wants to eat carrots and celery? You want to be able to eat a yummy glazed donut when you want to, wherever you want to. Am I read-ing you right?

That, in a nutshell, is why we resist giving up our favorite habits and ad-dictions. We want to feel good. We want our highs.

In my workshops, I often ask, "How many of you would like to lose some weight and get in really great physical shape?" Typically, two thirds of the hands go up. That reflects the extent of overeating in America. I then say:

*Well, you just made a mistake. In fact, you don't want to lose weight and get in great shape. You know why? Because there are only two things you can do to lose weight and get in great shape—and they both suck: diet and exercise.*

*If you want to lose weight, you have to give up your goodies and go out jogging, even if you're in terrible shape and it's raining and cold out.*

*This reflects a basic law of physics that nobody can violate. You can only lose weight by reducing the calories you take in, increasing your exercise, or both. There's simply no way around it.*

*Do you really want to do that? I don't think so. I don't either!*

We all want to be lean and attractive, and we also want to be in great physical shape, but most of us don't want to diet and exercise. It's a lot more fun to eat something that we really like. Some people make claims about how wonderful you'll feel after you work out, and some will also try to sell you on the "runner's high," but you know what? There is no darn runner's high! It's a scam, a myth, and a fraud—at least for most of us.

I've tried hard to get the runner's high. I once ran twelve miles uphill. And you know what I felt when I finally arrived at the top? Darn tired. Of course, some people do get the runner's high. My daughter is one of them. If so, more power to you. You're lucky.

But for most of us, here's the bottom line: We resist giving up our habits and addictions because that means giving up a tremendous source of pleasure and gratification. And if we decide we do want to change, then we have to use discipline and deprivation, and we may even have to tolerate some withdrawal effects as well.

That doesn't sound like a very good trade-off, which is precisely why there's such a high failure rate in the treatment of habits and addictions. Research shows that some people can lose weight or give up habits for a short period of time, but the long-term outcomes typically aren't all that great.

## OVERCOMING STUCKNESS

Hopefully you now have a better understanding of the four kinds of resistance that came to me in my dream. Let's make sure you understand what you've learned so far.

In the following table, briefly describe why you, or anyone, might resist change and cling to depression, anxiety, relationship problems, or a habit or addiction. Then briefly describe what you would have to do (that you might not want to do) if you did want to change. When you're done, you can look at the resistance chart earlier in the chapter to compare your answers.

| Target | Why Do We Resist Change? | What Will You Have to Do (That You Probably Won't Want to Do) if You Want to Change? |
|---|---|---|
| Depression | | |
| Anxiety | | |
| Relationship Problems | | |
| Habits and Addictions | | |

Now before you get too discouraged about resistance and how intense it can be, I have some good news. I have many new tools that can rapidly reduce or eliminate therapeutic resistance and accelerate recovery. In fact, the tools I describe in this book represent the next revolution in psychotherapy and behavior change. These techniques are powerful—and in most cases, I believe you'll be able to use them on your own, even if you're not in therapy.

In the next chapter, I'm going to show you how I helped a woman named Karen who'd struggled with intense feelings of depression, anxiety, guilt, hopelessness, and anger after a traumatic event involving her 12-year-old daughter.

As you'll see, Karen had many good reasons *not* to change. And then something totally amazing happened.

In chapter 10, I'll show you how you can apply the exact same techniques to yourself. So let's get started!

## Answers to the Magical Thinking Quiz

| Type of Anxiety | Magical Thinking<br>How does this type of anxiety help or protect you? |
|---|---|
| **Performance Anxiety.** You constantly worry that you'll blow it when you take a test, go on a job interview, or perform in public. | You may think your anxiety motivates you and is the price you must pay for doing the best you can. |
| **A Phobia.** You have a fear of cats, dogs, spiders, snakes, closed spaces, driving, storms, flying, heights, or elevators. | You probably believe your phobia protects you from something genuinely dangerous. |
| **OCD.** You may wash your hands over and over, compulsively count things, check the locks or stove repeatedly, or arrange things in a particular way. | You may believe your compulsive ritual—such as repeatedly washing your hands—protects you from something awful, like contamination, and that if you stop washing, something terrible will happen, like getting cancer. |
| **PTSD.** You have terrifying flashbacks or upsetting memories about some traumatic event. | You may believe that constant vigilance will protect you from another traumatic experience, like being raped, mugged, or worse. |
| **Shyness.** You feel intensely anxious around people. For example, you may be afraid to ask someone on a date or feel terrified about giving a talk in front of a group of people. | If your shyness disappears, you may be afraid that you'll make a fool of yourself when you interact with people or try to give a talk in front of other people. Your shyness protects you from rejection or embarrassment. |
| **Hypochondriasis.** You may go to the doctor for every little ache or pain, or for dizziness or some other symptom, but the doctor never finds anything wrong with you. | If you stop going to the doctor every time you get an ache or pain, you might not go to the doctor when you have a real illness, like a brain tumor. |

# 4 | Karen's Story: "I'm a Bad Mom."

In this chapter, I'm going to show you how to use a powerful tool called the Daily Mood Journal. It can help you change the way you feel, no matter what the circumstances of your life might be.

I based the Daily Mood Journal on the ancient notion that your thoughts, and not external events, create all of your feelings. And when you change the way you think, you can change the way you feel! To illustrate how the journal works, I'll walk you through a real example of a patient who volunteered to participate in a live therapy demonstration during one of my summer intensives in San Francisco.

The patient's name was Karen, and she'd been struggling with feelings of depression, guilt, anxiety, and anger following a traumatic event nine years earlier. I invited Dr. Jill Levitt to be my co-therapist. TEAM-CBT is usually done with a single therapist, but for live demonstrations, I like to have a co-therapist for teaching purposes because it adds depth and richness to the experience. Dr. Levitt and I are tremendously indebted to Karen for her courage to work before a large audience on an intensely personal and painful experience and for giving us permission to share her story with you as well.

Here's what happened: Nine years earlier, Karen's 12-year-old daughter, Ashley, asked if she could go out and play after dinner. Karen had mixed feelings because it was getting late but said it was okay since Ashley often went out to play at that time.

Unfortunately, some neighborhood boys with a high-powered pellet rifle snuck up on Ashley and shot her in the face. They said they didn't think the gun was loaded. Luckily, the bullet didn't kill her, but it did blow out her front tooth, including the roots. Ashley ran inside, sobbing, screaming, and bleeding profusely.

Over the next nine years, Ashley endured multiple dental surgeries to repair the damage to her mouth, along with extensive psychiatric treatment for PTSD. This tragic event was also enormously traumatic for Karen, who blamed herself for what happened. Since that night, Karen had not experienced one moment of happiness or relief.

We asked Karen to fill out a Daily Mood Journal so we could see exactly how she was thinking and feeling. The first step in the Daily Mood Journal is to briefly describe an upsetting event that you want help with. Here's what Karen wrote down:

*Sitting here in the workshop, feeling extremely upset about Ashley.*

Next, Karen circled all the negative feelings she was experiencing and rated how strong each one was on a scale from 0 (not at all) to 100 (the worst). As you can see in the emotions table of her Daily Mood Journal, Karen was feeling sad, anxious, guilty, inadequate, hopeless, and resentful—and all of these feelings were intense.

I love the Daily Mood Journal because it shows exactly how my patient is feeling. Those ratings often come as a surprise. If you'd met Karen, you would never dream that she was feeling so desperate inside. She was personable, articulate, friendly, and even upbeat. Sometimes people hide tremendous suffering behind the positive front they present to the world.

## Karen's Daily Mood Journal: Negative Emotions*

| Emotions | % Now | % Goal | % After |
|---|---|---|---|
| Sad, blue, depressed, down, unhappy | 90 | | |
| Anxious, worried, panicky, nervous, frightened | 100 | | |
| Guilty, remorseful, bad, ashamed | 100 | | |
| Worthless, inadequate, defective, incompetent | 80 | | |
| Lonely, unloved, unwanted, rejected, alone | | | |
| Embarrassed, foolish, humiliated, self-conscious | | | |
| Hopeless, discouraged, pessimistic, despairing | 75 | | |
| Frustrated, stuck, thwarted, defeated | 100 | | |
| Angry, mad, resentful, annoyed, irritated, upset, furious | 90 | | |
| Other | | | |

We told Karen that we would ask her to rate her feelings again at the end of the session to find out whether or not she'd improved. This is an incredibly important step because it holds the patient and therapist accountable for creating meaningful and measurable change in *today's* session and not at some vague time in the future.

Now I have a question for you. Why was Karen feeling so bad? What was causing her negative feelings? Was it the traumatic event? A chemical imbalance in her brain? Her upbringing or her genes?

Think about it before you continue reading, and put your best guess here:

_____

_____

_____

_____

_____

## My Answer

Why was Karen feeling so bad? That may seem like a foolish question, and most people would probably say, "The answer should be obvious. It's because her daughter was shot in the face!"

But that's *not* the reason. The cause of Karen's intense and prolonged negative feelings goes to the very heart of an idea that's been around for at least 2,000 years, ever since the time of the Greek Stoic philosopher, Epictetus. In his classic book, *The Enchiridion*, Epictetus wrote that we are disturbed, not by things, but by the views we take of them.

In other words, the events of this world do *not* cause our suffering. Instead, our thoughts about what's happening create all our negative and positive feelings. This is a powerful and simple notion that can change your life, but it is so basic that it can be hard to grasp at first—and it may be hard to believe too.

In Karen's case, although the traumatic event was truly horrible, it was not the cause of her suffering. Instead, her negative feelings resulted from her *thoughts* about the event. I think you'll see what I mean if you review the negative thoughts Karen recorded on her Daily Mood Journal on the next page.

## Karen's Daily Mood Journal: Negative Thoughts

| Negative Thoughts | % Now | % After | Distortions | Positive Thoughts | % Belief |
|---|---|---|---|---|---|
| 1. I never should have let her go out and play. She never would have suffered from severe PTSD and depression. | 100 | | | | |
| 2. She would never have been shot if I'd been a better disciplinarian and made her stay inside. | 100 | | | | |
| 3. I'm a bad mom. | 75 | | | | |
| 4. I should not have trusted the doctors who put her on all kinds of psychiatric medications that only made things worse. | 100 | | | | |
| 5. It's my fault that her childhood was ruined. | 100 | | | | |
| 6. I'll have to spend the rest of my life trying to make it up to her. | 100 | | | | |
| 7. I can never be truly happy because I never know if she's going to be stable. | 90 | | | | |
| 8. The therapists in the audience may judge me. | 100 | | | | |
| 9. They won't like me. | 100 | | | | |
| 10. They'll think I'm a bad mom. | 80 | | | | |

As you can see, Karen was telling herself that she was a bad mom, that she never should have let Ashley go out and play, that she should have been a better disciplinarian, and that she ruined her daughter's childhood. These negative thoughts were the cause of Karen's emotional distress.

I don't mean to minimize the awfulness of what happened. Seeing your beautiful and innocent daughter getting shot in the face is truly horrific. But Karen's thoughts about the event were the real cause of her intense negative feelings. And she was still suffering nine years later because her mind was flooded by the same negative thoughts.

Now if you look to the right of each of Karen's negative thoughts, you'll also see that she recorded how strongly she believed each thought on a scale from 0 (not at all) to 100 (completely). These ratings were all high, which makes sense because when you're upset, you'll always be convinced that your negative thoughts are true.

And this brings us to the *necessary* and *sufficient* conditions for emotional distress. To feel upset, two things are required:

1. **Necessary condition:** You must have a negative thought.

2. **Sufficient condition:** You must believe the negative thought.

Since you may not have studied logic or philosophy, I'll break this down in a manner that's easier to understand. To feel emotional distress, you must have a negative thought in your mind—that's the *necessary* condition. In addition, you have to believe that the negative thought is true—that's the *sufficient* condition.

If you have a negative thought that you don't believe, then it won't upset you. For example, dwell on this thought for a moment: "The world will end in five seconds." Does that thought upset you? I don't think so! You probably don't believe it, and that's why it doesn't make you anxious.

Do you see what I mean? You must believe a negative thought before it can upset you. If you don't believe it, then it will have no impact on you. And learning to challenge and disprove your own negative thoughts is one of the most important goals of this book. These are important concepts, so I'll give you a little quiz later in this chapter to see if you can remember these two requirements for emotional distress.

Let's return to Karen. Right now, she probably does not understand that her emotional distress results from her negative thoughts, even though she's very intelligent. She still believes, just like almost everybody, that her suffering results from the actual event—the horrific trauma that her daughter endured. This way of thinking is totally understandable and practically universal, but it can make you a victim of forces beyond your control.

That's because there's no way Karen can change or undo what happened. Her daughter really did get shot in the face. But if she can change the way she's thinking about the traumatic event, then she can change the way she feels.

Before we continue, let's briefly review what you've learned so far. What causes negative feelings, like depression and anxiety? Take the following quiz. Once you've completed it, continue reading on to find the answer. But don't look until you take the quiz!

| What Causes Negative Feelings? | (✓) |
|---|---|
| 1. A chemical imbalance in the brain | |
| 2. A bad childhood | |
| 3. Repressed feelings and conflicts | |
| 4. The circumstances in our lives, such as a lack of money or education, or being rejected by someone you love | |
| 5. Traumatic events | |
| 6. Negative thoughts | |

## My Answer

The correct answer is: 6. Negative thoughts.

All your emotions result from your thoughts in the here and now. *We all create our own emotional reality at every moment of every day.*

You are doing this at the very moment you are reading this. You are having thoughts about this book and perhaps some thoughts about me or the quiz, and those thoughts are creating your feelings right now. For example, if you are telling yourself that this is too good to be true and that it couldn't possibly work for you because your problems are so severe, then you are probably feeling skeptical or even hopeless.

Or if you're telling yourself that I am a con artist, a fraud, or a phony, then you are probably feeling angry or annoyed.

Or if you are telling yourself that this is kind of exciting and promising, something that could help you or even change your life, then you are probably feeling excited and hopeful.

Do you see what I mean? Everyone is reading the same thing, but everyone feels differently depending on the thoughts, or cognitions, they are having. My words cannot affect you—only your thoughts can make you feel the way you do.

The idea that our thoughts create our moods is a fantastic and potentially empowering notion. And here's another fantastic notion that I could hardly swallow when I first learned about it more than forty years ago: The negative thoughts that trigger our pain are usually distorted, illogical, and unrealistic. That is why they are called cognitive distortions.

You learned a little about cognitive distortions in chapter 2. Essentially, a cognitive distortion is a highly misleading way of thinking about yourself or the world—it's a way of fooling yourself. If you take a look at the following table, you'll see the list of ten cognitive distortions from my first book, *Feeling Good*. This list appears on every Daily Mood Journal and makes it easy to identify the distortions in your negative thoughts.

## Checklist of Cognitive Distortions*

| | |
|---|---|
| 1. **All-or-Nothing Thinking (AON).** You view things in absolute, black-and-white categories. | 6. **Magnification and Minimization (MAG/ MIN).** You blow things out of proportion or shrink their importance. |
| 2. **Overgeneralization (OG).** You view a negative event as a never-ending pattern of defeat: "This *always* happens!" | 7. **Emotional Reasoning (ER).** You reason from your feelings: "I *feel* like an idiot, so I must really *be* one." |
| 3. **Mental Filter (MF).** You dwell on the negatives and ignore the positives. | 8. **Should Statements (SH).** You use *shoulds, shouldn't*s, *musts, ought to*s, and *have to*s. |
| 4. **Discounting the Positive (DP).** You insist that your positive qualities don't count. | 9. **Labeling (LAB).** Instead of saying, "I made a mistake," you say, "I'm a jerk" or "I'm a loser." |
| 5. **Jumping to Conclusions (JC).** You jump to conclusions not warranted by the facts.<br>• **Mind Reading (MR).** You assume people are reacting negatively to you.<br>• **Fortune Telling (FT).** You predict that things will turn out badly. | 10. **Blame.** You find fault instead of solving the problem.<br>• **Self-Blame (SB).** You blame yourself for something you weren't entirely responsible for.<br>• **Other-Blame (OB).** You blame others and overlook ways you contributed to the problem. |

* Copyright © 1984 by David D. Burns, MD. Revised 2003, 2016.

Now let's see if any of Karen's thoughts are distorted. Take a look at Karen's third negative thought ("I'm a bad mom"). Then review the list of cognitive distortions, and check off all the distortions that seem to apply.

Please do this on paper, and not in your head, unless you are driving and listening to this. In that case, pay attention to your driving! You can do the quiz on paper later.

Once you're done, you can review the answers on the next page. But please don't look until you've completed the quiz. It should be pretty easy for you, and you don't need to worry about getting it "perfect."

| Cognitive Distortions Quiz | (✓) |
|---|:---:|
| 1. **All-or-Nothing Thinking.** You think about yourself or the world in black-or-white, all-or-nothing categories. Shades of gray do not exist. | |
| 2. **Overgeneralization.** You think about a negative event as a never-ending pattern of defeat by using words like *always* or *never*. | |
| 3. **Mental Filter.** You dwell on something negative and filter out or ignore things that are positive. This is like a drop of ink that discolors the beaker of water. | |
| 4. **Discounting the Positive.** This is an even more spectacular mental error. You tell yourself that your positives don't count. This way, you can maintain a universally negative view of yourself. | |
| 5. **Jumping to Conclusions.** You jump to conclusions that aren't warranted by the facts.<br>• **Mind Reading.** You assume you know what other people are thinking and feeling.<br>• **Fortune Telling.** You make negative predictions about the future. | |
| 6. **Magnification and Minimization.** You blow things out of proportion or shrink their importance inappropriately. I call this the "binocular trick" because things either look much bigger or much smaller depending on what end of the binoculars you look through. | |
| 7. **Emotional Reasoning.** You reason from how you feel. For example, you may *feel* like a loser, so you assume you really *are* a loser. Or you *feel* hopeless and conclude you really *are* hopeless. | |
| 8. **Should Statements.** You make yourself (or others) miserable with *should*s, *must*s, or *ought to*s. Self-directed shoulds cause feelings of guilt, shame, depression, and worthlessness. Other-directed shoulds trigger feelings of anger and relationship problems. World-directed shoulds cause feelings of frustration and entitlement. | |
| 9. **Labeling.** You label yourself or others instead of focusing on the specific problem. Labeling is an extreme form of overgeneralization because you see your entire self or someone else as totally defective or bad. | |
| 10. **Blame.** You find fault with yourself (self-blame) or others (other-blame). | |

## My Answer

You could make a case for lots of distortions and arguably all ten. Karen is involved in:

1. **All-or-Nothing Thinking.** She's telling herself that she's either 100% (a "good mom") or 0% (a "bad mom"). But no mother or father is at one extreme or the other. We're all somewhere in between.

2. **Overgeneralization.** Karen is generalizing one negative event (her daughter getting shot in the face) to her entire self.

3. **Mental Filter.** She spends almost all her time thinking about the trauma and overlooking all the loving things she has done for her daughter, both before and after the trauma occurred.

4. **Discounting the Positive.** This would be the case if she's also telling herself that her loving activities "don't count" because of the trauma.

5. **Jumping to Conclusions (Mind Reading or Fortune Telling).** The thought that she is a "bad mom" does not include mind reading since she's not imagining that others are judging her. But she is involved in mind reading when she tells herself that the therapists in the audience are probably judging her. And she's involved in fortune telling when she tells herself, "I'll have to spend the rest of my life trying to make it up to her."

6. **Magnification/Minimization.** Karen appears to be minimizing the value of the enormous love and support she's provided for her daughter.

7. **Labeling.** This is classic. Karen is labeling herself as a "bad mom" as if this were her entire essence or identity.

8. **Emotional Reasoning.** Karen *feels* guilty, so she concludes she *is* a bad mom and that she *must be* guilty for the shooting.

9. **Should Statements.** This is not a clear should statement, but there are many hidden shoulds in her negative thoughts, such as "I shouldn't have let her go out and play" and "As long as my daughter is suffering, I should suffer too!"

10. **Self-Blame.** Karen is clearly blaming herself for the trauma and feels pretty sure it is all her fault.

## Scoring the Quiz

To see how you did on the quiz, count how many check marks you put in the right-hand column and look at the scoring key provided here.

| Score | What Your Score Means |
|---|---|
| 0 | If you didn't check off any distortions, then it probably means you didn't try, or maybe you didn't want to put any check marks in your book! |
| 1–3 | That's pretty good! You found at least one and maybe several distortions. You're off to a good start! When you find one distortion in a negative thought, you can often find several more. |
| 4–7 | You did a fantastic job! Way to go! |
| 8–10 | Wow! You did an awesome job! You may be a cognitive therapy genius! Keep up the great work! |

When you identify the distortions in one of your own negative thoughts, you can record them in the distortions column in your Daily Mood Journal, using abbreviations. You can see how Karen did that right here. For example, AON stands for all-or-nothing thinking, OG stands for overgeneralization, and so forth.

| Negative Thoughts | % Now | % After | Distortions | Positive Thoughts | % Belief |
|---|---|---|---|---|---|
| 1. I'm a bad mom. | 75 | | AON, OG, MF, DP, JC, MAG/MIN, ER, LAB, SH, SB | | |

Why did I want Karen to write down her negative thoughts on the Daily Mood Journal? And why would I want you to do the same?

When you record your negative thoughts on paper, it makes it much easier to see exactly what you're telling yourself. In addition, it becomes vastly easier to identify the distortions in each negative thought. If you try to do this in your head, without the written work, you may just keep cycling painfully from one negative thought to the next without getting anywhere. But if you write them down, you can begin the process of challenging your thoughts and replacing them with more realistic, positive thoughts.

And that is where emotional change occurs.

## NECESSARY AND SUFFICIENT CONDITIONS FOR EMOTIONAL CHANGE

Before we talk about the necessary and sufficient conditions for emotional change, let's review the necessary and sufficient conditions for emotional distress. Do you remember what they are? Write them down here:

| The *Necessary* Condition for Emotional Distress | The *Sufficient* Condition for Emotional Distress |
|---|---|
|  |  |

Earlier in the chapter you learned that to experience emotional distress, you must have a negative thought (necessary condition) *and* you must believe that the negative thought is true (sufficient condition). If you don't buy into the negative thought, then it won't upset you.

Now let's examine the other side of the coin by looking at the conditions required for emotional change. Let's start with the necessary condition for emotional change: You have to challenge your negative thought with a positive thought that is true.

If the positive thought doesn't seem entirely true, then it won't help you. Sometimes, when you're upset, people will try to cheer you up with positive, reassuring statements, like "You're a good person" or "Look on the bright side"—or something lame like that. In most cases, these statements won't be helpful, and they might even be downright irritating! That's because rationalizations or half-truths simply won't help any human being. Most of us simply won't buy into a bunch of BS.

Now let's look at the sufficient condition for emotional change. The positive thought must crush the negative thought. In other words, the positive thought must drastically decrease your belief in the negative thought.

And when you suddenly realize that your negative thoughts are not valid and you stop believing them, then your emotional distress will decrease or disappear entirely.

In other words, when you change the way you *think*, you can change the way you *feel*. But this has to happen at the gut level. It has to be real and not just some intellectual nonsense or positive thinking that doesn't ring true.

For example, Karen will not be able to challenge and defeat the thought "I'm a bad mom" by telling herself "I'm a good mom" because she won't believe this positive thought. But once she's identified the distortions in the negative thought, it will be much easier for her to challenge and crush it.

---

**Teaching Point**

1. **The necessary condition for emotional change:** If you want to change the way you feel, then you will have to challenge the negative thought with a positive thought that is 100% true. You can record the positive thought in your Daily Mood Journal and indicate how much you believe it on a scale from 0 (not at all) to 100 (completely).

2. **The sufficient condition for emotional change:** The positive thought must put the lie to the negative thought. In other words, the positive thought must drastically reduce your belief in the negative thought. Ideally, you will reduce your belief in the negative thought all the way to zero, although that's not always needed. The very instant you stop believing the negative thought, you will suddenly feel better!

---

Here's the bottom line: The very moment Karen stops believing the distorted negative thoughts that have been causing so much pain for the past nine years, her negative feelings will instantly improve and may even disappear completely. This is true for you too.

But changing Karen's thoughts was not going to be easy because she was a smart lady who had been trying to fight her depression for nine years, and she was still convinced her negative thoughts were absolutely true. Perhaps you've felt the same way about your own negative thoughts.

Dr. Levitt and I were going to need some powerful tools if we hoped to end Karen's suffering that day. Fortunately, I have developed many awesome tools that can work amazingly quickly. However, before we jumped in and tried to "fix" Karen, we did a couple of important things.

First, we empathized with Karen and provided some warmth, compassion, and support. Karen tearfully and painfully told her story while Dr. Levitt and I listened, provided support, and shared our sadness about what had happened to her. We paraphrased her negative thoughts and feelings in the spirit of warmth and acceptance and followed several guidelines that helped us avoid common errors therapists and loved ones sometimes make when interacting with someone who is upset:

1. We didn't try to help Karen or give her any advice.

2. We didn't try to rescue or save Karen.

3. We didn't try to cheer her up.

4. We didn't try to challenge or correct any of her distorted thoughts.

5. We didn't try to encourage her.

6. We didn't try to help her solve any of her problems.

7. We didn't try to reassure Karen or insist she was a good mom.

It is surprisingly difficult for friends and loved ones of someone who's feeling down to avoid these errors. Many people have a compulsive urge to help or give advice. Unfortunately, this usually just irritates the person who's feeling down. It may come across as patronizing too. Someone once said that if you're always trying to fix the world, then it means you view the world as broken. Empathy involves learning to listen and let the person tell his or her story.

Dr. Levitt and I listened respectfully and gave Karen the space to express herself. Karen's anguish came pouring out for about thirty minutes. Then we asked Karen how we were doing. Had we accurately understood how she was feeling? Had we provided warmth, acceptance, and support? Karen said that we'd been doing great and that she felt understood. She gave us an A on empathy.

Next, we asked Karen if she wanted some help in the session or if she needed more time to just talk while we listened. Karen said she *did* want help and *was* ready to get started, so I asked her the miracle cure question:

*Karen, let's assume that a miracle happens here today, and you go out of the session feeling fantastic. What miracle would you be asking for?*

Karen said that after nine years of misery, she would like to feel happy and at peace again. Then I asked the magic button question, which you're already familiar with:

*Karen, let's imagine that there's a magic button right in front of you, and if you press it, all your negative feelings and thoughts will suddenly disappear, with no effort at all, and you'll be flooded with joy and self-esteem. Will you press that button?*

Like nearly every person I've worked with, Karen said she *would* press the button.

Now we're going to move in a direction that may surprise Karen, and it may surprise you too. Instead of helping Karen defeat the negative thoughts and feelings that were plaguing her, Dr. Levitt and I went in the opposite direction. We worked to reduce Karen's resistance—or stuckness—before we jumped in and tried to help her. That way, we had a much greater chance of making that miracle happen that day.

I said:

*Karen, as you know, there is no magic button, but we do have some wonderful tools to help you change the way you're thinking and feeling. And although I can't guarantee anything, it's entirely possible that a small miracle could happen here today. In fact, I predict that a miracle probably will happen. But first, I think we need to step back and ask if we really want to do that. I'm not so sure it would be a good idea.*

Karen seemed confused and asked why not.

Dr. Levitt and I explained it was because her negative thoughts and feelings might reflect some really positive and awesome things about her, and there might be some important benefits, or advantages, of her negative thoughts and feelings. Before we tried to change anything, we asked if we could list the advantages of her negative thoughts and feelings, as well as the many positive and awesome things that these negative thoughts and feelings showed about her.

If you recall from chapter 2, this technique is called positive reframing. It's one of the unique features of TEAM-CBT, and it has revolutionized the treatment of depression and anxiety. Before I show you the list of positives that we came up with, I want you to give it a try. Once again, I'm going to ask you to "fail joyously" if you're willing to do that.

First, let's think about Karen's guilt. You'll recall that Karen told herself "I'm a bad mom" and "It's my fault that her childhood was ruined." These thoughts triggered Karen's guilt. Now ask yourself these two questions:

1. Are there some advantages, or benefits, of Karen's guilt?

2. What does Karen's guilt show about her and her core values that's beautiful, positive, and arguably even awesome?

Put on your thinking cap and list your ideas on Karen's Positive Reframing Chart. You don't have to do a "perfect" job when you do this assignment. In fact, you may struggle with it since positive reframing is a really new concept. Experienced mental health professionals almost always struggle with this exercise at first too.

If you do find it challenging, perplexing, or frustrating, that's actually a good thing because when you see the answers, you will suddenly understand something really important that can be helpful to you, and that's one of the main goals of this book. Trying and struggling is the best way, and perhaps the only way, to learn how this powerful technique works.

There are a few things to keep in mind when you do positive reframing:

1. Everything on your list must be positive and flattering. Negative comments like "Karen probably wants to feel like a victim" won't be helpful. They're hurtful, and they're usually not accurate.

2. Everything you list must be realistic and true. Remember that rationalizations and half-truths will never help anyone.

3. Everything you list must be a direct, clear manifestation of Karen's guilt. General, vague compliments like "Karen is a survivor" miss the point and will not be helpful.

Once you've listed a few things, you can keep reading to see what we came up with. But make sure you've listed at least one positive thing about Karen's guilt first.

## Karen's Positive Reframing Chart

| Thought or Feeling | Advantages<br>What are some advantages, or benefits, of Karen's guilt? | Core Values<br>What does Karen's guilt show about her and her core values that is beautiful, positive, and awesome? |
|---|---|---|
| Guilt | | |

Did you put something down? If you wrote something down, then you're off to a good start! But don't worry if you drew a total blank. This exercise is challenging because most people aren't used to thinking about psychiatric symptoms in such a positive way.

If you look at the first row of Karen's Positive Reframing Chart on the next page, you will see there are some definite advantages to her guilt. You'll also see that her guilt is an expression of her core values as a mother and as a human being. For example, her guilt shows what an extraordinarily loving and responsible mother she is. It's actually an expression of her intense love for her daughter, and it motivates her to do everything possible to help her daughter.

These positives may be obvious to you, but they were a huge surprise to Karen. It had never dawned on her that there could be something positive about her guilt since she'd been feeling so horrible.

## Karen's Positive Reframing Chart

| Thought or Feeling<br>List each negative thought or feeling you are analyzing here. | Advantages<br>What are some advantages, or benefits, of this negative thought or feeling? | Core Values<br>What does this negative thought or feeling show about you that is positive and awesome? |
|---|---|---|
| Guilt | • My guilt has motivated me to do everything possible to help my daughter, physically and emotionally, for the past nine years.<br>• My guilt may prevent me from making a similar mistake in the future. | • My guilt is an expression of my intense love for my daughter.<br>• My guilt reveals my sense of responsibility as a parent.<br>• My guilt shows that I take my role as a mother seriously.<br>• My guilt shows that I have a moral compass and high standards. |
| Sadness | • My suffering makes me more compassionate in my interactions with others who are suffering.<br>• My sadness makes me feel much closer to my daughter and all that she's had to go through. | • My sadness is totally appropriate since my daughter has suffered greatly.<br>• If I didn't feel sad, then it might be like saying that I didn't really care about my daughter's suffering! |
| Anxiety | • My anxiety makes me vigilant so I can protect my daughter. | • My anxiety shows my love for my daughter and for myself since we both deserve protection. |
| Inadequacy | • My feelings of inadequacy propel me to work hard and do my best as a mother and as a professional woman. | • My feelings of inadequacy show that I'm honest and realistic since I do have many flaws. |
| Discouragement and hopelessness | • My hopelessness can protect me from getting my hopes up and then getting disappointed again. After all, I've had nine years of failure in overcoming my own depression, as well as my daughter's PTSD. | • My hopelessness shows that I'm realistic and willing to face the facts instead of living in a Pollyanna world where you deny problems and insist that everything will be fine.<br>• My discouragement shows that I'm facing the truth since the treatments my daughter received for PTSD (pills, pills, pills) were not effective. |

| Frustration | • My frustration with the poor treatment my daughter has received has motivated me not to give up! | • My frustration shows my dissatisfaction with how I'm feeling and how my daughter is feeling, and it shows that I'm a fighter who won't give up. |
|---|---|---|
| Anger and resentment | • My anger has energized me to take action against the parents of the boys who shot my daughter. | • My resentment and persistence show that I'm a fighter.<br>• My anger is justified— the parents should never have let the boys play with a loaded rifle. |
| "I'm a bad mom." | • My self-critical thoughts show that I have high standards.<br>• My high standards have motivated me to achieve a great deal in my career and to do my best for my family. | • When I say, "I'm a bad mom," it might actually show that I'm a good mom because I really care!<br>• My self-criticisms show that I'm humble and not arrogant.<br>• Humility is a spiritual quality, and I want to be a spiritual person. My religious faith is central to my life.<br>• My self-criticisms show that I'm willing to be accountable and examine my own mistakes rather than blaming everyone else. |
| "The therapists in the audience may judge me." | • My fear of being judged may protect me from saying something foolish or inappropriate in front of my peers. | • My fear of being judged by the therapists in the audience indicates my desire for meaningful relationships with my colleagues. |

If we had tried to reduce or eliminate Karen's feelings of guilt without considering the many truly positive things that came along with it, then she almost definitely would have resisted our efforts. If she were to press the magic button and her guilt had suddenly disappeared, it would be like saying she didn't really care.

Can you see that?

You can do positive reframing with any negative thought or feeling. When we continued listing positives, Karen soon got into the swing of it, and the three of us came up with an impressive list of twenty-five positives. I think it is fair to say Karen was stunned. She'd been so used to thinking that there was something wrong with her when her suffering was actually the expression of what was *right* with her!

At first, it can be hard to do positive reframing because we've been programmed to think about negative feelings as symptoms of this or that "mental disorder." For example, if, like Karen, you've been feeling depressed for two weeks or more, a psychiatrist might diagnose you with major depressive disorder using the criteria listed in the DSM-5. Suddenly your feelings have been converted into a "mental disorder."

This is an odd way of looking at things for a variety of reasons. First, why do you have to have two weeks of depression to be diagnosed with a mental disorder? Why not one week? Or three weeks? It's entirely arbitrary. Why not just say that the person has been feeling depressed, and how severe it's been, and how long it's been?

Second, when you're told that you have a mental disorder, you naturally conclude that there's something "wrong" with you. That there is a defect that has to be corrected. This puts patients in a one-down position and makes it sound like the doctor has some special diagnostic ability that you don't have. I don't believe this is true!

When we do positive reframing, we are turning this way of thinking upside down. In fact, we want Karen to feel *proud* of her negative thoughts and feelings and not *ashamed* of them!

Why do we have to think of sadness as a disease in the first place? Karen's suffering was an expression of her amazing love for her daughter. In fact, all of Karen's negative thoughts and feelings were manifestations of what was beautiful about her and her core values as a mother and human being.

That's why it might not be such a good idea for her to push the magic button: All her negative feelings will disappear in a flash, but all these positives will disappear as well.

Would Karen really want that to happen? Would you if you were in her shoes?

Karen hadn't been struggling with depression and anxiety for the past nine years because she liked to whine and complain, because she was afraid of change, or because of any other negative motive. Her feelings of depression and anxiety were not due to some genetic abnormality or a "chemical imbalance" in her brain either. Her negative thoughts and feelings were an expression of what was awesome and beautiful about her.

This is likely to be true of you, too, as you'll discover in chapter 10.

Now we have an interesting dilemma. Karen doesn't want to spend another nine years feeling miserable, but if she presses the magic button, all those beautiful things about her will go down the drain.

How will we resolve this dilemma? Can you think of any solutions?

Jot down your ideas here before you continue reading. Again, the goal is not to get the "right" answer but simply to get your brain circuits firing in some new and different ways. I make mistakes constantly and find they can often be the first step in learning something new.

_____

_____

_____

_____

_____

## My Answer

You may recall the magic dial from chapter 2. Dr. Levitt and I asked Karen to imagine we had a magic dial, instead of a magic button, so she could dial down each negative feeling to some optimal amount rather than trying to make the feeling disappear entirely. That way, she might be able to feel a whole lot better without losing any of the positive things about her negative thoughts and feelings.

For example, Karen's feelings of sadness are totally appropriate. Can you imagine how weird
it would be if she pressed the magic button
and suddenly felt happy? It would be like saying, "Oh, my daughter has suffered tremendously for the past nine years because she was
shot in the mouth, but I'm as happy as I can be!"

Can you see how bizarre that would sound?

Some sadness and depression about her daughter's trauma is totally appropriate, even desirable. But does she need to feel 90% sad and depressed? If
she had a magic dial, what would she want to dial down her sadness to?

Karen decided that 10% would be sufficient, so she put a 10 in the "%
Goal" column of her Daily Mood Journal, as you can see here. You can also
see that she decided she wanted to reduce her anxiety from 100 to 20, her
hopelessness and discouragement from 75 to 10, and all the other negative
feelings to 0.

| Emotions | % Now | % Goal | % After |
|---|---|---|---|
| Sad, blue, depressed, down, unhappy | 90 | 10 | |
| Anxious, worried, panicky, nervous, frightened | 100 | 20 | |
| Guilty, remorseful, bad, ashamed | 100 | 0 | |
| Worthless, inadequate, defective, incompetent | 80 | 0 | |
| Lonely, unloved, unwanted, rejected, alone | 0 | 0 | |
| Embarrassed, foolish, humiliated, self-conscious | 0 | 0 | |
| Hopeless, discouraged, pessimistic, despairing | 75 | 10 | |
| Frustrated, stuck, thwarted, defeated | 100 | 0 | |
| Angry, mad, resentful, annoyed, irritated, upset, furious | 90 | 0 | |

By using the magic dial, we were essentially making a deal with Karen's
subconscious mind. We were asking her what level of negativity she would
be comfortable with. That put Karen in control and allowed her to steer the
ship. We wouldn't have to try to sell her on anything, and she wouldn't have
to resist!

The magic dial allowed Karen's subconscious resistance to save face because we were honoring her negative thoughts and feelings as the expression of something good rather than labeling them as a manifestation of a "mental disorder."

That's the great thing about positive reframing: It can help you develop some empathy for yourself. Instead of hating yourself and feeling ashamed of being "damaged" or "defective," you can be proud of all of your negative feelings as you discover so many beautiful things about yourself. And that type of internal acceptance, or "self-empathy," is really the most important key to recovery. It's not something that others can give you, but it is something you can give yourself.

When I use tools like the magic button, positive reframing, and the magic dial, I am in a radically different kind of therapeutic role. Usually, we think about the therapist as the person who promotes change. The therapist typically tries to sell the patient on overcoming his or her negative thoughts and feelings using this or that therapeutic method.

In fact, that might be why you're reading this book. You may hope to learn how to overcome your own feelings of insecurity and self-doubt so you can feel greater joy, self-esteem, and productivity, and have more loving relationships with others.

But with these new tools, I'm no longer "selling," and I'm no longer trying to persuade the patient to change. Instead, I'm honoring all the good reasons *not* to change. This really amounts to a role reversal because now the patient has to argue for change, and I become the voice of the patient's subconscious resistance. This is the opposite of the helping or rescuing approach that many—and arguably most—therapists pursue.

But what if the patient says, "You're right, Dr. Burns. I *don't* want to change!"

What then?

Strangely, that almost never happens, unless a patient is coming to me because of external coercion. But if a patient truly does not want to change, for any reason at all, then I would honor that. And I'd let the patient know that if he or she ever has a change of heart, then I'd be pleased to work with him or her again. I call this technique sitting with open hands.

Fortunately, Karen said she was incredibly eager to get to work once we completed the positive reframing chart and used the magic dial.

So far, we've completed the TEA of TEAM:

The **T** = Testing, meaning that we tested Karen's negative feelings at the start of the session. We found out that she was severely depressed and anxious, and when we reviewed her Daily Mood Journal, we discovered that she had lots of additional negative feelings as well.

The **E** = Empathy, meaning that Dr. Levitt and I listened, without trying to "help" Karen, while she told her story and the tears flowed. We proved that we were listening and hearing by reflecting what she was saying, using her own words, and summarizing how she was feeling from time to time. We also tried to convey warmth, compassion, and acceptance.

The **A** = Assessment of Resistance, meaning that we found out what Karen wanted help with, brought her resistance to conscious awareness, and melted it away using the magic button, positive reframing, and the magic dial.

Now how will we now proceed with the **M** = Methods phase of the session?

Whenever I'm working with people who are depressed or anxious, I always ask them to select one negative thought from their Daily Mood Journal that they want to work on first. This is tremendously important. I can't help you, or anyone, in a general sort of way. We've got to work with something very narrow and very specific! But the impact and implications of that can be tremendous, as you're about to see.

Karen selected the first negative thought she identified in her journal: "I never should have let her go out and play. She never would have suffered from severe PTSD and depression."

You did a great job identifying the distortions in the thought "I'm a bad mom," so let's see how you do with this one. Check off all the distortions you can find in the thought "I never should have let her go out and play."

| **Cognitive Distortions Quiz** | (✓) |
|---|---|
| **1. All-or-Nothing Thinking.** You think about yourself or the world in black-or-white, all-or-nothing categories. Shades of gray do not exist. | |
| **2. Overgeneralization.** You think about a negative event as a never-ending pattern of defeat by using words like *always* or *never*. | |
| **3. Mental Filter.** You dwell on something negative and filter out or ignore things that are positive. This is like a drop of ink that discolors the beaker of water. | |
| **4. Discounting the Positive.** This is an even more spectacular mental error. You tell yourself that your positives don't count. This way, you can maintain a universally negative view of yourself. | |
| **5. Jumping to Conclusions.** You jump to conclusions that aren't warranted by the facts. <br> • **Mind Reading.** You assume you know what other people are thinking and feeling. <br> • **Fortune Telling.** You make negative predictions about the future. | |
| **6. Magnification and Minimization.** You blow things out of proportion or shrink their importance inappropriately. I call this the "binocular trick" because things either look much bigger or much smaller depending on what end of the binoculars you look through. | |
| **7. Emotional Reasoning.** You reason from how you feel. For example, you may *feel* like a loser, so you assume you really *are* a loser. Or you *feel* hopeless and conclude you really *are* hopeless. | |
| **8. Should Statements.** You make yourself (or others) miserable with *should*s, *must*s, or *ought to*s. Self-directed shoulds cause feelings of guilt, shame, depression, and worthlessness. Other-directed shoulds trigger feelings of anger and relationship problems. World-directed shoulds cause feelings of frustration and entitlement. | |
| **9. Labeling.** You label yourself or others instead of focusing on the specific problem. Labeling is an extreme form of overgeneralization because you see your entire self or someone else as totally defective or bad. | |
| **10. Blame.** You find fault with yourself (self-blame) or others (other-blame). | |

When you're done, you can review my answers on the next page. But don't look until you've completed the quiz!

## My Answer

Identifying distortions is not a pure science, but here are some distortions I spotted in Karen's thought: "I never should have let her go out and play. She never would have suffered from severe PTSD and depression."

1. **Mental Filter.** Karen was thinking only about her daughter's trauma and judging herself as a bad mother because of this one event.

2. **Discounting the Positive.** Karen was not thinking about all the loving things she had done for her daughter before the trauma and ever since. And she might even have been tempted to say those positive things "didn't count" since her decision led to the traumatic event.

3. **Jumping to Conclusions (Mind Reading or Fortune Telling).** Karen was engaging in what I call anticipatory fortune telling: She expected herself to be able to predict the future so she could prevent something bad from happening. When I pointed this out to her, she had an aha moment and saw that no human being could be expected to predict the future.

4. **Magnification/Minimization.** At first, I didn't think this distortion was present because Karen's daughter had endured nine years of emotional distress, and the incident was genuinely traumatic. However, a colleague pointed out that she *was* magnifying her role in the incident and minimizing the role of the perpetrators and their parents. Once you "see" this (or any) distortion, it becomes so clear!

5. **Emotional Reasoning.** We'd probably have to ask Karen to see what she really thinks, but it did seem that because she *felt* guilty, she had concluded that she *was* to blame for her daughter's suffering.

6. **Should Statements.** This is a clear and classic should statement. Karen was telling herself that she should have known her daughter was about to get shot, which is impossible.

7. **Self-Blame.** This is another classic example of self-blame. Karen was clearly blaming herself for the fact that her daughter got shot.

Here are some distortions I did *not* find in the negative thought.

8. **All-or-Nothing Thinking.** I did not check off this distortion because Karen did not see herself in black-or-white terms in this particular thought. She was just saying that she'd made a specific mistake that

had horrible consequences. However, she did engage in all-or-nothing thinking when it came to other negative thoughts ("I'm a bad mom").

9. **Overgeneralization.** If you selected this distortion, I would give you credit because she did use the word *never*. However, I don't think this negative thought is a very strong example of overgeneralization because Karen really meant that she shouldn't have let her daughter go out and play on that particular evening. She did not mean to imply that she was "always" screwing up this way or that she "never" did anything right.

10. **Labeling.** I don't see any labeling in this thought. However, she was certainly labeling herself when she called herself a "bad mom," as we discussed earlier.

How did you do? Most of the distortions are obvious. For example, Karen's negative thought is clearly a should statement since she's saying, "I never should have..." It's also a classic example of self-blame since she's blaming herself for the traumatic event. However, one of the most important distortions was subtle, and you might have missed it. I missed it at first too.

When Dr. Levitt and I were asking Karen about the distortions she could identify in that thought, we noticed that she had included fortune telling in the distortion column (with the abbreviation FT), as you can see here:

| Negative Thoughts | % Now | % After | Distortions | Positive Thoughts | % Belief |
|---|---|---|---|---|---|
| 1. I never should have let her go out and play. She never would have suffered from severe PTSD and depression. | 100 | | MF, DP, FT, ER, SH, SB | | |

Can you see why Karen's negative thought might be an example of fortune telling? Put your best guess here before you continue reading:

_____

_____

_____

_____

_____

Did you figure it out yet? Dr. Levitt and I didn't see it right away either!

It was puzzling at first because we usually think of fortune telling as making a negative prediction about something bad that's going to happen in the future. For example, individuals with depression sometimes tell themselves that things will never change, so they feel hopeless. Or individuals with anxiety tell themselves that something awful is about to happen, so they feel scared. But Karen was not making a negative prediction.

Suddenly a light bulb went off in my head. It dawned on me that Karen's negative thought was a somewhat unusual example of fortune telling: She was telling herself that she should have been able to predict the future so she could prevent this bad thing from happening.

But no human being can predict the future.

When I mentioned this, Karen had an aha moment and realized that she'd been expecting the impossible from herself. You could see the pain draining out of her face almost instantly, and she looked way more relaxed. I'm so glad we recorded the session on video because it was a remarkable moment to behold.

I asked Karen to explain this distortion to me in her own words, and she said:

*I can't predict the future. I had no way of knowing she would get shot when she walked out the door that night.*

From your perspective, this might seem obvious and not really an aha moment—because you're not Karen. But when you're struggling with your *own* feelings of self-criticism or self-doubt, your own negative thoughts will feel every bit as realistic and compelling as Karen's.

That's one of the truly amazing things about depression and anxiety: We convince ourselves that our own extremely distorted and unfair negative thoughts are absolutely valid. If you've ever struggled with depression or anxiety, I'm certain that you know exactly what I'm talking about. You can see how distorted Karen's negative thoughts are, but you are probably still convinced your own negative thoughts are totally true!

Dr. Levitt and I asked Karen to include her discovery in the positive thoughts column and to tell us how much she believed the positive thought. She said she believed it 100%. Then we asked how much she now believed the negative thought, and she said that she no longer believed it, so she put 0 in the "% After" column.

This is how her Daily Mood Journal looked at that point.

| Negative Thoughts | % Now | % After | Distortions | Positive Thoughts | % Belief |
|---|---|---|---|---|---|
| 1. I never should have let her go out and play. She never would have suffered from PTSD and depression. | 100 | 0 | MF, DP, FT, ER, SH, SB | It was her routine to go out and play every night. This night was no different. A loving mother lets her child go out to play. I'd been doing that for years and had no way of knowing she was about to get shot. | 100 |

In the early days of cognitive therapy, I rarely saw such incredibly rapid changes, but I see this all the time now. I'm convinced this is because of the powerful effect of positive reframing. Once you see the positive side of your negative thoughts and feelings, it becomes much easier to challenge and defeat them.

After Karen defeated the first negative thought, we worked on the other negative thoughts in her Daily Mood Journal. She was able to defeat most of them easily, as you can see on the next page. In the next chapter, you'll learn more about how to crush negative thoughts with something I call a recovery circle, though in Karen's case, the aha moment was all she needed to change the way she was thinking and feeling.

| Negative Thoughts | % Now | % After | Distortions | Positive Thoughts | % Belief |
|---|---|---|---|---|---|
| 1. I never should have let her go out and play. She never would have suffered from severe PTSD and depression. | 100 | 0 | SH, AON, MF, FT, SB | It was her routine to go out and play every night. This night was no different. A loving mother lets her child go out to play. I'd been doing that for years and had no way of knowing she was about to get shot. | 100 |
| 2. She would never have been shot if I'd been a better disciplinarian and made her stay inside. | 100 | 0 | SH, AON, MF, FT, SB | What happened wasn't my fault, and it wasn't a matter of needing to be a better disciplinarian. I've let her go out and play every night for many years. | 100 |
| 3. I'm a bad mom. | 75 | 0 | AON, LAB, SH, SB, DP, ER | Good mothers cannot protect their children from everything. I am very loving, caring, and supportive. While it is true that I cannot protect her from everything, that doesn't make me a bad mother. | 100 |
| 4. I should not have trusted the doctors who put her on all kinds of psychiatric medications that only made things worse. | 100 | 0 | SH, SB, MF, AON | I did the best that I could by seeking out professional help from qualified professionals. I can't blame myself for not knowing that some of them were going to make things worse. | 100 |
| 5. It's my fault that her childhood was ruined. | 100 | 0 | MF, DP, AON, SB, ER | It's not my fault that she's suffered from depression and PTSD or that she's had to spend so much time at the doctor's office. She's fortunate that we've had the resources to get the best dental services for her so she doesn't look disfigured. In fact, I have been so supportive and loving toward her, trying to get her the best possible help all these years. | 100 |

| | | | | | |
|---|---|---|---|---|---|
| 6. I'll have to spend the rest of my life trying to make it up to her. | 100 | 0 | SH, SB, DP, FT, MAG, AON | I'd rather spend the rest of my life enjoying my daughter and rejoicing that she's alive rather than feeling guilty. | 100 |
| 7. I can never be truly happy because I never know if she's going to be stable. | 90 | 0 | SH, SB, AON, MF, ER, OG | I can finally let go of the guilt I've been carrying around for years and reclaim my happiness. I've paid for this long enough! | 100 |
| 8. The therapists in the audience may judge me. | 100 | | MR | | |
| 9. They won't like me. | 100 | | MR | | |
| 10. They'll think I'm a bad mom. | 80 | | MR | | |

As you can see, Karen needed a little help with the last three negative thoughts in her Daily Mood Journal. She was still engaging in mind reading because she was convinced the therapists in the audience would judge her, dislike her, and think she was a bad mom.

Initially, she wanted to combat these thoughts with this positive thought: "If they're judging me, then that's their problem!" This thought brought a wave of cheers and applause from the audience because it sounded great!

But there was a problem with this thought. Can you see what it is? *It buys into the idea that the audience really is judging her.* But what if they aren't?

Instead, Dr. Levitt and I asked Karen if we could think of a way to test her belief that the audience was judging her, to which she replied, "I suppose I could ask them."

We asked Karen if this idea made her anxious, and she said it made her tremendously anxious. In fact, she practically fainted with fear.

Do you think that meant it was a good idea or a bad idea? Should we encourage Karen to face her fears and ask the people in the audience if they are judging her since it makes her so anxious?

Put your answer here before reading on to find my answer:

|  | (✓) |
|---|---|
| 1. I think it's a great idea for Karen to ask the therapists in the audience if they're judging her. |  |
| 2. I don't think it's good idea. It's too risky because she may find out that the therapists in the audience really *are* judging her. |  |
| 3. It will be a waste of time because the people in the audience won't be honest with her. They'll just shine her on! |  |
| 4. I'm not sure. |  |

## My Answer

It's a great idea! You may remember that exposure is the key to overcoming your fears. When you discover that the monster has no teeth, then you'll experience a joyous jolt of enlightenment.

Karen resisted this idea at first. She said the idea freaked her out and that the people in the audience probably wouldn't be honest with her.

I told her we could cross-examine them and ask if they were being honest or just being "nice." I also told her that her intense anxiety meant this was just the thing to do.

Karen courageously asked if some of the audience members would be willing to walk up to one of the microphones so she could ask them what they thought of her. Many people rushed to the front and told Karen, one by one, how they'd been touched and inspired by her courage and how she had become their hero that night. Most had tears streaming down their cheeks. Their comments were mind-blowing.

Karen could hardly believe what she was hearing, and her belief in the last three negative thoughts also dropped to zero. She looked stunned—even dazed.

To find out if the session had been helpful, Dr. Levitt and I asked Karen to re-rate the negative feelings she had listed in her Daily Mood Journal, just as she'd done at the beginning of the session. You may recall that T = Testing is one of the key features in TEAM-CBT. I test every patient at the start and end of every session, with no exceptions.

As you can see in the "% After" column, the results were phenomenal—all of Karen's negative feelings had completely disappeared. In fact, two of them *more* than disappeared. She re-rated her feelings of guilt and shame at minus 1,000 and her feelings of being stuck at minus 1,000,000!

| Emotions | % Now | % Goal | % After |
|---|---|---|---|
| (Sad,) blue, depressed, down, unhappy | 90 | 10 | 0 |
| Anxious, worried, panicky, nervous, frightened | 100 | 20 | 0 |
| Guilty, remorseful, bad, ashamed | 100 | 0 | −1,000 |
| Worthless, inadequate, defective, incompetent | 80 | 0 | 0 |
| Lonely, unloved, unwanted, rejected, alone | 0 | 0 | -- |
| Embarrassed, foolish, humiliated, self-conscious | 0 | 0 | -- |
| Hopeless, discouraged, pessimistic, despairing | 75 | 10 | 0 |
| Frustrated, stuck, thwarted, defeated | 100 | 0 | −1 million |
| Angry, mad, resentful, annoyed, irritated, upset, furious | 90 | 0 | 0 |

We asked Karen if these changes were real or if she was just being "nice" for the demonstration. And if the changes were real, what were the healing elements of the session? After all, she'd been struggling with intense feelings of sadness, guilt, anxiety, and anger for nine years, and now it looked like she had totally recovered in one therapy session. Was this possible? And if so, how and why did this happen?

Karen said: "I don't know what the hell just happened! Wow! It was amazing! It was a miracle!"

While you're reading this book, we'll see if we can work a little miracle for you too!

# 5 | Melanie's Story: "She'll Tell Others Who Will Judge Me!"

In the last chapter, you saw how rapidly TEAM-CBT works and often in just a single extended therapy session. The sudden and dramatic changes we see with TEAM-CBT have been amazing and rewarding. I never get over the thrill of seeing someone's transformation from tears and despair to joy and laughter right before my eyes. It really is, to use Karen's words, "a miracle."

As you read about Karen, you got a feel for how some of the new techniques—the magic button, positive reframing, and the magic dial—work to melt away resistance or stuckness. However, those techniques, while vitally important, are not enough. You will also need powerful techniques to challenge and crush your negative thoughts.

Over the past several decades, I've developed more than fifty methods to crush the negative thoughts that cause depression, anxiety, relationship problems, and habits and addictions. You can see a list with descriptions at the beginning of chapter 33 ("Fifty Ways to Untwist Your Thinking").

But what methods should you use? And how can you select the ones that are most likely to be helpful for you?

In this chapter, I'm going to answer those questions by describing the treatment of a woman named Melanie. Melanie had felt defective and ashamed for nearly ten years because she believed she hadn't lived up to her personal, moral standards. In addition, she was terrified that others would find out about her failures and judge her.

Have you ever felt like that? Do you ever worry about being judged or not being good enough? I know I have! I'm sure the details of your life are very different from Melanie's and different from mine, but these concerns are almost universal.

Melanie volunteered to let me film a live therapy session so I could create a teaching product to show how TEAM-CBT works. Dr. Angela Krumm was my co-therapist for the session. As the session unfolded, Melanie tearfully explained that she'd received an upsetting call from a member of her church a few days earlier. The woman who called had expressed condolences for the death of Melanie's mother-in-law.

Melanie explained that her tears were not because of the death of her mother-in-law. Melanie was upset because she had to tell the woman who called that her mother-in-law had *not* died—it was her ex-mother-in-law.

With tears still running down her cheeks, Melanie confessed that she was actually in her third marriage and had *two* ex-mothers-in-law. She felt intensely ashamed and was afraid the woman who called would tell other people about her failed marriages, and then her reputation would be ruined.

Melanie explained that her current marriage of nine years was very successful and that she and her husband were very much in love, but she'd been hiding her two failed marriages from nearly everybody. She said that when she and her husband were out with friends having fun, she'd feel good for a couple of hours because she'd "forget" about her failed marriages. But then she'd suddenly remember, and her heart would sink because she'd start worrying about people finding out and judging her. She said these concerns plagued her every day and robbed her of feelings of freedom, peace, self-esteem, and joy.

If you look at Melanie's Daily Mood Journal on the next page, you'll see that she identified the phone call as the upsetting event, and she had many intensely negative thoughts and feelings about it.

You'll see that she was telling herself she was a failure, that people would judge her when they found out about her failed marriages, and that she was defective. She was also afraid people would think she couldn't maintain relationships. Her belief in all these negative thoughts was high.

Melanie's fifth negative thought was especially interesting, as she was afraid that her children would be humiliated at her funeral. Although she wasn't even ill, she had the fantasy that people would be chuckling and gossiping about her when she was being buried!

## Melanie's Daily Mood Journal*

**Upsetting Event:** Telephone call from a church member offering condolences after my ex-mother-in-law died.

| Emotions | % Now | % Goal | % After | Emotions | % Now | % Goal | % After |
|---|---|---|---|---|---|---|---|
| **Sad**, blue, depressed, down, unhappy | 50 | | | **Embarrassed**, foolish, humiliated, self-conscious | 100 | | |
| **Anxious**, worried, panicky, nervous, frightened | 100 | | | **Hopeless**, discouraged, pessimistic, despairing | 25 | | |
| **Guilty**, remorseful, bad, ashamed | 100 | | | **Frustrated**, stuck, thwarted, defeated | 80 | | |
| **Inferior**, worthless, inadequate, defective, incompetent | 95 | | | **Angry**, mad, resentful, annoyed, irritated, upset, furious | 75 | | |
| **Lonely**, unloved, unwanted, rejected, alone, abandoned | | | | **Other** | | | |

| Negative Thoughts | % Now | % After | Distortions | Positive Thoughts | % Belief |
|---|---|---|---|---|---|
| 1. I'm a failure. | 100 | | | | |
| 2. She'll tell other people who will judge me. | 100 | | | | |
| 3. I'm defective. | 85 | | | | |
| 4. People will think I can't maintain a relationship. | 95 | | | | |
| 5. My children will be humiliated at my funeral. | 90 | | | | |
| 6. People will think I deserve to be punished. | 95 | | | | |
| 7. I might be abandoned. | 100 | | | | |
| 8. It's only safe to share my failures with others who've had failed marriages. | 100 | | | | |

One of the really sad things Dr. Krumm and I learned was that Melanie had received numerous civic awards for her work with disadvantaged individuals in the community. Sometimes she'd even been honored at events with hundreds of people in the audience.

And yet what do you think she did with all those awards? She hid them in her office closet!

Do you know why? What do you think? Put your best guess here:

_____

_____

_____

## My Answer

You may have guessed that Melanie hid her awards because she didn't think she deserved them. That's what almost everyone thinks.

But that's *not* why Melanie hid them. She kept her awards hidden because they had three different names on them. And she was afraid her colleagues and students might look at the plaques and ask, "Gee, Melanie, it's great that you got all these awards. But who are all these different people? Why are there three different names on these plaques?" And then she'd have to reveal the "horrible" truth that she was in her third marriage.

Isn't that sad?

Melanie also told us she was active in the marriage ministry of her church, where she helped troubled couples. But this only added to her feelings of anxiety and shame because she felt like a fraud. My heart went out to Melanie because she was a beautiful, humble, gentle, and giving person.

How can we help Melanie change the way she's thinking and feeling? I'll walk you through it step by step, with some exercises to do along the way. If you complete these exercises, then it will be much easier for you to crush your own negative thoughts when we start working on them in chapter 10.

The first thing Dr. Krumm and I did was simply listen and provide warmth while Melanie shared her negative thoughts and feelings for the first thirty minutes or so of the session. Once again, we didn't try to intervene or "help" her. We just paraphrased her words and acknowledged the pain she'd been in.

Then we asked if she was ready get some help with the anxiety, shame, and defectiveness that had been plaguing her or if she needed more time to talk and get support. Melanie said she definitely wanted help and felt ready to get started.

I asked Melanie what kind of help she'd want. If a miracle happened during today's session, what was she hoping that miracle would be?

Melanie said she hoped she'd feel free from the feelings of anxiety and shame that had been plaguing her for nine years and that she'd stop worrying about people finding out about her two failed marriages and judging her. And if they did find out and judge her, she wouldn't care or worry about it so much anymore.

I asked Melanie to imagine we had a magic button, and if she pressed it, all of her negative thoughts and feelings would instantly disappear, with no effort at all. She'd walk out of the session on a high, feeling joyous and free.

Melanie said she *would* press the magic button "as long as there was no work involved!" Almost everyone says they want to press the button, but as you've learned, people often have conscious and subconscious reasons that keep them stuck. That's why it's important to melt away some of that stuckness if we hope to see meaningful change.

If you take another look at Melanie's Daily Mood Journal, you'll see that she had many negative thoughts and feelings. Now I want you to focus on her negative thoughts and feelings, one at a time, and ask yourself these two questions:

1. What does this negative thought or feeling show about Melanie and her core values that's positive and awesome?

2. What are some benefits, or advantages, of this negative thought or feeling?

List all the positives you can think of on the Positive Reframing Chart on the next page. You can use any of her negative thoughts or feelings when you do this exercise. Just make sure that you focus on them one at a time.

Remember that you don't need to do a "perfect" job. Just jot some things down. When you're done, you can turn the page and see what Melanie and I came up with. And remember, if you came up with different answers, that's just fine. You may have some insights that we missed. And if some of your answers seem lame, that's even better. I want you to fail shamelessly and joyfully when you do this exercise and all the exercises in this book!

## Melanie's Positive Reframing Chart

| Negative Thought or Feeling from Melanie's Daily Mood Journal | Advantages and Core Values |
|---|---|
|  |  |
|  |  |
|  |  |
|  |  |
|  |  |
|  |  |
|  |  |

Here's what Melanie and I came up with:

## Melanie's Positive Reframing Chart

| Negative Thought or Feeling | Advantages and Core Values |
|---|---|
| Sadness | • Melanie's feelings of sadness are appropriate since one of her ex-mothers-in-law has just died. She has maintained close relationships with both ex-mothers-in-law following her divorces, so the grief is normal.<br>• Her feelings of sadness about her two failed marriages are also appropriate and show that she has a sense of loss. |
| Guilt and shame | • These feelings show that Melanie has a moral compass and that she values love and marriage. |
| Anxiety | • Melanie's anxiety reminds her not to tell people about her failed marriages. This protects Melanie, as well as her friends, family, students, and church members who look up to her so they won't have to feel ashamed or disappointed in her. Of course, Melanie might change her thinking about this after today's session, but up until now, her policy has been to keep the failed marriages secret, and her anxiety helps her remain vigilant. |
| Feelings of inadequacy, defectiveness, and incompetence | • When Melanie labels herself as defective, she is being realistic since she does have many flaws and defects, just like the rest of us.<br>• These feelings also show her humility, which is a spiritual quality. Melanie's warmth and humility are very real and part of what makes her so likable.<br>• These feelings also show that she has high standards, and her high standards have motivated her to accomplish a great deal. |
| Anger | • Her anger is justified and shows that she will stick up for herself since many people are judgmental, including some churchgoers who claim to be devoutly religious. |
| Hopelessness | • Melanie only feels slightly hopeless, which is good. Her hopelessness can protect her from getting her hopes up and then feeling disappointed. |
| "I'm a failure." | • This negative thought shows that Melanie has high standards. Her self-criticisms also show that she's willing to be accountable and examine her own shortcomings rather than blaming everyone else the way so many people do. |
| "People will think I deserve to be punished." | • Melanie's fears of being judged show that she values meaningful, loving relationships with her friends, students, and the people in her church. She wants to feel close to people, and she wants people to value her. That's a good thing! |

If you came up with even more positives, that's great. This is subjective. It's not a pure science.

Once we completed our lists, Melanie decided she didn't want to push the magic button since there were so many good things about her negative thoughts and feelings. She said she'd prefer instead to dial down her negative feelings to lower, more manageable levels.

For example, she wanted to keep her anxiety at a healthy 40% since her anxiety was keeping her vigilant and protecting her, but she wanted to dial her feelings of depression all the way to 0%. She wanted to reduce the rest of her negative feelings as well.

| Emotions | % Now | % Goal | % After |
|---|---|---|---|
| **Sad**, blue, depressed, down, unhappy | 50 | 0 | |
| **Anxious**, worried, panicky, nervous, frightened | 100 | 40 | |
| **Guilty**, remorseful, bad, ashamed | 100 | 30 | |
| **Inferior**, worthless, inadequate, defective, incompetent | 95 | 10 | |
| **Lonely**, unloved, unwanted, rejected, alone, abandoned | | | |
| **Embarrassed**, foolish, humiliated, self-conscious | 100 | 30 | |
| **Hopeless**, discouraged, pessimistic, despairing | 25 | 0 | |
| **Frustrated**, stuck, thwarted, defeated | 80 | 0 | |
| **Angry**, mad, resentful, annoyed, irritated, upset, furious | 75 | 0 | |
| **Other** | | | |

However, these "goals" are not set in stone. Once we show Melanie how to challenge and crush her negative thoughts, something will suddenly change in her brain, and she may decide to lower some of her negative feelings even further.

Now before we move on, I want to make sure you have a clear understanding of what happened with Melanie because it may still feel new to you. By using these techniques (magic button, positive reframing, magic dial),

Dr. Krumm and I didn't jump in and try to "help" her change the way she was thinking and feeling. Doing so probably would have just fired up her resistance—and for several good reasons!

Do you know why? Why might the attempt to help Melanie fire up her resistance? Put your ideas here before you continue reading.

_____

_____

_____

_____

_____

## My Answer

First, Melanie strongly believed all her negative thoughts, and most of us will not give up any thought or idea that seems absolutely true. Truth is a tremendous motivator and guide of the human mind.

Second, most of us don't like a sales pitch. When anyone tries to push us in this or that direction, we have an automatic urge to push back.

Third—and this is crucial—Melanie's negative thoughts and feelings were expressions of her core values, and no one wants to give up or betray their core values.

And, finally, many of Melanie's negative thoughts and feelings helped and protected her. No one willingly gives up help or protection.

So instead of trying to help Melanie, Dr. Krumm and I went in the opposite direction. We gave up our voice as the therapist, expert, or helper and took on the voice of Melanie's subconscious resistance by pointing out all of the really great reasons *not* to change.

Like almost every patient, Melanie still reported that she wanted to change in spite of all the many positives and benefits we listed—but only to the levels she recorded in the goal column of her Daily Mood Journal.

## THE RECOVERY CIRCLE

Now that we've made a deal with Melanie's subconscious resistance and melted away most of her stuckness, how do we help her change the way she's thinking and feeling? And how will I help you change the way you're thinking and feeling?

As you learned in the last chapter, the first thing is to select one negative thought that you'd like to work on first. Melanie selected the second negative thought on her journal: "She'll tell other people who will judge me."

The second step involves putting this thought in the middle of what we call a recovery circle, like this:

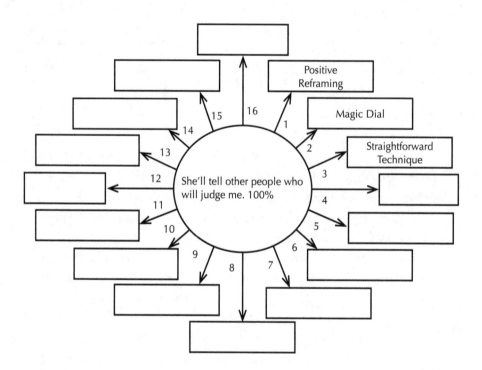

The recovery circle represents a kind of trap or prison you're in when you're feeling down, and the arrows represent ways of escaping from this trap. There are many ways to escape. At the end of the arrows, there are sixteen boxes. Each box represents a method—from the list of "Fifty Ways to Untwist Your Thinking" you'll find in chapter 33—that you can use to smash the thought in the middle of the circle.

The first three boxes are filled in because the first three techniques will always be the same:

- **Positive Reframing.** You are already familiar with this technique. You ask yourself what the negative thought says about you that's positive and awesome. And you also ask yourself how the negative thought might help you. What are the advantages of giving yourself this message?

- **Magic Dial.** You imagine that you have a magic dial that would allow you to reduce each negative feeling to some lower level so you could keep all the positive qualities associated with that feeling.

- **The Straightforward Technique.** The straightforward technique is simple: You just ask yourself if you can come up with a realistic and undistorted positive thought that will challenge or contradict the distorted negative thought in the middle of your recovery circle.

Sometimes these three techniques are sufficient to drastically reduce your belief in the negative thought (as in Karen's case in chapter 4) but not necessarily. No problem! We've got tons of great techniques. Your job is to select many additional techniques that could be helpful and to put one technique in each of the boxes surrounding the recovery circle.

Why are we filling out the recovery circle? The recovery circle is your guide to challenging and smashing a negative thought with one or more positive thoughts. But in order to help, remember that each positive thought must fulfill the two basic requirements for emotional change:

1. It must be 100% true (necessary condition).

2. It must drastically reduce or eliminate your belief in the negative thought (sufficient condition).

Let's assume Melanie comes up with this positive thought when she tries the straightforward technique: "Other people will not judge me for having two broken marriages."

Will this thought be helpful to Melanie? What do you think?

Put a check mark in the corresponding column to let me know what you think. There's one correct answer, but don't look until you've made a guess!

|  | (✓) |
|---|---|
| Yes, I think this positive thought will be helpful. |  |
| No, I don't think this positive thought will be helpful. |  |
| I'm not sure. |  |

## My Answer

The positive thought probably won't be helpful to Melanie because it's not 100% true. Some people probably will judge her for having two broken marriages. So trying to convince herself that people won't judge her simply won't cut it. As the Buddha once said, "Nobody was ever helped by phony baloney!"

However, a positive thought that's 100% true may not help either. Truth is necessary but not sufficient for change. The positive thought also has to reduce your belief in the negative thought—that's the sufficient condition for change. This is a very basic and crucial idea!

Let's imagine Melanie comes up with this positive thought: "Lots of people have had broken marriages." This thought is 100% true.

Will this positive thought help her? What do you think?

| | (✓) |
|---|---|
| Yes, I think this positive thought will be helpful. | |
| No, I don't think this positive thought will be helpful. | |
| I'm not sure. | |

## My Answer

Once again, it probably won't help because Melanie will still be worried about people judging her. In other words, even though a positive thought is 100% true, if it doesn't reduce your belief in the negative thought, then it won't be effective.

## MELANIE'S ESCAPE

Now I have an important exercise for you. It will be challenging and might be a bit frustrating as well because it will be the first time you've done it. Are you willing to give it a shot?

Sometimes I will teach you things that are easy to grasp. Other times I'll give you exercises that will be a bit harder at first. Be patient with yourself on this exercise, and don't worry about doing a perfect job. I promise you're going to learn a lot even if you struggle or stumble a bit at first. Please struggle and stumble shamelessly!

To get started, I want you to look at the following four techniques and see which ones might help Melanie challenge the negative thought "She'll tell other people who will judge me." Check off any techniques that you'd include on her recovery circle.

| | (✓) |
|---|---|
| **Examine the Evidence:** Melanie could ask herself: What's the evidence that this thought is true? What's the evidence that this thought might not be true? | |
| **Experimental Technique/Survey Technique:** Instead of jumping to conclusions about what other people think, Melanie could ask them. If they say they're not judging her, she could ask if they're being honest or simply being nice. | |
| **Reattribution:** Melanie seems to be blaming herself entirely for her failed marriages and also seems to be willing to blame herself if others judge her or gossip about her. She could ask herself, "Is this completely fair and realistic?" | |
| **Cost-Benefit Analysis:** Melanie could list the advantages and disadvantages of believing this thought. How will it help her, how might it hurt her, and are the advantages or disadvantages greater? | |

What did you check off? All of these methods could be helpful, so all of your check marks represent correct choices. Here's why:

- **Examine the Evidence.** This is a great choice. Melanie could ask herself if she knows of other people who've had one or more failed marriages, and if she still liked and respected them, or knew of other people who liked and accepted them.

  She could also use examine the evidence another way. At the start of the session, Melanie mentioned that she had told a few of her friends about her two failed marriages, so she could also ask herself, "How did they react? Did they seem judgmental? Did my disclosure seem to hurt our friendship?" In fact, they all seemed supportive, accepting, and loving when she opened up. That's at least some evidence she could use to challenge the negative thought.

  So if you selected this technique, you got an A on this exercise. Way to go!

- **Experimental Technique/Survey Technique.** These techniques are quite daring and could be incredibly helpful. Melanie could tell a number of friends, colleagues, church members, or students that she's in her third (and very happy) marriage but has felt ashamed of having two failed marriages and has been hiding this information from people.

  She could also say, "I'm tired of feeling ashamed, so I've decided to start telling people, and that's why I'm telling you. I hope we can still be friends because I've always liked you a lot. But I would like to know what you think and how you feel. Do you feel disappointed in me?"

If you selected the experimental technique or the survey technique for the recovery circle, I like your style! You're off to a great start. Way to go!

In this example, the experimental technique and survey technique are just the same thing. But sometimes they are different. A survey is just one type of experiment you can do to test a negative thought, but there are other kinds of experiments you can do that are not surveys.

- **Reattribution.** This technique can be really helpful for self-blame, and Melanie is definitely blaming herself from at least two perspectives. First, she thinks if people judge her and gossip about her, then it's her fault and it means there's something wrong with her. For my money, I'd be more likely to point the blame at the people who are judging her!

  Second, she seems to think the two divorces were entirely her fault. While it's definitely laudable that she is holding herself accountable and willing to look at her own role in the conflict, we have to ask if her previous husbands also played a role in the problems in her marriages. What do you think?

  Reattribution is such a sophisticated method that few people select it for the recovery circle. But you're absolutely right if you selected reattribution. It's a thoughtful option, so kudos to you!

- **Cost-Benefit Analysis.** This is a great technique. Melanie would list all the advantages and disadvantages of believing the negative thought. For example, Melanie's negative thought will help her in many ways. For one thing, she will keep her failed marriages secret, and this will protect her from any potential criticisms. There will be other potential benefits as well. But at the same time, the thought also hurts her because hiding her past has made her miserable for many years, and she's always worrying about being "found out."

  Once she lists the advantages and disadvantages, she can balance them against each other on a 100-point scale to see whether the advantages or disadvantages are greater.

As you can see, it's not terribly difficult to select methods for the recovery circle. And since these four techniques are all suitable for Melanie's situation, you can add them to her recovery circle on the next page. Please do that now.

Have you done that?

If so, you already have seven techniques Melanie could use to challenge the negative thought "She'll tell other people who will judge me."

Now see if you can add more techniques to Melanie's recovery circle, using the "Fifty Ways to Untwist Your Thinking" from chapter 33. Although you may not have a clear understanding of exactly how each technique works just yet, don't worry about that. I'll be teaching you the *what, how,* and *why* of most of these techniques in section II of this book. Right now, you can just guess: If you think a particular method sounds promising, write it down in one of the boxes on Melanie's recovery circle.

### Melanie's Recovery Circle*

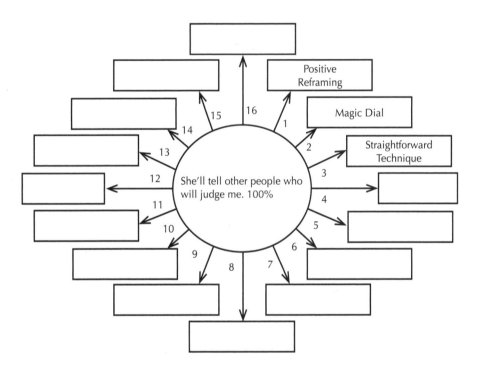

If you add a technique that you later decide was not the best choice, you will have learned something, and that's good. Rest assured that the recovery circle police are not going to arrest you!

If you are still feeling a bit intimidated about doing this exercise, then I'll make your job even easier. Before you dive in, I have created a cheat sheet on the next page to help you. As it turns out, different distortions tend to respond to different techniques. On the cheat sheet, you'll notice there is a row for each of the ten distortions and a column for each of the fifty methods. On each row, there are some white check marks and some gray check marks. A white check mark means "This technique has promise" and a gray check mark means "This technique has a lot of promise for this distortion."

---

## Cheat Sheet

| Distortion | Positive Reframing | Magic Dial | Straightforward Technique | Double Standard Technique | Examine the Evidence | Experimental Technique | Survey Technique | Reattribution | Socratic Method | Thinking in Shades of Gray | Semantic Method | Let's Define Terms | Be Specific | Worst, Best, Average | Self-Monitoring | Negative Practice/Worry Breaks | Paradoxical Magnification | Shame-Attacking Exercises | Externalization of Voices | Feared Fantasy | Acceptance Paradox | Time Projection | Humorous Imaging | Cognitive Hypnosis |
|---|---|---|---|---|---|---|---|---|---|---|---|---|---|---|---|---|---|---|---|---|---|---|---|---|
| All-or-Nothing Thinking | ✓ | ✓ | ✓ | ✓ | ✓ | | | | | ✓ | ✓ | | ✓ | ✓ | | | | | ✓ | | ✓ | | | |
| Overgeneralization | ✓ | ✓ | ✓ | ✓ | ✓ | | ✓ | | | | ✓ | ✓ | ✓ | | | | | | ✓ | | ✓ | | | |
| Mental Filter | ✓ | ✓ | ✓ | ✓ | ✓ | | | ✓ | | ✓ | ✓ | | ✓ | ✓ | ✓ | | | | ✓ | | ✓ | | | ✓ |
| Discounting the Positive | ✓ | ✓ | ✓ | ✓ | ✓ | | | | | ✓ | | | ✓ | ✓ | ✓ | | | | ✓ | | ✓ | | | ✓ |
| Jumping to Conclusions | | | | | | | | | | | | | | | | | | | | | | | | |
| • Mind Reading | ✓ | ✓ | ✓ | ✓ | ✓ | ✓ | ✓ | | ✓ | | | ✓ | ✓ | | ✓ | ✓ | ✓ | ✓ | ✓ | ✓ | ✓ | | ✓ | ✓ |
| • Fortune Telling | ✓ | ✓ | ✓ | ✓ | ✓ | ✓ | ✓ | | ✓ | | | ✓ | ✓ | | ✓ | ✓ | ✓ | ✓ | ✓ | ✓ | ✓ | ✓ | ✓ | ✓ |
| Magnification & Minimization | ✓ | ✓ | ✓ | ✓ | ✓ | | | | | ✓ | ✓ | | | | ✓ | | ✓ | ✓ | ✓ | | ✓ | | | |
| Emotional Reasoning | ✓ | ✓ | ✓ | ✓ | ✓ | ✓ | ✓ | | ✓ | | ✓ | ✓ | ✓ | ✓ | | | ✓ | | ✓ | | ✓ | ✓ | | ✓ |
| Should Statements | ✓ | ✓ | ✓ | ✓ | ✓ | | | ✓ | ✓ | ✓ | ✓ | | | | ✓ | | | | ✓ | | ✓ | ✓ | ✓ | ✓ |
| Labeling | ✓ | ✓ | ✓ | ✓ | ✓ | | | ✓ | ✓ | ✓ | ✓ | ✓ | ✓ | ✓ | ✓ | ✓ | ✓ | | ✓ | | ✓ | ✓ | ✓ | ✓ |
| Blame | | | | | | | | | | | | | | | | | | | | | | | | |
| • Self-Blame | ✓ | ✓ | ✓ | ✓ | ✓ | | | ✓ | ✓ | ✓ | ✓ | ✓ | ✓ | ✓ | ✓ | ✓ | ✓ | | ✓ | | ✓ | ✓ | | ✓ |
| • Other-Blame | ✓ | ✓ | | | | | ✓ | | | | | | | | | | | | ✓ | | ✓ | ✓ | ✓ | ✓ |

Column groupings:
- **Basic** (All): Positive Reframing, Magic Dial, Straightforward Technique
- **Cognitive** (Depression and Anxiety Disorders):
  - Compassionate: Double Standard Technique
  - Truth-Based: Examine the Evidence, Experimental Technique, Survey Technique, Reattribution
  - Logic-Based: Socratic Method, Thinking in Shades of Gray
  - Semantic: Semantic Method, Let's Define Terms, Be Specific
  - Quantitative: Worst, Best, Average; Self-Monitoring; Negative Practice/Worry Breaks
  - Humor-Based: Paradoxical Magnification, Shame-Attacking Exercises
  - Role-Play: Externalization of Voices, Feared Fantasy, Acceptance Paradox
  - Philosophical/Spiritual: Time Projection
  - Visual Imaging: Humorous Imaging, Cognitive Hypnosis

| | Uncovering | | | | Motivational | | | | | | | | Exposure | | | | | | | | Interpersonal | | | | |
|---|---|---|---|---|---|---|---|---|---|---|---|---|---|---|---|---|---|---|---|---|---|---|---|---|---|
| Individual Downward Arrow | Interpersonal Downward Arrow | What-If Technique | Hidden Emotion Technique | Cost-Benefit Analysis | Devil's Advocate Technique | Stimulus Control | Decision-Making Tool | Daily Activity Schedule | Pleasure-Predicting Sheet | Anti-Procrastination Sheet | Gradual Exposure and Flooding | Response Prevention | Distraction | Cognitive Flooding | Image Substitution | Memory Rescripting | Smile and Hello Practice | Talk Show Host | Self-Disclosure | Flirting Training | Rejection Practice | Blame/Relationship Cost-Benefit Analysis | Relationship Journal | Five Secrets of Effective Communication | One-Minute Drill |
|---|---|---|---|---|---|---|---|---|---|---|---|---|---|---|---|---|---|---|---|---|---|---|---|---|---|
| ✓ | ✓ | | | ✓ | | | | | | | | | | | | | | | | | | | | | |
| ✓ | ✓ | | | ✓ | | | | | | | | | | | | | | | | | | | | | |
| ✓ | | | | ✓ | | | | | | | | | | | | | | | | | | | | | |
| ✓ | | | | ✓ | | | | | | | | | | | | | | | | | | | | | |
| | | | | | | | | | | | | | | | | | | | | | | | | | |
| ✓ | ✓ | ✓ | ✓ | ✓ | ✓ | | | ✓ | ✓ | ✓ | ✓ | ✓ | ✓ | ✓ | ✓ | | | ✓ | ✓ | ✓ | ✓ | ✓ | ✓ | | |
| ✓ | ✓ | ✓ | ✓ | ✓ | ✓ | | | ✓ | ✓ | ✓ | ✓ | ✓ | ✓ | ✓ | ✓ | | | ✓ | ✓ | ✓ | ✓ | ✓ | ✓ | | |
| ✓ | | ✓ | | ✓ | ✓ | | | ✓ | ✓ | ✓ | ✓ | ✓ | | ✓ | ✓ | ✓ | | | | | | | | | |
| ✓ | | | | ✓ | ✓ | ✓ | ✓ | ✓ | ✓ | ✓ | ✓ | ✓ | | | | | | | ✓ | | | | | | |
| ✓ | ✓ | ✓ | | ✓ | | | ✓ | | | | | | | | | | | | | | | | | | |
| ✓ | ✓ | | | ✓ | | | | | | | | | | | | | | | | | | | | | |
| ✓ | ✓ | | | ✓ | | | | | | | | | | | | | | | | | | ✓ | ✓ | ✓ | |
| | ✓ | | | ✓ | | | | | | | | | | | | | | | | | | ✓ | ✓ | ✓ | ✓ |

All    Habits and Addictions    Anxiety Disorders    Relationship Problems

Once you pinpoint one or more distortions in a negative thought, you can use the cheat sheet to easily find more methods to include on the recovery circle.

For example, Melanie's first negative thought ("I'm a failure") is a classic overgeneralization. Here are the techniques with gray check marks that have a lot of promise:

- Positive reframing
- Double standard technique
- Examine the evidence
- Be specific
- Let's define terms
- Externalization of voices
- Acceptance paradox
- Individual downward arrow
- Cost-benefit analysis
- Worst, best, average

And these are some techniques with white check marks that have some promise:

- Straightforward technique
- Survey technique

Now you've got a lot of methods to add to the recovery circle if the negative thought in the middle is an overgeneralization.

Is Melanie's thought "She'll tell other people who will judge me" an overgeneralization? Tell me what you think!

|  | (✓) |
|---|---|
| Yes, I think this negative thought is an overgeneralization. |  |
| No, I don't think this negative thought is an overgeneralization. |  |
| I'm not sure. |  |

## My Answer

This is not a slam dunk one way or the other, but I think you could argue that the thought is an overgeneralization since Melanie seems to think that *everyone* will judge her because of her two failed marriages, and this is clearly not true. In addition, she seems to be overgeneralizing from her behavior to her "self" in thinking that people will judge her entire "self" as bad because of her two failed marriages.

Overgeneralizing from some specific failure to your "self" is the cause of a great deal of emotional distress because you begin to feel like you're defective or not good enough. I see this thinking error all the time when I'm working with people who feel depressed or anxious.

Do you ever fall into this trap at times? Most of us do. Almost all my students and colleagues feel like this at times. So do I!

Any thought with an overgeneralization is likely to have many additional distortions, so using the cheat sheet allows you to identify even more techniques you can add to the recovery circle. Let's see if you can pinpoint more distortions in Melanie's negative thought "She'll tell other people who will judge me." Check off all the distortions you can find in this thought.

| **Cognitive Distortions Quiz** | (✓) |
|---|---|
| **1. All-or-Nothing Thinking.** You think about yourself or the world in black-or-white, all-or-nothing categories. Shades of gray do not exist. | |
| **2. Overgeneralization.** You think about a negative event as a never-ending pattern of defeat by using words like *always* or *never*. | |
| **3. Mental Filter.** You dwell on something negative and filter out or ignore things that are positive. This is like a drop of ink that discolors the beaker of water. | |
| **4. Discounting the Positive.** This is an even more spectacular mental error. You tell yourself that your positives don't count. This way, you can maintain a universally negative view of yourself. | |
| **5. Jumping to Conclusions.** You jump to conclusions that aren't warranted by the facts. <br> • **Mind Reading.** You assume you know what other people are thinking and feeling. <br> • **Fortune Telling.** You make negative predictions about the future. | |
| **6. Magnification and Minimization.** You blow things out of proportion or shrink their importance inappropriately. I call this the "binocular trick" because things either look much bigger or much smaller depending on what end of the binoculars you look through. | |

| 7. **Emotional Reasoning.** You reason from how you feel. For example, you may *feel* like a loser, so you assume you really *are* a loser. Or you *feel* hopeless and conclude you really *are* hopeless. | |
|---|---|
| 8. **Should Statements.** You make yourself (or others) miserable with *should*s, *must*s, or *ought to*s. Self-directed shoulds cause feelings of guilt, shame, depression, and worthlessness. Other-directed shoulds trigger feelings of anger and relationship problems. World-directed shoulds cause feelings of frustration and entitlement. | |
| 9. **Labeling.** You label yourself or others instead of focusing on the specific problem. Labeling is an extreme form of overgeneralization because you see your entire self or someone else as totally defective or bad. | |
| 10. **Blame.** You find fault with yourself (self-blame) or others (other-blame). | |

Don't continue reading until you've checked them off!

## My Answer
You could make a pretty good case for all ten distortions.

1. **All-or-Nothing Thinking**. This is definitely present because Melanie is assuming *everyone* will judge her in a totally negative way because of her two failed marriages.

2. **Overgeneralization.** As we've pointed out already, Melanie is thinking that if one person judges her, then everyone will judge her. In fact, people are different and don't all think the same way. Some people might even like her more and feel closer to her when they learn of her struggles. I know that's how Dr. Krumm and I felt during the session!

3. **Mental Filter.** Melanie is focusing entirely on her shortcomings and filtering out everything that's good or even great about her. There are a lot of positives that she's filtering out!

4. **Discounting the Positive.** She's telling herself that her current wonderful marriage, her volunteer work for the community, her civic awards, and her warmth and generosity don't really count.

5. **Jumping to Conclusions.** She assumes others will judge her (mind reading) and is making negative predictions about the future (fortune telling).

6. **Magnification and Minimization.** Although most people would prefer not to have two failed marriages, Melanie is blowing it out of proportion, as if she's a terrible, despicable human being. She's also minimizing her inner beauty, as well as the love that so many people have for her.

7. **Emotional Reasoning.** Melanie *feels* guilty and ashamed, so she concludes she really *must be* bad. She also *feels* anxious and afraid, so she assumes she's in grave danger of widespread condemnation, judgment, and rejection.

8. **Should Statements.** Melanie is filled with hidden shoulds because she believes she *should not* have failed marriages and that she *should be* way better than she is.

9. **Labeling.** When she uses the phrase "judge me," she is using emotionally charged language, as if she's on trial for serial killing.

10. **Blame.** Melanie is blaming herself big-time.

Now we've got an abundance of riches! If you use the cheat sheet I've provided, then you'll find lots of techniques to include in Melanie's recovery circle. For example, since this negative thought is an example of all-or-nothing thinking, you might want to use thinking in shades of gray. And since it's a hidden should statement, you might want to include the acceptance paradox and the semantic technique.

As you continue to read, you will develop a much deeper appreciation for how these techniques work and how you can use them to crush your own negative thoughts. Remember, we're just getting started. Don't put yourself under pressure to get it all right now. You're on board now and the boat is just leaving the dock as we head toward a new destination.

One last thing: You don't have to use the cheat sheet when you do this exercise. If you prefer, you can just skim through the list of "Fifty Ways to Untwist Your Thinking" in chapter 33 and add any techniques to the recovery circle that appeal to you. That's the way I prefer to do it, but the cheat sheet is okay too.

Take a stab at it now. If you haven't already done so, identify all the techniques Melanie could use to crush her negative thought "She'll tell other people who will judge me." This exercise should take you fifteen or twenty minutes, but don't worry if it takes a bit longer. I think it will be well worth the time. If you spend an hour thinking about how the various techniques might work, that's great!

When you're done, you can check out the recovery circles that Melanie, Dr. Krumm, and I completed on the following page, but don't look at them until you're done. You'll see that we filled up two recovery circles, but I only asked you to complete one because I didn't want you to feel overwhelmed.

## Melanie's Recovery Circles

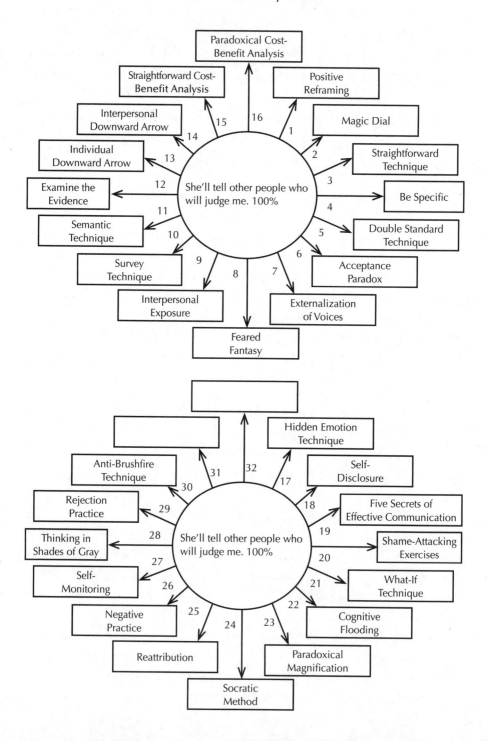

You'll see that we came up with lots of methods to help Melanie challenge the thought "She'll tell other people who will judge me."

Why have I created so many methods?

It's because all human beings are different, and you never know what method will lead to recovery. When you complete your recovery circle for one of your own negative thoughts, you can set yourself up for success by following a philosophy we call "failing as fast as you can."

Why would you want to fail as fast as you can? Well let's say you find out that one of the techniques on your recovery circle isn't helpful, and you still feel anxious and depressed.

No problem! You can just move on to the next technique. The faster you fail, the quicker you'll get to the technique that does work.

Isn't that cool? It always gives me great relief to know that I've got tons of ways of helping any patient so I don't have to keep trying the same approach over and over again. I think this philosophy might also help you because you can see that if one or even several approaches don't work, there are still tons of other options. The goal is rapid, substantial, and lasting change—and, for the most part, I don't care too much what technique brings that result about.

Although all the methods are different, every technique is designed to change how you feel at the gut level. And the change has to be proven in two ways. First, you will suddenly report, "Hey, I'm feeling better now. In fact, I feel GREAT!" Second, your improvement will be reflected by a profound reduction in the negative feelings in your Daily Mood Journal.

Once you complete the recovery circle, try the techniques you listed one at a time. After each technique, try to come up with a positive thought that fulfills the two requirements for emotional change:

1. The positive thought has to be 100% true.

2. It has to drastically reduce your belief in the negative thought that is the source of your emotional distress.

During the session, it took the three of us about fifteen minutes to populate Melanie's recovery circles, working together as a group, so we had many techniques to choose from. Melanie said she wanted to try a gentle technique first, so we started out with the double standard technique. As I mentioned in earlier chapters, this technique involves asking yourself if you'd be willing to talk to yourself in the exact same way you'd talk to a dear friend who was just like you.

Dr. Krumm and I used the role-play version of the double standard technique to add a bit more drama and zip to it since we were working together live. Here's the way it worked: Dr. Krumm agreed to play the role of a dear friend named Angela, who was like Melanie's long-lost identical twin. We explained that Angela was the same age and looked a lot like Melanie, and she had all of Melanie's strengths and weakness. However, this Angela was a different person who was a dear friend of Melanie's. Melanie agreed to play herself in the exercise.

Dr. Krumm began by explaining that she had a problem that was remarkably similar to Melanie's problem. She said:

> *Melanie, I don't know if you're aware of this, but I've been married for nine years, and I'm in my third marriage. My third marriage has been wonderful, and I've finally found my knight in shining armor, but I've been hiding the fact that I've had two failed marriages, and I'm really feeling ashamed and worried. I'm concerned people will judge me if they find out. What do you think?*

Melanie immediately responded with gusto. She said:

> *Although some people might judge you, most people will see the beautiful parts of your personality, and those who do judge you will simply make themselves look bad.*

Melanie looked very confident and self-assured when she said this. The sudden change in her affect and demeanor was startling.

Dr. Krumm continued role-playing and told Melanie that what she said was encouraging, but she asked if Melanie was telling the truth or simply being nice. This cross-examination was very important because we wanted Melanie to prove in a convincing way that the negative thought was false.

Melanie insisted that what she was saying *was* true and explained that although some people might judge her, most people would not.

Angela continued to cross-examine Melanie, still in the role of a friend, and asked:

> *But what if some people do judge me? Are you saying that's okay and that I should be happy about that?*

Melanie came up with another powerful response. She said:

*I'm not saying it's okay or that you should be happy if someone judges you. But the bottom line is that you've found someone you love, and you have a beautiful marriage now, and you can be really happy about that. And if people want to judge you, let them go ahead and judge you. They can just go home and eat popcorn and get fat!*

Melanie was clearly knocking it out of the park! Every time Angela challenged her, Melanie crushed it.

She was clearly a changed person, and the change had happened almost instantly, the moment they started the role-play exercise. You could see the change in Melanie's face and body language. She had suddenly found a strong, loving voice within herself and appeared extraordinarily confident and self-assured. This was dramatically different from the way she had looked and felt just minutes earlier when she was in tears.

I asked Melanie how strongly she believed the things she was saying to Angela, the woman who was just like Melanie. She said, "100%." I replied, "Well, if it's true of Angela, it must also be true of you since Angela is essentially your clone."

Melanie agreed, so I asked her to record those statements in the positive thoughts column of her Daily Mood Journal, which now looked like this:

| Negative Thoughts | % Now | % After | Distortions | Positive Thought | % Belief |
|---|---|---|---|---|---|
| 2. She'll tell other people who will judge me. | 100 | | AON, OG, MF, DP, MR, FT, MAG, ER, SH, SB | Some people may judge me. Most people will see the beautiful parts of my personality. Those who judge me will make themselves look bad. | 100 |

As you will recall, the necessary condition for emotional change is that the thought must be 100% true. Do you remember what the sufficient condition is? The sufficient condition is that the positive thought must lead to a significant reduction in your belief in the negative thought.

I asked Melanie how much she now believed the negative thought. She said it no longer had much credibility and that her belief in it had dropped to 35%, so she recorded that in the "% After" column in her Daily Mood Journal, as you can see here:

| Negative Thoughts | % Now | % After | Distortions | Positive Thought | % Belief |
|---|---|---|---|---|---|
| 2. She'll tell other people who will judge me. | 100 | 35 | AON, OG, MF, DP, MR, FT, MAG, ER, SH, SB | Some people may judge me. Most people will see the beautiful parts of my personality. Those who judge me will make themselves look bad. | 100 |

Melanie said the negative thought had lost its hold over her. She was absolutely convinced most people would not judge her, and even if a few people did judge her, this no longer seemed like much of a threat.

Most of the time, the moment you crush one negative thought, there will be an almost instantaneous change in how you think and feel, and it will usually be easy to crush the rest of your negative thoughts.

This was the case for Melanie. As you can see on her completed Daily Mood Journal on the next page, she was able to smash all of her negative thoughts, and her negative feelings changed dramatically as well.

## Melanie's Daily Mood Journal*

**Upsetting Event:** Telephone call from a church member offering condolences after my ex-mother-in-law died.

| Emotions | % Now | % Goal | % After |
|---|---|---|---|
| **Sad**, blue, depressed, (down), unhappy | 50 | 0 | 0 |
| **Anxious**, worried, panicky, nervous, frightened | 100 | 40 | 5 |
| (Guilty), remorseful, bad, (ashamed) | 100 | 30 | 10 |
| **Inferior**, worthless, (inadequate), defective, incompetent | 95 | 10 | 5 |
| **Lonely**, unloved, unwanted, rejected, alone, abandoned | | | |
| **Embarrassed**, foolish, humiliated, self-conscious | 100 | 30 | 10 |
| **Hopeless**, discouraged, pessimistic, despairing | 25 | 0 | 0 |
| **Frustrated**, stuck, thwarted, defeated | 80 | 0 | 0 |
| **Angry**, mad, resentful, annoyed, irritated, upset, furious | 75 | 0 | 0 |
| **Other** | | | |

| Negative Thoughts | % Now | % After | Distortions | Positive Thoughts | % Belief |
|---|---|---|---|---|---|
| 1. I'm a failure. | 100 | 0 | AON, OG, MF, DP, MAG, LAB, SH, SB | I've successfully rebounded from past mistakes and unwise choices. I was successful in refraining from allowing adversity to rob me of my current happy nine-year marriage. Besides, no one has ever said I'm a failure because of my three marriages. | 100 |
| 2. She'll tell other people who will judge me. | 100 | 35 | AON, OG, MF, DP, MR, FT, MAG, ER, SH, SB | Some people may judge me. Most people will see the beautiful parts of my personality. Those who judge me will make themselves look bad. | 100 |

| # | Negative Thought | % Now | % After | Distortions | Positive Thought | % Belief |
|---|---|---|---|---|---|---|
| 3. | I'm defective. | 85 | 10 | AON, OG, MF, DP, MAG, ER, LAB, SB | All humans are imperfect, so I must be normal in my imperfection. I'm from the human species. | 95 |
| 4. | People will think I can't maintain a relationship. | 95 | 0 | AON, OG, MF, DP, MAG, SB | I made a mistake with my first two choices. It is unhealthy to remain in a bad relationship. I've been married to my third husband for nine years, and we are both very, very happy and compatible. I maintain great relationships with my ex-in-laws from both previous husbands. Now *that's* maintaining a relationship. | 100 |
| 5. | My children will be humiliated at my funeral. | 90 | 5 | AON, MF, DP, MR, FT, ER | They will be older and understand the complexity of relationships. Their grief will supersede their possible fleeting moments of shame. They love me and are proud of me for many things I have done. They are close to my third husband who has helped them in so many ways. They might even say, "Mom had it going on!" | 100 |
| 6. | People will think I deserve to be punished. | 95 | 0 | AON, OG, MR, FT, DP, ER | I was already punished when I was still in the unhappy marriages. I paid my dues in advance. I have been punished by the shame I have carried. People are more compassionate than cruel to divorced women. | 100 |
| 7. | I might be abandoned. | 100 | 0 | AON, MF, MR, FT, MAG, SB, ER | No one has distanced from me yet because of it. In fact, I have kept many of my old friends from both marriages and made many new ones that are my third husband's friends. The handful of people I'm not in contact with may have disappeared for other reasons. | 100 |
| 8. | It's only safe to share my failures with others who've had failed marriages. | 100 | 0 | AON, MF, MR, FT, ER, MAG | Some of my single friends, who have never been married, say I am lucky or blessed. They did not condemn me despite the shame in my thoughts. In fact, no one who has been married only once has ever actually said anything condemning. | 100 |

Melanie's recovery was dramatic, and it happened in a single therapy session—just as it had happened for Karen, who you read about in the last chapter.

I know what you might be thinking right now.

- This couldn't have been real. It happened too fast. Melanie was just trying to please Dr. Burns and Dr. Krumm. Her feelings did not really change at the gut level.

- This is too good to be true. Recovery from years of depression, anxiety, defectiveness, and shame could never happen that fast.

- Even if Melanie did have a temporary "flight into health" (Freud's expression for sudden recovery), the positive feelings could not last.

These are all important concerns. And if you have any of those doubts, then I'm glad you're being skeptical. I was skeptical of much of what I was taught during my residency training in psychiatry, and that skepticism led to new discoveries. If you're not a bit skeptical, you're probably too gullible!

Here are my answers to your concerns:

- The sudden change in Melanie *was* real. I see equally dramatic, rapid changes most of the time when I'm doing therapy. I believe this is primarily the result of the new tools I've developed, like positive reframing, which are beginning to look like a significant breakthrough in the treatment of depression and anxiety disorders. Once your resistance is diminished or gone, genuine miracles become possible.

- Recovery from years of depression, anxiety, and self-doubt *can* happen rapidly. In fact, the very moment you put the lie to your negative thoughts and you stop believing them, your feelings will almost instantly change. Recovery, in my experience, nearly always happens in a flash.

  But it's not easy since you have to crush the negative thoughts that trigger your negative feelings. Rationalizations, intellectualizations, and half-truths simply won't do the trick. You have to really grasp that you've been fooling yourself with your distorted, negative thoughts. That's why I've included so many methods in this book: so you'll know we've got plenty of firepower to get the job done.

- Rapid recovery is highly desirable, but your negative thoughts and feelings *will* return at some point. No one is entitled to be happy all the time.

This includes Melanie, you, me, and practically everyone. Negative thoughts and feelings are part of the human condition.

We will all fall into black holes from time to time. It only becomes a problem if you get stuck in a black hole for weeks, months, or years. But if you do relapse prevention training (which I'll discuss in section IV), then you can prepare for these relapses ahead of time. That way you'll have a little ladder so you can climb right back out of the black hole and feel good—or even GREAT—again.

You'll also discover the same techniques that worked for you the first time you recovered will always work for you—that's one of the interesting things about this approach and the way our minds work.

If you are still in a state of doubt or disbelief about the incredibly rapid changes Melanie experienced, then I have some good news for you. The session with Melanie was recorded by two television camera professionals, and it's available if you'd like to watch it and see for yourself what happened. It is one of the most dramatic therapy sessions ever recorded, and you could learn a great deal from it. If that interests you, you can find further information about the video in the store on my Feeling Good website.

And if you still think this sort of rapid recovery isn't possible for you, then that's understandable—especially if you've been suffering for some time. But in the next few chapters, I'll show you evidence that treatment *can* happen at a high speed—sometimes even in a single session! To demonstrate how it works, I'll provide a few more case studies of some wonderful individuals I've worked with who experienced what I call the "single session cure." I'll even provide you with links to some of these sessions so you can see their recovery for yourself.

Then we'll roll up our sleeves and see what we can do for you!

# 6 | High-Speed Treatment—Is It Possible? Desirable? Or Just Fool's Gold?

Many people believe that recovery from depression or anxiety has to be a long, slow process that unfolds over a period of years. In fact, that's what I was taught as a psychiatric resident. And my experience seemed to confirm that it was true. No matter how much listening I did and how many medications I prescribed, the majority of my patients seemed to improve slowly, if at all.

Now my experience is radically different, and I actually see ultra-rapid recovery pretty routinely now. This profound change often happens in just a few sessions using the techniques described in this book. Many times, my patients experience a significant reduction or even a complete elimination of negative feelings in a single extended therapy session! You've seen some examples of this kind of rapid recovery already with Karen and Melanie.

But the idea that people can recover quickly from depression and anxiety is controversial and can be threatening to some therapists. Some therapists don't believe rapid recovery is possible even when they see it with their own eyes! At one of my annual four-day intensives, I treated a young woman with a history of severe trauma who experienced an amazing and jubilant recovery in a little over an hour. In fact, I had to try to stretch out the session because her recovery seemed almost *too* fast.

When people turned in their evaluations for the day, a number of therapists wrote rather hostile comments indicating that they were angry and convinced she was an actress. They believed the live therapy session was fake and had been staged!

I read these criticisms out loud on the second morning of the workshop and asked our patient what she thought. She explained that her depression and trauma were *very* real and that her suffering had been agonizing and prolonged. She also explained that she now felt incredibly joyous and that these new feelings were equally intense and real.

The audience stood and gave her a much-deserved standing ovation. If you're also feeling skeptical, and you'd like to see a brief follow-up video with her a couple of months later, just to satisfy yourself that it did happen and was real, you can check it out at my website ("Was it Real? Or a Hoax?").

Because some of you might still be skeptical, I decided to look through my charts and analyze the last forty or so individuals I've treated in workshops, as I've saved the before-session and end-of-session mood ratings for most of them. As you can see, the reduction in feelings of depression, anxiety, and anger during the session were dramatic.

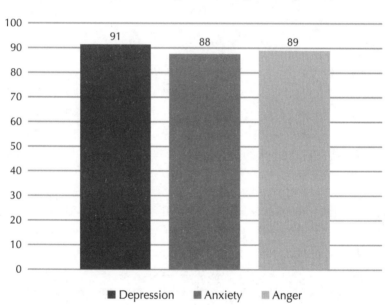

% Reduction in Negative Feelings During Session

Of course, a reduction in negative feelings does not necessarily imply an improvement in positive feelings because you can be relatively undepressed but still be unhappy with your life. But as you can see on this next chart, the increases in positive feelings from the start to the end of the session were equally dramatic.

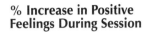

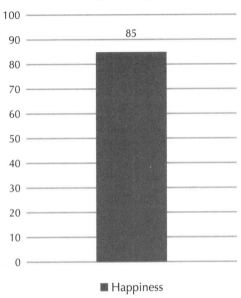

■ Happiness

These single-session changes are quite impressive when you consider two facts:

1. Nearly all of these individuals had been depressed and anxious for years—decades in some cases—prior to the time I worked with them.
2. All the published outcome studies examining the efficacy of antidepressants and/or individual psychotherapy for depression have found that generally fewer than 50% of patients experience even a 50% reduction in symptom severity.

Why have the individuals I've treated in the past several years recovered so rapidly? There are lots of competing ideas about this, and we'll have to wait for more research on TEAM-CBT before we can draw any firm conclusions, but here are some things that might contribute to the amazingly rapid changes I've seen:

1. The patients I work with in public settings are highly motivated. After all, they have to get up in front of a crowd of strangers to share deeply

personal feelings and problems, and this takes tremendous courage and determination.

2. I have somewhat of a high profile, so patients may get excited to work with me and may expect miracles. In this case, these miracles might just be the result of a super placebo effect.

3. The patients I treat in workshops are fairly high functioning, and some of them have been familiar with my work prior to coming to the workshops.

4. I've been getting data from every patient I've treated for the past forty years. The feedback has sometimes been painful, but it has radically shaped how I do therapy. I've worked hard to polish my craft.

5. TEAM-CBT may really be a superior form of therapy. In particular, the methods I've developed to reduce or eliminate therapeutic resistance could be largely responsible for the incredibly rapid changes I'm seeing.

6. I treat people for free, so I have no motive to prolong the treatment—I'm not getting paid anyway! My only reward is seeing them recover. Most people also know they'll just get one shot with me since I'm seeing them in the context of workshops around the country.

   I believe this could be a powerful factor. I let them know that I'll see them just this once and that I anticipate, but clearly cannot guarantee, complete recovery. This may function as a self-fulfilling prophecy for recovery.

   This is in contrast to how private practice works, where therapists are rewarded financially by a more prolonged treatment. The therapist may inform the patient that therapy will take weeks, months, or more—and that message can function as a self-fulfilling prophecy too.

7. There might be something about the way I do therapy that is especially helpful to people. When I've watched recordings of myself doing therapy, I've been surprised, and even shocked, by how much humor plays a role in the therapy I do. Even in sessions with people who've experienced horrific abuse or trauma, a good 25% of the session seems to involve laughter, even giggling. Although that might appear unprofessional, I do think that laughter can have an incredible healing effect and can also convey genuine warmth and affection.

8. I never try to operate within the traditional, 50-minute therapy session. I use an extended session, which usually lasts about 2 hours. That's the amount of time I need to go through all four parts of TEAM.

9. Many of the people I work with on stage reveal incredibly personal information that they have been hiding in shame for years or decades. And most are pretty convinced that the people in the audience are judging them.

   We often test this using the survey technique toward the end of the session. I encourage the patient to ask the people in the audience if they're judging him or her. When they discover amazing warmth and admiration rather than rejection, it has a mind-blowing effect on the patient and usually on the audience as well.

In my opinion, all of these factors probably play a role, except for number three. When I've worked with individuals with few resources and little education, they've been exceptionally easy to work with. I don't buy the theory that high-functioning individuals are easy to treat. They're not! And when I've worked with people who are not familiar with my work, they've responded just as rapidly as those who've read my books.

To my way of thinking, the factor that towers above all the others is number five. The positive reframing I've developed seems to unleash the possibility of incredibly rapid change in nearly all individuals struggling with depression and anxiety.

Of course, more research is needed to learn how effective TEAM is when it's administered by therapists I've trained. Just because I'm getting excellent results with this approach doesn't mean other therapists will. Therapy is part art, part science. I've been working at it for a long time, and I believe my skills have evolved tremendously over the years.

In the next few chapters, I'm going to present a number of brief and inspiring descriptions of patients who recovered rapidly with TEAM, along with exercises in every chapter that will help you develop and refine your own positive reframing skills. These exercises will *not* be difficult or time-consuming, and if you do them on paper, I think good things will be in store for you as well!

Because seeing is believing, I'll also provide internet links to some of the sessions so you can witness what happened firsthand and judge the results for yourself. If you take the time to follow some of the links, I think it will be time well spent. When you see or hear someone recovering right before your eyes, and you witness the transformation from tears to laughter, it can inspire and inform you at the same time.

As they say, sometimes a picture is worth a thousand words! So let's take a look.

# 7 | Mark's Story: "I've Been a Failure as a Father."

In April 2017, I published a podcast of a live therapy session with Mark, a physician who felt he was a failure as a father. My co-therapist during the session was Dr. Jill Levitt. Although it was just a single therapy session, we broke it into smaller segments and included some teaching and commentary with each segment so it became seven consecutive *Feeling Good* podcasts. Those podcasts have received tens of thousands of downloads. This chapter is based on that remarkable session.

During our session with Mark, he told us that he'd been haunted for decades by a problem with his oldest son, whom he'd never gotten close to. Although Mark's problem will probably be very different from your own, you might also understand what it's like to feel like a failure or to tell yourself that you're defective or simply not good enough.

Mark explained that he had two goals in life when he was a young man. He hoped to have a large, loving family and wanted to become a skillful and compassionate physician. Although he felt he had achieved the second goal, he felt sad and guilty because he'd failed to develop a loving relationship with his oldest son from a previous marriage. He said that he'd felt bad about this for several decades.

If you take a look at Mark's Daily Mood Journal on the next page, you'll see he was consumed by a variety of negative thoughts. For example, he thought he was a failure and that his brain was defective. He also worried that he wasn't doing a good enough job for Dr. Levitt and me—perhaps thinking that we needed someone with a more severe or dramatic problem.

You'll notice that Mark also blamed his ex-wife for the problems with his son. This is not unusual. When you're not getting along with someone, you may spend part of your time telling yourself that the problem is all your fault and part of your time telling yourself that it's someone else's fault.

## Mark's Daily Mood Journal at the Start of the Session*

**Upsetting Event:** My role as a father for my oldest son.

| Emotions | % Now | % Goal | % After | Emotions | % Now | % Goal | % After |
|---|---|---|---|---|---|---|---|
| **Sad,** blue, depressed, down, **unhappy** | 60 | | | **Embarrassed,** **foolish,** humiliated, self-conscious | 60 | | |
| **Anxious,** worried, panicky, nervous, frightened | 30 | | | **Hopeless,** **discouraged, pessimistic,** despairing | 80 | | |
| Guilty, remorseful, bad, **ashamed** | 60 | | | **Frustrated,** stuck, thwarted, **defeated** | 80 | | |
| Worthless, **inadequate,** defective, incompetent | 50 | | | Angry, mad, **resentful,** annoyed, irritated, **upset,** furious | 30 | | |
| **Lonely,** unloved, unwanted, rejected, alone | 40 | | | Other | | | |

| Negative Thoughts | % Now | % After | Distortions | Positive Thoughts | % Belief |
|---|---|---|---|---|---|
| 1. I've been a failure. | 70 | | | | |
| 2. There's something defective in my brain that has prevented a loving relationship with my son. | 90 | | | | |
| 3. Someone else could have had a better therapy session with Jill and David. | 70 | | | | |
| 4. This should not happen to me because I'm a caring person. | 75 | | | | |
| 5. Other family members (ex-wife) have contributed to this conflict. | 80 | | | | |

\* Copyright © 2016 by David D. Burns, MD.

In the early days of my career, I would have assumed that Mark wanted help—after all, he'd been in pain for a long time and came to the session to get some help. So I would have jumped in with a variety of techniques to help him challenge his negative thoughts.

Although this might have been effective, there's a good chance it might not have worked. Mark might have yes-butted me and insisted that he really *was* a failure.

Do you know why? Put your ideas here before you continue reading, and don't worry about getting it "right."

_____

_____

_____

_____

_____

## My Answer

By now, you've learned that attempts to change without first dealing with your ambivalence about change is the cause of nearly all therapeutic failure. Although Mark *is* suffering and *does* want help, he may have some mixed feelings about giving up his negative thoughts and feelings.

That's because he's pretty convinced his negative thoughts are valid. You may feel that way about your own negative thoughts too! Most of us are extremely reluctant to let go of thoughts or beliefs that seem absolutely true.

So before we jump in and try to help Mark, let's see if we can melt away his resistance. I asked Mark the familiar magic button question. If he could simply press a magic button, and all of his negative feelings would suddenly disappear, and he'd feel absolutely joyful without any effort at all, would he press the button?

Just like most people respond, he said he'd *definitely* press it!

**MAGIC BUTTON**

Then Dr. Levitt and I pointed out that although there was no magic button, we did have lots of powerful techniques that could reduce his negative feelings today and maybe even make them disappear entirely.

But before we did that, we told Mark that maybe we should take a look at what his negative thoughts and feelings showed about him that was positive and awesome, as well as the benefits of his negative thoughts and feelings. Doing this type of positive reframing was important so we could melt away any of Mark's subconscious resistance and open the door to rapid change.

Before I show you the list of positives that Mark came up with, I'm going to ask you to come up with a list too. This will be a valuable chance for you to practice and refine positive reframing, which is one of the most important skills in this book.

Look over Mark's Daily Mood Journal again, and ask yourself these two questions about each negative thought and feeling:

1. What does this negative thought or feeling show about Mark and his core values that is beautiful, positive, and awesome?

2. What are some benefits, or advantages, of this negative thought or feeling?

You can record your ideas on the positive reframing list on the next page. Remember that it may be difficult for you to come up with a list of positives at first. Just do the best you can, and don't worry about getting it "right" or doing a great job. Jot down anything you can think of.

Once you've practiced positive reframing several times, it will get easier! And then you'll have a new and deeper understanding of an incredible tool that can help you—whether you're a therapist or are struggling with your own feelings of depression, anxiety, and inadequacy.

## Mark's Positive Reframing List

1. _____

2. _____

3. _____

4. _____

5. _____

6. _____

7. _____

8. _____

9. _____

10. _____

11. _____

12. _____

13. _____

14. _____

15. _____

When you're done, continue reading to find out what Mark and I came up with.

At first, it was hard for Mark to come up with even one positive for his list. Like so many people, he was used to thinking about his problems as some kind of shameful "defect." But with some help, he was able to come up with a pretty impressive list. I think you'll be impressed too!

## Mark's Positive Reframing List

1. My negative thoughts and feelings show that I care deeply about having a loving relationship with my oldest son.

2. My negative thoughts and feelings motivate me to not give up so I will continue to try even after decades of failure.

3. My negative thoughts and feelings show that I'm accountable and willing to examine my own role in this problem rather than just blaming others, like my ex.

4. My self-criticisms show that I'm honest about my flaws.

5. Perhaps my feelings of inadequacy show that I'm humble, which is one of my core values.

6. Humility is a spiritual quality.

7. My self-criticisms show that I have high standards.

8. My high standards have motivated me to be productive and to achieve a great deal in my life and in my career as a physician.

9. My suffering and sadness reflect my strong desire to make my oldest son happy. My sadness and depression are actually expressions of my love for my son.

10. My frustration shows that I still haven't given up on my goal of having a more loving relationship with my oldest son. If I weren't frustrated, it would mean that I didn't really care.

11. My third negative thought shows that I admire others, including Jill and David.

12. My negative thoughts and feelings show that I want to learn and that I'm open to learning.

13. My hopelessness protects me from disappointment. I'm so tired of getting my hopes up only to fail again and again.

14. My anger shows that I have a sense of fairness and justice and that I'm aware that others have also contributed to this problem.

Mark was surprised but agreed that all the positives we listed were absolutely real and incredibly important. At this point, Dr. Levitt and I asked Mark why in the world he'd want to press the magic button since it would cause all these positive qualities to disappear along with the negatives. In addition, the real problem would not disappear, just his thoughts and feelings. So he'd be happy, but would he *want* to feel happy, given that he still wouldn't have a loving relationship with his oldest son?

Paradoxically, this question nearly always unleashes a tremendous determination to change, and that's exactly what happened with Mark. He said he was tired of feeling so down and ashamed and that these feelings really weren't helping him get any closer to his son.

At this point, we asked Mark to imagine that he had a magic dial rather than a magic button. That way, he could dial down each negative feeling to some lower level that would still allow him to keep all these positives. Would some lower level of depression, shame, or anger be enough?

MAGIC DIAL

As you can see here, Mark decided that 10% or less would be sufficient for each negative feeling.

| Emotions | % Now | % Goal | % After |
|---|---|---|---|
| Sad, blue, depressed, down, unhappy | 60 | 10 | |
| Anxious worried, panicky, nervous, frightened | 30 | 0–5 | |
| Guilty, remorseful, bad, ashamed | 60 | 5 | |
| Worthless, inadequate, defective, incompetent | 50 | 5 | |
| Lonely, unloved, unwanted, rejected, alone | 40 | 10 | |
| Embarrassed, foolish, humiliated, self-conscious | 60 | 5 | |
| Hopeless, discouraged, pessimistic, despairing | 80 | 5–10 | |
| Frustrated, stuck, thwarted, defeated | 80 | 10 | |
| Angry, mad, resentful, annoyed, irritated, upset, furious | 30 | 5–10 | |
| Other | | | |

Now that we had melted away Mark's stuckness, we were ready to work on changing how he was thinking and feeling. Mark decided he wanted to work on this negative thought first: "There must be something defective in my brain that prevents me from forming a loving relationship with my oldest son."

If you recall, Mark believed this thought 90%, so how can we challenge this belief? Remember that he's been hooked on this negative thought for decades. So we can't just tell him to cheer up, encourage him to think more positively, or reassure him that his brain is fine. Not only will those simplistic approaches fail, but they may annoy him because they sound patronizing. They may even convey the message that we think he's an idiot for believing something so ridiculous.

Instead, it's usually a good idea to start by identifying the distortions in the negative thought. Once you do so, it will be much easier to challenge the thought.

See how many distortions you can find in Mark's negative thought: "There must be something defective in my brain that prevents me from forming a loving relationship with my oldest son."

| Cognitive Distortions Quiz | (✓) |
|---|---|
| 1. **All-or-Nothing Thinking.** You think about yourself or the world in black-or-white, all-or-nothing categories. Shades of gray do not exist. | |
| 2. **Overgeneralization.** You think about a negative event as a never-ending pattern of defeat by using words like *always* or *never*. | |
| 3. **Mental Filter.** You dwell on something negative and filter out or ignore things that are positive. This is like a drop of ink that discolors the beaker of water. | |
| 4. **Discounting the Positive.** This is an even more spectacular mental error. You tell yourself that your positives don't count. This way, you can maintain a universally negative view of yourself. | |
| 5. **Jumping to Conclusions.** You jump to conclusions that aren't warranted by the facts.<br>• **Mind Reading.** You assume you know what other people are thinking and feeling.<br>• **Fortune Telling.** You make negative predictions about the future. | |
| 6. **Magnification and Minimization.** You blow things out of proportion or shrink their importance inappropriately. I call this the "binocular trick" because things either look much bigger or much smaller depending on what end of the binoculars you look through. | |
| 7. **Emotional Reasoning.** You reason from how you feel. For example, you may *feel* like a loser, so you assume you really *are* a loser. Or you *feel* hopeless and conclude you really *are* hopeless. | |
| 8. **Should Statements.** You make yourself (or others) miserable with *shoulds*, *musts*, or *ought tos*. Self-directed shoulds cause feelings of guilt, shame, depression, and worthlessness. Other-directed shoulds trigger feelings of anger and relationship problems. World-directed shoulds cause feelings of frustration and entitlement. | |

| 9. **Labeling.** You label yourself or others instead of focusing on the specific problem. Labeling is an extreme form of overgeneralization because you see your entire self or someone else as totally defective or bad. | |
|---|---|
| 10. **Blame.** You find fault with yourself (self-blame) or others (other-blame). | |

Once you're done, continue reading to see the answers.

## My Answer

You could argue that Mark's negative thought contains every single distortion.

1. **All-or-Nothing Thinking.** Mark seems to think about his brain and his relationship with his son in black-or-white categories, as if everything is either perfect or a complete failure.

2. **Overgeneralization.** Mark is generalizing from his long-standing conflict with his oldest son to his "self" or "brain" in thinking that he has some kind of global, irreversible flaw.

3. **Mental Filter.** He is dwelling on all of his failed attempts to connect with his son and ignoring all the other information that indicates his brain is not defective.

4. **Discounting the Positive.** He ignores or overlooks his pretty tremendous communication skills. In fact, he is viewed by his colleagues as the only physician on his team who can connect with angry, devastated patients.

5. **Jumping to Conclusions.** He is assuming his son has no love for him at all (mind reading), and he is predicting that things won't or can't improve (fortune telling).

6. **Magnification and Minimization.** Although his conflict with his son is important and painful, he is perhaps exaggerating his own role in the relationship and minimizing his son's repeated rejections of his attempts to get close.

7. **Emotional Reasoning.** Mark is definitely reasoning from how he feels. He feels defective, so he thinks he really *is* defective.

8. **Should Statements.** He is telling himself that he *should* have a better relationship with his son or that he *should* have resolved it by now.

9. **Labeling.** He is labeling himself, as well as his brain, as defective.

10. **Blame.** He is blaming himself for sure!

Although Mark's negative thought contained all ten distortions, four really stood out in my mind:

- Overgeneralization
- Mental filter
- Discounting the positive
- Emotional reasoning

The conflict with Mark's son was real, but he was making a pretty huge overgeneralization by assuming the conflict meant there was something wrong with his brain. In addition, he was clearly focusing on the conflict with his son (mental filtering) and ignoring a wealth of data that suggested his brain was functioning pretty darn well! And he was clearly reasoning from his feelings: He *felt* defective, so he thought he *was* defective.

Once you've identified the distortions in a thought, it's relatively easy to pick out some methods you can use to challenge the thought using the cheat sheet from chapter 5. You can see some of the techniques we selected for Mark's recovery circle here.

## Mark's Recovery Circle*

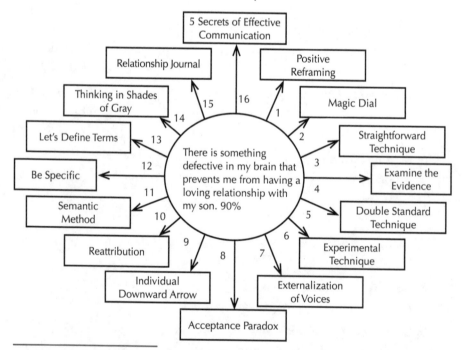

Although we came up with a variety of strategies to combat Mark's negative thought, we only ended up needing to use two of these methods: examine the evidence and the double standard technique. This happens a lot these days, and it's almost definitely because of positive reframing. That's the key to rapid recovery!

We started with examine the evidence because this technique can work really well for mental filtering and discounting the positive. We asked Mark to list the evidence that he had a "brain defect," along with the evidence that he didn't.

This was a bit of a slam dunk because the only real evidence he could come up with was the fact that he'd had trouble developing a loving relationship with his oldest son, as well as the fact that he "felt" defective. But an awful lot of moms and dads have conflicts with their children, and feeling defective is not evidence of a brain disorder. It's just a symptom of depression.

When trying to diagnose a brain tumor, neurologists don't ask, "Do you sometimes feel defective or have problems getting along with family members?" In addition, Mark confessed that he'd actually consulted with experts about this on several occasions and that none of them had ever suggested he had a defective brain. In fact, his colleagues often praised his skill in dealing with angry, challenging patients and their families.

This technique reduced his belief in the negative thought considerably because he had to admit that there simply wasn't any convincing evidence to support it.

Of course, some people *do* have brain defects. One of the students in my Tuesday group had brain surgery for a tumor recently, and another had a cerebral hemorrhage following a traumatic brain injury. But they're doing just fine! And my mother told me that the right side of my skull was squashed during delivery because they had to use forceps to pull me out, and I think that might be why I have trouble recognizing people's faces and remembering people's names. But this has never been a huge barrier for me either.

Once we finished examining the evidence, we tried the double standard technique. I asked Mark what he would say to a dear friend who was going through the same exact situation. Would Mark say that his friend's brain was defective?

Mark said he definitely wouldn't say that! Instead, this is what he'd tell his friend:

*I'm not convinced that you have a defect in your brain. You've consulted with lots of experts, and none of them has ever said you had a brain defect. In ad-*

*dition, your conflict with your son is not unusual, and it sounds like it's not entirely your fault either. You've definitely had a role, but blaming everything on your brain is unfair!*

Mark said he believed this new thought completely, so we asked him to write it down in the positive thoughts column of his Daily Mood Journal. He also re-rated his belief in the negative thought, and it dropped all the way to zero.

We then used several additional techniques to help Mark smash the rest of his negative thoughts, which did not take long. As I've suggested, once you crush one negative thought, the circuits in your brain suddenly change, and it usually becomes easier to challenge the rest of your negative thoughts. You can see Mark's completed Daily Mood Journal at the end of the chapter.

Once Mark successfully smashed his negative thoughts, there were dramatic reductions in all of his negative feelings, with most of them disappearing entirely.

At this point, we talked about the fact that some problems require an internal solution as well as an external solution. We'd completed the internal solution, which involved changing the way Mark was thinking and feeling. But the external solution would require changing the way he'd been communicating with his son.

We gave Mark a homework assignment to try again to connect with his son using the five secrets of effective communication, which you'll learn more about in chapter 17. We practiced this technique during his session, and we offered to schedule another session in case he needed more help with this.

He never did schedule another session. The changes in Mark's feelings were both rapid and phenomenal. At the end of the session, I asked Mark if these ratings were genuine or, if as some people might suspect, faked in order to try to please Dr. Levitt and me. Surprisingly, Mark burst into tears and said, "This was a life-changing experience!"

But here's the big problem: Will the changes last? And what will happen when he tries to connect with his oldest son?

I had a wonderful opportunity to sit down with Mark on the second anniversary of his therapy session. The interview was pretty mind-blowing and deeply moving. He confessed that he'd also been skeptical that his years of suffering could be reversed in a single therapy session. His tears flowed as he recalled the feelings of failure he'd had for so long at being unable to connect with his oldest son. I asked Mark if he'd tried to connect with his son using the five secrets of effective communication. And if so, what happened?

Mark said that right after his session, there was an amazing and almost instantaneous transformation in his relationship with his son. He used the five secrets of effective communication, and his oldest son opened up for the first time. He said he felt extremely happy—overjoyed, really—and that his relationships with *all* of his children and grandchildren were now wonderful and amazing.

Again, I want to say how incredibly indebted we all are to Mark for giving us such a transformative and illuminating experience! It probably won't quiet all the critics, but I am hopeful his story may be inspiring and helpful for some of you.

And my message to those who are still critical and skeptical of TEAM-CBT: Please continue to use your critical thinking and skepticism when you evaluate TEAM or any other approach. It was my own skepticism about the things I learned during my residency training and clinical work that actually led to the emergence of TEAM therapy. I don't want to quiet my critics—I want to praise all of you!

If you'd like to listen to Mark's session for yourself, here are the links.

| Podcast # | Title | Link |
|---|---|---|
| 29 | Introduction/Testing | https://feelinggood.com/2017/03/27/029-live-session-mark-introduction-testing-phase-part-1/ |
| 30 | Empathy | https://feelinggood.com/2017/04/03/030-live-session-mark-empathy-phase-part-2/ |
| 31 | Assessment of Resistance | https://feelinggood.com/2017/04/10/031-live-session-mark-agenda-setting-phase-part-3/ |
| 32 | Assessment of Resistance (cont'd) | https://feelinggood.com/2017/04/11/032-live-session-mark-agenda-setting-phase-part-4/ |
| 33 | Methods | https://feelinggood.com/2017/04/17/033-live-session-mark-methods-phase-part-5/ |
| 34 | Methods (cont'd) | https://feelinggood.com/2017/04/24/034-live-session-mark-methods-phase-contd-part-6/ |
| 35 | Conclusion/Testing | https://feelinggood.com/2017/05/01/035-live-session-mark-final-testing-wrap-up-part-7/ |
| 141 | Two-Year Follow-Up | https://feelinggood.com/2019/05/20/145-two-year-follow-up-with-mark-ive-been-a-failure-as-a-father/ |

## Mark's Daily Mood Journal at the End of the Session*

Upsetting Event: My role as a father for my oldest son.

| Emotions | % Now | % Goal | % After | | Emotions | % Now | % Goal | % After |
|---|---|---|---|---|---|---|---|---|
| Sad) blue, depressed, down, unhappy | 60 | 10 | 0 | | Embarrassed, foolish, humiliated, self-conscious | 60 | 5 | 0 |
| Anxious) worried, panicky, nervous, frightened | 30 | 0–5 | 0 | | Hopeless, discouraged, pessimistic, despairing | 80 | 5–10 | 10 |
| Guilty, remorseful, bad, ashamed | 60 | 5 | 5 | | Frustrated, stuck, thwarted, defeated | 80 | 10 | 10 |
| Worthless, inadequate, defective, incompetent | 50 | 5 | 20 | | Angry, mad, resentful, annoyed, irritated, upset, furious | 30 | 5–10 | 0 |
| Lonely, unloved, unwanted, rejected, alone | 40 | 10 | 0 | | Other | | | |

| Negative Thoughts | % Now | % After | Distortions |
|---|---|---|---|
| 1. I've been a failure. | 70 | 0 | AON, OB, MF, DP, MR, MAG/MIN, SH, ER, LAB, SB |
| 2. There's something defective in my brain that has prevented a loving relationship with my son. | 90 | 0 | OG, MF, DP, JC, FT, MAG/MIN, SH, ER, LAB, SB, OB |
| 3. Someone else could have had a better therapy session with Jill and David. | 70 | 0–5 | DP, MR, FT, ER, SH, SB |
| 4. This should not happen to me because I'm a caring person. | 75 | 0 | ER, SH, BL |
| 5. Other family members (ex-wife) have contributed to this conflict. | 80 | 5–10 | OG, MF, MAG/MIN, ER, BL |

| Positive Thoughts | % Belief |
|---|---|
| 1. My life has not been a failure. Any relationship involves two people. | 100 |
| 2. There is absolutely no proof that I have a defect in my brain, and no expert has ever suggested that I do. Of course I am not as close to my son as I would like, but blaming my brain for everything is unfair! | 100 |
| 3. There will be many other good sessions, but this session was not too shabby either! | 100 |
| 4. Good and bad things can and do happen to everyone. | 100 |
| 5. There is some truth to this, but my wife passed years ago, and the relationship is all in my hands now. I am the only parent now. | 100 |

# 8 | Marilyn's Story: "I've Got Stage 4 Lung Cancer."

In 2017, I published a live therapy session with Marilyn, a colleague who'd just been diagnosed with stage 4 lung cancer, as a series of four consecutive *Feeling Good* podcasts. My co-therapist was Dr. Matthew May, a compassionate and superbly skillful psychiatrist and dear friend. I also published a follow-up session eight weeks later when Marilyn experienced a painful metastasis to one of her ribs. Although the subject matter of this chapter is exceptionally grim and disturbing, I believe Marilyn's story will inspire you and give you courage when you face losses, traumas, and problems in your own life. If you'd like to listen to the sessions with commentaries, you'll find the links at the end of this chapter.

Marilyn had never smoked and was shocked and devastated when she discovered, unexpectedly, that she had lung cancer. I am enormously grateful to Marilyn for her courage and generosity in making this extremely private and intensely personal experience available to all of us.

You've learned that the theory behind cognitive therapy is that our thoughts, and not external events, create all our feelings. However, many people cannot accept this idea, especially when something truly horrific happens, like learning you have terminal cancer. In this case, many people argue that it is the event, and *not* your thoughts, that triggers your negative feelings. They insist that depression and anxiety are *inevitable* when terrible things happen. As you read about Marilyn, you'll have a chance to draw your own conclusions.

At the beginning of the session, Marilyn was in shock, as you might expect. If you review her scores on the Brief Mood Survey on the next page, you'll see that her negative feelings were about as severe as you can imagine, and her positive feelings were practically nonexistent.

These feelings were also reflected in her Daily Mood Journal. She rated eight different categories of negative feelings at 100%. That's about as bad as it gets.

## Marilyn's Before-Session Brief Mood Survey*

**Instructions:** Use checks (✓) to indicate how you're feeling right now.
**Answer all items.**

**How depressed do you feel *right now*?**

| | Before Session | | | | | After Session | | | | |
|---|---|---|---|---|---|---|---|---|---|---|
| | 0—Not at all | 1—Somewhat | 2—Moderately | 3—A lot | 4—Extremely | 0—Not at all | 1—Somewhat | 2—Moderately | 3—A lot | 4—Extremely |
| 1. Sad or down in the dumps | | | | | ✓ | | | | | |
| 2. Discouraged or hopeless | | | | | ✓ | | | | | |
| 3. Low in self-esteem, inferior, or worthless | | | | ✓ | | | | | | |
| 4. Unmotivated to do things | | | | ✓ | | | | | | |
| 5. Decreased pleasure or satisfaction in life | | | | ✓ | | | | | | |
| Total → | | | | 17 | | | | | | |

**How suicidal do you feel *right now*?**

| | | | | | | | | | | |
|---|---|---|---|---|---|---|---|---|---|---|
| 1. Do you have any suicidal thoughts? | ✓ | | | | | | | | | |
| 2. Would you like to end your life? | ✓ | | | | | | | | | |
| Total → | | | | 0 | | | | | | |

**How anxious do you feel *right now*?**

| | | | | | | | | | | |
|---|---|---|---|---|---|---|---|---|---|---|
| 1. Anxious | | | | | ✓ | | | | | |
| 2. Frightened | | | | | ✓ | | | | | |
| 3. Worrying about things | | | | | ✓ | | | | | |
| 4. Tense or on edge | | | | | ✓ | | | | | |
| 5. Nervous | | | | | ✓ | | | | | |
| Total → | | | | 20 | | | | | | |

**How angry do you feel *right now*?**

| | | | | | | | | | | |
|---|---|---|---|---|---|---|---|---|---|---|
| 1. Frustrated | | | | ✓ | | | | | | |
| 2. Annoyed | | | | | ✓ | | | | | |
| 3. Resentful | | | | ✓ | | | | | | |
| 4. Angry | | | | | ✓ | | | | | |
| 5. Irritated | | | | | ✓ | | | | | |
| Total → | | | | 18 | | | | | | |

## Positive Feelings Survey*

**Instructions:** Use checks (✓) to indicate how you're feeling *right now*.
**Answer all items.**

**Positive Feelings:** How do you feel right now?

| | 0—Not at all | 1—Somewhat | 2—Moderately | 3—A lot | 4—Extremely | 0—Not at all | 1—Somewhat | 2—Moderately | 3—A lot | 4—Extremely |
|---|---|---|---|---|---|---|---|---|---|---|
| 1. I feel worthwhile. | ✓ | | | | | | | | | |
| 2. I feel good about myself. | | ✓ | | | | | | | | |
| 3. I feel close to people. | | ✓ | | | | | | | | |
| 4. I feel I am accomplishing something. | | ✓ | | | | | | | | |
| 5. I feel motivated to do things. | | ✓ | | | | | | | | |
| 6. I feel calm and relaxed. | ✓ | | | | | | | | | |
| 7. I feel a spiritual connection to others. | | ✓ | | | | | | | | |
| 8. I feel hopeful. | | ✓ | | | | | | | | |
| 9. I feel encouraged and optimistic. | | ✓ | | | | | | | | |
| 10. My life is satisfying. | | ✓ | | | | | | | | |
| Total → | | | | 8 | | | | | | |

## Marilyn's Daily Mood Journal, page 1*

**Upsetting Event:** Being recently diagnosed with incurable stage 4 (nonsmoker) lung cancer

| Emotions | % Now | % Goal | % After | Emotions | % Now | % Goal | % After |
|---|---|---|---|---|---|---|---|
| Sad, blue, depressed, down, unhappy | 100 | | | Embarrassed, foolish, humiliated, self-conscious | | | |
| Anxious, worried, panicky, nervous, frightened | 100 | | | Hopeless, discouraged, pessimistic, despairing | 100 | | |
| Guilty, remorseful, bad, ashamed | 100 | | | Frustrated, stuck, thwarted, defeated | 100 | | |
| Inferior, worthless, inadequate, defective, incompetent | 100 | | | Angry, mad, resentful, annoyed, irritated, upset, furious | 100 | | |
| Lonely, unloved, unwanted, rejected, alone, abandoned | 100 | | | Other | | | |

| Negative Thoughts | % Now | % After | Distortions | Positive Thoughts | % Belief |
|---|---|---|---|---|---|
| 1. This cannot be true—I've never smoked. | 100 | | | | |
| 2. I'm going to die (sooner than later). | 100 | | | | |
| 3. I'm terrified of dying. | 100 | | | | |
| 4. Is there life after death? There is no life after death. | 100 | | | | |
| 5. I can't believe I have cancer. | 100 | | | | |
| 6. I've wasted a lot of my life because of my alcoholism. | 100 | | | | |

* Copyright © 2016 by David D. Burns, MD.

## Marilyn's Daily Mood Journal, page 2

| | | | |
|---|---|---|---|
| 7. I've been duped by religions. | 100 | | |
| 8. I don't want to have cancer. | 100 | | |
| 9. I'm defective because I have never had and never will have a life partner. | 100 | | |
| 10. I'm not as spiritual as others. | 100 | | |
| 11. I may be a burden to others. | 100 | | |
| 12. I may suffer with physical pain. | 100 | | |
| 13. There may be no life after death. | 100 | | |
| 14. I'm not spiritual enough. | 100 | | |

## Checklist of Cognitive Distortions*

1. **All-or-Nothing Thinking (AON).** You view things in absolute, black-and-white categories.

2. **Overgeneralization (OG).** You view a negative event as a never-ending pattern of defeat: "This *always* happens!"

3. **Mental Filter (MF).** You dwell on the negatives and ignore the positives.

4. **Discounting the Positive (DP).** You insist that your positive qualities don't count.

5. **Jumping to Conclusions (JC).** You jump to conclusions not warranted by the facts.
   - **Mind Reading (MR).** You assume that people are reacting negatively to you.
   - **Fortune Telling (FT).** You predict that things will turn out badly.

6. **Magnification and Minimization (MAG/MIN).** You blow things out of proportion or shrink their importance.

7. **Emotional Reasoning (ER).** You reason from your feelings: "I *feel* like an idiot, so I must really *be* one."

8. **Should Statements (SH).** You use *shoulds*, *shouldn'ts*, *musts*, *ought tos*, and *have tos*.

9. **Labeling (LAB).** Instead of saying, "I made a mistake," you say, "I'm a jerk" or "I'm a loser."

10. **Blame.** You find fault instead of solving the problem.
    - **Self-Blame (SB).** You blame yourself for something you weren't entirely responsible for.
    - **Other-Blame (OB).** You blame others and overlook ways you contributed to the problem.

If you review Marilyn's Daily Mood Journal, you'll notice that her negative thoughts focused on several themes, including:

- Her fears of cancer, pain, and death.
- Her feelings of spiritual inadequacy.
- Her doubts in the existence of God and the afterlife.
- Her anger, as she felt that she'd been duped by religion.
- Her feelings of incompleteness and failure at never having found a life partner.
- Her feelings of self-blame for drinking excessively during her life.

Before Dr. May and I could help Marilyn, we had to deal with her ambivalence about change. Although her negative thoughts and feelings were unbearable and added enormously to her suffering, they also reflected some truly positive things about her and her core values.

Dr. May and I suggested that we look at Marilyn's Daily Mood Journal and see if we could find some positives in her negative feelings. Before I share the list of positives that we came up with, let me ask you to give it a try. I want you to do this exercise, even though it may be challenging, because it's a manifestation of one of the most important messages of this book.

Remember the underlying concept:

*Wouldn't it be awesome if our suffering was not the result of what is* wrong *with us but what is* right *with us?*

That idea can change your life, but it's not easy to "get it" at first. That's why I've included many exercises for you in this book. The repeated practice will create new healing networks in your brain!

So roll up your sleeves and ask yourself the two familiar questions about each of Marilyn's negative feelings:

1. What does this feeling show about Marilyn and her core values that's positive and awesome?

2. How does this feeling help Marilyn? What are some potential benefits of feeling this way?

You can write your answers on the positive reframing table on the next page. When you're done, you can check out the list that Marilyn, Dr. May, and I came up with.

## Marilyn's Positive Reframing Table

| Emotions | Positives |
|---|---|
| Sad, blue, depressed, down, unhappy | |
| Anxious, worried, panicky, nervous, frightened | |
| Guilty, remorseful, bad, ashamed | |
| Inferior, worthless, inadequate, defective, incompetent | |
| Lonely, unloved, unwanted, rejected, alone, abandoned | |
| Hopeless, discouraged, pessimistic, despairing | |
| Frustrated, stuck, thwarted, defeated | |
| Angry, mad, resentful, annoyed, irritated, upset, furious | |

Here is the list of positives that we came up with in the session with Marilyn:

| Emotions | Positives |
|---|---|
| Sad, blue, depressed, down, unhappy | These feelings:<br>• Show that I'm very sensitive.<br>• Show that I have a sense of awe for life, a profound appreciation for life, and an awareness of the beauty and preciousness of life.<br>• Are appropriate, given what has happened.<br>• Make me feel alive. |
| Anxious, worried, panicky, nervous, frightened | These feelings:<br>• Protect me.<br>• Are a form of self-love.<br>• Show compassion for myself.<br>• Show wisdom and courage to face reality.<br>• Show I'm facing it and not sitting home drunk every night. |
| Guilty, remorseful, bad, ashamed | These feelings:<br>• Show that I care about what I've done and am willing to own up to it.<br>• Show that I have a good value system.<br>• Motivate me to get involved in social justice.<br>• Show that I'm willing to be accountable. |
| Inferior, worthless, inadequate, defective, incompe-tent | These feelings:<br>• Show that I have high standards, and these standards have motivated me to accomplish a great deal—I have a PhD and four master's degrees!<br>• Help me to have empathy and compassion for others who are suffering.<br>• Show humility, and humility is a spiritual quality.<br>• Are a reminder that I need to learn and grow.<br>• Give me a sense of control.<br>• Show honesty since I have many defects.<br>• Show that I'm accountable and not just blaming others. |
| Lonely, unloved, unwanted, rejected, alone, abandoned | My loneliness:<br>• Shows that I have a desire to be of service to others and to have something to bring to the table.<br>• Shows gratitude in being with others.<br>• Shows a yearning for loving relationships with others. |
| Hopeless, discour-aged, pessimistic, despairing | My hopelessness:<br>• Is motivating.<br>• Can be a relief.<br>• Can protect me from disappointment.<br>• Shows honesty since there are some pretty awful things happening right now. |
| Frustrated, stuck, thwarted, defeated | My frustration:<br>• Motivates me to pray.<br>• Shows that I haven't given up. |

| Angry, mad, resentful, annoyed, irritated, upset, furious | My anger:<br>• Shows that I really care and want things to be different.<br>• Is a source of power—I can *feel* it.<br>• Gives me the courage to fight.<br>• Shows that I have a good value system and a moral compass.<br>• Shows my love for others who have been duped or taken advantage of by unscrupulous spiritual teachers. |
|---|---|

Marilyn was surprised by all the positives we found in her negative feelings. We could have done positive reframing with her negative thoughts as well, but that would have been overkill.

Once you've realized that your so-called "symptoms" actually result from what is most beautiful and positive about you, your resistance to change will usually drop dramatically, and that's exactly what happened to Marilyn.

We asked Marilyn what she'd want to dial her negative feelings down to if she had a magic dial. As you can see, she wanted to keep her depression fairly high (45%) and her anxiety, guilt, and anger somewhat elevated (20%), but she felt like it would be okay to lower the rest of her negative feelings to pretty low levels (5% to 15%).

| Emotions | % Now | % Goal | % After |
|---|---|---|---|
| Sad, blue, depressed, down, unhappy | 100 | 45 | |
| Anxious, worried, panicky, nervous, frightened | 100 | 20 | |
| Guilty, remorseful, bad, ashamed | 100 | 20 | |
| Inferior, worthless, inadequate, defective, incompetent | 100 | 15 | |
| Lonely, unloved, unwanted, rejected, alone, abandoned | 100 | 10 | |
| Embarrassed, foolish, humiliated, self-conscious | | | |
| Hopeless, discouraged, pessimistic, despairing | 100 | 5 | |
| Frustrated, stuck, thwarted, defeated | 100 | 5 | |
| Angry, mad, resentful, annoyed, irritated, upset, furious | 100 | 20 | |
| Other | | | |

Keep in mind that these "goals" are not fixed in stone. Once you begin to change, your goals may change as well. All we did was put Marilyn in charge of where we'd sail the ship, and we made a deal with her subconscious mind so she'd feel free to reduce her negative feelings.

This is really important, and it's based on common sense as well. If you told someone recently diagnosed with stage 4 lung cancer that you were going to make them feel really happy, they'd simply dismiss you as either a kook or someone who was incredibly lacking in compassion. The "% Goal" column in the Daily Mood Journal is just one of many innovations in TEAM-CBT, and it's been incredibly helpful!

Now that we'd reduced Marilyn's resistance, it was time to use some methods to help her challenge and crush the negative thoughts that were causing her so much pain. Identifying the distortions in these thoughts is usually the best place to start.

Marilyn said she wanted to work on this negative thought first: "I'm not as spiritual as others." See how many distortions you can find in this thought using this checklist. When you're done, continue reading to see the distortions that we came up. But don't look until you've completed the quiz. It's not very difficult, and I think you'll enjoy it and find it illuminating.

| **Cognitive Distortions Quiz** | (✓) |
|---|---|
| 1. **All-or-Nothing Thinking.** You think about yourself or the world in black-or-white, all-or-nothing categories. Shades of gray do not exist. | |
| 2. **Overgeneralization.** You think about a negative event as a never-ending pattern of defeat by using words like *always* or *never*. | |
| 3. **Mental Filter.** You dwell on something negative and filter out or ignore things that are positive. This is like a drop of ink that discolors the beaker of water. | |
| 4. **Discounting the Positive.** This is an even more spectacular mental error. You tell yourself that your positives don't count. This way, you can maintain a universally negative view of yourself. | |
| 5. **Jumping to Conclusions.** You jump to conclusions that aren't warranted by the facts. Two common forms are called mind reading and fortune telling. • **Mind Reading.** You assume you know what other people are thinking and feeling. • **Fortune Telling.** You make negative predictions about the future. | |
| 6. **Magnification and Minimization.** You blow things out of proportion or shrink their importance inappropriately. I call this the "binocular trick" because things either look much bigger or much smaller depending on what end of the binoculars you look through. | |
| 7. **Emotional Reasoning.** You reason from how you feel. For example, you may *feel* like a loser, so you assume you really *are* a loser. Or you *feel* hopeless and conclude you really *are* hopeless. | |

| | |
|---|---|
| **8. Should Statements.** You make yourself (or others) miserable with *shoulds*, *musts*, or *ought tos*. Self-directed shoulds cause feelings of guilt, shame, depression, and worthlessness. Other-directed shoulds trigger feelings of anger and relationship problems. World-directed shoulds cause feelings of frustration and entitlement. | |
| **9. Labeling.** You label yourself or others instead of focusing on the specific problem. Labeling is an extreme form of overgeneralization because you see your entire self or someone else as totally defective or bad. | |
| **10. Blame.** You find fault with yourself (self-blame) or others (other-blame). | |

## My Answer

As you'll see here, Marilyn was engaging in all ten distortions:

1. **All-or-Nothing Thinking.** Marilyn seems to think about spirituality in black-or-white categories. Spiritual feelings, like all feelings, tend to come and go and change greatly over time. Most human beings, including renowned spiritual leaders, have had some, or many, moments when they questioned their belief in God or in life after death.

2. **Overgeneralization.** Initially, I did not check this one off, but upon further thought, I think it is okay to include overgeneralization. Marilyn seems to believe that her current crisis of faith is something permanent and fixed, something that will go on forever. In addition, she seems to think that she has a "self" that is not sufficiently spiritual.

3. **Mental Filter.** Marilyn is thinking about the moments, including the current moment, when she has doubted her religious faith and her belief in God.

4. **Discounting the Positive.** Marilyn is overlooking or discounting the many times when she's felt a profound feeling of spirituality, such as when she meditates. She is also discounting the fact that she has a master's degree in theology and has been a faithful member of the Catholic church, attending morning services on an almost daily basis.

   In addition, Marilyn is discounting the importance and value of her own critical thinking, as well as the spiritual importance of feeling suddenly "lost." Many religious mystics have taught that this "dark night of the soul" is actually a crucial step on the path to enlightenment.

5. **Jumping to Conclusions.** Marilyn is mind reading when she assumes other religious people do not also have moments of doubt when they question or even lose their faith.

6. **Magnification and Minimization.** Although I don't see her thought as a classic example of this distortion, you could argue that Marilyn is definitely magnifying the "awfulness" of her temporary loss of faith and minimizing her tremendous dedication to the church ever since she was a little girl.

7. **Emotional Reasoning.** Marilyn is definitely reasoning from how she feels. She feels like a lost sinner, so she assumes she really is one.

8. **Should Statements.** Marilyn is clearly telling herself that she *should* have a stronger belief in God and that she *should not* doubt the existence of the afterlife.

9. **Labeling.** Marilyn is not labeling herself in this thought. If she were to call herself a "sinner" or a "bad person," then she'd be labeling herself.

10. **Blame.** She is blaming herself for her feelings of doubt.

As you can see, we found a lot of distortions in this thought. This was good news because it meant we could use lots of techniques to challenge the thought and perhaps bring Marilyn some relief.

We began with the double standard technique and asked Marilyn what she'd say to a dear friend who was just like her, someone who had just been diagnosed with cancer and began to doubt her belief in God and the afterlife. Would she say, "You should feel more spiritual" or "You're not spiritual enough"?

Marilyn said she would *never* say something that harsh to a dear friend because it would be mean, and it would also be unrealistic since most of the world's greatest religious leaders have at times experienced profound feelings of doubt about the existence of God. Instead, Marilyn said she would say this to her friend:

*You've had many experiences of profound spiritual awe. In addition, doubting your faith shows that you're a person with integrity who's capable of critical thinking. Doubt is part of the religious experience.*

Dr. May and I asked Marilyn if what she'd just said was true or if she was just rationalizing. She said it was absolutely true. We asked Marilyn if she'd be willing to talk to herself in the same gentle way, with compassion and acceptance rather than with harsh self-criticism and judgment. Because Marilyn is an extremely compassionate woman, it "clicked" and she was able to crush her negative thought immediately.

Next, I shared a story that Marilyn seemed to like. I told her about a visit I once had with God when I was jogging home from the train station in Philadelphia. I can remember exactly where I was too—on a steep hill on Conshohocken State Road, about half a mile from our house. I told Marilyn that God told me, "David, if you believe in me, I'm going to be deeply disappointed."

I replied, "Don't worry, big guy, I've got your back!"

Marilyn seemed to love this story and burst into laughter. I just *love* it when we can laugh during a therapy session, even when you're dealing with something as grim as terminal cancer.

At this point, there seemed to be an almost immediate change in how Marilyn was feeling. She emerged as a powerful partner in her recovery and was easily able to crush the rest of her negative thoughts, even though they had seemed so real, devastating, and overwhelming at the start of the session.

Here's how she challenged some of these negative thoughts:

| Negative Thoughts | % Now | % After | Distortions | Positive Thoughts | % Belief |
|---|---|---|---|---|---|
| 11. I may be a burden on others. | 100 | 5 | MR, FT, MAG, ER, SH, LAB, SB | It can be an honor to allow others to help me, just as it's been an honor for me to help others who were struggling and suffering on so many occasions. Most people probably would not feel like I'm "a burden" but, rather, someone they love and care about deeply. We will take turns being burdens at some point or another in our lives. | 100 |

| 12. I may suffer physical pain. | 100 | 15 | AON, MF, DP, FT, MAG/ MIN | I've dealt with physical pain in the past, and I've done well with it. I'm blessed to have wonderful medical care. | 100 |
|---|---|---|---|---|---|
| 13. There may be no life after death. | 100 | 10 | FT | If there's no life after death, there will literally be nothing to be afraid of. If there is life after death, that will be pretty awesome! A wonderful surprise! | 100 |

It seemed like a tremendous session, but I've mentioned that therapists' perceptions can often be way off base, so even though Marilyn appeared to change—fairly dramatically—we didn't know for sure until we reviewed Marilyn's Daily Mood Journal at the end of the session to see how her mood changed.

As you can see here, she easily surpassed her goals, and all of her negative feelings fell to incredibly, almost impossibly, low levels.

| Emotions | % Now | % Goal | % After |
|---|---|---|---|
| Sad, blue, depressed, down, unhappy | 100 | 45 | 5 |
| Anxious, worried, panicky, nervous, frightened | 100 | 20 | 2 |
| Guilty, remorseful, bad, ashamed | 100 | 20 | 0 |
| Inferior, worthless, inadequate, defective, incompetent | 100 | 15 | 0 |
| Lonely, unloved, unwanted, rejected, alone, abandoned | 100 | 10 | 0 |
| Embarrassed, foolish, humiliated, self-conscious | | | |
| Hopeless, discouraged, pessimistic, despairing | 100 | 5 | 1 |
| Frustrated, stuck, thwarted, defeated | 100 | 5 | 1 |
| Angry, mad, resentful, annoyed, irritated, upset, furious | 100 | 20 | 1 |
| Other | | | |

You can view this session as a powerful psychological experience—Marilyn described it as "mind-blowing." You can also see it as a profound spiritual experience. Marilyn suddenly emerged from what mystics have called the "dark night of the soul" and experienced a sudden and profound spiritual rebirth.

Technically, the key to the change she experienced was self-acceptance. Her recovery involved the death of the "self." Marilyn had been telling herself that she "should" be far better than she was, and this—not the cancer—was the main cause of her suffering. The moment she accepted her very flawed self, a kind of miracle occurred.

Eight weeks after our first session, Marilyn experienced her first painful metastasis to a rib and panicked, causing her symptoms of depression, anger, and anxiety to return. Negative feelings have a way of creeping back in during moments of vulnerability and self-doubt, which is why relapse prevention training is so crucial following recovery. If you've prepared for this ahead of time, then you can learn to pop out of relapses fairly quickly. And that's what happened with Marilyn: She came in for a tune-up session and experienced an equally mind-blowing change in her thoughts and feelings once again.

Now that you've heard Marilyn's story, let's return to the highly controversial theory I mentioned at the start of this chapter: that our emotional pain results from our thoughts and not from the circumstances of our lives. I hope this dramatic session has clarified your thinking on this topic. We really *do* create our own emotional reality at every moment of every day. And you really CAN change the way you FEEL when you change the way you THINK!

If you'd like to listen to the recordings of our session with Marilyn, the links are provided here. I think you'll find them inspiring. Although these sessions have received nearly 20,000 downloads so far, they have not been nearly as popular as podcasts with more positive titles involving "happiness" or "finding the meaning of life." I think people are probably frightened by a topic as grim as coping with terminal cancer.

However, we have been flooded with emails from listeners expressing profound gratitude and admiration for Marilyn. Oddly enough, many people wanted Marilyn to know that she had become their spiritual hero because of her integrity, vulnerability, and genuineness! I hope Marilyn's story has touched and inspired you as well.

| Podcast # | Title | Link |
|---|---|---|
| 49 | Live Session with Marilyn (Part 1)—Testing, Empathy | https://feelinggood.com/2017/08/07/049-live-session-marilyn-testing-empathy-part-1/ |
| 50 | Live Session with Marilyn (Part 2)—Assessment of Resistance | https://feelinggood.com/2017/08/14/050-live-session-marilyn-agenda-setting-part-2/ |
| 51 | Live Session with Marilyn (Part 3)—Methods, Relapse Prevention | https://feelinggood.com/2017/08/22/051-live-session-marilyn-methods-relapse-prevention-part-3-2/ |
| 52 | Your Responses to Marilyn (Part 4)—Were the Changes Real? Will they Last? | https://feelinggood.com/2017/09/11/052-your-responses-to-the-live-work-with-marilyn-are-people-honest-in-their-ratings-and-do-the-improvements-stick/ |
| 59 | Live Session with Marilyn (Part 5)—The 8-Week Tune-Up | https://feelinggood.com/2017/10/26/059-live-session-marilyn-the-tune-up/ |
| 159 | Live Therapy with Marilyn (2-Year Follow-Up)—"What if I die without having lived a meaningful life? | https://feelinggood.com/2019/09/23/159-live-therapy-with-marilyn-what-if-i-die-without-having-lived-a-meaningful-life/ |

# 9 | Sara's Story: "I'm Afraid of Germs!"

Could someone with a *super* severe disorder be rapidly helped with TEAM-CBT? Or is this new approach limited to people with less severe problems?

OCD is generally considered one of the most severe and difficult psychiatric disorders to treat. Psychiatrists push medications and psychotherapy, often with limited effectiveness, and many patients end up struggling with their obsessions and compulsive rituals for years or even decades.

OCD is a severe form of anxiety characterized by obsessions and compulsive rituals. The obsessions are frightening thoughts about something terrible that might happen. For example, you may lie in bed wondering if you turned off the burners on the kitchen stove and have fears that the house will burn down. That's the obsession. So you get out of bed and check the burners, just to make sure you turned them off. That's the compulsion.

This gives you some temporary relief. But soon the thought comes back, so you get out of bed to check the stove again… and again and again! That's classic OCD, and it can really interfere with your life and with your emotional well-being.

In severe cases, OCD can be crippling. The obsessions and compulsions may become so severe that you end up spending most the day worrying and checking things out. That was the case for a woman named Sara, who kindly agreed to visit my Tuesday evening Stanford training group so I could do a live demonstration of TEAM-CBT for my students and colleagues.

Sara described her agonizing struggles with a debilitating germ phobia for more than twenty years. You probably know that this is the same problem that plagued the life of the late billionaire business tycoon Howard Hughes. He also had a germ phobia and lived for a time in the penthouse suite of a Las Vegas hotel, isolated from practically all human contact, with elaborate rituals to protect himself from germs.

Sara explained how she showered for an hour every day, with elaborate cleaning rituals, and washed her hands repeatedly throughout the day.

The skin on her hands was chapped and painful, but even then she didn't stop. She even opened all canned goods at home with a paper towel.

Because of her OCD, Sara also made demands on her family. For example, she asked her daughter to wash her hands anytime she touched something "yucky," and she never let her daughter sit on the floor at home, at school, or at parties.

You can see Sara's Daily Mood Journal on the next page. She identified the upsetting event as walking into the psychiatry building and feeling intensely panicky and grossed out as she opened the door. She'd told herself that the door handle was yucky and contaminated, so she covered it with a napkin. But she tried to do this secretly, when no one was looking, because she felt ashamed and humiliated.

This type of shame is common among individuals with anxiety. You feel like there's something terribly wrong with you and tell yourself that others will judge you if they were to find out about your symptoms. So you try to hide your symptoms in shame, like Sara had been doing for two decades.

It was heartbreaking to see how she'd been suffering for such a long time.

## Sara's Daily Mood Journal*

**Upsetting Event:** Walking in the front door of the Stanford psychiatry building and not wanting to touch the front door.

| Emotions | % Now | % Goal | % After |
|---|---|---|---|
| **Sad**, blue, depressed, down, unhappy | | | |
| **Anxious**, worried, panicky, nervous, frightened | 100 | | |
| **Guilty**, remorseful, bad, ashamed | 100 | | |
| **Inferior**, worthless, inadequate, defective, incompetent | 40 | | |
| **Lonely**, unloved, unwanted, rejected, alone, abandoned | | | |

| Emotions | % Now | % Goal | % After |
|---|---|---|---|
| **Embarrassed**, foolish, humiliated, self-conscious | 100 | | |
| **Hopeless**, discouraged, pessimistic, despairing | 50 | | |
| **Frustrated**, stuck, thwarted, defeated | 30 | | |
| **Angry**, mad, resentful, annoyed, irritated, upset, furious | 30 | | |
| **Other** Grossed out | 100 | | |

| Negative Thoughts | % Now | % After | Distortions | Positive Thoughts | % Belief |
|---|---|---|---|---|---|
| 1. God only knows what's on that front door handle! | 100 | | | | |
| 2. Who knows who touched it? They could have contaminated hands! | 100 | | | | |
| 3. I'll get sick if I touch it without a napkin. | 100 | | | | |
| 4. I don't really know what's on there. | 100 | | | | |
| 5. Maybe somebody touched it and they didn't wash their hands after going to the bathroom. | 100 | | | | |
| 6. It's yucky! | 100 | | | | |
| 7. I'll get contaminated if I touch it. It looks really dirty! | 100 | | | | |

After Sara told her story, I asked if she wanted help. That's not a totally obvious question because nearly all individuals with OCD are intensely ambivalent about wanting to change. That's because they believe that the dangers they're avoiding are very real.

I was pleased that Sara clearly wanted help, so I asked what type of help she hoped for in the session. Although I obviously couldn't promise a miracle, if a miracle happened by the end of our session, what would she be hoping for?

She said she wanted to be cured of her OCD and freed from the anxiety and shame that had been plaguing her for so long. I asked Sara to imagine that we had a magic button, and if she pushed it, her germ phobia and all of her cleaning rituals would instantly disappear, with no effort at all, and she'd walk out of today's session in a state of joy, completely cured.

I asked Sara if she'd press the magic button. What do you think she said?

Nearly everyone says yes, and Sara was no exception.

I explained that although we didn't have a magic button, we did have some pretty powerful techniques that could free her from OCD. But before we got too excited about curing her, I explained that maybe we should take a look at some of the benefits of her germ phobia, as well as some of the positive and awesome things that her negative thoughts and feelings said about her and her core values as a human being.

Sara said that she'd never thought there was anything positive or beneficial about her phobia.

To prime the pump, I pointed out that her elaborate cleaning rituals had at least one huge benefit: They protected her from getting sick. She immediately agreed with that, so we put that first on Sara's list of positives.

Before you continue reading, see if you can come up with a few more positives. Put yourself in Sara's shoes, and ask yourself these two questions:

1. What are some advantages of Sara's negative thoughts, feelings, and compulsive cleaning rituals?

2. What do they show about her that's positive and awesome?

I really want to encourage you to complete Sara's positive reframing list before you continue reading. The practice will make it much easier for you to use this powerful tool with your own thoughts and feelings.

## Sara's Positive Reframing List

1. My germ phobia and rituals protect me from getting sick—and that's a *very* good thing!

2. _____

3. _____

4. _____

5. _____

6. _____

7. _____

8. _____

9. _____

10. _____

Once you're done, turn the page to see the list that Sara and I came up with.

As you can see here, there were lots of positives!

## Sara's Positive Reframing List

1. My germ phobia and rituals protect me from getting sick—and that's a *very* good thing!

2. My cleaning rituals reassure me and give me peace of mind.

3. They show my commitment to staying healthy.

4. I won't get sick and be a burden on others.

5. I can follow through on my commitments to others since I'll be healthy and able to function.

6. This is flu season, so there really *are* lots of dangerous germs around.

7. My rituals of washing my hands and carefully showering for an hour every day show that I've got discipline.

8. My germ phobia shows my love for my family and friends since I don't want them to get sick.

9. My daily rituals show that I'm conscientious.

10. My phobia and rituals show that I have high standards.

11. My high standards have motivated me to work hard and accomplish quite a bit.

12. My shame shows that I have humility.

13. My shame shows that I'm honest and willing to examine my flaws.

14. My hopelessness and discouragement protect me from disappointment and from getting my hopes up too much since I've been struggling with this problem for nearly twenty years.

15. My hopelessness also shows that I'm realistic since most experts say that OCD is a brain disorder that is difficult to treat.

Once we completed this list, I asked Sara why in the world she would want to press the magic button. After all, if she *was* cured tonight, then she'd start touching all kinds of contaminated surfaces, and who knows what might happen!

This "pivot question" is one of the unique features of TEAM-CBT. I do *not* try to persuade patients to change, as this usually fires up the patient's resistance. Instead, I take the role of the patient's subconscious resistance—in this case, Sara's fear of change—and let my patients talk *me* into working with *them*.

Some therapists resist this approach because they're afraid the patient will say, "Actually, I *don't* want to change!" This possibility strikes fear—even terror—into the heart of most therapists. Nearly all therapists go into the field because of their extreme desire to help. In fact, helping becomes our professional identity, and the idea that a patient may *not* want help threatens this sense of identity.

It can happen on occasion, but it usually doesn't. Instead, the pivot question seems to have the opposite effect of suddenly activating the patient's determination to change.

And that's exactly what happened with Sara. She told me she'd do *anything* if I'd only work with her and cure her OCD that night. She said the burden of carrying all the anxiety, loneliness, and shame far outweighed any real or imaginary danger from germs and contamination that she'd been struggling so hard to avoid.

This was good to hear, so I asked if she'd be willing to pay the price of being cured tonight.

Sara asked what the price would be. I said that she'd have to confront the monster she feared the most. To make this clear, I told her that we would all leave the seminar room together and begin touching all kinds of contaminated surfaces—like the toilet seats in the bathroom and the door handles in the building, including the immensely frightening front door.

If you recall from chapter 3, this is called exposure, and it's a vitally important component in the treatment of anxiety. If you confront your fears, then your chances of success are almost 100%. But if you refuse, then you almost certainly won't recover.

On the spur of the moment, I described my favorite episode of *The Twilight Zone*, a TV show from decades ago. The episode features an elderly woman, Wanda, who refuses to leave her dilapidated apartment because she's afraid Mr. Death is lurking outside. Even though Mr. Death is invisible to other people, she's seen him on several occasions since she was a young girl, and she thinks he's coming for her now. If Mr. Death touches you, then you will instantly die, and Wanda is not ready to die.

Wanda hears a commotion outside and sees an incredibly handsome police officer, Harold, lying in the snow. He says he's been shot and begs for help. Although Wanda is very suspicious, she reluctantly helps him inside so he can lie down on her bed. She expresses her surprise when she doesn't die after touching him.

Once inside, Wanda tells Harold of her fears of Mr. Death, explaining that he has been trying to come and take her for several months. She says that he comes in different disguises, and when it's your time, he touches you and you die. But she's determined not to let Mr. Death trick her.

She explains that earlier in the day, a man came to her door claiming to be a building foreman, and he told her that her apartment building had been condemned and she'd need to leave. She was pretty sure it was Mr. Death, so she didn't let him into her apartment.

There is a sudden knock on the door, and although Wanda is reluctant to answer it, Harold convinces her to do so. She opens it a crack, keeping it chained, and sees that the building foreman has returned, saying, "I'm sorry lady, but I've got my orders." He pushes his way in, breaking the chain and accidentally knocking Wanda to the floor.

The foreman apologizes but explains that the building is set to be demolished in an hour and that she *must* vacate. Wanda protests and says she has to help Harold, the wounded police officer on her bed. The foreman protests that he's unable to see anyone on her bed and leaves, telling Wanda, once again, that she must vacate *immediately*.

Wanda suspiciously asks Harold why he didn't help her when the foreman barged in. Harold tells her to look in the mirror, and when she does, she realizes she can't see any reflection of Harold. Like lightning, it hits her that Harold *is* Mr. Death, and she angrily cries out, "You *tricked* me!"

Harold explains that death is nothing to fear and that Wanda is simply afraid of the unknown. He gently takes her hand and says, "You see? No shock!"

When Wanda asks if she's about to die, Harold asks her to look at the bed—where she sees her own dead body—and Harold gently says, "You see, Wanda, our journey has already begun." And together, they walk out of the building in a joyous, peaceful, and loving way, on a great adventure together.

After I told the story, I asked Sara to take my hand, and we led the group on an incredibly courageous adventure as Sara confronted her own version of Mr. Death.

We began in the women's bathroom, with more than twenty therapists who crowded in and watched as Sara and I rubbed our hands on one of the toilet seats. She estimated her anxiety as 125 a scale from 0 to 100.

Incredible!

Then she went further and lifted the toilet seat and rubbed her hands on the lower portion. I was so proud of her!

Next, we walked to the dreaded front door, touching all the door handles along the way. She was still in a state of sheer terror.

When we got to the front door, she rubbed her hands all over the glass where you could see other people's fingerprints. That was especially terrifying for her.

Then we went outside and noticed a large trash barrel that had been recently emptied, but it was really dirty and still had some gooey garbage at the bottom. I told her to reach inside and rub her hands around in the gooey mess.

She initially resisted, so I rubbed my hands around inside first. After watching me, she finally touched the inside gingerly but then immediately backed off, saying it was too much.

I told Sara that she *had* to put her hands *really* down deep in the garbage can, and I modeled this for her again. She forced herself to do this and said she almost vomited. But she did it!

Then we both rubbed our hands on our faces!

Some of the students were really anxious and asked if they could offer her some of the sanitary wipes that were next to the door! It is interesting how infectious fear can be. But we ignored them and returned to our seminar room.

I asked Sara how she was feeling now. The tears flowed as she described how enormously relieved and grateful she was. She said her anxiety was now only 1 or 2 on a scale from 0 to 100.

This was mind-blowing to me, as well as the students in the group. There were lots of tears flowing in the room.

But did Sara's remarkable and rapid recovery last? Such rapid results are really difficult for some people to believe, especially since so many therapists have been taught that the treatment of OCD is slow and that the prognosis is guarded at best.

Before we left, I gave Sara some exposure assignments for homework so she could continue with her healing after the group. I asked her to email our training group in a day or two to let us know how she was doing.

Here's the email we received two days later:

*First of all, what a magical evening and amazing transformation I had on Tuesday night. And YES!!! I was able to keep my hands contaminated all day long and only washed them after using the restroom. I didn't even wash them before I ate. What is even more amazing is that I had a smile on my face and giggled every time I touched something "gross" and yucky. What a JOY!!!*

*However, the awesomeness does not stop there. I would like to share the profound change that Tuesday night's healing has had on my daily life.*

*Today I had a very productive day that started very early. I got up a half an hour earlier and was able to complete my shower in 20 minutes instead of an hour. (Yes, sadly enough, I was taking 1-hour long showers thanks to the ridiculously "stupid" rituals—pardon the language.)*

*Best of all, because I didn't engage in my normal OCD rituals, I was out of the house in 35 minutes compared to 2 hours or more sometimes. It's mind-blowing how much time I was dedicating to this suffering and self-defeating monster.*

*And another beautiful thing happened: I visited my mother-in-law, who resides in an assisted living facility, and was able to connect with her fellow residents in a more personal and warm manner. I shook their hands, helped with their walkers, and enjoyed a cup of tea without feeling any anxiety or the need to go wash my hands. I wouldn't have been able to do this last week without anxiety and the need to run to the restroom to wash my hands. And even more beautiful and joyful was when, just like a 4-year old, I ran both of my hands on the railing from one side of the hallway to the other with great delight.*

*And if that is not enough proof of the powerful healing of TEAM in just one session, how about my licking my hands after I rubbed them on the dirty floor—not only once but twice—and laughing about it while doing it. This is how I proved to my daughter and husband that I had been "cured" after they made a comment about my happy mood and being healed from "my germs."*

*I felt so happy and validated to witness my husband and daughter noticing the change. They were blown away when I showed them the fantastic video and picture Erik took. My daughter was beyond herself and could not believe I had my hands inside the garbage can. Thank you so much Erik for preserving such a profound moment in my life. It has made a tremendous impact.*

*In summary, today I have experienced 0 anxiety about touching public door handles, toilets, floors, garbage cans, hallway railings, wheelchairs, and walkers, and I have only washed my hands after using the restroom. And when I washed my hands, it was only for a quick 10 seconds compared to the previous 3- to 4-minute intense hand washing. This is what I call freedom from the sink!*

*My contamination anxiety began in the mid 90s and had just gotten progressively worse. As you can imagine, it was taking a toll on my life and my family. Interestingly enough, the image of my dirty hands and the wonderful video playing in my head have provided so much relief, comfort, and joy. This is just amazing to me!*

*Thank you for the unconditional support and this life changing gift! I feel like I won the lottery.*

Thank *you* Sara! You were so courageous—and fantastic! What an amazing gift you've given to all of us!

We recently featured Sara on *Feeling Good* Podcast 162, many months after her recovery, to see if the effects lasted. It was one of our most popular podcasts ever.

# 10 | How to Change the Way You Feel: Part 1—Your Daily MoJo (Daily Mood Journal)

Now I'm inviting you to work with me in the same way I worked with the patients I've described thus far so I can show you how to change the way you think and feel. To make this easy for you, I'm going to lead you through your own Daily Mood Journal (Daily MoJo) in a step-by-step manner.

I'll ask you to do some written work while you read this chapter. The written work is important if you're hoping for real change. Even if you're not seriously depressed or anxious, the written work will show you how this really works.

By the way, if you'd like to download a copy of the Daily Mood Journal, go to https://feelinggood.com/daily-mood-journal.

## STEP 1. SELECT AN UPSETTING EVENT OR MOMENT

I want you to focus on a specific moment when you were feeling down. We all hit bumps in the road at times, and you can focus on any moment when you felt upset. Put a brief description of the situation at the top of your own Daily Mood Journal on page 172.

Why do we always start out with one specific moment when you were upset? There are two reasons:

1. All of your problems will be encapsulated in that brief moment. So when you understand why you were upset at that specific moment, you'll understand why you get upset at any moment. It will nearly always be some version of the same thing.

2. When you learn how to change the way you think and feel at that specific moment, you'll understand how to change the way you think and feel at any moment. That's because the techniques that help you at one specific moment will almost always help you.

The upsetting event can be anything that makes you depressed or anxious now or at any time in the past. It might involve a failure, loss, or being put down by someone you care about. It might be something frightening, like having to give a talk at work or talking to strangers if you're super shy.

If you're feeling guilty, the upsetting event might be something you said or did that hurt someone you care about. If you're feeling embarrassed, it might be something you said or did that seemed stupid or foolish. The upsetting event could even be something as simple as sitting here right now, reading this book, feeling depressed, anxious, or discouraged.

For example, yesterday, a 25-year-old computer programmer named Ben told me he'd had sex with an attractive man named Richard whom he met at a bar. Ben was really interested in Richard and had fantasies of a romantic relationship, but his spirits suddenly plunged when he discovered Richard was already involved in a serious relationship and was just having a fling.

Ben wrote "Rejection by Richard" in his description of the upsetting event on the top of his Daily Mood Journal. A short description like this is ideal.

The upsetting event can be anything, but it has to be real and specific. For example, "life sucks" won't work because it's general and vague. There's nothing wrong with feeling like life sucks—sometimes life *does* suck! But I need a specific moment when life seemed sucky.

Make sure the moment you select is a time when you were feeling down and would like to feel better. The reason I say that is sometimes people feel upset, but they're not really looking for help. That's okay—I've felt like that myself at times. I have to confess there have even been times when I just wanted to feel sorry for myself! But for this example, select a moment or upsetting event that you *would* like help with.

In addition, make sure the problem you want help with is an individual mood problem and not a relationship conflict. Individual mood problems involve feelings of depression or anxiety, and your negative thoughts will, for the most part, be directed at yourself ("I'm a loser") rather than someone else ("She's a loser").

The tools for resolving relationship conflicts are quite different from the tools for overcoming feelings like depression and anxiety. I'll show you how to resolve relationship problems later in this book, but that's not what we're going to focus on in this chapter.

You might be a bit confused since Ben and Melanie were both struggling with relationship problems. Melanie felt ashamed of her two divorces and was intensely worried about other people judging her, and Ben was depressed about being rejected. Those are certainly relationship problems, but their negative thoughts were mostly directed at themselves. They were both blaming themselves (not others), and they were primarily struggling with feelings of depression, shame, inferiority, and anxiety. So a relationship problem can be the upsetting event if your negative thoughts and feelings are directed mainly at yourself.

At this point, you should have written a brief description of an upsetting moment or event at the top of your Daily Mood Journal. Have you written it yet? Or did you skip that step and just continue reading?

Oh, you skipped that step? I had a hunch that might happen!

Hey, I'm glad you purchased this book and appreciate the chance to share these new ideas and methods with you. But I'm hopeful I can persuade you to give the exercises a try—now or later on—because I want to help you change the way you feel. That would give us both a lot of joy!

If you just want to read the chapter without doing the written work, then that's a great first step. In that case, I'd suggest you read it twice and do the written work on the second go-round.

# Daily Mood Journal*

**Upsetting Event:** _____

| Emotions | % Now | % Goal | % After | | Emotions | % Now | % Goal | % After |
|---|---|---|---|---|---|---|---|---|
| **Sad**, blue, depressed, down, unhappy | | | | | **Embarrassed**, foolish, humiliated, self-conscious | | | |
| **Anxious**, worried, panicky, nervous, frightened | | | | | **Hopeless**, discouraged, pessimistic, despairing | | | |
| **Guilty**, remorseful, bad, ashamed | | | | | **Frustrated**, stuck, thwarted, defeated | | | |
| **Worthless**, inadequate, defective, incompetent | | | | | **Angry**, mad, resentful, annoyed, irritated, upset, furious | | | |
| **Lonely**, unloved, unwanted, rejected, alone | | | | | **Other** | | | |

| Negative Thoughts | % Now | % After | Distortions | Positive Thoughts | % Belief |
|---|---|---|---|---|---|
| 1. | | | | | |
| 2. | | | | | |
| 3. | | | | | |
| 4. | | | | | |

| | | | | |
|---|---|---|---|---|
| 5. | | | | |
| 6. | | | | |
| 7. | | | | |
| 8. | | | | |
| 9. | | | | |

## Checklist of Cognitive Distortions

1. **All-or-Nothing Thinking (AON).** You view things in absolute, black-and-white categories.

2. **Overgeneralization (OG).** You view a negative event as a never-ending pattern of defeat: "This *always* happens!"

3. **Mental Filter (MF).** You dwell on the negatives and ignore the positives.

4. **Discounting the Positive (DP).** You insist that your positive qualities don't count.

5. **Jumping to Conclusions (JC).** You jump to conclusions not warranted by the facts.
   - **Mind Reading (MR).** You assume people are reacting negatively to you.
   - **Fortune Telling (FT).** You predict things will turn out badly.

6. **Magnification and Minimization (MAG/MIN).** You blow things out of proportion or shrink their importance.

7. **Emotional Reasoning (ER).** You reason from your feelings: "I *feel* like an idiot, so I must really *be* one."

8. **Should Statements (SH).** You use *shoulds, shouldn'ts, musts, ought tos,* and *have tos.*

9. **Labeling (LAB).** Instead of saying, "I made a mistake," you say, "I'm a jerk" or "I'm a loser."

10. **Blame.** You find fault instead of solving the problem.
    - **Self-Blame (SB).** You blame yourself for something you weren't entirely responsible for.
    - **Other-Blame (OB).** You blame others and overlook ways you contributed to the problem.

Even if you're a therapist and your primary goal in reading this book is to learn new ways of helping your patients, I would still encourage you to do the written exercises for two reasons:

1. The written exercises will greatly enhance your understanding and your skills.

2. Doing your own personal work is crucial if you want to be a healer, as opposed to a mere technician. The Biblical notion "Physician, heal thyself" is as true today as it was nearly 2,000 years ago.

Of course, you might be listening to this as an audiobook while driving. In that case, do the written part later when you get home. I don't want you to be writing while you're driving!

## STEP 2. CIRCLE AND RATE YOUR EMOTIONS

Once you've described the upsetting event or moment, the next step is easy. On the Daily Mood Journal, you'll find a list of negative emotions arranged in categories. Circle the feelings in each category that resonate with how you've been feeling.

For example, Ben circled *depressed* and *down* because that resonated the most with how he felt when he learned Richard was not interested in an ongoing relationship.

| Emotions | % Now |
|---|---|
| Sad, blue, depressed, down, unhappy | |

Once you've circled your negative feelings, indicate how intense the feelings are on a scale from 0 (not at all) to 100 (the worst possible), and put these ratings in the "% Now" column. You can rate how you were feeling when the upsetting event happened or how you're feeling right now. It's probably best to rate how you were feeling when the event happened, but you can rate how you're feeling now if it's still bothering you.

Ben estimated his feelings at 100, as you can see:

| Emotions | % Now |
|---|---|
| Sad, blue, depressed, down, unhappy | 100 |

Once you've done this for the first category of emotions, continue by circling and rating the rest of your negative feelings. For example, you might also be feeling anxious, guilty, worthless, lonely, hopeless, and hurt.

You'll notice there's also a space for *other* feelings. This is for any feelings you have that aren't listed. For example, you might be feeling trapped, overwhelmed, betrayed, or stressed out. If so, you can add some additional emotion words and rate their intensity as well.

The emotions portion of the journal shows me exactly how my patient is feeling in nine different categories at the start of the session. Many therapists will claim they have lots of patients who don't seem to know how they're feeling. There's a technical term for this—*alexithymia*—which is a big word with a simple meaning!

Alexithymia is the inability to identify and describe your emotions, and some experts report that about 10% of the population has this problem. Most therapists will say they have lots of patients with alexithymia.

This used to puzzle me because I've never had a patient who didn't know exactly how he or she was feeling. I think that's because I've always used the Daily Mood Journal. Once you focus on a specific upsetting moment, it's easy to circle all your negative feelings about that event and to indicate how strong each feeling is.

The emotions table also gives me a good before-and-after reading so I can find out exactly how much a patient has improved or not improved. By T = Testing a patient's emotions, therapists are held accountable for the first time. It's much like having an emotional X-ray machine that allows the therapist to actually "see" exactly how a patient feels at the start and end of each session and to know how effective—or ineffective—the session was.

To me, that's cool because the therapist can no longer get away with nonspecific, seemingly endless sessions that involve schmoozing behind closed doors, month after month, year after year. The goal becomes rapid, profound, and measurable change.

That concept represents a massive change in how psychotherapy is practiced in the United States and throughout the world as well. I wish all therapists would incorporate testing, and I believe it will soon be required by insurance companies and licensing agencies, just as scientific testing is now required in medicine.

If you tried to practice medicine without the use of the thermometer, blood tests, or an X-ray machine, you'd soon lose your license. I think mental health professionals should be held to the same standard.

## STEP 3. RECORD YOUR NEGATIVE THOUGHTS

Next, I want you to write down the negative thoughts associated with your negative feelings. Ask yourself questions like, "What am I telling myself when I'm feeling sad? Or ashamed? Or hopeless?" You can do this with all the negative emotions you circled in your Daily Mood Journal.

Record your negative thoughts using short, complete sentences and number them. Then indicate how strongly you believe each negative thought on a scale from 0 (not at all) to 100 (completely) in the "% Now" column.

According to Dr. Aaron Beck's theory of cognitive content specificity, each type of negative feeling is caused by a specific type of negative thought. For example, when you tell yourself that you've done something bad or hurt someone you love, this triggers feelings of guilt. When you tell yourself that you're in danger, this causes feelings of anxiety. When you tell yourself that you're a failure or a loser, this causes feelings of depression.

Beck's theory of cognitive content specificity makes it really easy to identify how your negative feelings are connected to your negative thoughts. Simply use the chart on the next page to look up your negative feelings and ask yourself, "What am I thinking when I'm feeling this way? What am I telling myself? What thoughts are floating across my mind?"

## Thoughts and Feelings: The Theory of Cognitive Content Specificity

| Type of Feeling | Thought | Example |
|---|---|---|
| Depression | You tell yourself that you're a failure or that you're unlovable because you've lost something important to your sense of self-esteem. | You'll recall that Mark told himself he was a failure as a father because he hadn't developed a loving relationship with his oldest son. |
| Anxiety | You predict danger and tell yourself that something awful is about to happen. | • **The fear of flying:** "What if the plane runs into turbulence and crashes?"<br><br>• **The fear of heights:** "Yikes, if I get too close to the edge of the cliff on this lookout point, I'll fall!"<br><br>• **Public speaking anxiety:** "My mind will go blank, and I'll look like a total fool when I get up to give my talk!"<br><br>• **OCD:** "If I don't wash my hands again, they'll get contaminated and something awful will happen!"<br><br>• **Generalized Anxiety:** "What if there's drinking at the high school party my kids are going to? What if they get in a car accident after the party? What if my boss doesn't like my report?"<br><br>• **Shyness/Social Anxiety:** "What if this person notices how nervous I feel? He won't be interested in anything I have to say and probably thinks I'm a loser!"<br><br>• **Panic Attacks:** "I'm about to die or go crazy! This is horrible!" |
| Guilt or shame | You tell yourself that you're bad, that you've violated your personal values, or that you've hurt someone you love.<br>You tell yourself that others will judge you and see you as bad, defective, or flawed. | You may recall that Melanie was ashamed because she was convinced people would judge her if they found out that she'd had two failed marriages. |

## Thoughts and Feelings (cont'd)

| Type of Feeling | Thought | Example |
|---|---|---|
| Inadequacy, worthlessness, inferiority | You focus on your flaws and shortcomings or compare yourself with others, and you tell yourself that you're not good enough. | A woman who endured years of domestic violence told herself, "I must be defective." A clinical social worker told me, "I'm inferior because there's nothing really special about me. I'm just average." |
| Loneliness | You tell yourself that you need others or that you're doomed to unhappiness because you're alone. | After she discovered her husband was about to leave her because of an affair with his secretary, a woman named Maria told herself, "I could never be happy without Jim's love." |
| Hopelessness | You tell yourself that things will never change. | "I'll be depressed forever. My problems will never be solved." |
| Embarrassment, humiliation | You tell yourself that others will judge you because of some flaw or shortcoming. | When sitting on a chair during a presentation, I moved my chair backward and fell off the stage! I told myself, "They must think I'm a nut!" Fortunately, the audience was incredibly kind and supportive. |
| Frustration | You tell yourself that some situation is far more difficult than it should be. | You might tell yourself, "Why is this flight so far behind schedule when I have to make a connecting flight? They should speed up and take off!" Or you might be thinking, "Darn it! This new software keeps crashing! It doesn't work as advertised!" |
| Anger | You tell yourself that someone is treating you unfairly or trying to take advantage of you. | "All he thinks about is himself!" or "She shouldn't act like that!" or "He is a self-centered jerk!" |

Here are a few additional tips when writing down your negative thoughts:

1. Don't put descriptions of events in the negative thought column. The description of the upsetting event goes at the top of the Daily Mood Journal. That's because you cannot challenge or change an event—you can only change the way you think and feel about it. The negative thought column is for your *thoughts* about the event. In most cases, those thoughts will be distorted.

2. Don't put emotions or feelings in the negative thought column. Instead, circle and rate your emotions on the emotions table. That's because you cannot challenge a feeling. You can only challenge the distorted thought that triggers the feeling.

3. Use short sentences and try to limit each negative thought to one sentence or two at most. Avoid long and rambling descriptions of problems.

4. Use complete sentences. Don't put down single phrases like "worthless" or "totally sucked." It isn't clear who or what is worthless or what totally sucked. A complete, negative thought would be "I'm worthless" or "My presentation totally sucked."

5. Do not include rhetorical questions like "Why am I so screwed up?" Instead, convert questions to declarations or should statements, like "I'm really screwed up" or "I *shouldn't* be so screwed up."

To help me illustrate, let's return to Ben. When Ben was rejected, he recorded the following negative thoughts on his Daily Mood Journal:

1. There is some deep, worthless thing about me that makes me unlovable.

2. I am worthless because I am physically and sexually inferior.

3. I feel worthless and hurt because Richard rejected me.

The first two negative thoughts contain many distortions. However, the third thought is not a suitable negative thought. Can you see why? See if you can identify any problems with this thought. There may be one, many, or no correct answers. When you're done, continue reading to find out my answer.

|  | (✓) |
|---|---|
| 1. It's a description of a negative event. |  |
| 2. It's a description of negative feelings. |  |
| 3. It contains a Freudian slip. |  |
| 4. It contains a rhetorical question. |  |

## My Answer

The answer is (1) It's a description of a negative event ("Richard rejected me"), and (2) It's a description of negative feelings ("I feel worthless and hurt"). Richard's rejection of Ben is an event that actually occurred, and as painful as it was, Ben cannot change what happened. By stating, "Richard rejected me," Ben is just describing the event instead of describing his thoughts about the event. In addition, Ben's feelings of worthlessness and hurt are very real, but they reflect his *emotions* related to the event and not his *thoughts* about it.

Here's one final tip that may help you pinpoint your negative thoughts: If you're feeling upset but can't identify your negative thoughts, you can just make up some negative thoughts. That usually works just fine.

For example, a man named Rameesh recently emailed me to say he loved my book, *When Panic Attacks*, but he was feeling really anxious about a talk he had to give at work and couldn't identify any negative thoughts that triggered his anxiety. He wanted to know what to do.

I told Rameesh to just write down some negative thoughts someone *might* have in his situation. He responded with this email:

*Hi Doctor Burns! Thanks for writing back! A person in my situation could be thinking:*

- *I will stutter a lot.*
- *As a non-native English speaker, my English is not great. People might think less of me if I use the wrong words.*
- *People may ask questions about my research that I don't know how to address, and then I'll look dumb.*
- *They may argue that my methodology is weak and that I'm not finding the real causal relation I think I am. Then everything else I say won't matter, and I'll feel awkward for the rest of the seminar.*
- *I won't be able to present everything in 30 minutes, so I'll rush at the end and forget important parts.*

*I think I understand what you wanted me to get. Even though I'm not aware of the thoughts explicitly, they are there, right? May I call these silent thoughts?*

Rameesh was correct! You can definitely think of them as "silent thoughts," and if you write them down, then it will be far easier to pinpoint what you're thinking. And that's the first step toward feeling great.

I was so pleased with Rameesh's email that I scheduled a *Feeling Good* podcast just to address his negative thoughts. If you want to listen to it, you can find at the Feeling Good website (Podcast 150).

Okay, now it's time for you to record your negative thoughts in your Daily Mood Journal. Please do this before you continue reading.

## STEP 4. IDENTIFY YOUR COGNITIVE DISTORTIONS

Once you've recorded your negative thoughts, take a look at your thoughts, one by one, and list the distortions in each thought in the distortions column using abbreviations.

Don't worry about finding many distortions in a thought. This is common. There is a lot of overlap among the various distortions. Sometimes you'll even find all ten distortions in a negative thought!

If you can't identify any distortions in a thought, it's probably a description of an event or a feeling instead of a thought. Remember, it's what you *think* about the event—that is, how you think about it and interpret it—that upsets you.

When you pinpoint a distortion, it can be really helpful to ask yourself these questions:

1. Why exactly is this negative thought an example of this cognitive distortion?

2. Why might this be an unrealistic and misleading way to think?

3. Why might this distortion be hurtful or upsetting to me?

## STEP 5. THE MIRACLE CURE QUESTION

Have you identified the cognitive distortions in your negative thoughts? Good!

Now I'm going to ask you a question that might sound ridiculous. Do you want some help with your negative thoughts and feelings? Would you like to feel better?

If the answer is no, I get it.

But if the answer is yes and you *do* want help with your negative thoughts and feelings, that's great! In that case, I have a second question for you. What kind of help are you looking for? In other words, if a miracle happened today, and you ended up feeling fantastic after you completed your work with the Daily Mood Journal, what would happen?

Most of my patients tell me they'd want to feel happy and joyful instead of feeling anxious, depressed, inferior, hopeless, worthless, angry, and ashamed. They say they want their negative thoughts and feelings to disappear.

Is this also true for you? Would you like your negative thoughts and feelings to disappear?

## STEP 6. THE MAGIC BUTTON

If the answer is yes, then I have another question for you, and I think you know what it is. Imagine that the magic button is right in front of you. If you push it, then all your negative thoughts and feelings will instantly disappear, with no effort at all, and you'll suddenly feel happy and joyous. Will you push the button?

Of course, we both know there is no magic button, but I do have some tremendous tools that will help you change the way you're thinking and feeling. And although I cannot guarantee any particular outcome, if we work together, then there's a good chance that you *will* improve and that your negative feelings may even disappear completely.

But I'm not so sure it would be a good idea to use those tools.

Do you remember why?

It's because there may be some advantages of your negative thoughts and feelings that might also disappear if you press the magic button. In addition, your negative thoughts and feelings almost definitely reveal some positive and awesome things about you that would also disappear if you were to press the magic button.

## STEP 7. POSITIVE REFRAMING

So before we jump in and try to change things too quickly, let's examine your negative thoughts and feelings from a radically different perspective, using the Positive Reframing Tool on page 197. Here's how it works.

First, list your negative thoughts and feelings, one at a time, in the left-hand column, and ask yourself these two questions:

- Are there some advantages, or benefits, of this negative thought or feeling? How might it be helpful to me?
- What does this negative thought or feeling show about me and my core values that's beautiful, positive, or even awesome?

Then list all the advantages and core values you can think of in the right-hand column.

Don't just do this in a general sort of way. Instead, focus on one negative thought or feeling at a time. That's because different kinds of advantages and core values will be embedded in each negative thought or feeling. They won't all be the same.

To make this easy, we can start with one of the categories of negative feelings you circled in your Daily Mood Journal. For example, if you circled *sad, down,* or *depressed,* then you would record those feelings in the left-hand column of the Positive Reframing Tool, like this.

| Negative Thought or Feeling | Advantages and Core Values |
|---|---|
| Sad, down, depressed | |

Now ask yourself these two questions:

1. What are some possible advantages, or benefits, of feeling sad, down, and depressed?
2. What do these feelings show about me and my core values that's positive or maybe even awesome?

Does anything come to mind? If so, put it in the right-hand column.

For example, let's assume you're feeling sad because you've had years of failed treatment for depression and anxiety. Many of my patients feel this way when they first start treatment with me. In fact, some have endured decades of failed therapy with medications, psychotherapy, and even electroconvulsive therapy, and nothing has been helpful. I even treated a woman from Europe who'd had nearly 200 electroconvulsive treatments and two failed lobotomies for her depression and anxiety!

I'd say that some feelings of depression and discouragement are totally appropriate in that situation. Would you agree?

If so, your Positive Reframing Tool might look like this:

| Negative Thought or Feeling | Advantages and Core Values |
|---|---|
| Sad, down, depressed | These feelings are appropriate and understandable because none of the treatments I've had for my depression and anxiety have worked. |

Of course, you may be feeling down and depressed for other reasons. For example, if you lost a loved one, then your feelings of sadness may reflect an expression of your love for the person you've lost. Or if you were let go from your job or experienced a setback in your career, then your sadness might reflect your passion for your career and your commitment to being productive and earning a decent living for your family.

You might also be struggling with feelings of guilt. Luckily, guilt is one of the easiest feelings to do positive reframing with, as you saw in chapter 4 when we were working with Karen. You can ask yourself:

1. Are there any benefits of feeling guilty? In what ways is my guilt helping me?

2. What does my guilt show about me and my core values that's positive and beautiful?

See what comes to mind and jot down your thinking here before you continue reading:

| Negative Thought or Feeling | Advantages and Core Values | |
|---|---|---|
| | 1. | |
| | 2. | |
| Guilt | 3. | |
| | 4. | |
| | 5. | |

## My Answer

Guilt can:

1. Show that you have a moral compass.

2. Show that you care about others.

3. Make you more sensitive to how others feel.

4. Motivate you to apologize and modify your behavior. It would be rather cold and callous if you hurt someone but didn't feel guilty about it. For example, most psychopaths do not have strong or even any feelings of guilt.

5. Show that you're realistic about your flaws and willing to be accountable.

6. Show that you're humble.

7. Show that you don't want to hurt or exploit others.

8. Show that you have high standards.

As you can see, guilt hurts, but it's a little like physical pain—it can cause you to suddenly change direction and protect you from further injury. Without pain, you might leave your hand on a hot stove and get badly burned.

What about hopelessness? Hopelessness is one of the more challenging feelings to do positive reframing with. For a while, it was even difficult for me to see how there could be anything positive about hopelessness. In fact, hopelessness is one of the most painful emotions a human being can have.

Dr. Aaron Beck pointed out that we can endure almost any suffering if we know that it will come to an end. But if you feel hopeless, then you may be convinced there will be no end to your suffering, and this belief can trigger suicidal urges when you think that's the only possible escape from pain.

So how could hopelessness possibly be positive? That seems to make no sense! Think about this for a moment before you continue reading, and ask yourself:

1. Are there any benefits of hopelessness? How might this feeling help or protect me?

2. What might feelings of hopelessness show about me and my core values that's positive and awesome?

Once you've thought of something, jot down a few ideas here and then continue reading to find out my answer. But give it a moment and see what you can come up with before you look!

| Negative Thought or Feeling | Advantages and Core Values |
|---|---|
| Hopelessness | 1. |
| | 2. |
| | 3. |
| | 4. |
| | 5. |

## My Answer

Feelings of hopelessness can:

1. Protect you from getting your hopes up and then feeling devastated if you experience another failure. For example, in this book I've been telling you that I have developed powerful new tools to fight depression and anxiety and that many people recover quickly. That sounds good, but if you get your hopes up and this book doesn't help you, it might be incredibly painful. If, in contrast, you tell yourself this book won't or can't possibly be helpful, then you won't have to risk disappointment.

2. Show that you're honest and facing the facts since you may have had many disappointments, rejections, failures, and setbacks. Feelings of hopelessness often reveal a kind of integrity.

3. Show a kind of intelligence or critical thinking. It makes sense to be skeptical about new treatment methods—after all, I might be just another snake oil salesman trying to peddle his latest tonic!

4. Give you a good reason to stop beating your head against the wall. It can stop you from trying things over and over that don't seem to work. The hopelessness can relieve the pressure to keep trying and failing.

5. Motivate you to reach out to others and let them know how much you're hurting.

Do you see what I mean? Hopelessness can be incredibly demoralizing and painful, but it can also be beneficial, and it may also be an expression of your integrity and intelligence, as well as a way of having some compassion for yourself.

To make it easier to identify how negative feelings might have benefits and how they might reflect some beautiful things about you, I've developed a Positive Reframing Map for Negative Feelings on the next page. This tool will make it super easy for you to identify the positives in every conceivable type of negative emotion. You can just look up any type of negative feeling and find many suggestions for positive things you can add to the right-hand column of your Positive Reframing Tool.

## Positive Reframing Map for Negative Feelings

| Advantages<br>What are some benefits of feeling this way?<br>How will this type of feeling help you? | Core Values<br>What do these kinds of feelings show about you that is awesome and beautiful? |
|---|---|

### Sad, down, depressed, unhappy

| | |
|---|---|
| Feelings of sadness and depression can:<br>• Let you know something is not right.<br>• Show that you are realistically looking at a problem or loss that has been difficult and painful for you.<br>• Make you more compassionate and understanding of others who are suffering.<br>• Be a celebration of life. If we can grieve the loss of a loved one or the loss of something we care deeply about, then it means we are alive and have the capacity to care. | These feelings may:<br>• Be appropriate if you've experienced loss, rejection, trauma, or failure, or if things haven't been going very well for you.<br>• Reflect your passion for life and for the thing or person you have lost.<br>• Show that you are willing to wrestle with pain rather than running from it and living in a state of denial.<br>• Show that you have high standards. |

### Anxious, nervous, worried, panicky, afraid

| | |
|---|---|
| Anxiety can:<br>• Keep you vigilant.<br>• Protect you from danger.<br>• Prevent you from getting complacent and letting your guard down.<br>• Motivate you to prepare and do really great work.<br>• Prepare you for failure or disappointment so you aren't taken by surprise. | Anxiety may show that you:<br>• Care deeply about being on top of things.<br>• Want to protect yourself and others from danger.<br>• Are responsible and not reckless.<br>• Care greatly about others and what others think of you.<br>• Have high standards and want to do your best. |

## Guilty, bad, ashamed

| Guilt and shame may show that you: |
|---|
| • Have high standards and a strong moral code. |
| • Hold yourself accountable instead of blaming others for your problems. |
| • Are willing to face your shortcomings instead of denying them. |
| • Care about the impact of your behavior on others. |
| • Don't want to let others down or let yourself down. |
| • Have strong moral values. |
| • Want others to like and respect you. |

| Guilt can: |
|---|
| • Remind you that you might not have been living up to your core values. For example, you may have lashed out and said or done something that hurt someone you love during a moment of irritability or frustration. |
| • Motivate you to examine your behavior and make a commitment to doing things differently next time. |

## Inferior, defective, worthless, inadequate

| These feelings may show that you are: |
|---|
| • Courageously honest and realistic since you do, in fact, have many flaws and shortcomings. |
| • Humble and not arrogant or overly high on yourself. |
| • Have integrity to admit when you are falling short. |

| These feelings can motivate you to: |
|---|
| • Examine your flaws and shortcomings rather than denying them or settling for second best. |
| • Improve or change your behavior. |

## Lonely, alone, rejected, abandoned

| These feelings may show that you: |
|---|
| • Care about others and value loving relationships with the people who are important to you. |
| • Desire deep and meaningful relationships rather than just superficial connections. |

| These feelings can motivate you to: |
|---|
| • Reach out to others rather than giving up on people or drifting into isolation, bitterness, or cynicism. |
| • Make personal changes that would make you more appealing to others. For example, you might decide to lose weight or improve your flirting or communication skills. |

## Humiliated, self-conscious, embarrassed

These feelings may:
- Prevent you from doing something foolish and risking disapproval or censure.
- Prompt you to examine and modify your behavior.

These feelings show that you:
- Value the opinions of others and want their respect.
- Are willing to admit and examine your flaws.

## Hopeless, discouraged, pessimistic, demoralized, defeated

Feelings of hopelessness can:
- Protect you from getting your hopes up and risking disappointment.
- Let you know when it is time to surrender and accept defeat graciously so you can save your energy for something or someone more promising.

These feelings can show that you are:
- Honest and realistic since you may have had many failures or disappointments.
- Intelligent and skeptical and that you question and challenge things.

## Frustrated, stuck, thwarted

Sometimes anger at yourself or others can:
- Be healthy and appropriate.
- Alert you that something is not right or that you are being taken advantage of.
- Motivate you to take action and stick up for yourself rather than giving in to someone who is hostile, unfair, or exploitative.
- Empower you when others are breaking the rules or trying to hurt you or someone you love.
- Be more effective than being calm. For example, if your child runs into the street to chase a ball, an angry rebuke may be more effective than a rational discussion about the dangers of traffic.
- Show that you mean business!

These feelings can show that you:
- Are aware of the dark side of human nature.
- Are not in a state of denial about others' mean-spirited thoughts or actions.
- Have high standards about the way others treat you or the people you care about. You can feel proud of your high standards!
- Value fairness, kindness, honesty, and integrity.
- Care deeply and aren't indifferent to the way others are behaving or treating you.
- Won't be a pushover and let others use you or walk all over you!

So far, we've discussed how to reframe negative feelings. But you can do positive reframing with negative *thoughts* as well. Let's say that you've recorded a self-critical thought in your Daily Mood Journal. For example, you may be criticizing yourself for some failure or flaw and telling yourself that you're a failure or a loser. You may also be telling yourself that you should be better than you are or that you shouldn't have made this or that mistake.

You can also record your negative thoughts, one by one, in the left-hand column of the Positive Reframing Tool. Then ask yourself these two familiar questions:

1. Are there some advantages of this negative thought?
2. What does this negative thought show about me and my core values that's awesome and positive?

Self-critical negative thoughts can be very beneficial and will nearly always reflect many of your core values. For example:

- Your negative thought may show that you have high standards and that you don't want to settle for mediocrity. That could be a good thing!
- In addition, your high standards may motivate you to work hard and do the very best you can. You may have accomplished many things because of your high standards and hard work.
- Your self-criticisms may also mean you're being honest about your shortcomings since you probably do have lots of flaws and shortcomings. That type of honesty could be a form of strength.
- Your self-criticisms may also show you're willing to be accountable and look within for answers rather than blaming others or blaming the universe for your problems.
- Your self-criticisms may also be an expression of your humility rather than arrogance or narcissism. Humility is a spiritual quality.

As you can see, although your suffering may be incredibly painful, there will always be many advantages, or benefits, of your negative thoughts. And your negative thoughts will nearly always reveal positive and awesome things about you too.

To help you reframe your negative thoughts, I've developed another handy tool on the next page called the Positive Reframing Map for Negative Thoughts. This tool groups negative thoughts into three categories:

1. "I'm no good." These are the kinds of thoughts that trigger depression, inferiority, guilt, and hopelessness.

2. "I'm in danger." These are the kinds of thoughts that trigger anxiety and fear.

3. "You're no good." These are the kinds of thoughts that trigger anger and conflict.

This map will help you identify the advantages and core values of any negative thought you list on the Positive Reframing Tool.

## Positive Reframing Map for Negative Thoughts

| Depressing Thoughts: "I'm No Good." |
|---|

These thoughts trigger depression, unhappiness, guilt, inferiority, worthlessness, and hopelessness.

- **All-or-Nothing Thinking:** "I'm a complete failure."
- **Overgeneralization:** "I think I'm unlovable."
- **Mental Filter:** "I screwed up again! I've made so many mistakes!"
- **Discounting Positives:** "I'm just average. There's really nothing special about me."
- **Fortune Telling:** "Things are hopeless. I'll never be able to solve my problems."

- **Magnification/Minimization:** "I can't stand feeling this way!"
- **Labeling:** "I'm a bad mother (or father)."
- **Emotional Reasoning:** "I *feel* like a failure, so I must *be* a failure."
- **Self-Directed Shoulds:** "I shouldn't be so screwed up."
- **Self-Blame:** "It's all my fault."

| Advantages | Core Values |
|---|---|
| These kinds of thoughts can: <br><br>• Motivate you to pinpoint and overcome your shortcomings. <br>• Make you aware that you may have hurt someone you care about or violated your personal values. <br>• Motivate you to ask for forgiveness and change your own behavior. <br>• Keep you alert so you don't deny or overlook your problems and shortcomings. <br>• Make you aware that bad outcomes are possible. <br>• Protect you from disappointment. <br>• Highlight things that are important to you and that are not working as well as they could be. <br>• Remind you when you're falling short of your goals. <br>• Show that you've experienced the loss of someone or something you love. | These kinds of thoughts can show that you: <br><br>• Have worthy and challenging goals for yourself. <br>• Have high standards for your performance. <br>• Don't want to do mediocre work or settle for second best. <br>• Have a strong sense of integrity and a willingness to examine your flaws. <br>• Are humble and aware of your shortcomings. <br>• Care about what others think about you and that you want to deserve their respect. <br>• Want to treat others in a loving and fair manner. <br>• Are honest and willing to face your shortcomings and failures. <br>• Are accountable and willing to examine your own failures rather than always blaming others or blaming the world. <br>• Are realistic and facing the facts since you may have tried many things that did not work. |

## Frightening Thoughts: "I'm in Danger!"

These kinds of thoughts trigger anxiety, fear, worry, nervousness, insecurity, and panic:

- **All-or-Nothing Thinking:** "I'll totally screw up when I talk to my boss."
- **Overgeneralization:** "This always happens! Everyone will look down on me and think I'm a loser."
- **Mental Filter:** "Air travel is *so* danger-ous!"
- **Discounting Positives:** "No matter how hard I study, I know I'll screw up when I take the test."
- **Fortune Telling:** "My mind will go blank, and I'll probably pass out when I give my talk."

- **Mind Reading:** "People will think I'm a loser."
- **Magnification/Minimization:** "I'm so panicky! What if die, pass out, or lose my mind?"
- **Labeling:** "Why do I feel so anxious? I must be a mental case."
- **Emotional Reasoning:** "I feel really scared. This means something terrible is about to happen."
- **Self-Directed Shoulds:** "I shouldn't feel so anxious."
- **Self-Blame:** "I'm really screwed up!"

| Advantages | Core Values |
|---|---|
| These kinds of thoughts can: | These kinds of thoughts can show that you: |
| • Protect you from harm by reminding you to avoid dangerous or threatening situations. | • Are careful and don't want to act in a reckless or thoughtless manner. |
| • Motivate you to prepare and work hard so you don't get complacent and flunk a test. | • Want to protect yourself and the people you love from dangerous situations. |
| • If you have a phobia, like fear of flying, your negative predictions will protect you and remind you to avoid the thing you're afraid of. | • Want to prepare carefully and do high-quality work. |
| • Keep you vigilant and prevent you from getting mugged if you're alone at night in a dangerous part of town. | • Want meaningful and genuine relationships with others. |
| • Protect you from assuming that everyone likes you when they actually don't. | • Care deeply about what others think about you. |
| • Alert you to the fact that people can be very judgmental or critical. | • Don't always take people for face value but think deeply about feelings they may be hiding. |
| • Be a way of letting others know that your problems are severe or urgent. | • Are taking a problem seriously rather than writing it off as unimportant. |
| • Motivate you to seek help from others. | • Are a sensitive person and that you're in touch with your feelings. |
| | • Are cautious, thoughtful, and aware of the dangers in the world. |

## Angry Thoughts: "You're No Good!"

These kinds of thoughts trigger anger, annoyance, irritation, frustration, and resentment:

- **All-or-Nothing Thinking:** "All he thinks about is himself."
- **Overgeneralization:** "She never listens!"
- **Mental Filter:** "He always has to be right!"
- **Discounting Positives:** "She says all the right things but doesn't really mean it."
- **Fortune Telling:** "I've tried everything, and nothing works. She will never change."
- **Mind Reading:** "He thinks he's better than everyone else."
- **Magnification/Minimization:** "I can't stand him."
- **Labeling:** "She is a jerk."
- **Emotional Reasoning:** "I feel like there's nothing good about him."
- **Other-Directed Shoulds:** "She shouldn't feel that way."
- **World-Directed Shoulds:** "This computer shouldn't keep crashing. It's brand new!"
- **Other-Blame:** "This is all his fault."

| Advantages | Core Values |
|---|---|
| The benefits of these kinds of thoughts include: <br>• It's easy to blame others. <br>• You won't have to change, which involves hard work. <br>• Blaming others can give you a feeling of moral superiority. <br>• It can be rewarding to look down on the people you're not getting along with. <br>• You won't have to examine your own role in the problem, which can be humiliating. <br>• You can get others to support you and agree that the person with whom you're at odds really is a jerk. <br>• Feelings of anger and injustice can be exciting and can give your life a greater meaning and purpose. <br>• Blaming others can mobilize you to take action rather than just giving up and feeling defeated. <br>• You can deny or minimize your role in the conflict. <br>• You can play the role of the victim. <br>• You'll have an excuse for doing nothing since the other person or the universe is to blame. <br>• You can think about the shortcomings and flaws in the world and in other people. <br>• You can feel sorry for yourself (sometimes a delicious secret pleasure!) | These kinds of thoughts can show that: <br>• You have a moral compass. <br>• You're willing to stick up for yourself or others. <br>• You recognize the dark side of human nature and realize that sometimes people will intentionally try to hurt or exploit others. <br>• You have a strong sense of justice. <br>• You won't let other people take advantage of you or walk all over you. <br>• You're willing to hold other people accountable for their behavior. <br>• You realize that people can be intentionally unfair and act in a mean-spirited fashion. <br>• You have high standards and won't settle for less than the best from other people. <br>• You value fairness and accountability. <br>• You feel that people should follow through on their commitments and that products should work as advertised. |

Now that you have a feeling for how positive reframing works, let's focus on your negative thoughts and feelings using the Positive Reframing Tool on the next page. I suggest you start with a negative feeling instead of a negative thought. Remember to ask yourself:

1. What are the advantages of this type of feeling (or thought)?

2. What does this feeling (or thought) show about me and my core values that's beautiful, positive, and awesome?

Remember to focus on one negative thought or feeling at a time when you do positive reframing.

In doing this exercise, you will discover that your negative thoughts and feelings show some really neat things about you. Paradoxically, those discoveries will make the next and most crucial step—*changing* the way you think and feel—far easier.

Please complete the Positive Reframing Tool now. Do this exercise on paper and not just in your head. When you're done, you can continue reading on.

## Positive Reframing Tool*

**Instructions:** Review the negative thoughts and feelings in your Daily Mood Journal and fill in the two columns below. Ask yourself these two questions about each negative thought or feeling you list in the left-hand column:

1. What are some advantages, or benefits, of this negative thought or feeling?
2. What does this negative thought or feeling show about me that is positive and awesome?

Some negative thoughts or feelings may have *only* advantages, some may have *only* core values, and some may have advantages *and* core values. You will find many helpful tips on the Positive Reframing Map for Negative Feelings and the Positive Reframing Map for Negative Thoughts. Remember to work on one negative thought or feeling at a time.

| Negative Thought or Feeling | Advantages and Core Values |
|---|---|
| 1. | |
| 2. | |
| 3. | |
| 4. | |
| 5. | |
| 6. | |
| 7. | |
| 8. | |
| 9. | |
| 10. | |

Once you've completed the Positive Reframing Tool, you will see why there's a downside to pressing the magic button. If you pressed the magic button to make all of your negative thoughts and feelings go away, all these positive and awesome things about you would disappear at the same time. That could be a huge loss, and it might amount to a betrayal of many of your core values and beliefs.

And that gives us an answer to the question Freud asked more than 100 years ago: Why do we sometimes cling to our negative feelings and resist change?

Could it be because our negative thoughts and feelings are not symptoms of "mental disorders," as the DSM-5 would have us believe, but might instead be the expressions of what is most awesome and beautiful about us? Could it be that our negative thoughts and feelings may sometimes even help and protect us? If so, it makes perfect sense that we might push back against anyone who tries to persuade us to think or feel differently!

*As I've said, our negative feelings, as well as our "resistance" to change, are not really the result of what's wrong with us but what's right with us!*

## STEP 8. THE MAGIC DIAL

But now we have a dilemma. On the one hand, you may be struggling with painful negative thoughts and feelings, and you may desperately want to feel better. In fact, that could be why you're reading this book.

But if you suddenly recovered, and all your negative feelings disappeared, then you might lose some things that are extremely precious. So if you have mixed feelings about change, with one foot in the water and one foot on the shore, I completely understand.

How can we resolve this dilemma?

If you think back to what you learned in chapter 4, you probably know the answer.

Instead of pressing the magic button, let's imagine that we had a magic dial, and you could turn the dial on each negative feeling down to some lower level. That way, you can improve the way you feel without sacrificing any of the positive aspects of your negative thoughts and feelings.

For example, let's say that you've been feeling sad, depressed, down, and unhappy, and you rated this feeling at 90%, like this:

| Emotions | % Now | % Goal | % After |
|---|---|---|---|
| (Sad,) blue, (depressed, down, unhappy) | 90 | | |

After you've completed positive reframing, you can ask yourself this question: "In light of all these positives, how sad and depressed do I want to feel? If I could dial these feelings down to any level between 0 and 100, how sad and depressed would I want to feel?" In other words, what level would allow you to feel better and still preserve all the positives you listed on the Positive Reframing Tool?

Let's say that you decide 20 would be enough. If so, you could write it in the "% Goal" column, like this:

| Emotions | % Now | % Goal | % After |
|---|---|---|---|
| (Sad,) blue, (depressed, down, unhappy) | 90 | 20 | |

Does that make sense? You're in charge, and you can decide how you want to feel. I'm working for you, and you're the boss!

Now I want you to fill in the remaining goal columns for each emotion in your Daily Mood Journal. That way, we can see what your goal is for each type of negative feeling.

Once you've completed this, we can use some terrific tools to help you smash your negative thoughts and improve the way you feel. Keep in mind, however, that the methods we're going to use are quite powerful, and in some cases, we might overshoot. For example, your feelings of sadness and depression might go all the way to 10% or even to 0%.

But don't worry, if your negative feelings get too low, I can help you work them back up a bit higher before we finish up. That way, you won't have to worry about getting *too* happy.

Now let's roll up our sleeves and start challenging the negative thoughts that are making you unhappy!

# 11 | How to Change the Way You Feel: Part 2—The Great Escape

In the last chapter, you completed the first several steps of your Daily Mood Journal. You had the chance to describe an upsetting event and to rate your negative feelings about that event. You also had the chance to record your negative thoughts about the event, to rate how strongly you believed each thought, and to identify the distortions in these thoughts.

We also did some positive reframing to help you see that your negative thoughts and feelings are not necessarily "symptoms" of some "mental disorder." Rather, they are expressions of your core values as a human being and can be of tremendous benefit to you. Finally, we used the magic dial so you could dial down each negative feeling to some lower level without losing all the positive, wonderful qualities that come along with them.

Now we're going to take the next and most important step. I'm going to show you how to change the way you think and feel. We have talked about the necessary and sufficient conditions for emotional distress, as well as for emotional change. Do you remember what they are?

Although this is a review, I want to make sure that you grasp these ideas, so please fill in the four blank areas on this table before you turn the page.

|  | Necessary Condition | Sufficient Condition |
|---|---|---|
| Emotional Distress |  |  |
| Emotional Change |  |  |

## My Answer

|  | Necessary Condition | Sufficient Condition |
|---|---|---|
| **Emotional Distress** | You must have a negative thought, like:<br>• "I'm a loser"<br>• "I shouldn't have screwed up!" | You must believe the negative thought and feel convinced that it's true. |
| **Emotional Change** | You must come up with a positive thought that's 100% true. Remember, we're not aiming for rationalizations or half-truths. | The positive thought must crush the negative thought. This means that your belief in the negative thought is drastically reduced, possibly all the way to zero. |

What's so cool about this process is that the change in how you feel can happen rapidly, sometimes even in the blink of an eye. In fact, the very moment you stop believing the negative thought that's upsetting you, you will feel relieved or even euphoric.

But how do you do that? How can you generate a positive thought that fulfills the necessary and sufficient conditions for emotional change? This is not a trivial question because most people who feel depressed and anxious have had the same negative thoughts for years.

Is that how it's been for you?

Friends, family members, and even therapists may have tried to cheer you up or encourage you to change the way you think and feel—and probably without much success. Challenging and crushing your negative thoughts is rarely easy because they may seem totally and absolutely true when you're depressed or anxious. And even if you can rationally pinpoint the cognitive distortions in your negative thoughts, they may still seem like some ultimate, horrible, and inescapable truth about you.

That's the amazing thing about depression and anxiety. They are cruel and deceptive illusions that seem absolutely real. After you recover, you'll look back and wonder how in the world you could have believed things about yourself and the world that were so incredibly misleading.

Fortunately, I've got many powerful techniques to help you challenge and crush your negative thoughts. My goal for you (and every person with whom I work) is not only to experience rapid and substantial changes in how you think and feel right now. It's to have lasting change so you'll be empowered to deal with painful mood swings in the future as well.

Take a look at your Daily Mood Journal and select one negative thought you'd like to work on first. Now put the negative thought you've selected in the middle of the two blank recovery circles at the end of this chapter. Make sure you've identified the distortions in this thought before you place it in the recovery circle.

Remember that the arrows represent different ways to escape from the circle you're trapped in, using techniques from the "Fifty Ways to Untwist Your Thinking" in chapter 33. Review that list and put techniques that look promising in the boxes at the ends of the arrows.

If you put one technique in each box in the first recovery circle, you'll have sixteen tools to help you challenge and defeat the negative thought in the middle. I've already selected the first three techniques since they will always be the same. But just in case you need even more techniques, I've included a second recovery circle you can fill out as well. That way, you'll have room to select as many as thirty-two techniques to challenge the negative thought. Sometimes you might need only one or two techniques. But it's great to include lots of methods on your recovery circle because you never know what method is going to work for you.

You probably won't need nearly that many techniques, but it might be comforting to know that we have a great deal of firepower available. If you've been struggling with feelings of depression, anxiety, and inferiority for a long time, like so many people, then you probably know change is not easy, and you may appreciate having so many powerful tools to help you challenge the distorted thoughts that are making you unhappy.

And if you're struggling to figure out what techniques to list, don't worry! Once you've identified the distortions in the thought, you can use the cheat sheet from chapter 5 to select techniques. If there are many distortions in your thought, you'll have tons of techniques to list. In the next section of this book, I'll go into more detail about the specific techniques that can be especially helpful for each distortion.

Once you've selected at least ten or fifteen techniques and put them in the boxes around your recovery circle, you can try them, one at a time, and see if you come up with positive thoughts that fulfill the two requirements for emotional change:

1. The positive thought must be 100% true.
2. The positive thought must cause a substantial reduction in your belief in the negative thought that's upsetting you.

When you generate positive thoughts that are 100% true, you can record them in the positive thoughts column of your Daily Mood Journal. Then you can re-rate how much you now believe the negative thought. Sometimes the positive thought will reduce your belief in the negative thought all the way to zero. But sometimes a reduction to a lower level will be good enough.

If your positive thought is not 100% true or if it does not reduce your belief in the negative thought, then it won't be helpful to you. What should you do then?

Just move on to the next technique in your recovery circle and try again. Remember that a positive thought won't be effective if it's not completely true. Half-truths and rationalizations are rarely or never helpful. TEAM-CBT is based on the Biblical notion "The truth shall make you free."

---

### Teaching Point

Once you've completed the first several steps of the Daily Mood Journal, select the negative thought you want to work on first, and put it in the middle of your recovery circle.

Next, review the list of "Fifty Ways to Untwist Your Thinking" and select at least ten to fifteen methods you can use to challenge the negative thought in the middle. Put the names of the techniques in the empty boxes around your recovery circle.

Each method will help you come up with a positive thought you can use to combat the negative thought. Indicate how strongly you believe the positive thought on a scale from 0% (not at all) to 100% (completely).

Then indicate how strongly you now believe the negative thought. If the positive thought is 100% true, and if it causes a drastic reduction in your belief in the negative thought, then your negative feelings will probably improve immediately.

If the positive thought does not substantially reduce your belief in the negative thought, then you can move on to the next technique on your recovery circle, following the philosophy of "failing as fast as you can"!

---

You can generate positive thoughts as many times as you need to until you've crushed the negative thought. When you find the technique that works, you can often use the same technique to crush the rest of the negative thoughts in your Daily Mood Journal. You'll learn much more about this in the coming chapters.

So let's get on with the show and start your great escape!

## Your Recovery Circles*

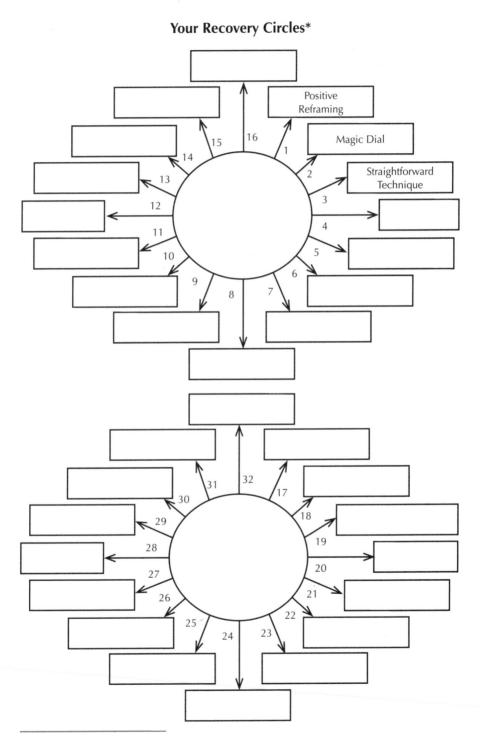

Positive Reframing

Magic Dial

Straightforward Technique

# Section II

---

*How to Crush Distorted Thoughts*

# 12 | All-or-Nothing Thinking

A man named Saul recovered from years of depression after only a dozen sessions of TEAM-CBT. He became euphoric and told himself:

*This is fantastic. I'm not a loser after all! My problems are finally solved! I'll never have to deal with depression again!*

Three weeks later, Saul got into an argument with his wife and went to bed feeling grumpy, frustrated, angry, and dejected. When he woke up the next morning in a state of severe depression, he told himself:

*My improvement was just a fluke. The therapy didn't really work. I'm worthless after all. I'll be miserable for the rest of my life!*

As you can see, Saul's angst results from **all-or-nothing thinking,** one of the most common cognitive distortions. With this type of distortion, you think about yourself or the world in absolute, black-or-white, all-or-nothing terms.

There are two opposite forms of this (or any) distortion:

- **Positive All-or-Nothing Thinking.** This distortion is dominated by the "all" side of the equation: You tell yourself that if you do well, then you're a winner and that everything is always going to be wonderful.

  This type of thinking was evident when Saul told himself, "My problems are finally solved! I'll never have to deal with depression again!"

- **Negative All-or-Nothing Thinking.** This distortion is dominated by the "nothing" side of the equation: You tell yourself that if you're not a complete success, then you're a total failure, a zero.

  This type of thinking was evident when Saul told himself, "The therapy didn't really work. I'm worthless after all."

Please write a brief explanation of why Saul's thought when he recovered was a classic example of positive all-or-nothing thinking.

_____

_____

_____

_____

Now explain why Saul's thought when he relapsed into depression several weeks later was an example of negative all-or-nothing thinking.

_____

_____

_____

_____

## My Answer

This is perhaps overly obvious. When Saul suddenly recovered, he jumped to the "all" side of the equation, thinking that he'd be happy forever. This created unrealistic expectations since no one can be happy all the time.

But when Saul woke up feeling depressed again, he jumped back to the "nothing" side of the equation, thinking that he was worthless and that the therapy hadn't worked. These all-or-nothing thoughts are unrealistic because, in actuality, Saul has many faults and strengths, much like the rest of us. In addition, his treatment was extremely effective, but that doesn't guarantee never-ending bliss.

As you can see, both forms of all-or-nothing thinking can be problematic. Negative all-or-nothing thinking triggers feelings like:

- Depression, despair, and hopelessness
- Anxiety and panic
- Shame and guilt
- Inadequacy, inferiority, and worthlessness

Positive all-or-nothing thinking leads to:

- Mania
- Narcissism
- Relationship conflicts
- Anger and violence
- Habits and addictions

Sometimes it's hard to avoid all-or-nothing thinking. It's really easy to slip into this distortion without being aware of it.

Go ahead and review the negative thoughts you recorded in your Daily Mood Journal from chapter 10. Can you spot all-or-nothing thinking in any of your negative thoughts, including the one you selected for your recovery circle? If so, write down the negative thought here.

_____

_____

_____

_____

Now write a brief explanation of why that thought might be unrealistic. In other words, why doesn't the all-or-nothing thinking reflect reality?

_____

_____

_____

_____

Can you now see why all-or-nothing thinking might contribute to your negative feelings? Can you also see why your all-or-nothing thinking might be unrealistic and arguably even unfair?

## POSITIVE REFRAMING

Before we jump in and try to challenge your all-or-nothing thinking, take a deep breath and ask yourself this question first: Are you sure this is something you really want to do?

As you've learned, there are likely many benefits of all-or-nothing think-ing, and it also reflects some pretty positive and awesome things about you. Can you see why?

Think about it for a moment before continuing.

For one thing, all-or-nothing thinking can make life really dramatic. When things go well, you may think of yourself as a "winner" and feel elated. That's pretty awesome.

And when you fail, you may think of yourself as a "total loser." That's painful, of course, but your intense negative feelings can motivate you to figure out why you failed and how to do better next time. That's definitely a *good* thing, and it's real.

In addition, all-or-nothing thinking is at the heart of perfectionism, and perfectionism can be a good thing. It shows that you have really high stan-dards, that you care deeply about your work, and that you're not willing to settle for mediocrity or second best. People who didn't give up—like Einstein, Edison, and so many others—changed the world.

We could easily add to the list, but I think you get the idea. We get hooked on cognitive distortions for the same reasons we get hooked on nega-tive thoughts and feelings. They are the expression of our core values, and they can be incredibly helpful.

So here's what I want to ask: Why would you want to give up all those benefits of all-or-nothing thinking? If you don't want to, I totally get it. When I was younger, I was totally hooked on perfectionism and had no desire whatsoever to give it up.

But if you *do* want to dial down your all-or-nothing thinking, the next technique is a great place to start.

## THINKING IN SHADES OF GRAY

If you look at the cheat sheet from chapter 5, you'll see that lots of techniques can be helpful. But a really simple solution is called **thinking in shades of gray**. You avoid extreme, black-or-white judgments and try to look at things more realistically, somewhere between 0% and 100%. It's an easy fix for the "all" and "nothing" sides of all-or-nothing thinking.

For example, when Saul recovers from his depression, he could tell himself:

*Hey, this is great. I feel terrific, and I can see that I'm not a worthless loser after all! I do have a lot of flaws, but I've got some strengths as well. I'm sure*

*I'll fall into the black hole of self-doubt again since no one can be happy all the time, but I've got some helpful tools that I can use to deal with my negative thoughts and feelings whenever they return.*

Then when he runs into a bump in the road, as we all do, he can think about it like this:

*Wow, I feel crappy again. The doctor warned me that this would happen. Now why am I so upset? Well, I had an argument with my wife last night. Nearly all couples fight from time to time, and if we talk it out, then I'm sure we'll feel more loving again.*

Can you see that these "shades of gray" messages might help prevent the extreme ups and downs that result from Saul's all-or-nothing thinking?

All-or-nothing thinking is nearly always a distortion because the world, for the most part, cannot be accurately described in all-or-nothing terms. For example, would you say that this book is the most fantastic book ever written? Is it better than Shakespeare or even the Bible? I don't think so!

Well then, if this is not the most fantastic book ever, then is it a total zero? Worse even than rotting poop? I must confess that there have been times when I felt like rotting poop, but I don't think my writing is nearly that bad!

Thinking about this book in all-or-nothing terms would not only be unrealistic, but it would be a barrier to my creativity too. That's because I'd feel tremendous pressure to write "perfectly" and come up with something stupendous. But I don't know how to write "perfectly" or "stupendously." So if I succumb to all-or-nothing thinking, then I may end up with a case of writer's block.

And that did happen to me once in the past, when I tried to revise my first book, *Feeling Good.* I had just gotten a contract and an advance from my publisher, and my editor, Maria, said I needed to rewrite the book—which she (rightfully) thought was "boring"—and turn it into a "best seller."

I sat at my desk for ten days, unable to write a single sentence! Finally, I wrote down the negative thought that was bugging me: "I don't know how to write a best seller. Maria will be disappointed in me."

Then I noticed my all-or-nothing thinking and decided to think about it like this instead: "I don't know how to write a best seller, and that's not even my job. My publisher will have to help with the publicity and marketing of the book. My job is just to talk to my readers the same way I talk to my patients. That's something I *can* do, and that might turn out to be really helpful for some people who are depressed, whether or not it's a 'best seller.'"

I immediately felt a surge of excitement and creativity, and the revision turned out to be really easy and fun!

If you think about anything in the world, or any human quality, you'll see that it can't be described very accurately in all-or-nothing terms. For example, think about your IQ or your physical strength. You're probably not as smart as Einstein, but you're probably pretty darn smart about lots of things. And you're probably not as strong as an Olympic weightlifting champion, but you probably have quite a lot of physical strength.

And my singing voice is terrible, certainly below average, but I can sing way better than a dog I saw on television. The dog was howling in a very sincere and enthusiastic way while his owner played the piano. And when I make up songs and sing for our new kitty, Miss Misty, she seems to love it!

Here's the typical type of song that I make up as I go and sing in my rather awful singing voice:

*Miss Misty! Oh Miss Misty!*

*You are the cutest girl*

*In all of Los Altos*

*By far, by far.*

*With your silky black fur*

*And your yellow-green eyes,*

*You are the prettiest kitty I've ever seen!*

*Prettier even than the skies,*

*And the sweetest one too—*

*So I love you!*

David and Miss Misty just before a Sunday hike.

She loves it!

We're all somewhere between 0% and 100% in all respects. Nobody is a zero, and nobody is perfect.

It's the same with the world. Some things in the world are positive, even fantastic—like medical breakthroughs, new discoveries about the origin of the universe, and acts of great compassion. And many things in the world are negative and horrible. But most things are somewhere in between these extremes.

So if you want to think about yourself and the world more realistically, try thinking in shades of gray. It may sound a bit drab compared to the drama of all-or-nothing thinking, but the world becomes far more colorful when you learn to think in shades of gray.

Now I have a final exercise for you. Take a moment and see if you can rephrase your all-or-nothing thought in terms of thinking in shades of gray. Try to make a more accurate statement that's in between the extremes of "all" or "nothing."

_____

_____

_____

_____

_____

I can't give you feedback on your new thought or presume that this particular technique is going to be effective for you, but it will be good practice to give it a try. I'm going to show you tons of ways to smash any negative thought, so don't worry if any particular technique does not do the trick. We've got many more great methods!

# 13 | Overgeneralization

A young professional woman named Ariella became depressed when her boyfriend for the past two years, Alan, suddenly broke up with her. She thought it was because she was too pushy, bossy, or controlling.

Alan and Ariella had been planning a weekend outing, and Ariella had carefully scheduled every minute so they could do all the things they wanted to do. Alan said he preferred to hit the road and just see what came their way. This led to an argument, a blowup, and eventually a painful breakup, which was heartbreaking for Ariella.

Ariella explained that although she'd had several fairly good romantic relationships, they all had ended because of the same kinds of conflicts. She concluded that she was unlovable and doomed to endless rejections and loneliness.

This is a classic example of **overgeneralization** because Ariella was generalizing from a negative event—breaking up with her boyfriend—to her "self" in thinking that she was "unlovable." In addition, Ariella was generalizing from a painful event in the here and now to the future by telling herself she'd be alone forever.

There are negative and positive versions of overgeneralization:

- **Negative Overgeneralization.** You generalize from a negative event to a never-ending pattern of defeat using words like *always* or *never*. Or you generalize from a flaw, screwup, or failure to your entire "self" by telling yourself that because you failed at X, this means you are a failure.

- **Positive Overgeneralization.** You generalize from a positive event to a never-ending pattern of success and tell yourself that you're *always* going to win. You may also see yourself as "a winner" or as an especially worthwhile human being because of some accomplishment or positive thing you did.

Overgeneralization, like all-or-nothing thinking, is one of the most common cognitive distortions. Did you spot that distortion in any of the negative thoughts you wrote down in your own Daily Mood Journal? If so, I'll ask you to work on that thought a little later in this chapter.

Negative and positive overgeneralizations can both be problematic. It might seem obvious why the negative version can cause problems, but it might be less obvious why this would also be the case for the positive version. To illustrate the drawbacks of positive overgeneralization, it can help to think about compulsive gamblers.

Compulsive gamblers often tell themselves that they're "on a roll" when they win a couple of hands in a row at the blackjack table. That feels great at the time, but if they buy into what they're telling themselves, then they may go home with a big loss at the end of the day! Positive overgeneralizations can be seductive because they cause a mental rush.

Let's return to Ariella. She's telling herself that since all her romantic relationships in the past have ended, that means that all her romantic relationships in the future will fail as well.

Is Ariella's thinking valid? Can you see why this is an overgeneralization? Put your ideas here before reading on.

_____

_____

_____

_____

_____

## My Answer

Here's one problem with Ariella's thinking: Millions of people in the world are married. Prior to getting married, what percent of their romantic relationships ended in a breakup? 100%!

So it can hardly be true that people who've had failed relationships in the past are doomed to never-ending rejections and loneliness in the future.

There's also another way that Ariella may be overgeneralizing. She is telling herself that she's "unlovable." Can you see why this is a classic overgeneralization as well? Put your ideas here before you continue reading.

_____

_____

_____

_____

_____

### My Answer

When Ariella thinks of herself as "unlovable," she's jumping from the specific to the "self." She's gotten lost in the clouds of abstraction. Ariella has many strengths and weaknesses, but her "self" can't be accurately described based on any single trait. In other words, Ariella is not all "this" or all "that." You and I aren't either.

Ariella is an attractive and charismatic young woman, a leader in her field, and her many colleagues and friends adore her. But her enthusiasm and leadership may also turn some people off. Our greatest strengths are almost always our greatest weaknesses as well. But does this mean that Ariella is "unlovable"? Or simply that she's human?

Eventually, Ariella will find a cool guy who's a good fit for her. But sometimes there are bumps in the road along the way—we all get rejected or put down at times, and that can hurt. To be honest, I've had some pretty painful rejections and put-downs at times. But the main cause of our pain is rarely or never the actual rejections or criticisms we receive—it's the distorted way we think about them.

What's the best way to overcome an overgeneralization?

## POSITIVE REFRAMING

Anytime you're trying to challenge a distorted negative thought, it's a good idea to start out with **positive reframing**. That will help melt away any resistance that might prevent you from letting go of your negative thoughts and feelings.

To show you how this works, let's focus on Ariella's thought "I'm unlovable." Ask yourself these two questions:

1. What are some advantages, or benefits, of believing this thought?
2. What does this thought show about Ariella and her core values that's positive and awesome?

See if you can come up with at least five positives:

_____

_____

_____

_____

_____

When you're done, continue reading, and I'll show you what we came up with.

## My Answer
Here's what Ariella and I came up with:

1. This thought is painful but helps me understand why I was rejected.
2. It shows that I'm accountable since I'm looking at my own flaws instead of blaming everything on my boyfriend.
3. The thought protects me from future disappointments. If I tell myself that I'm unlovable, then I won't get my hopes up and get disappointed again.
4. This thought shows that I have high standards. My high standards have motivated me to achieve a great deal and helped me grow as a person.
5. This thought shows humility as opposed to arrogance.
6. The thought is realistic since I do have many flaws. After all, several guys have broken up with me.
7. This thought gives me an excuse to take a vacation from the dating game, which can be time-consuming, frustrating, and exhausting.
8. This thought shows that I'm reflective, brave, and willing to examine my flaws and shortcomings so I can grow as a person and hopefully become more lovable and likable.

9. The thought makes me really sad. It's appropriate to feel sad after you've been rejected.

10. This thought reduces the chance that I'll get angry and start thinking about my boyfriend's flaws. I'm kind of protecting him and some of my positive memories of our time together.

Once we listed these positive aspects of Ariella's negative thought, I asked Ariella why in the world she'd want to challenge the idea that she was "unlovable." This is an important key to the rapid recovery I see all the time when I'm using TEAM-CBT. Instead of trying to sell my patients on change, I ask them to persuade *me* to work with them. And most of the time, they do!

Ariella insisted that in spite of all these positives, she *did* want to reduce her belief in the negative thought, if possible, because she was tired of feeling worthless, anxious, guilty, hopeless, inadequate, defeated, and depressed, and she did not want to give up on her dream of a loving and lasting relationship.

Next, I'll show you some specific techniques that were helpful for her.

## BE SPECIFIC

There are many techniques for challenging overgeneralizations, but one of the best is called **be specific**. When you use this technique, you come down from the clouds of abstraction and focus instead on your *specific* flaws, errors, or shortcomings. Once you've pinpointed a specific error or flaw, you can accept it, work on correcting it, or both. When you use this technique, it can sometimes be helpful to focus on your specific strengths as well.

For example, instead of telling herself that she's "unlovable," Ariella might ask herself, "What are some things I do that lead to problems in my relationships? And what could I do to grow and develop more loving relationships in the future?"

As we explored this, it became clear that she was making a significant error in her relationships with boyfriends and friends as well. She often assumed that if she was very enthusiastic about an activity she had planned, then the other person would feel pretty much the same way. Then she'd get disappointed and feel betrayed if the other person backed out at the last minute.

Ariella wasn't in the habit of checking with others to see how they actually felt about her planned activities and perhaps wasn't always tuning in to clues that the other person might have mixed feelings. This is a solvable problem. It's not a fatal flaw that makes you "unlovable."

As one part of the solution, Ariella decided to check in with others more frequently and ask if they had any negative feelings or doubts about some event she
was planning. That way, she could make sure everyone was on the same page.
This is called the **survey technique**, and it's pretty simple. You simply check
things out by asking people how they feel, rather than trying to read minds.

The survey technique was helpful to Ariella in another way. She was telling herself she was unlovable because she was too pushy, and she also assumed
everyone else felt the same way about her. I suggested she might ask several
friends and colleagues if they sometimes felt she was too pushy and controlling, and how she came across to them.

She was pleasantly shocked to receive extremely positive responses from
her friends and colleagues. They told her they did not find her pushy or controlling. In fact, they all said she was a friendly and warm leader, and they
appreciated her energy and enthusiasm. They said she was a spark plug who
made lots of fun things happen.

Ariella told me, "No one felt that I took up too much time or attention
when we were hanging out together, and they said they were grateful for me
just the way I am!"

Their acceptance made self-acceptance a sudden possibility, and Ariella
said her feelings of depression almost instantly vanished. Self-love and self-
acceptance are two of the most important keys to sex appeal, as well as loving
relationships with others.

Ariella decided to change her thinking about the breakup like this:

| Negative Thoughts | % Now | % After | Distortions | Positive Thought | % Belief |
|---|---|---|---|---|---|
| I'm unlovable. | 100 | 10 | AON, OG, MF, DP, MR, FT, MAG, ER, SH, LAB, SB | I have strengths and weaknesses, just like everyone. | 100 |
| | | | | Many guys have been attracted to me in the past. | 100 |
| | | | | Sometimes I may be a bit too pushy, but I also have a ton of positive qualities that people seem to appreciate and love. | 100 |
| | | | | There are lots of other fish in the sea! | 100 |

As you can see, her belief in the negative thought went down all the way to 10%, which was her goal.

By coincidence, I met with Ariella last night after not seeing her for several months. I was curious to see how she was doing and to find out if our previous work together had been helpful.

She said she wanted a little help with a new problem. Can you guess what her new problem was?

It was one that brought a lot of joy to my heart. Ariella had a new boyfriend, and there'd been a complete role reversal. He was pursuing her with such zeal that she was losing interest in him, and he was getting desperate. She said many other guys were chasing her as well, and she needed some help figuring out what to do.

Not bad for someone who's "unlovable"—and so much for overgeneralizations!

## OTHER TECHNIQUES

There are other techniques that can be helpful to challenge overgeneralizations as well. The **semantic technique** is a fairly humble and simple method, but it can be effective. For example, let's say that something negative happens, and you start telling yourself that this *always* happens or that you'll *never* get it right. This type of overgeneralization may make you feel frustrated, doomed, and defeated.

Instead, you can tell yourself that this "sometimes" happens. In other words, you simply substitute language that is less extreme. In some cases, this can take the edge off the negative thought that's upsetting you.

As another example, let's say you're depressed and feeling worthless or inferior because you're telling yourself, "I'm defective." This is a classic overgeneralization, and it's extremely common among people who are depressed.

Here are some techniques you could use to challenge this thought.

| Technique | "I'm Defective." Questions You Can Ask Yourself |
|---|---|
| Positive Reframing | What does this thought show about me and my core values that's positive and awesome? For example, does it show I have high standards and that I'm honest about my flaws? And what are some benefits of telling myself that I'm defective? For example, do my high standards sometimes motivate me to work hard and do my best? |
| Be Specific | Can I focus on the specific error I made instead of labeling my entire self as defective? |

| Double Standard Technique | What would I say to a dear friend who felt defective because of some failure or painful experience? Would I say, "Well you must be defective!" If not, why not? What would I say to a dear friend? |
|---|---|
| Examine the Evidence | What are some of my flaws, and what are some of my strengths? Is *everything* about me defective? Am I *always* screwing up? |
| Semantic Method | Can I substitute language that is less extreme? For example, instead of thinking of myself as a "defective human being" could I think of myself as "a human being with defects"? |
| Acceptance Paradox | Can I accept the fact that I have many flaws and defects without hating myself? |
| Let's Define Terms | What's the definition of a human being who is "defective"? Is it someone who screws up sometimes or someone who screws up all the time? If it's someone who screws up sometimes, then we're all defective. If it's someone who screws up all the time, then no one is defective. Either way, we're all in the same boat! |
| Cost-Benefit Analysis | I can list the advantages and disadvantages of thinking of myself as "defective." How will this thought help me, and how will it hurt me? Are the advantages or disadvantages greater? |
| Self-Disclosure/ Survey Technique | I can tell friends and colleagues that I sometimes feel defective when I screw up and ask them if they ever feel that way. I can also ask them if they judge me or think less of me when I screw up. |

Now that you have a feel for how to challenge overgeneralizations, review your list of negative thoughts from your Daily Mood Journal, and see if any of your thoughts have this distortion. Select one thought, and record it here:

_____

_____

Once you've written a thought down, see if you can explain *why* this thought is an overgeneralization. For example, you may be generalizing from some flaw or bad experience to your "self" by thinking that you are a "failure," "loser," or "bad person."

Or you may be generalizing from some current problem to the future and thinking that you're *always* going to screw up or get rejected and that things will *never* change.

Put your thinking here:

_____

_____

_____

_____

_____

Now let's see if you can challenge the negative thought with any of the techniques you've read about in this chapter. Remember that your positive thought has to be 100% true, and it has to crush your belief in the negative thought. You can record it here:

_____

_____

_____

_____

_____

What should you do if you weren't able to smash the negative thought and you still believe it as much as ever?

You don't need to worry about that for the reasons I mentioned earlier. If you recall, most negative thoughts contain many cognitive distortions, not just overgeneralization. In fact, Ariella's negative thought "I'm unlovable" contained all ten distortions. And there are tons of additional techniques you can try for each type of cognitive distortion. When one method doesn't work, you can try another, and then another, until you find the method that *is* effective.

# 14 | Mental Filtering and Discounting the Positive

Following my appearance on a morning talk show in Cincinnati, the host pulled me aside and asked if I could help him with a personal problem. He explained that after each show, he typically received several hundred emails from fans, almost all with glowing comments about his show. But sometimes there was a critical email. He said he'd ruminate about the one negative email for hours and feel miserable, while ignoring all the positive letters.

That's classic **mental filtering**, in which you dwell on negatives and filter out or ignore the positives. There are negative and positive forms of this cognitive distortion:

- **Positive Mental Filtering.** You think about all the positives and filter out or ignore the negatives. This type of mental filtering often triggers romantic intoxication. For example, if you get all excited about some wonderful person you met, then you may think about all of his or her positive qualities and end up thinking that person is fantastic. But as you get to know him or her, you may start to notice all the warts, and now you think, "Yuck!"
- **Negative Mental Filtering.** You dwell on all the negatives and filter out or ignore the positives. Do you sometimes do that? Do you dwell on the flaws in your appearance or personality, ruminate about your thinning hair or tendency to sweat excessively, or harp on some other flaw and conclude that you're inferior or that others will be totally turned off by you? Those are all examples of negative mental filtering.

Negative mental filtering often goes hand in hand with **discounting the positive**, in which you insist that your good qualities or positives don't count.

Do you sometimes discount compliments? For example, if a friend tells you that you look good, or that she really liked your proposal or the talk you gave at work, do you tell yourself, "Oh, she's just saying that to be nice. She doesn't really mean it." Those are all classic examples of discounting the positive.

The opposite of this distortion is called **discounting the negative**, in which you insist that your bad qualities, or someone else's, don't count.

Have you ever argued with someone who criticized you instead of finding the truth in what he or she said? Or have you ever lashed out at someone during a moment of frustration and later told yourself that you "didn't really mean it" and that you're not "that kind of person"? These are both examples of discounting the negative. You discount your flaws so you can maintain a uniformly positive view of yourself.

Positive mental filtering and discounting the negative help to fuel habits and addictions. For example, if you're trying to lose weight, you might tell yourself, "I'll just have one little bite of this donut. One little bite can't hurt!"

That sounds great, but how many times have you told yourself that? And how many times did you actually stop after one little bite? If you discount all that negative data, you can binge on some tasty donuts right now!

As you can see, positive distortions are rewarding. That can make it harder to challenge these distortions because they make us feel good. In contrast, the negative versions of these distortions hurt.

You saw a sad example of the pain caused by mental filtering and discounting the positive in the introduction to this book. You may recall that Frank, the carpenter, was telling himself that his life had never amounted to anything and that his hard work over the years didn't count for much.

Mental filtering and discounting the positive often account for the depression that people experience as they age. You may dwell on:

- All the things you wanted to do but didn't.
- All the places you dreamed of visiting but never traveled to.
- The loving, exciting partner you never found.
- The meaningful, rewarding career you never developed.
- The goals you didn't fulfill and the dreams that never came true.

But once again, it's not aging that's getting you down but your distorted thoughts. You can make yourself miserable with mental filtering and discounting the positive at any age, and no matter how much you've accomplished!

For example, I once read a story about an ancient pharaoh who was the wealthiest man in the world. When he died, all his family and closest advisors gathered excitedly for the reading of his will, eager to find out what riches and lands they had inherited.

The will was a bound papyrus volume thousands of pages long. But when they opened it, they were surprised to find that all the pages were blank except for the first. On that page, he had written one sentence, which read, "In all of my life, I had only seven happy days."

## COUNTING THE POSITIVES

What's the best way to overcome mental filtering and discounting the positive? One simple solution is called **counting the positives**.

For example, instead of dwelling on what you haven't achieved or enjoyed, you focus on some of the things you *have* enjoyed, some of the people you *do* love, and some of the goals you *have* achieved.

When you think about it, we would all make ourselves miserable if we constantly ruminated about all the things we can't do. For example, I'm too old to be an astronaut, and I can't play in the NBA because I'm average—at best—at basketball. And I can't fly to Paris in my jet to have dinner with some of the "beautiful people" because I don't have a jet and don't know any of the "beautiful people"!

There are countless things that I can't do and that you can't do either. So what!

How about noticing all the things you are doing and giving yourself some credit for those? If I think about the things I *am* doing, it makes me happy! For example, today I got up early, made myself a tall cup of coffee after feeding the cats, and started editing one of the chapters in this book.

Then I made an outline of my *Feeling Good* podcast for this coming Sunday and did some emailing—I always get a ton of emails, and many include good questions from thoughtful fans. I like to answer as many as I can, although it's impossible to keep up with all of them.

Then I did my jogging, even though I was tired. After that, I made some lunch and watched the news on TV, which was a bit distressing, and now I'm editing again.

And tonight I'm going to teach at my Tuesday night psychotherapy training group and do live therapy with one of our members who's been depressed and a bit at odds with her husband. My dear colleague, Dr. Jill Levitt, is going to be my co-therapist.

I'm pretty sure it's going to be incredibly rewarding! I love teaching at Stanford even though I'm not paid. It's just volunteer work, but my real payment is the joy I feel.

Hey, that ain't bad! The list made me feel good!

Counting the positives is a pretty humble technique and can sometimes be a nice antidote to mental filtering and discounting the positive.

## DOUBLE STANDARD TECHNIQUE

What are some other techniques you can use to combat mental filtering and discounting the positive? There are tons of helpful tools, but the **double standard technique** is one of the best. It's really easy to learn too.

Several years ago, I was asked by a colleague if I'd be willing to consult with a beloved, 45-year-old university administrator named Gabriella who was hospitalized for the evaluation of a pelvic mass her doctor discovered during a routine OB-GYN checkup.

Sadly, the biopsy indicated ovarian cancer that was already in an advanced stage, and there was no curative treatment at that time. Gabriella learned that she would have only about two years to live. She felt extremely depressed, guilty, worthless, and anxious, which is understandable.

My colleague told me that Gabriella was the type of person who always went out of her way to help others, like helping faculty and students on their research projects and grant proposals. Although she'd never been married, she was also helping three relatives with disabilities who lived with her in a large house in Redwood City, California.

Now you might argue—and most people would—that Gabriella was depressed and anxious because she had cancer. However, one of the cornerstones of cognitive therapy is the idea that only your thoughts, and not the events of your life, can cause you to feel depressed or anxious. But how can this be? If you've just learned that you're going to die from cancer, doesn't the event itself cause you to feel the way you do? Aren't depression and anxiety inevitable?

Well, you'd certainly think so! But let's find out.

When I met with Gabriella at the bedside in the hospital, she reported three negative thoughts that were making a huge impact on the way she felt:

1. I'm letting my family down.

2. They can't survive without me.

3. It's my fault that I got cancer.

She believed these thoughts 100%. However, they contained a bunch of distortions, like self-blame, mind reading, fortune telling, and emotional reasoning, as well as mental filtering and discounting the positives. That's because Gabriella was telling herself that she was failing her family and that everything she had done for them didn't count or wasn't good enough.

You can also see that these distorted thoughts, and not the cancer, were causing her despair. There's no way in the world the cancer could make Gabriella—or any human being—feel guilty or worthless!

Remember: Your negative feelings will *always* result from your thoughts and not from the actual events in your life. And if you're depressed and anxious, your thoughts will nearly *always* be distorted.

So while I couldn't change the facts of Gabriella's situation—the cancer was real—I could help her change the way she was thinking and feeling.

Because Gabriella seemed like a kind person, I thought the double standard technique might be a good place to start. You may recall that this technique is based on the idea that most of us operate on a double standard. When we fail or screw up at something, most of us scold ourselves mercilessly.

But if we were talking to someone else who had the exact same problem, then we'd probably talk to him or her in a far more compassionate and realistic way. When you use the double standard technique, you decide to talk to yourself the same way you would talk to someone else whom you really care about.

Although Gabriella was in a private hospital room, I told her to imagine there was another woman in the bed next to her and that this woman was a lot like her. She was also 45, had several relatives with disabilities living with her, and had just been diagnosed with ovarian cancer.

I told her to talk to that woman, out loud, the exact same way she was talking to herself. I said:

*Tell her that she's letting her family down, that they won't be able to survive after she dies, and that it's her fault that she got cancer.*

There was a long silence, and Gabriella looked puzzled. She finally said, "I can't *possibly* say those things to another woman, Doctor."

When I asked why not, she said, "Because they're *not* true!"

I replied, "Why not? Isn't it a plain fact that her family feels like she's letting them down?"

Gabriella said, "No, they *don't* feel that way. They love her and feel sad about her diagnosis and feel grateful for all the help she's given them over the years. They definitely don't feel like she's letting them down. Not at all!"

Then I asked Gabriella why she wouldn't tell this other woman that her family couldn't survive without her.

She said, "Because that's not true either. She's helped her family a lot, but they have excellent coping skills, and they'll continue to prosper after she dies. They'll miss her because they love her, but they'll do well."

Then I asked why she wouldn't tell this other woman that she was to blame for her cancer, and she said, "That's ridiculous too! We don't even know the cause of ovarian cancer. She couldn't cause it even if she wanted to!"

I asked Gabriella how much she believed what she'd just said about this other woman—the woman who was just like her—and she said it was absolutely true. I then asked Gabriella if this thought would be true for her as well, and she replied, "I guess it would be true for me as well."

Once Gabriella came to this realization, her thoughts about her illness changed to reflect the following:

| Negative Thoughts | % Now | % After | Distortions | Positive Thoughts | % Belief |
|---|---|---|---|---|---|
| 1. I'm letting my family down. | 100 | 0 | AON, MF, DP, MR, SH, ER, SB | No, they don't feel that way. They love me and feel sad about my diagnosis and probably feel grateful for the help I've given them over the years. They don't feel like I'm letting them down. Not at all! | 100 |
| 2. They can't survive without me. | 100 | 0 | FT, DP, ER | My family has excellent coping skills and their own resources. They love me and will miss me, but they will continue to thrive after I'm gone. | 100 |
| 3. It's my fault that I got cancer. | 100 | 0 | ER, SB | This is impossible. The cause of ovarian cancer is not even known! | 100 |

And the very moment she realized her thoughts were simply not true, her depression suddenly disappeared. She was still sad, but no longer depressed. Her treatment took only forty-five minutes.

I did not see Gabriella again as a patient, but our paths crossed from time to time over the next two years and she continued to do well. Unfortunately, the cancer metastasized right on schedule two years later, and she eventually passed away.

It was extremely sad, but I was happy and proud that Gabriella did not have to spend the last two precious years of her life feeling depressed, anxious, guilty, worthless, and alone. Instead she felt loved, productive, and happy with her life.

Now look back to your Daily Mood Journal and see if any of your negative thoughts involve mental filtering or discounting the positive. If so, record one of those thoughts here.

_____

_____

_____

_____

Next, explain why that thought is an example of mental filtering or discounting the positive and why that thought might not be accurate.

_____

_____

_____

_____

Finally, see if you can challenge the negative thought using counting the positives or the double standard technique. Remember that this positive thought must be true, and it must substantially reduce your belief in the negative thought.

_____

_____

_____

_____

Now you may be wondering what I would have done with Gabriella if the double standard technique had not been effective, and you may be wondering what to do if this technique was not helpful when you tried to talk back to your own negative thoughts.

Remember that different people respond to different techniques. That's why I've developed so many methods for smashing distorted thoughts. When one method doesn't work, just move on to the next one until you find one that's effective for you. You'll have plenty of opportunities to try out more techniques in the chapters that follow!

# 15 | Jumping to Conclusions— Mind Reading

Dave, a friend from the neighborhood, was riding his bicycle up Old La Honda Road toward Skyline Boulevard recently. This is a steep uphill climb, and Dave was feeling tired, so he decided not to push too hard.

But he noticed someone on a bicycle right behind him, and his competitive juices kicked in. He didn't want to let the fellow pass him, so he sped up. The man behind him sped up as well and stayed right on his tail.

Dave felt irritated and told himself that the other rider was trying to beat him and ruining his leisurely morning ride, so he went all out, but no matter how fast he went, the man behind him stayed right on his tail. Dave told me that when he got to the top, he was furious and stopped on the edge of the road, braced for an angry confrontation.

The man on the other bicycle pulled up next to him with a huge smile on his face and said, "Thanks for the push! I never could have made it that fast without your help!"

Dave realized that he'd been involved in a cognitive distortion called **jumping to conclusions.** This is where you automatically assume something that isn't warranted by the facts at hand. Dave had assumed the man behind him was trying to beat him, or best him, when the man on the other bicycle was actually thinking about the ride in an entirely different manner.

There are two common examples of jumping to conclusions:

- **Mind Reading.** You assume, without convincing evidence, that others are judging you or having negative feelings about you.
- **Fortune Telling.** You predict, without convincing evidence, that things will turn out badly.

In this chapter, we'll focus on mind reading, and in the next two chapters, we'll focus on fortune telling.

There are negative and positive versions of mind reading:

- **Negative Mind Reading.** You assume others are reacting far more negatively to you than they really are.
- **Positive Mind Reading.** You assume others are reacting far more positively to you than they really are.

I've often been misled by both forms of mind reading. We usually think we know how other people feel about us, but it's really easy to get fooled.

For example, during an inpatient cognitive therapy group at my hospital in Philadelphia, I was working with a severely depressed woman named Lucretia who had experienced two traumatic events in the same week. On Monday, her husband walked out on her, and on Tuesday, she lost her job. She felt hopeless and suicidal, and she was telling herself that she was a worthless human being.

During the group, I showed Lucretia how to talk back to her negative thoughts, and she seemed to be feeling much better by the end. I thought I'd done a fantastic job.

At the start and end of each group, I ask all the patients to complete my Brief Mood Survey so I can see how severe their symptoms are and how much they've improved during the group. It only takes them about a minute. At the end of each group, I also ask them to rate me on several scales that assess empathy and helpfulness.

I expected glowing ratings from Lucretia but was shocked to discover that her depression and suicidal urges had gotten much worse. In addition, she gave me the lowest scores I've ever seen on the empathy and helpfulness scales.

I was perplexed and convinced she'd made a mistake when filling out the forms, so I asked her to review her answers to make sure they were correct. Sometimes people get confused by the response options and fill out the scales in the opposite way they intended.

Lucretia glanced over her answers and said, "There's no mistake here, Dr. Burns."

I said, "What do you mean? We just had a terrific session!"

Lucretia responded, "Terrific for *you* maybe!"

I asked what she meant. She explained that when I said she'd had a double whammy—losing her job and husband at the same time—she thought I was making fun of her since "double whammy" sounded like a phrase in a comic book.

I had *no idea* that she'd reacted so negatively to my comment. Fortunately, we had a good talk and quickly resolved the problem, but if I hadn't used the assessment tests, I would have been totally deceived into thinking I'd done a terrific job.

This was a classic example of positive mind reading, though I've been fooled by negative mind reading as well.

For example, at the start of the group the next week, I noticed that a newly admitted patient named Rose was feeling extremely depressed, anxious, and angry. She'd just been hospitalized involuntarily on our locked unit because of a failed suicide attempt the night before. She defiantly announced that she intended to complete the job the first chance she got.

Rose explained that she'd been treated for depression for years, but nothing had ever helped, and she felt horrible every minute of every day. She said that she'd struggled with a crack cocaine habit and had been living in a recovery house in Philadelphia. She'd been clean and sober for two months but had slipped up and used crack following an argument with her roommate. The staff threatened to kick her out of the program, so she got mad and tried to kill herself. She said she felt utterly worthless and had decided it was time to face the facts about her life and cash it in.

I asked how many other patients in the group sometimes felt worthless and hopeless or even suicidal. Every hand went up. I asked Rose if she'd like some help during the group and if she'd ever been treated with cognitive therapy.

She practically bit my head off! She said I sounded like every other "stupid fucking shrink" she'd wasted time with and loudly announced that she had no interest whatsoever in any of my "fucking cognitive therapy."

I felt about two inches tall and decided Rose wasn't going to be the best person to work with during the group. I backed off and worked with a woman on the other side of the room who also felt hopeless and worthless. Rose didn't utter a word the entire time. I was afraid to look in her direction but could sense that she was staring at me with daggers in her eyes.

We had a reasonably good group, but I dreaded having to review Rose's feedback at the end of the session. I was taken aback when I saw that her depression, suicide, anxiety, and anger scores had all fallen to zero, which would seem to indicate complete recovery. I was even more surprised to see that she'd given me perfect scores on empathy and helpfulness.

At the bottom of the feedback form, I ask patients to describe how they felt about the group. For the section on "what did you like the least," Rose had simply written, "nothing."

For the section on "what did you like the best," she wrote:

*Doctor Burns, when you worked with that other woman, I felt like you were working with me. Her negative thoughts and feelings were just like mine. I've never had cognitive therapy before, and I didn't even know what a cognitive distortion was.*

*I always thought my problem was that I really* was *a worthless and horrible human being, but now I see that the real problem is the way I've been thinking, and now I can see how distorted and unfair my negative thoughts have been.*

*I can hardly believe I'm saying this, but I'm feeling joy and full of self-esteem right now. In fact, this is the first happiness I've experienced in my entire life. Thank you so much! The last hour and a half has changed my life.*

If I hadn't been using the assessment tests, then I wouldn't have known that the group had been so helpful to her, and I probably would have gone out of my way to avoid making eye contact with her if I saw her on the psychiatric unit. In this case, I was fooled by negative mind reading.

Positive and negative mind reading is far more common than you might think. We're usually convinced that we know how people think and feel, including how they feel about us, but most of the time we don't. Therapists often miss the boat, and family members do too. The results can sometimes be disastrous.

For example, I did a study at a community mental health clinic in New York to evaluate the accuracy of therapists' and caregivers' evaluations who brought children in for treatment. I asked the children, their therapists, and their mothers to rate how they thought the children were feeling.

When I analyzed the data, I was amazed to discover that the therapists' accuracy was about *zero*. And the mothers didn't do any much better! There was pretty much *no* correlation between how the children felt and how their therapists (or mothers) thought they felt.

The errors were not trivial. For example, the mother of one little boy rated his depression and suicidal urges at zero. She was convinced that her son did not feel depressed, and the therapist agreed with this assessment.

How did the boy actually feel?

His depression and suicidal scores were at the top of the scale! In the margin of the assessment test, he wrote that he had borrowed a gun from a friend and had plans to kill himself on Friday. In this case, mind reading almost resulted in the death of a little boy, but the assessment test alerted the mother and therapist to what was really going on and likely saved his life.

It's not only therapists or family members who may be off base. When you're involved in positive or negative mind reading, you may not realize it either. Do you know why?

It's because when people are annoyed with you, most of the time they'll hide their feelings and act polite. They may not tell you how they feel because they're unassertive or trying to avoid a conflict. That's what happened when I was treating Lucretia. I got completely fooled by positive mind reading, thinking she'd really liked the session.

We get fooled by negative mind reading for another reason. If you think people are judging you or having negative thoughts and feelings about you, then you probably won't ask them how they feel for the same reason—it's embarrassing, and you may want to avoid a conflict. As a result, you never get the information you need.

In addition, you may assume that people are annoyed with you when they're not. As a result, you may feel upset and react to the other person defensively, or you may say something aggressive because you don't like being judged. In turn, the other person will pick up on the tension and feel annoyed or frustrated with you, and the negative interaction you imagined becomes a reality.

That's why I always use assessment tests in my teaching and in my therapy sessions. The information is sometimes shocking but always illuminating. My students and patients have been my best teachers by far!

Of course, you can't usually use written feedback to find out how others feel about you. So what can you do?

## INQUIRY AND SELF-DISCLOSURE

Lots of techniques can be helpful, but inquiry and self-disclosure are especially useful.

- **Inquiry.** You ask people what they're thinking and feeling rather than jumping to conclusions. This is one of the five secrets of effective communication, and it's an art form that requires practice and courage.

You may recall that Karen, the woman in chapter 4, was involved in mind reading when she told herself that the therapists in the audience were judging her. When she asked them how they felt, she discovered that they actually had tremendous admiration for her. This was a huge surprise to her.

- **Self-Disclosure.** This is the opposite of inquiry. Instead of asking people how they feel, you tell them how *you* feel since others can't read your mind either.

For example, if you're shy, then you may be intensely ashamed of your shyness and try to hide your insecurities in social situations. You may try to act "normal" or "cool" because you're convinced that your shyness indicates some shameful defect. Of course, hiding your true self intensifies the feeling of shame and the shyness as well.

When you use self-disclosure, you simply open up about your feelings instead of trying to fake it. This can open up a much more meaningful connection with the other person, but it can be frightening.

For example, I once treated a handsome fellow named Robert who was incredibly lonely because he was painfully shy in social situations. He wanted to get married and settle down but said he was way too shy to make meaningful connections with single women.

Robert would go to singles bars and stand at the side watching everyone mingle, feeling terrified, and telling himself he *shouldn't* feel so anxious and insecure. Every night, he went home alone feeling ashamed and dejected. I encouraged him to use self-disclosure and simply tell the women he met that he felt shy and awkward. He stubbornly refused because he was absolutely convinced that he'd sound like a loser and get rejected.

This is classic mind reading, and it is common in people who struggle with shyness. You feel certain that you know how other people feel about you.

I told Robert he *had* to use self-disclosure if he wanted me to keep working with him, no matter how hard it seemed. This is called the "gentle ultimatum," and it's really important in the treatment of anxiety because individuals who are anxious will nearly always resist confronting their fears.

The following Saturday night, Robert bit the bullet and approached a woman in the bar. He told her he felt really shy and awkward but thought she was attractive. After a brief conversation, she said she also felt uncomfortable in singles bars, and she suggested they drive to the beach instead.

Robert was quite surprised!

Once they arrived at the beach, she suggested they might take a midnight swim in the ocean. Robert pointed out that they had no suits. She said, "So...?"

Robert was even more surprised!

They took a skinny-dip in the ocean, under the full moon. Their adventure turned out to be extremely exciting, and they started dating regularly. Robert declared himself "cured" and terminated therapy after a couple more sessions.

I didn't see Robert again for several years, until one evening when I was eating dinner with my family at a local restaurant. Robert came in with an attractive woman and three children. He spotted me and proudly introduced his wife and children. Then he said, "See Dr. Burns, your therapy worked!"

Self-disclosure is definitely scary, and it has to be done thoughtfully because it can backfire if you do it in a self-effacing or clumsy manner. For example, I'm not recommending you just walk down the street and talk about your deepest fears or worst flaws with every stranger you meet. And I'm not suggesting that you talk to your boss or customers in a totally uninhibited way either.

But if you do self-disclosure thoughtfully, it can be incredibly helpful. Other people cannot read your mind—and vice versa—but if you open up and share your feelings instead of acting phony and hiding them, then you will often connect with others at a much deeper level.

Still, this *is* scary. I get it!

I'm a big believer in practicing what you preach, so I'll do that right now! For years I struggled with anxiety—from crippling public speaking anxiety to anxiety about urinating in public restrooms for fear that people would notice that I couldn't pee. This is called "shy bladder syndrome."

I've also had dozens of phobias, and I fall into hypochondriasis from time to time when I'm under stress, thinking I have some dreaded disease like cancer when there's nothing whatsoever wrong with me.

For example, during my postdoctoral research fellowship at the University of Pennsylvania, I became concerned about a lump in my right armpit and began to worry that it might be a lymphoma. I finally worked up the courage to tell my wife, who pointed out that I could pop right over to the ER and have it checked out.

One of the medical residents evaluated me and did a careful examination of my right armpit. He told me there was no lump there and that I was fine. I told him he was wrong, that there *was* a lump, and that I could feel some pain in my armpit from the lump. I insisted on a second opinion from another ER doctor.

Because I was on the staff of the hospital, the director of the ER kindly came in and examined my right armpit. He told me the same thing—there definitely was no mass in my armpit and I was fine.

I demanded an X-ray. He protested that there was no medical reason to do so.

I pushed hard, so they finally gave in and ordered an X-ray. Once it was completed, the resident and ER director invited me to look at the results with them. They had long faces, and I was pretty sure they'd found something awful, like a mass in my lung or a tumor in my armpit.

They asked me to take a careful look at the X-rays and tell them what I saw. I told them I couldn't see any abnormalities and that the results looked totally normal.

They said the X-rays *were* normal and asked if I'd been under stress lately.

It suddenly dawned on me that my oral board examination for licensure in psychiatry was coming up in one week and that I was incredibly worried about it. It also dawned on me that just before I got the pain in my armpit, I'd been carrying around a heavy suitcase on a trip to London, and that I'd probably pulled a muscle, and that was what was causing my pain.

What a relief! And I was overjoyed to pass the exam a week later with flying colors.

There you have it. Now that I've done some self-disclosure, you see how neurotic I am, so you can either burn the book in disgust, or you can continue reading. Hopefully, we'll have a more human connection now.

## FEARED FANTASY

When I write about these techniques, I try to make them seem simple so you can see exactly how each technique works. But we all know it's not always so simple, and things don't always have happy endings. What then?

For example, if you're mind reading that someone is annoyed with you, judging you, or rejecting you, it's possible that you're right! So when you use the inquiry technique to ask them how they feel, you might not experience a kumbaya moment.

What then?

You can try the feared fantasy technique:

- **Feared Fantasy.** You enter an *Alice in Wonderland* nightmare world where there are two really weird rules. First, people really *are* having negative thoughts about you. Second, they aren't polite but get right up in your face and tell you what they think. For example, if you're afraid of rejection or disapproval, in this world, people really *do* reject you and disapprove of you. In addition, they aren't nice about it and tell you what they really think. They try hard to put you down and humiliate you.

This technique might sound scary, but by facing your worst fear, you often realize that the monster has no teeth.

To use this technique, start off by writing down all the negative thoughts you think other people may be having about you. These are the things that people might think but won't ordinarily say.

Continuing with my own self-disclosure, here are some things that I'm worried judgmental readers may be thinking about me:

1. He really sounds disturbed.

2. He's a phony because he's more screwed up than his patients.

3. He can't even pee in a public restroom! That's weird!

4. I'm going to tell everyone about him.

5. I'm going to throw this stupid book away or ask for a refund.

Of course, your own list of feared judgmental thoughts will be different, but I'll show you how it works with mine.

You can respond to the criticisms of this feared fantasy person by using a combination of self-defense and the acceptance paradox. When you use self-defense, you argue with the feared fantasy person and insist that what he or she is saying simply isn't true. When you use the acceptance paradox, you win by agreeing with the critic with a sense of humor or inner peace.

I'll show you how it works. We can stick with my personal example, and you can be the feared fantasy person. I don't know if you want to address me as David or Dr. Burns, but we can use the more familiar David. Hope that's okay!

**You (as feared fantasy person):** Gee, David, I read your book and now I can see how screwed up you are!

**David:** I have tons of flaws, even more than I wrote about in the book. What do you think?

**You (as feared fantasy person):** Well, to be totally honest, I'm judging you. You sound more screwed up than most of your patients.

**David:** Well, that might be, but in a way, it's helped me because I think I have more understanding and compassion for my patients. In addition, working to overcome some of my own flaws and insecurities has given me more powerful tools to help my patients. I know what works and what doesn't.

**You (as feared fantasy person):** Well, you can say anything you want, but no one would want to work with such a screwed-up psychiatrist.

**David:** Actually, you might be surprised! I've had many patients who've seemed to appreciate the work we've done together. Perhaps they have low standards! But they seem far more interested in some compassion and help with their own problems than in judging me for my flaws. And when they found out I was flawed, most of them seemed to like me even more! Totally weird, don't you think?

**You (as feared fantasy person):** Yes, that might be, but you can't even pee in a public restroom!

**David:** That was incredibly embarrassing for me for a long time, and I tried to hide it, but to be honest, I've more or less gotten over it, and I use public restrooms all the time now. It's not a problem at home either.

Of course, I probably wouldn't want a group of friends pointing and staring at me derisively when I pee, as I might freeze up. But that's not much of a problem since no one seems to want to stare at me while I'm peeing.

**You (as feared fantasy person):** Well, I've never had that problem with peeing in public restrooms!

**David:** I know, I know! I've heard you pee really well! Kudos to you. I may even nominate you for the Peeing Award. Or perhaps it's the Peabody Award? I can't remember what the exact name is.

**You (as feared fantasy person):** I'm going to tell everyone about what a nut you are! And I'm going to reject you too!

**David:** Oh, I hope you tell lots of people. It might boost sales for this book. I would appreciate that, really. But one thing you said does make me sad.

**You (as feared fantasy person):** What's that?

**David:** I'm sad that you're going to reject me because I've always liked you and enjoyed hanging out with you. But gosh, you sound really angry and upset with me.

Is it hard for you to have a friend who's got so many flaws? Do you prefer to hang out with people who are really confident and well-adjusted?

**You (as feared fantasy person):** I don't want to listen to you anymore. I'm going to throw your stupid book away!

**David:** I'm sad that my book wasn't helpful for you, but if you give it to me instead of throwing it away, I can probably give it to someone who needs a copy. I think there are lots of people who might appreciate a free copy.

Remember that this technique is not preparation for real life. When you do a feared fantasy dialogue, the feared fantasy person is simply the projection of your own self-critical thoughts. You're really doing battle with yourself. For example, the feared fantasy person in this example was just the projection of my own negative thoughts. It was the self-critical David.

If you'd like to try this technique, make a list of the negative, judgmental things you're afraid other people might be thinking about you. Then write out your own feared fantasy dialogue.

If you're brave, you can act it out with a friend or family member. Let your friend start out as the feared fantasy person, who attacks you with the list of your own imagined negative thoughts.

Use lots of role reversals if your friend hits you with something you can't easily defeat. Remember these simple guidelines:

- If you cannot respond effectively to one of the imaginary criticisms and you're using self-defense, try the acceptance paradox instead.

- If you cannot respond effectively to one of the imaginary criticisms and you're using the acceptance paradox, try self-defense instead.

- If neither strategy is effective, try a combination of the acceptance paradox and self-defense.

In this chapter, we've reviewed three strategies for challenging mind reading: inquiry, self-disclosure, and the feared fantasy technique, along with the self-defense paradigm and the acceptance paradox.

But there are many additional techniques that may be helpful as well. And remember that any negative thought that involves mind reading probably has many additional distortions, so if you consult your cheat sheet, then you'll have tons of potentially helpful ways to challenge and crush the thought.

Now take a look at your Daily Mood Journal and see if any of your negative thoughts involve mind reading. If so, record one of those thoughts here.

_____

_____

_____

_____

Next, explain why that thought is an example of mind reading and why it might not be accurate.

_____

_____

_____

_____

Finally, see if you can challenge the negative thought with a positive thought that fulfills the necessary and sufficient conditions for emotional change. Do you remember what they are? First, the positive thought must be 100% true or nearly 100% true. Second, the positive thought must substantially reduce your belief in the negative thought.

_____

_____

_____

_____

In the next chapter, we'll tackle fortune telling, the other common form of jumping to conclusions. I'm looking forward to showing you how to challenge and crush this distortion too because it is the cause of all anxiety, and it leads to feelings of hopelessness and despair as well.

# 16 | Fortune Telling: Part 1—Hopelessness

In the last chapter, you learned about mind reading, one of the two most common forms of jumping to conclusions. In the next two chapters, we're going to focus on fortune telling, which is equally common. Fortune telling accounts for a great deal—arguably most—of the depression and anxiety in the world. It's really easy to get fooled by this deceptive distortion. In this chapter, we'll focus on depression, and in the next chapter, we'll focus on anxiety.

Fortune telling involves drastic and upsetting predictions that aren't necessarily based on real evidence. For example, if you're depressed and feeling hopeless, then you tell yourself that things will never change and that you'll never recover or improve. Or if you're anxious, you tell yourself that something bad is about to happen.

There's a positive version of fortune telling too. You tell yourself, without convincing evidence, that everything is going to turn out great. For example, when you put a dollar in the slot machine, you may feel excited because you tell yourself that this is your lucky day and that you're about to hit the jackpot. But after pouring in dollar after dollar, you discover that your glowing prediction felt great but wasn't terribly accurate.

Of course, there's nothing wrong with a positive outlook on life. In fact, optimism can trigger hard work, creativity, and invention. Edison told himself his inventions would change the world. This gave him enormous motivation and energy, and his prediction turned out to be right.

But overly optimistic predictions can lead to huge financial losses, as well as mania, impulsive acts, criminal behavior, addictions, relationship conflicts, and even violence.

To help me illustrate how easy it is to get fooled by fortune telling, let me introduce you to Bennie, a violent and suicidal gang member who once attended a cognitive therapy group I was leading at my hospital in Philadelphia. Prior to the group, the nurses had warned me that Bennie was a local drug dealer and gang member and that he'd just been admitted for suicidal depression, but he also had a diagnosis of intermittent explosive disorder. This was just a polite way of saying that he liked to beat people up. The nurses cautioned me that he was dangerous and warned me not to confront him during the group. Although Bennie had been well-behaved so far, they said he could explode violently if provoked.

I assured them that I would not confront Bennie!

At the start of the group, about a dozen patients were seated in a circle, and there was a young, muscle-bound fellow covered with tattoos pacing about behind the chairs. He looked angry and threatening, and he was wearing a T-shirt with his cigarette pack rolled up in his left sleeve.

I figured it was Bennie and asked if he wanted to join us and sit in the one of the chairs in the circle. He scowled and said he wasn't about to sit in one of the "goddamn fucking" chairs and wanted to know what I intended to do about it.

I was on the spot, and all the patients were staring at me, as if to say, "What's the young doctor going to do?" The group had only been going on for one minute, and I was already in a power struggle with Bennie. Yikes!

My thoughts were spinning. How could I reply?

I said:

*You know, Bennie, we have just one rule here. And that is that you* must *sit in one of the chairs during the group… or stand and pace about. Or both. And if you stand and pace about, then you have to stay here in the room so you can hear what's going on, or out in the hall, or both. And as long as you obey that rule, Bennie, we'll get along just fine.*

This seemed to silence him, but he would not sit down and continued to pace about angrily, staring at me with a scowl.

Then I asked patients to tell me their scores on the depression, anxiety, and anger tests in their workbooks so I could record them in my data sheet and see how each patient was doing. But when I got to Bennie, he said his scores were none of my "fucking" business. Another confrontation!

I thought Bennie might be feeling embarrassed to have to admit that he was depressed, so I offered to look in his workbook and record his scores for him. That way, he wouldn't have to say his scores out loud. He said if I tried to look in his workbook it would be the last thing I ever did.

I was frightened and backed off immediately, and I pushed ahead with the group, which was on the topic of self-esteem. I explained that self-esteem has to be unconditional and that you can't earn self-esteem through status or achievements, by being loved, or in any other way. It's a gift you decide to give yourself, an act of self-love.

I also explained that the negative thoughts that rob us of self-esteem are always distorted and illogical, and I emphasized that depression and low self-esteem are ways we con ourselves into believing that we aren't good enough.

I asked people in the group to talk about times they felt a loss of self-esteem. Group members were getting very emotional, and many were crying. I thought to myself, "Oh, this is a terrific group. They're really getting it and opening up."

Then out of the blue, Bennie started shouting:

*Doc, I'm so sick and tired of hearing about self-esteem and all the things you have to do to be worthwhile. You have to be a good little boy and follow all the rules and do what you're told. As far as I'm concerned, Doc, you can take your self-esteem and stick it up your fucking ass!*

All the patients were staring at me, and I was on the spot again. I thought, "There he goes again, having to be the center of attention and ruining everything again."

But instead, I said:

*Bennie, I think we're on the same page. In fact, that's the exact point I was just making. You can't earn self-esteem by following the rules, by being a good little boy, or by having lots of money, status, or success. No amount of achievement or love can give you self-esteem. It has to be unconditional.*

*You seem to know this stuff already. You could almost be my assistant and help me teach the group today!*

*In fact, what I'm teaching today is based on the teachings of the Buddha, who taught us that there's no such thing as self-esteem. It's just a marketing term. And there's no such thing as a "self" either. Thinking you have a "self" is just another trap.*

*I'm amazed you know all this stuff. Tell me, were you raised as a Buddhist?*

He said, "I'm no fucking Buddhist. I'm in the fucking Mafia if you want to know the truth!"

I told him that was really interesting because the Mafia and Buddhism were very similar concepts. At that point, Bennie got excited and plunged into the circle of chairs. He sat down in the chair in the middle that I'd been using for role-playing and said defiantly, "Well, if you think you're so smart, let's see if you can prove that *my* negative thought is wrong!"

I told Bennie I would be happy to do so and asked what it was. He replied, "Doc, I'm a hopeless case, and there's nothin' you can do about it!"

Of course, that's a classic example of fortune telling mixed with a big dose of defiance. Bennie was telling himself that recovery was impossible, and he felt absolutely certain this was true. In fact, that's why he got suicidal and had to be admitted to our hospital.

I wrote his negative thought on the flip chart at the front of the room and asked myself what techniques might be effective. Since Bennie was clearly oppositional and trying to bust me, I realized that trying to disprove his belief would not work. He would just defeat me by yes-butting me and insisting that he really *was* hopeless. I decided to try a paradoxical cost-benefit analysis instead since this technique zeros in on therapeutic resistance or stuckness.

## PARADOXICAL COST-BENEFIT ANALYSIS

To do a **paradoxical cost-benefit analysis** with Bennie, I started by drawing a vertical line down the middle of the flip chart, right under the thought "I'm a hopeless case." I then labeled the left-hand column "advantages" and the right-hand column "disadvantages."

### Cost-Benefit Analysis

"I'm a hopeless case."

| Advantages | Disadvantages |
|------------|---------------|
|            |               |
|            |               |
|            |               |
|            |               |

I told Bennie I could easily show him his negative thought was distorted and not really true, but it wouldn't do any good if he *wanted* to believe that thought. I also mentioned there were actually tons of advantages, or benefits, of telling himself he was a hopeless case, and I wondered if we could list them off before we tried challenging that thought.

Bennie seemed taken aback and said:

> *Doc, you don't know what the hell you're talkin' about. I've flunked out of every drug abuse program in Philadelphia and some of them two or three times. No one has been able to help me. And I'll tell you this, Doc. I'll be dead in two years. You can count on it! So you can put that in your disadvantages column.*

So I put "Dead in two years" in the disadvantages column, as you can see here:

### Cost-Benefit Analysis

"I'm a hopeless case."

| Advantages | Disadvantages |
|---|---|
| | Dead in two years. |

Then I turned to the other group members and said, "There are lots of advantages of Bennie telling himself he's hopeless. What are they, group?"

They started coming up with all kinds of advantages, like these:

- If Bennie tells himself he's hopeless, then he won't have to do any hard work, like the rest of us, like writing down our negative thoughts and learning about the ten distortions.
- He can take drugs and get high all day long.

I said:

*Bennie, that's huge. I've heard that you're a drug dealer and have some of the best cocaine and heroin in Philadelphia. I've never had cocaine or heroin even once, but I've heard it's a terrific high! So if you tell yourself you're hopeless, then you can get stoned all the time.*

The other patients in the group came up with even more advantages:

- If he says he's hopeless, then he can't fail. It will protect him from disappointment.
- He's very important and gets a lot of attention.

I said:

*That's right Bennie, you are very important. Even before the group, the nurses told me about you and said, "Don't confront Bennie. Be careful with Bennie. He's the big man in the neighborhood, and he's very dangerous." You're by far the most important person in this room. And you are getting a lot of attention too. In fact, you're sitting right in the middle of the circle.*

Bennie seemed to like that comment!

The group continued listing advantages of Bennie's hopelessness. They came up with several, including the fact that he could intimidate people he didn't like, that he was very powerful, and that he made a ton of money from drug dealing and didn't have to pay income tax.

Then Bennie got into it and suggested another advantage—he got laid a lot. I pointed out that was another huge benefit of being a handsome bad boy. At that point, I said:

*Bennie, you're actually a cultural icon. You remind me of James Dean with your motorcycle and black leather jacket. You don't have to follow the rules, you make the rules! You're as free as the breeze, and you do whatever you want whenever you want. In fact, you're the kind of man I've always wanted to be!*

If you look on the next page, you can see how the cost-benefit analysis now looked.

## Cost-Benefit Analysis

"I'm a hopeless case."

| Advantages | Disadvantages |
|---|---|
| No work, it's easy. | Dead in two years. |
| Can get stoned all the time. | |
| Can't fail. No disappointments. | |
| Important. | |
| Big man in the neighborhood. People admire me. | |
| Joys of violence—can beat people up. | |
| Powerful—can defeat all the stupid shrinks who try to help me. | |
| Get laid a lot. | |
| Make lots of easy money, no tax. | |
| Cultural hero. Don't have to follow the rules. I do what I *want* to do! | |

If you notice, I ignored the disadvantages of Bennie's negative thought when going through his paradoxical cost-benefit analysis. That's because listing disadvantages would have simply invited a battle. Instead, I said:

*Bennie, I'm noticing that the advantages of telling yourself that you're hopeless include pretty much all the best things in life—easy money, no tax, an unlimited supply of sex and drugs, not having to work or obey the rules, prestige, power, euphoria, freedom, and adulation, to mention just a few.*

*So now I'm confused. Ten minutes ago, you asked for help disproving your belief that you're a hopeless case. But look at all the benefits of that belief!*

*Why in the world would you want to give all that up? It makes no sense! It seems you've got a pretty good thing going!*

At that moment I was no longer Dr. Burns. I was Bennie. I'd become the voice of his resistance and rebelliousness, and I was no longer trying to "help" or "save" him. In fact, at that moment I really could not see any reason for him to change! I was no longer the shrink—I *was* Bennie.

Bennie suddenly softened for the first time and said, "Doc, you read me like a book."

Paradoxically, the very moment you suddenly see why a patient should *not* change, the resistance almost always disappears. But this requires the death of the therapist's ego. The therapist has to "die" for a moment and give up the traditional role of "expert" or "helper."

Bennie was quiet for a moment and asked if he could talk about something that had happened to him when he was a little boy, something he'd never talked about before. I told him we'd be eager to hear anything he had to say.

Bennie described how much he had loved his grandfather when he was a little boy. He explained that his grandfather was the only one who would talk to him and spend time with him. He said his grandfather was a lot like him and explained that his grandfather also went into dark depressions and was involved in the same line of work—drug dealing.

He said that one day, his grandfather was talking in a very dark way, complaining that he had a problem with "the family" and that there was "no way out." Bennie said this scared him because his grandfather had a sawed-off shotgun in his lap.

Bennie then explained how his grandfather put the barrel of the gun in his mouth, pulled the trigger, and blew his head off. Bennie began sobbing uncontrollably. Tears were coming down most group members' cheeks.

After a few minutes, Bennie pulled himself together and asked, "Doc, do you remember when I wouldn't let you see my mood test scores earlier in the group? It's because I can't fucking read or write, and I didn't want the other group members to see that about me because I'm so ashamed." Then he began sobbing again.

Why did Bennie suddenly make himself vulnerable? It's because I honored his resistance and saw the value in what appeared to be a very painful thought. You could argue that it was a deep form of empathy because I saw where he was coming from and didn't try to "fix" or "rescue" him.

The paradoxical cost-benefit analysis is not a gimmick to manipulate someone. It has to be done respectfully. I really *did* like Bennie, and he could sense it. Even when you're working with someone who seems to be hard and violent, the use of respect, compassion, and acceptance can sometimes be surprisingly powerful.

Of course, a paradoxical cost-benefit analysis will not provide a sudden "cure" for someone like Bennie—who had severe problems involving drug-dealing and drug abuse, as well as depression—but at least it provided a chance for us to connect in a very real way. And for people with less severe problems, a paradoxical cost-benefit analysis can often be the first step to lasting change.

## STRAIGHTFORWARD COST-BENEFIT ANALYSIS

If you're feeling hopeless, but you're not as oppositional as Bennie, you might find that a **straightforward cost-benefit analysis** might be more effective for you. First, look over the negative thoughts in your Daily Mood Journal and see if any involve fortune telling. These are thoughts that you're hopeless and that things will never get better.

Then list the advantages of telling yourself that you're hopeless in the left-hand column of the cost-benefit analysis chart on the next page. Here are some advantages you might want to include:

1. Hopelessness will protect me from disappointment.
2. My hopelessness is based on the facts since medication and psychotherapy have not been helpful for me. I'm still depressed.
3. My hopelessness shows that I'm realistic and not involved in denial or false hope.
4. If I'm hopeless, then I can give up and won't have to keep trying or banging my head against the wall.
5. I may get extra support from people because my hopelessness lets them know how severe my suffering is.
6. I can defeat and frustrate people who try to help or "rescue" me without really listening.
7. I can feel sorry for myself, which is sometimes comforting.
8. My problems are real and overwhelming, so my hopelessness is realistic.
9. My hopelessness shows that I'm a critical thinker. I'm suspicious of all these quick "cures" for depression.

You can probably think of other advantages as well.

## Cost-Benefit Analysis

"I'm hopeless and will never recover or improve."

| Advantages | Disadvantages |
|---|---|
|  |  |

Next, list the disadvantages of telling yourself that you're hopeless in the right-hand column. Here are a few disadvantages you might want to include.

1. If I tell myself I'm hopeless, then I'll give up and things *won't* change.

2. If I tell myself I'm hopeless, then I'll feel really horrible.

3. If I insist that things are hopeless, then people who are trying to help me might get frustrated and annoyed with me.

4. Since I have improved at times, this suggests that I'm not hopeless, so I might be telling myself something that isn't true.

5. Just because I feel something very strongly, it doesn't make it true.

6. I may become suicidal. If I try to end my life, then it will have a devastating impact on the people who love me.

7. If I take my life, then my chances for joy and intimacy will end forever. This won't prove that I really *was* hopeless. It will just prove that I *felt* hopeless and acted on those feelings.

Once you've listed all the advantages *and* disadvantages you can think of, balance them against each other on a 100-point scale. Ask yourself whether the advantages or disadvantages are greater, and put two numbers adding up to 100 in the circles at the bottom that reflect your evaluation.

For example, if the advantages feel a lot more desirable, then you might put 70–30 in the two circles. But if the disadvantages feel greater, then you might put 45–55, or 25–75, or some other variant in the two circles.

What should you do if the advantages are greater or if it's a 50–50 standoff? In that case, you probably won't be motivated to challenge your belief. But that doesn't mean you *are* hopeless, it just means you *feel* hopeless and may even *want* to feel hopeless. And like Bennie, you may have lots of really good reasons for feeling that way.

In that case, it would be important to seek treatment with a mental health professional. Sometimes things can seem so overwhelming that it gets awfully hard to find your way out of the trap you're in without some help. Another person with skill and compassion can often provide the support you need.

If, on the other hand, the disadvantages of hopelessness are greater, then you might want to do some work challenging your belief that things will never change. Many techniques can be helpful. In the next section, I'll describe a technique that can help you realize your feelings of hopelessness may not be based on the truth.

But I want to caution you that this technique probably won't be helpful and may even be annoying if you *want* to feel hopeless—so it's important that the disadvantages of your hopelessness outweigh the advantages if this technique is going to be effective.

## EXAMINE THE EVIDENCE/LET'S DEFINE TERMS

If you look at the list of "Fifty Ways to Untwist Your Thinking" in chapter 33, you'll see that **examine the evidence** is a truth-based technique you can use to challenge fortune telling, especially the belief that you are "hopelessly depressed" and "will never get better." You can sometimes combine it with a logic-based technique called **let's define terms**.

Suppose, for example, that you *feel* hopelessly depressed. To use this technique, you'd ask yourself, "What's the definition of someone who is hopelessly depressed?"

You might say that a hopelessly depressed person is someone whose mood cannot improve.

Now that we've defined what we mean, let's examine the evidence. I think you will discover that this definition does not apply to you—or anyone.

For example, you probably have to admit that your moods have been constantly changing since the moment you were born. When you popped out of your mother's birth canal, you were probably crying, frightened, and upset.

You might have been pissed off as well! It was no fun being squeezed through such a small space and then being hit by lots of noise and bright lights when you'd been feeling quiet, peaceful, and warm for months. But when you were in your mother's arms a few moments later, you suddenly felt happy and content.

And since that time, your moods have been constantly changing. You've probably felt worse on thousands of occasions. And if you examine the evidence, then you'll have to admit that on every one of those occasions, you felt better later on.

So if a hopelessly depressed person is someone who cannot improve, then the evidence is overwhelming that you *cannot* be hopeless since you *always* improve.

Hmm. That might not help, so let's try another definition.

You might define a hopelessly depressed person differently—as someone who cannot improve beyond a certain point. For example, you might tell yourself that a hopeless person is someone whose depression will always be greater than 60 on a 100-point scale.

Can you see any problems with this definition? Put your ideas here:

_____

_____

_____

_____

_____

This definition doesn't work very well either because you'd have to say that someone whose depression is at 59 is non-hopeless, whereas someone who's depression is at 60 is hopeless. That doesn't make sense because these levels are practically identical.

In addition, there is no invisible barrier at 60. If you can reduce your depression to 60, then you can certainly get it to fall to 59 or even further, at least for a little while. There's simply no logical cut-off point for depression that makes someone hopeless.

Let's try again.

Perhaps we could define a hopelessly depressed person as someone who can improve a little but cannot improve completely.

Now we'll have to define what we mean by "completely." Completely might mean that your depression score has fallen all the way to zero. So a hopelessly depressed person is someone whose depression score cannot fall all the way to zero.

Can you see any problems with that definition? Put your ideas here:

_____

_____

_____

_____

_____

This definition probably won't work very well either. Here's why. We would have to claim that someone whose depression score has dropped all the way to 5 is hopeless, but someone who's score has dropped to 0 is non-hopeless. But both people have improved tremendously, and their mood scores are nearly identical, so it makes no sense to say that one is hopeless and the other is not.

In addition, if someone's score can drop as low as 5, that's an incredibly encouraging prognostic sign. It would make a lot more sense to label that person as incredibly hopeful.

If you still feel like you really *are* hopeless and haven't yet proved your point, then you might want to try one last definition. You could say that a hopelessly depressed person is someone who can become non-depressed for a short period of time but can't remain non-depressed indefinitely. In other words, a hopelessly depressed person is someone who will just relapse back into depression sooner or later.

Can you see any problems with that definition? Put your ideas here:

_____

_____

_____

_____

_____

According to this definition, pretty much all human beings are hopeless. That's because no one can be happy all the time. We all get upset at times. That makes us human, not hopeless. We'll talk about how to climb out of these black holes when I discuss relapse prevention training in chapter 29. Once you learn how to pop out of a relapse, then you won't have to worry about relapses anymore.

In addition, if you can learn to become non-depressed for a short period of time, that shows there are things that can greatly improve your mood. Over time, you can get better at using the tools that work for you so you can enjoy longer and longer depression-free periods of time.

These techniques might seem adversarial, like two attorneys arguing a case in court. If so, I apologize. Most of us get turned off by arguments, and other methods may be more helpful to you. However, for some people, using these techniques is one way to show that it simply *isn't true* that you're hopeless.

## POSITIVE REFRAMING

Sometimes trying to fight back against fortune telling with evidence and logic doesn't work. This was the case with a woman I once worked with, Keisha, who was absolutely certain that she was hopeless, and she felt she had concrete, irrefutable proof too. This case may also interest you because it highlights one of my (rather frequent) therapeutic errors.

Keisha was a severely depressed medical student at the University of Pennsylvania. She reached out to me and wanted to know if I could refer her to a therapist who used the techniques in my first book, *Feeling Good*. She explained that she'd been treated for depression for twenty years with medications and psychotherapy, but nothing had helped.

I told Keisha I had many excellent clinicians to recommend but wondered if she was aware that I treated medical students for free as part of my volunteer work for the department of psychiatry. I told her I didn't know if I'd be the best fit for her, but at least she couldn't beat the price.

Keisha said she'd love to work with me.

I told her there were two unusual things about the way I worked with people, and I wanted to make sure she was comfortable with those requirements before she agreed to treatment.

First, I explained that since I wasn't being paid, I didn't care how long my sessions lasted, and I typically worked with patients until their symptoms improved dramatically or disappeared entirely. And that usually required an extended, two-hour session or sometimes a little longer.

Second, I told Keisha that she'd have to do homework between sessions and that this was not negotiable.

Keisha said she'd be fine with both requirements, but she thought I was crazy if I thought I could cure her in a single session since she really *was* a hopeless case.

I explained that nearly all depressed patients feel hopeless, but this feeling results from cognitive distortions. Keisha insisted this wasn't true in her case and that she really was hopeless.

I asked Keisha why she was so sure. She explained that when she was young, she'd experienced horrific abuse from her brothers and was still tormented by the memories. She said the abuse certainly wasn't any kind of cognitive distortion.

In addition, she explained that there was only one thing she'd ever wanted in life—a baby—but it could never happen. In the first place, she was 40 and didn't even have a boyfriend, but on top of that, she had a gynecological problem that would make it impossible for her to conceive.

She explained that she was first in her medical school class and that everyone thought she had everything—her research had been published in some of the world's top scientific journals—but all of those accomplishments meant nothing to her since she would never have the *only* thing she ever wanted: a baby.

Keisha arrived at my house on a Saturday morning for her session, and I gave her the Brief Mood Survey, which not surprisingly indicated severe depression, anxiety, and anger.

I was determined to do a stellar job, and we had what I thought was a tremendous session. I showed her how to crush her distorted negative thoughts and figured we'd made a warm and trusting connection. The session took about two hours, as I'd anticipated, and I was convinced her depression was gone.

As you know, I ask patients to repeat the Brief Mood Survey at the end of each session, and I also have them rate me on empathy and helpfulness. Keisha was happy to complete the end-of-session survey and did it in front of me.

When I looked at her scores, I was shocked. Her mood had not improved but had gotten even worse. Her depression, anger, and anxiety scores had increased from the severe range to the extreme range. She also gave me failing grades on empathy and helpfulness. Yikes!

I felt embarrassed and ashamed since not only had I failed big-time, but I hadn't even realized it. I told Keisha I was disappointed, but perhaps we could pinpoint the mistakes I'd made so I could try to be more effective at our next session.

I told her that I thought I'd made two mistakes. First, instead of listening to how horrible her childhood had been and encouraging her to vent, I'd jumped in too quickly to try to "help" her. Second, I tried to convince her that she wasn't hopeless instead of listening and perhaps finding the wisdom in her hopelessness.

She nodded. Both mistakes were true.

I said that if she'd be open to trying again, I'd try to correct those errors the next time we met. She was fine with that. I find that most patients are very gracious and generous if I admit my mistakes in the spirit of improving the treatment.

At the next session, I used a lot more empathy without trying to "help" while Keisha described the horrors of her childhood and cried a lot. After a while, I asked her to close her eyes so we could travel back in time to her childhood and she could tell me what she saw.

She described being curled up in the fetal position in her bedroom crying, after her brothers had beat up on her. She reported feeling alone, unloved, and worthless, like there was no one to support her, not even her parents.

I told Keisha that this little girl needed love and support, and I asked if she could walk into that room and tell herself what she needed to hear when she was little. To tell that little girl that she was loved and worthwhile and that the abuse was not her fault.

This was a dramatic and emotional moment for Keisha, and after lots more tears, she seemed to be feeling a bit more relaxed.

Then I asked Kesha if we could take today's session in the opposite direction of what I did last time. Instead of arguing against her hopelessness, I asked if we could list some advantages of feeling hopeless, as well as what her hopelessness showed about her that was positive and awesome.

Keisha said she couldn't think of any positive things about her hopelessness.

Can you? See if you can list a few positives here before you continue reading. I know this may be redundant with things you've already read about in this book, but this exercise is a useful review of some really important ideas and skills you've learned. So please jot down a few positives before you continue reading.

1 _____

2. _____

3. _____

4. _____

5. _____

I told Keisha I thought there were, in fact, quite a few really good things about her hopelessness. For example, her hopelessness might protect her from disappointment if it turned out that I couldn't help her. Her hopelessness might also be realistic since she'd had two decades of treatment from experts who hadn't been able to help.

Keisha agreed and seemed to brighten up immediately, and she put both these qualities at the top of her list of positives.

She then began to come up with a lot more things to add to her list. For example, her hopelessness was a form of intellectual skepticism that showed her capacity to doubt and challenge claims that people make. Her intense depression also showed her passion and commitment to her dream of being a mother and having a baby.

I suggested that her suffering might also make her more compassionate with her own patients when she completed her training, especially if she went into psychiatry, but also in any branch of medicine. She added that to her list as well.

Together, we came up with more than ten positive things about her hopelessness and extreme depression. It was a pretty impressive list.

Given all those benefits, I told Keisha I now realized how ridiculous I must have sounded last week when I was trying to talk her out of her hopelessness. I told her maybe this was something we shouldn't be working on.

When I said that to Keisha, I became Keisha's subconscious resistance and allowed my "helpful self" to die. Although Keisha was not at all like Bennie, this was a similar moment. I was looking at all the good reasons *not* to change, which allowed her to let go of her stuckness.

In response, Keisha said she *did* want to work on not feeling hopeless anymore. She wanted to recover from her depression, and that required letting go of her hopelessness. She said she was ready for those tools I had mentioned and wanted to get to work.

I pulled out a Daily Mood Journal and asked Keisha to write down her negative thoughts. She quickly identified the distortions in them, and I then suggested a really aggressive method called the externalization of voices.

## EXTERNALIZATION OF VOICES

The **externalization of voices** is one of the most powerful techniques I've developed. You (in this case, me) and another person (in this case, Keisha) take turns playing the role of that person's negative thoughts and that person's positive thoughts. In this role-play, I assumed the role of Keisha's negative thoughts and spoke in the second person ("you"). Keisha played the role of her positive thoughts and spoke in the first person ("I").

I explained to Keisha that my job in this role-play was to attack her with her own negative thoughts, and her job—as the positive, self-loving version of herself—was to defeat me using the self-defense technique, the acceptance paradox, or a combination of both.

I told her we'd do role reversals until Keisha could knock it out of the park. Partial victories are not enough when you use this incredibly powerful technique.

Keisha was up for that, so I started to verbalize the negative thoughts she'd recorded on her Daily Mood Journal. Keisha rose to the occasion and ripped me to shreds. She was actually way more intelligent than I was, and the moment she decided to defend herself, she turned into a fighter! It was a joy to behold.

It went something like this:

**David (as the negative Keisha):** Face it, you're a hopeless case. No one's been able to help you!

**Keisha (as the positive Keisha):** Well, the treatments I've had have not been effective, but that doesn't mean this treatment or future treatments won't be effective. This treatment is new to me and very different from endlessly taking pills and complaining about the past.

I asked who won the exchange, and Keisha said that the positive Keisha had won huge.

So I attacked again and said:

**David (as the negative Keisha):** Well, that might be true, but the only thing that could ever make you happy is having a baby. But you have no boyfriend, and it's physiologically impossible for you to have a baby. So you'll always be miserable. Things really are hopeless, and that's a plain fact. It's not a distortion.

**Keisha (as the positive Keisha):** Well, I would certainly love to have a husband and a baby. But I have been happy at times, especially when I've been absorbed in my research. And sometimes I've been extremely happy when I've been hanging out with friends. So it simply isn't true that I *need* to have a baby to feel happy.

She said she won this exchange as well. I hit her with the rest of her negative thoughts, but she blew them all out of the water really quickly. It only took a few minutes.

Why did it happen so fast? It's because her resistance was gone. Once that barrier to recovery had been removed, a powerful, self-loving voice emerged. I'm convinced that you also have a powerful, self-loving voice within you, and I'm hoping you'll let it emerge while you're reading this book.

The entire session took a little less than two hours. At the end, Keisha's depression, anxiety, and anger scores had dropped to zero, and she gave me perfect scores on empathy and helpfulness too. She said she was flooded with feelings of joy and relief.

Keisha came in for one final session the next week for relapse prevention training, after which I never saw her again as a patient, though I often wondered how she was doing.

A year and a half later, I got an email from Keisha. She wrote:

*I decided to contact you since you might be wondering how I'm doing. Well, I'm still on a high, and although it might sound impossible, I'm even happier today than the day I completed my treatment with you. If you look at the photos I've attached, I think you'll understand why.*

I opened the first photo, and it was her wedding party. Very cool! I was so happy for her! When I opened the second photo, tears came to my eyes. It was a picture of Keisha holding her newborn baby in her arms. There was a note attached to the photo that read:

*Dr. Burns, you were right after all. Sometimes hopelessness really is a distortion!*

That was mind-blowing! But what was even uncannier was that I ran into Keisha the next day at the psychiatric resident lounge. Keisha was standing in the lounge next to her husband with her baby in her arms. Apparently, she was applying to our residency program. I was excited to see her. She turned to her baby and said, "I'd like you to meet Dr. Burns. You need to thank him for your existence!"

If you've been feeling down, discouraged, or even hopeless, and you've noticed some fortune telling in the negative thoughts in your Daily Mood Journal, then you might want to try some of the techniques I've described in this chapter. Do you remember what they are?

I illustrated cost-benefit analysis, let's define terms, examine the evidence, positive reframing, and the externalization of voices. However, these are just a few techniques that you can add to your recovery circle, so keep in mind that there are many more. In addition, the techniques in this chapter are not limited to fortune telling, and you can use them with just about any cognitive distortion.

In the next chapter, we'll examine the other common form of fortune telling: when you tell yourself, without convincing evidence, that you're in danger and that something terrible is about to happen. This is the distortion that triggers feelings of anxiety, worry, panic, nervousness, and fear. But with the right tools, I'll show you how to challenge and crush this type of fortune telling as well.

# 17 | Fortune Telling: Part 2—Anxiety

The second common form of fortune telling is telling yourself that you're in danger and that something terrible is about to happen.

This distortion is the cause of all anxiety and fear. Here are some examples:

1. **Public Speaking Anxiety.** You tell yourself that when you get in front of the audience, you're going to blow it and make a fool of yourself.

2. **Fear of Flying.** You tell yourself that the plane may run into turbulence and crash.

3. **Panic Attacks.** You tell yourself that you're on the verge of dying, losing control, or going crazy.

4. **Hypochondriasis.** You tell yourself that you might die of some terrible disease like cancer if you don't go to the doctor and get your symptoms checked out (again, and again, and again!)

5. **Shyness.** You tell yourself that if you try to schmooze with people, then you'll say something stupid and sound like an idiot.

6. **Shy Bladder Syndrome.** You tell yourself that if you try to pee in a public restroom, then you'll freeze up and be unable to pee. Then people will notice and judge you.

7. **Agoraphobia.** You tell yourself that if you leave home alone, then you'll end up having a panic attack somewhere, like at a grocery store or on a bus, and there will be no one to help or rescue you.

8. **PTSD.** You tell yourself that something awful will happen again—like getting raped, mugged, or attacked— if you're not constantly vigilant and afraid.

9. **OCD.** You tell yourself that if you don't check the burners on the stove repeatedly, then the house will burn down.

10. **Phobias.** You tell yourself that the thing you fear—like cats, dogs, bees, blood, heights, or lightning—is extremely dangerous.

11. **Test or Performance Anxiety.** You tell yourself that if you don't worry constantly, then you're going to flunk the test or screw up during your musical or athletic performance.

12. **Generalized Anxiety.** You constantly worry and frighten yourself with fantasies about awful things that could happen, like your children getting into a car accident after a high school party or your husband suddenly having a heart attack and dying.

Do any of those fears sound familiar? And that's only a partial list! Anxiety is one of the most common emotional problems around the world. In fact, anxiety is probably number one on the list. But no matter what kind of anxiety you have, it's a certainty that fortune telling is involved, as well as many additional distortions, such as mind reading, all-or-nothing thinking, should statements, emotional reasoning, labeling, and magnification.

These distortions are always present in anxiety and neurotic worrying. Anxiety, like depression, results from a mental con—from distorted thoughts that aren't really true. In contrast, healthy fear results from negative thoughts that are true. For example, if you're in a neighborhood with lots of gang violence and muggings, your fear may keep you alive!

Shame is another hallmark of almost every form of anxiety. This is especially true if you have social anxiety and panic attacks. You may tell yourself that you *shouldn't* feel the way you do and that there is something terribly wrong with you. In turn, you struggle to hide your anxiety because you're afraid people will judge you and think you're a basket case or a weirdo if they find out how insecure you feel.

Although anxiety is different from depression, the two often walk hand in hand. Fifty percent of people who struggle with anxiety also have elevated scores on my Depression Test. And if you look at people who are struggling with depression, nearly all of them also struggle with some feelings of anxiety.

If you want a "cure," then I have some really good news. The prognosis for rapid and lasting recovery from anxiety is exceptionally high. However, there are two kinds of stuckness or resistance that you'll have to confront if you want complete recovery. Recall from chapter 3 that these are called outcome resistance and process resistance.

Outcome resistance means that you have mixed feelings about pressing the magic button and being instantly cured. Process resistance means that recovery is not as easy as pushing a magic button and that there's something you'll *have* to do—something you won't want to do—to recover.

What causes outcome resistance? Why might you have mixed feelings about recovery if you have anxiety?

And what does process resistance have to do with? What is the unpleasant thing you're going to have to do if you want to get over the anxiety?

Hint: If you want to cheat, you can look back at the resistance table in chapter 3. I don't mind if you take a look. We'll call it "research"! In fact, I hope you'll refer back to certain sections of this book frequently.

Please put your ideas here before reading on:

| What Causes Outcome Resistance in Anxiety? | What Does Process Resistance in Anxiety Have to Do With? |
|---|---|
| | |

## My Answer

What is the cause of pretty much all outcome resistance in anxiety?

The answer is **magical thinking**. This means that although you are struggling with anxiety and want to get over it, a part of you may not be excited about treatment because you think your anxiety magically protects or helps you.

This becomes pretty obvious if you think about any specific type of anxiety. For example, I recently treated a woman named Annie for OCD. Annie had been washing her hands fifty to eighty times a day because of her fears of contamination, and the skin on her hands was red, rough, and dry.

When I asked Annie if she would push the magic button—allowing her to be suddenly cured of OCD—she had mixed feelings at best. That's because if she was cured, it would mean that she'd stop washing her hands over and over again all day long, and then her hands would get "contaminated."

And she was afraid that if her hands got contaminated, then she might touch her children, and then *they* would get contaminated, and then they might get leukemia and die.

Perhaps you can see why Annie had mixed feelings about pressing the magic button. Her magical thinking led her to believe that her intense anxiety was keeping her children alive.

That might sound nutty, but if you're anxious, you're probably involved in magical thinking too! For example, if you've got test anxiety, you probably think that you *need* the anxiety to study and perform your best on tests. And if you have a fear of heights, you tell yourself that your anxiety will keep you safe because you'll be very careful to avoid places where you might risk falling.

But what's the process resistance in anxiety all about?

The answer is **exposure**. Exposure means that you will have to confront the thing you fear the most if you want complete recovery.

But that's no fun at all. Exposure sucks! Anxiety can be intensely uncomfortable and unbearable, really. I know this from personal experience. I've struggled with just about every type of anxiety you can think of. And that's why I *love* treating anxiety. No matter what you've had, I can say, "Oh, I've had that too! I know how much that sucks. And what a joy it will be to show you how to defeat it!"

If you resist and avoid exposure, then your chances of a complete cure are close to zero. In contrast, if you agree to confront your fears, then the chances of being cured are close to 100%.

If Annie wants to get over her OCD, what's one thing that she'll *have* to do that she won't want to do? What type of exposure will be crucial to her cure? Put your ideas here before you continue reading.

---

---

---

---

---

## My Answer

I hope that wasn't too difficult to figure out! She'll have to touch things she believes are contaminated and not wash her hands. Then she'll have to touch her kids!

The first thing I did was ask Annie to touch a whole box of appointment cards I was using. I told her that way she could kill off about 100 people at once! She thought this was funny but was terrified to touch all those appointment cards. Although she knew her negative thoughts were ridiculous, on some level she still believed she was endangering the lives of everyone who would touch the cards later on.

But she did it. Good for Annie! I greatly admire my patients when they show courage. And it *does* take courage to beat anxiety.

Then I told her that if she wanted to work with me, she'd have to do a homework assignment, and it was nonnegotiable. She'd have to agree to stop washing her hands all day long, no matter how anxious she got. And she'd also have to keep touching and hugging her children all day long to see if she could kill them off.

Yikes, that's not easy either! But she did it. Another gold star for Annie!

And what happened? Sadly, her children passed away shortly after that session.

I'm just kidding! Sorry! That's my dark sense of humor. Her kids were just fine, and Annie completely recovered from OCD, although she had three pretty terrifying days when she agreed to stop washing her hands.

Before we continue, I want to expose three myths about exposure that can really get in the way of effective treatment.

1. **Myth 1: Exposure is all you need.**

   Exposure is absolutely necessary in the treatment of anxiety, but it is not a treatment per se. I always work with many techniques when I generate a recovery circle for someone with anxiety. Exposure has to be included, but for full recovery, you may need to use quite a few additional techniques too.

2. **Myth 2: Exposure doesn't work.**

   Many, and perhaps most, people struggling with anxiety wrongly believe that they've already tried exposure and that exposure doesn't work. But what they really mean is that every time they're around the thing they fear, they get tremendously anxious and try to fight, control, or get away from the feared situation as fast as possible.

This is not exposure but avoidance. The attempt to fight, control, or avoid the thing you fear is the actual cause of your anxiety. It's not the cure.

Exposure is quite different. You intentionally confront your fear and make yourself as anxious as possible for as long as possible. If you stick with the anxiety and refuse to run away, then you'll discover that your anxiety will diminish and disappear after a while.

3. **Myth 3: Exposure is dangerous.**

For the most part, exposure is not dangerous. You are not too fragile to use and benefit from exposure. I say this because patients are extremely good at hypnotizing their therapists into thinking that they aren't ready for exposure or that the exposure will be too dangerous or disturbing for them. If you give in to this myth and don't use exposure, your treatment will be doomed!

## SELF-DEFEATING BELIEFS

So far, we've been focusing on the distorted negative thoughts that make you miserable in the here and now. These negative thoughts only pop up when you're feeling depressed or anxious. However, underneath these thoughts, you may have any number of self-defeating beliefs that make you especially vulnerable to painful mood slumps in certain kinds of situations or when certain kinds of negative events occur.

For example, if you have what I call the approval addiction, then you base your self-esteem on what others think about you. When you get approval, you feel terrific because you feel worthwhile. But you'll be prone to anxiety and depression anytime you think people are judging or criticizing you.

Self-defeating beliefs are present whether or not you're feeling upset. When you identify and modify those beliefs, it makes you less vulnerable to feelings of depression and anxiety in the future. On the next page, you'll find a list of some of the most common self-defeating beliefs.

## Twenty-Three Common Self-Defeating Beliefs*

| Achievement | Depression |
|---|---|
| 1. **Perfectionism.** I must never fail or make a mistake.<br>2. **Perceived Perfectionism.** People will not love and accept me as a flawed and vulnerable human being.<br>3. **Achievement Addiction.** My worthwhileness depends on my achievements, intelligence, talent, status, income, or looks. | 13. **Hopelessness.** My problems could never be solved. I could never feel truly happy or fulfilled.<br>14. **Worthlessness/Inferiority.** I'm basically worthless, defective, and inferior to others. |

| Love | Anxiety |
|---|---|
| 4. **Approval Addiction.** I need everyone's approval to be worthwhile.<br>5. **Love Addiction.** I can't feel happy and fulfilled without being loved. If I'm not loved, then life is not worth living.<br>6. **Fear of Rejection.** If you reject me, then it proves that there's something wrong with me. If I'm alone, then I'm bound to feel miserable and worthless. | 15. **Emotional Perfectionism.** I should always feel happy, confident, and in control.<br>16. **Anger Phobia.** Anger is dangerous and should be avoided at all costs.<br>17. **Emotophobia.** I should never feel sad, anxious, inadequate, jealous, or vulnerable. I should sweep my feelings under the rug and not upset anyone.<br>18. **Perceived Narcissism.** The people I care about are demanding, manipulative, and powerful.<br>19. **Brushfire Fallacy.** People are clones who all think alike. If one person looks down on me, the word will spread like brushfire, and soon everyone will look down on me.<br>20. **Spotlight Fallacy.** Talking to people feels like having to perform under a bright spotlight on a stage. If I don't impress people by being sophisticated, witty, or interesting, then they won't like me.<br>21. **Magical Thinking.** If I worry enough, then everything will turn out okay. |

| Submissiveness | |
|---|---|
| 7. **Pleasing Others.** I should always try to please others, even if I make myself miserable in the process.<br>8. **Conflict Phobia.** People who love each other shouldn't fight.<br>9. **Self-Blame.** The problems in my relationships are bound to be my fault. | |

| Demandingness | Other |
|---|---|
| 10. **Other-Blame.** The problems in my relationships are the other person's fault.<br>11. **Entitlement.** You should always treat me in the way I expect.<br>12. **Truth.** I'm right and you're wrong. | 22. **Low Frustration Tolerance.** I should never be frustrated. Life should be easy.<br>23. **Superman/Superwoman.** I should always be strong and never be weak. |

So how do we uncover and pinpoint these self-defeating beliefs? The **downward arrow technique** is one great method. Here's how it works.

You start with a negative thought from your Daily Mood Journal and draw a downward arrow under it. The downward arrow means, "If that thought were true, what would it mean to me? Why would it be upsetting to me?" Asking this question will usually cause a new negative thought to pop into your head.

This second version is called the **what-if technique**, and it's very similar but was developed specifically for anxiety. With this technique, you ask yourself, "What if that actually happened? What am I the most afraid of? What's the worst that could happen?" Again, asking yourself this question will usually trigger a new negative thought to pop into your head.

With both of these techniques, you write down the new negative thought, draw another downward arrow under it, and ask the question again. You continue following this chain of thoughts until you uncover the underlying self-defeating belief that is at the root of your depression or anxiety.

To illustrate how this works, let me introduce you to a man named Roberto, whom I recently did a live therapy demonstration with during a workshop in Minneapolis. Roberto was 66 years old and had struggled with shyness and public speaking anxiety ever since he was a kid, and he'd made very little progress in spite of years of treatment.

Roberto was planning to retire from his counseling job at a mental health clinic so he could start his own private practice. This was a lifelong dream of his. However, in order to generate referrals, he'd have to start giving talks to community groups, and he was terrified people would notice his anxiety and not want to refer anyone to him.

Roberto had quite a few negative thoughts that were contributing to his anxiety:

1. The audience will see how anxious I am and judge me.

2. The audience will get bored and tune out. They'll yawn, look at their cell phones, and start texting.

3. I'll get anxious and forget my material.

4. I don't have what it takes to be an effective public speaker because I lack the confidence.

5. I haven't found my "voice."

6. You have to be captivating to impress people, but I'm just not captivating!

7. The people here in the workshop may be judging me right now.

You can see fortune telling in most of these thoughts. Roberto was making negative predictions about what was going to happen. That's classic. He was also involved in mind reading—telling himself that others would be intensely critical of him.

You can probably spot tons of additional distortions, including hidden should statements. For example, he seemed to be telling himself that he *should* have found his "voice" by now, that he *should not* have this problem, and that he *should* be more confident.

When I used the downward arrow approach with Roberto, this is how it went:

> **David:** Let's assume that people here are judging you right now. What would that mean to you? Why would that be upsetting to you?
>
> **Roberto:** That would mean I was inadequate.
>
> **David:** Let's assume that's also true and that you are, in fact, inadequate. What would that mean to you? Why would that be upsetting to you?
>
> **Roberto:** Then I won't be accepted or valued because at my age, I should not feel inadequate.
>
> **David:** Let's assume that you are not accepted or valued. What would that mean to you? Why would that be upsetting to you?
>
> **Roberto:** Then I'd be rejected and alone.
>
> **David:** And then what? What would that mean to you? Why would it be upsetting if you were rejected and alone?
>
> **Roberto:** Then I'd be a miserable failure, and I'd be unhappy and worthless for the rest of my life.

By using the downward arrow technique, I was able to identify quite a few self-defeating beliefs that were contributing to Roberto's thinking. Can you spot them? Review the list of self-defeating beliefs and see how many you can find. List them here:

1. _____

2. _____

3. _____

4. _____

5. _____

6. _____

7. _____

8. _____

9. _____

10. _____

This is not an exact science, so just do your best. When you're done, you can continue reading to see what Roberto and I came up with.

## My Answer

This is the list of self-defeating beliefs that Roberto and I came up with, but your own list may differ, which is totally fine.

1. **Perfectionism.** It sounds like Roberto is afraid of making mistakes.

2. **Perceived Perfectionism.** He seems to believe that others will also expect him to be perfect and won't love or respect him if they see he's flawed and not perfect.

3. **Approval Addiction.** He seems to be basing his feelings of self-esteem on getting everyone's approval.

4. **Fear of Rejection.** It sounds like Roberto thinks he can't feel happy or fulfilled if he's rejected or alone.

5. **Pleasing Others.** It sounds like Roberto assumes a submissive role and is focused on pleasing other people.

6. **Self-Blame.** It sounds like Roberto would blame himself if someone judged or rejected him because he wasn't good enough.

7. **Brushfire Fallacy.** He thinks that if one person judges him, then the word will spread like brushfire, and pretty soon everyone will be judging and rejecting him.

8. **Spotlight Fallacy.** It sounds like he thinks he has to impress people to make them like him. It's like he's always a performer on stage, in the spotlight, and he thinks people will constantly judge his performance and find him lacking.

**9. Superman.** It sounds like he thinks he has to be charismatic and captivating and blow people away and that he should never appear vulnerable, human, or flawed.

## OVERCOMING OUTCOME AND PROCESS RESISTANCE

Now that we've identified Roberto's self-defeating beliefs, how can we help him overcome his anxiety?

First, we'll need to deal with Roberto's outcome resistance, and one of the best tools for that is **positive reframing**. Ask yourself these two questions:

1. What are some benefits, or advantages, of Roberto's shyness and public speaking anxiety?

2. What do Roberto's shyness and public speaking anxiety say about him and his core values that's positive or even awesome?

List as many as you can think of here before you continue reading.

| Benefits/Advantages | Core Values |
|---|---|
|  |  |

Here's what Roberto and I came up with:

| Benefits/Advantages | Core Values |
|---|---|
| My fears:<br>• Keep me safe and protect me from public humiliation.<br>• Might make it easier for others to feel close to me since they may be flawed as well.<br>• May motivate me to prepare really well when I decide to give talks to community groups.<br>• Probably make me a more effective counselor since I have a lot of compassion for others who suffer.<br>• Keep me from being overly controlling or trying to dominate interactions with others. I'm a really good listener and know how to provide support. | My fears show that:<br>• I'm sensitive and caring.<br>• I want to be with people.<br>• I want to be genuine and real.<br>• I have a passion for meaningful relationships.<br>• I'm self-aware and willing to admit my shortcomings.<br>• I have a strong desire to change.<br>• I'm humble.<br>• I'm realistic and honest since I do have many flaws.<br>• I have high standards and want to do a good job.<br>• I want to present myself in a positive and appealing light so people will like me and feel that I have something to offer.<br>• I have courage and am willing to confront my fears.<br>• I have determination and am still willing to work hard to overcome my fears in spite of decades of failure and frustration. |

The list, as usual, was a huge surprise to Roberto, since he'd viewed his anxiety as something bad and had felt ashamed of his anxiety since childhood.

Now that I had dealt with Roberto's outcome resistance, I moved on to addressing his process resistance. In particular, I asked Roberto if he'd be willing to face his worst fear in order to get over his shyness that very day. Of course, he'd already partially done that by agreeing to treatment in front of a live audience. That huge first step took a lot of courage! But he said that if he had to do more, he would.

Since Roberto was convinced that his shyness and insecurity were his greatest flaws and defects, I suggested he ask the audience what they thought about him based on the intensely personal feelings of insecurity and inadequacy he'd just disclosed. You'll recall that he was pretty convinced people would judge him if he revealed his anxiety.

He was shocked when numerous people in the audience offered warm and admiring responses about his performance during the live demonstration. In fact, one woman said that she found him very captivating.

At that moment, he suddenly found his "voice" and was catapulted into enlightenment. Not only did his anxiety completely disappear, but he became absolutely euphoric. It happened suddenly. Do you see why? Put your thoughts here before you continue reading.

_____

_____

_____

_____

_____

## My Answer

Roberto suddenly recovered because he realized that his negative thoughts were not valid. First, he discovered that he didn't have to be some charismatic showboat speaker to connect with an audience. He only had to be authentic.

Second, he discovered that his worst "flaws"—his shyness and insecurity—were actually his greatest assets in terms of getting close to others. He finally understood that the problem was never his flaws but his failure to accept them. And the moment he accepted himself exactly as he was, warts and all, he suddenly made the greatest change a human being can make.

If you want to think about my session with Roberto from a technical perspective, you could say that his amazingly rapid recovery from fifty years of shyness and public speaking anxiety resulted from:

- **Identify the Distortions.** We identified the distortions in his negative thoughts, like fortune telling (predicting he'd blow it if he gave a talk), mind reading (assuming people would judge him if he was anxious), emotional reasoning (he *felt* defective, so he assumed he *was* defective), and hidden should statements (he thought he *should* be flashy and charismatic).

- **Downward Arrow Technique.** We pinpointed his self-defeating beliefs, like perceived perfectionism, the approval addiction, and others.

- **Positive Reframing.** We highlighted the many benefits of Roberto's anxiety and listed what his anxiety and shyness showed about him that was positive and awesome. This reduced his shame.

- **Exposure.** He confronted his fears in front of a live audience and discovered that the monster had no teeth.

- **Self-Disclosure.** He shared his insecurities openly instead of hiding them in shame and secrecy.
- **Survey Technique.** He asked people what they thought about him. That was really frightening, but he did it!
- **Acceptance Paradox.** He decided to accept his anxiety and insecurities instead of trying to overcome them, as he'd been doing for decades. Paradoxically, the very moment he accepted his anxiety, it disappeared.

Roberto and I also did some **shame-attacking exercises** after the session was over. When you do a shame-attacking exercise, you do something crazy or ridiculous in public to make a fool of yourself on purpose. That way, you can discover that the world won't come to an end if you do, in fact, appear foolish. Shame-attacking exercises can be incredibly frightening at first, but they can also be amazingly liberating.

I encouraged Roberto to walk around the hotel lobby and approach several strangers and say:

*Hi, I just want to talk to you for a moment if I can. I've struggled with shyness and feelings of shame about my shyness ever since I've been a little boy. But today I've decided to stop hiding it and just start telling people. So that's why I'm telling you!*

He was reluctant and scared at first, but I insisted. In fact, I stopped a hotel employee and said, "This man needs to speak with you." That way Roberto couldn't wriggle out of it!

He was shocked that every person he approached responded with tremendous warmth and kindness. He did something he thought was totally foolish and discovered that the world didn't come to an end. In fact, the opposite happened.

He went home that night on a tremendous high.

Now you're asking, "But did it last? Maybe it was just a flash in the pan."

I asked Roberto if he'd like to be on my podcast and just received this email from him:

*Hope you're doing well! Yes, I would like to do a podcast of the live session we did last week at the workshop, and I have the recording on my cell phone! It was an amazing experience, and I have been feeling great!*

*My mood has improved, and I'm walking up to strangers and continuing with the exercise we did at the hotel. What a breakthrough! I'm planning to do public speaking soon.*

## HIDDEN EMOTION TECHNIQUE

Before we leave the topic of fortune telling and anxiety, I want to share a powerful tool called the **hidden emotion technique**. Here's the gist of it: The vast majority of people who struggle with anxiety are exceptionally "nice" people. In many cases, this excessive "niceness" is the actual cause of the anxiety.

What does this mean? Sometimes people with anxiety have a really hard time expressing certain kinds of feelings, so when they get upset, they have a tendency to sweep these feelings under the rug. In doing so, these feelings then come out indirectly—disguised as anxiety—and people lose sight of the hidden conflict or feeling that's really bugging them.

Anger is a common feeling that anxious people tend to avoid, but it's not the only feeling by a long shot. It can be any feeling you subconsciously think you're not supposed to have.

And here's the really neat thing. If you can bring the hidden emotion to conscious awareness and express it, or solve the problem you've been avoiding, then your anxiety will usually disappear completely. So it's a great technique to keep in mind when you're battling any form of anxiety.

I'll give you an example since this technique could be really helpful to you.

I recently treated a woman called Lillya who was extremely anxious about having a second child. She and her husband, Lyle, had planned to have another child when their first child was 5, but now that their first child—a happy and healthy girl named Masha—was 4 years old, Lillya was beginning to get cold feet. This was surprising to Lillya since the birth of their first child had been smooth and there'd never been any significant problems raising her.

When I asked Lillya to record all her negative thoughts, it became clear that she was making herself anxious from two opposite perspectives. First, she was telling herself that if they had a second child, there could be several pretty negative outcomes. For example, she wouldn't be able to bounce back to her pre-baby body. In addition, another child would cause problems with her career, which was just starting to blossom. She was also worried that the second child might be born with some kind of terrible illness or birth defect.

But the more puzzling thing was that Lillya was also telling herself that equally awful things might happen if they *didn't* have a second child. For example, she thought that her first child might die unexpectedly, so she and Lyle would end up without any children at all. She was also concerned that her first child would grow up lonely without a sibling.

You can see that both forms of negative thoughts involved fortune telling. Lillya was telling herself she was damned if she did get pregnant and damned if she didn't—and for no obvious reason. What's going on?

I asked Lillya if there was anything bothering her that she wasn't telling me about. I had been suspicious of a hidden problem since Lillya had reported some feelings of anger and anxiety at the start of the session, and she also had a low score on the Relationship Satisfaction Test.

For example, was there a problem that she'd been sweeping under the rug, like a problem at work or a conflict with her husband? Could there be more to the story than just anxiety? Could there be a hidden problem she wasn't owning up to, perhaps because she was too "nice"?

If you have any suspicions, put on your Sherlock Holmes cap and tell me what you're thinking. You don't have to get it right, but if you can come up with something, even something that turns out to be way off base, it will help you learn how to use the hidden emotion technique.

---

---

---

---

---

When you're done, keep reading, and I'll tell you what happened next!

## My Answer

Lillya initially brushed off the notion of marital conflict. She insisted everything was fine and that all she needed help with was her anxiety about having a second child.

This is not unusual. Most individuals with anxiety will insist there's nothing wrong, even when something is eating away at them. They're not lying or being intentionally deceptive. *They just can't bring the hidden emotion or problem to conscious awareness.* This "hidden emotion" phenomenon seems to be very specific for people with anxiety. I've seen it in about 75% of the anxious people I've treated.

After empathizing with Lillya for about thirty minutes, I asked what type of help she was hoping for. If the session was really super and she walked out feeling terrific, what would change? What miracle was she hoping for?

She said she wanted help with two things: First, she wanted to get over her anxiety about having a second child. And second, she wanted to get rid of her anger.

I told Lillya I'd be happy to help her with her anxiety but had mixed feelings about eliminating her anger because suppressed anger is frequently the cause of anxiety. I explained it was important to learn how to express her anger in a loving and respectful way instead of ignoring it or suppressing it.

I asked Lillya if her anger had to do with Lyle and if something was bugging her. She finally admitted she was frustrated and resentful because Lyle didn't help out much with tasks involving their daughter, like making sure their daughter was ready to go before they all went out together in the car.

Now that the hidden emotion was out in the open, her anxiety made much more sense. Do you see why? Lillya's anxiety was really her symbolic way of saying, "I'm not sure I want another child given the fact that I'm shouldering most of the burden of raising our first child without much help from my husband." But because Lillya was a very "nice" person, like most people who struggle with anxiety, she'd been trying to sweep it under the rug.

If you remember, Lillya was also afraid that if she didn't have a second child, then their first child might die, and they'd be left with no children. But at the same time, she was afraid that if they *did* have a second child, he or she might be born with some terrible illness or birth defect. Why is she so preoccupied with the death of her children?

Are we allowed to make a psychoanalytic interpretation here? Could Lillya have been subconsciously angry about the burden of having to raise children without more support from her husband? After all, she was killing them off in her anxious fantasies! But because she was sweeping her anger under the rug, it came out indirectly, as anxiety.

And if you struggle with anxiety, there's a really good chance you may be doing the same thing—denying some conflict or problem because you're so "nice"!

Now that I had completed the first part of the hidden emotion technique—figuring out what Lillya's hidden feeling or problem was—it was time to help her express the anger she had been avoiding. I asked her to focus on one specific moment when she and Lyle were at odds with each other and to write down one thing Lyle said to her and what she said in return. These are the first two steps of the **relationship journal**, a powerful new tool I've created for individuals with troubled relationships. In Step 1, you write down exactly what the other person said to you, and in Step 2, you write down exactly what you said next. You also circle all the feelings you think the other person might have had, along with all the feelings you had at that moment.

Here is how Lillya completed these first two steps:

### Lillya's Relationship Journal*

| Step 1: Write down *exactly* what the other person said. Be brief: | Step 2: Write down *exactly* what you said next. Be brief: |
|---|---|
| Lyle said, "It's time to go!" | I said, "No! It's *not* time to go! She still needs her shoes, her coat, and her vitamins!" (I said this in a scolding, critical voice.) |
| Circle the emotions *he or she* might have been feeling | Circle the emotions *you* were feeling |
| **Sad**, blue, depressed, down, (unhappy) | **Sad**, blue, depressed, down, (unhappy) |
| (**Anxious**,) worried, panicky, nervous, frightened | (**Anxious**,) worried, panicky, nervous, frightened |
| **Guilty**, remorseful, bad, (ashamed) | **Guilty**, remorseful, bad, ashamed |
| **Inferior**, worthless, (inadequate,) defective, (incompetent) | **Inferior**, worthless, inadequate, defective, incompetent |
| **Lonely**, unloved, unwanted, (rejected,) alone, abandoned | **Lonely**, unloved, unwanted, rejected, alone, abandoned |
| **Embarrassed**, foolish, humiliated, (self-conscious) | **Embarrassed**, foolish, humiliated, self-conscious |
| **Hopeless**, (discouraged,) pessimistic, despairing | (**Hopeless**, discouraged, pessimistic,) despairing |
| (**Frustrated**, stuck,) thwarted, (defeated) | (**Frustrated**,) stuck, thwarted, defeated |
| (**Angry**, mad,) resentful, (annoyed, irritated,) upset, furious | (**Angry**,) mad, (resentful, annoyed, irritated,) upset, furious |
| **Other** (specify (hurt) | **Other** (specify (disappointed) |

As you can see, Lillya's husband had gotten impatient because they were about to get in the car for an outing with their daughter, and Lillya seemed to be stalling.

---

* Copyright © 1991 by David D. Burns, MD. Revised 2007, 2016.

Lillya responded in a scolding, critical tone of voice because Lyle had not done anything to help their daughter get ready. Of course, he defended himself, and the interaction escalated into an argument. Lillya admitted that this type of combative interaction occurred frequently even though they loved each other a lot. Perhaps you've experienced similar conflicts with someone you love. Have you?

Next, I asked Lillya to complete Step 3 of the relationship journal. At this step, you examine your response to the other person and ask if it was an example of good or bad communication using the EAR Checklist. This can be painful but really helpful.

As you can see here, Lillya checked off all three forms of bad communication. She did not acknowledge any of Lyle's feelings (no E = empathy), did not share any of her own feelings (no A = assertiveness), and her response was adversarial (no R = respect).

## EAR Checklist

|  | Good Communication | ✓ | Bad Communication | ✓ |
|---|---|---|---|---|
| E =<br>Empathy | 1. You acknowledge the other person's feelings and find some truth in what he or she said. |  | 1. You ignore the other person's feelings or argue and insist he or she is "wrong." | ✓ |
| A =<br>Assertiveness | 2. You express your feelings openly and directly. |  | 2. You fail to express your feelings or express them aggressively. | ✓ |
| R =<br>Respect | 3. Your attitude is respectful and caring. |  | 3. Your attitude is not respectful or caring. | ✓ |

Step 3 of the relationship journal can be a bit disturbing if, like most of us, you're used to blaming the other person and feeling like you're the victim. But when you examine how you responded to the other person, and you discover that you made all three communication errors—no empathy, no sharing of your feelings, and no communication of love, liking, or respect—then the finger of blame suddenly points to you.

In Step 4, this often becomes even more obvious and painful. You ask yourself how your response affected the other person. How did it make that person feel? What did he or she say or do next? And how did your response affect the very problem you've been complaining about? Did it make it better or worse? Here is what Lillya came up with:

> *Lyle felt hurt and put down because I was snapping at him. He shut down, started arguing, and became more determined to win. He didn't want to be helpful to me. So although it is painful to admit this, you could argue that I'm forcing him to not want to be helpful to me!*

Now before you throw the book down in disgust and accuse me of being a male chauvinist, let me say that if Lyle had been my patient and he had gone through this same process, then he would have discovered the same thing: that he was provoking the exact problem that he was complaining about in their marriage.

I call this the "theory of interpersonal relativity." The person who asks for help will nearly always discover that he or she is creating the very problem that he or she is complaining about. This discovery can be painful, but it is also liberating because it means we all have far more power than we think to create frustrating—or rewarding—relationships with others.

In Step 5 of the relationship journal, you revise your response in Step 2 using the five secrets of effective communication:

### Five Secrets of Effective Communication (EAR)*

---

#### E = Empathy

1. **The Disarming Technique.** Find some truth in what the other person is saying even if it seems totally unreasonable or unfair.
2. **Empathy.** Put yourself in the other person's shoes and try to see the world through his or her eyes.
   - **Thought Empathy.** Paraphrase the other person's words.
   - **Feeling Empathy.** Acknowledge how the other person is probably feeling based on what he or she said.
3. **Inquiry.** Ask gentle, probing questions to learn more about what the other person is thinking and feeling.

#### A = Assertiveness

4. **"I Feel" Statements.** Express your own ideas and feelings in a direct, tactful manner. Use "I feel" statements (such as "I feel upset") rather than "you" statements (such as "You're wrong!" or "You're making me furious!")

#### R = Respect

5. **Stroking.** Convey an attitude of respect even if you feel frustrated or angry with the other person. Find something genuinely positive to say to the other person even in the heat of battle.

---

* Copyright © 1991 by David D. Burns, MD. Revised 2006.

After writing down each sentence, indicate which of the five secrets you used in that sentence. For example, Lillya and I revised her response to her husband to look like this:

*You're saying it's time to go, and I think you might be feeling frustrated and angry with me, and maybe even hurt too* (thought empathy, feeling empathy). *I think I've been snapping at you, and that's probably why you feel annoyed* (disarming technique). *I'm feeling hurt too because I love you, but I've felt kind of overwhelmed because I'm not getting much support when it comes to raising our daughter* ("I feel" statement, stroking). *In addition, I want you to know that I feel awful when we fight like this* ("I feel" statement). *Can you tell me more about how you're feeling right now and what this has been like for you?* (inquiry)

As you can see, Lillya began by summarizing what Lyle had just said and acknowledging how he was probably feeling. Then she admitted she'd been treating him unkindly. She openly and respectfully shared her feelings and expressed love for him. She concluded her statement with some open-ended questions, encouraging him to open up as well.

After we generated a response she liked on paper, we practiced role-playing during the session so she'd have the skills she needed to do it in real time with Lyle.

Did it work? The next week, Lillya confided that there'd been a dramatic change in their relationship and that the five secrets had been tremendously helpful. In fact, she said that Lyle was practically hand-feeding her grapes! In addition, her anxiety about having another child had mysteriously vanished.

## THE TAKE-HOME MESSAGES

If you're feeling anxious and you've found a good bit of fortune telling in your negative thoughts, what can you do?

First, you'll want to include lots of cognitive techniques in your recovery circle. In addition, make sure you include several exposure techniques as well. Facing your fears will be crucial to your recovery. And make sure that you include the hidden emotion technique too. Once you bring your hidden problem or feeling to conscious awareness (and express your feelings or solve the problem), the anxiety will often improve or disappear completely, as was the case with Lillya.

How can you figure out what the hidden problem or feeling is? Here are some hints:

1. It will rarely be some traumatic event that's buried in the past, although some people have experienced traumatic events that still haunt them. But this phenomenon is different. The hidden feeling or problem will be buried in the present, not the past.

2. The hidden feeling will often be an emotion you think you're not supposed to have, like anger. But it can be any positive or negative feeling you're sweeping under the rug because you think you're not supposed to feel that way.

3. Your anxiety will often be a disguised, symbolic, almost poetic expression of the hidden conflict. Remember that in her anxious fantasies, Lillya was "killing off" her current child and her unborn child as well. This was her way of saying she was turned off by the idea of having a second baby because her husband wasn't helping out enough.

If you discover that the hidden conflict involves a relationship problem of some sort, then you can use the relationship journal, as I did with Lillya. I've provided a blank template at the end of this chapter that you can use.

And remember, if you're struggling with anxiety, the first step is to reduce your own outcome and process resistance. You can overcome your outcome resistance by listing all the ways your anxiety is helping you and protecting you, as well as what it shows about you that's positive and awesome.

And you can overcome your process resistance by facing the thing you fear the most and allowing yourself to be flooded with anxiety until it disappears. That's what you'll probably resist the most because exposure is so frightening.

There are many techniques to overcome anxiety in addition to those described in this chapter. If you want to take a deeper dive into this topic, I recommend my book, *When Panic Attacks*. You'll learn about many additional techniques to overcome every conceivable type of anxiety.

# Relationship Journal*

| **Step 1:** Write down *exactly* what the other person said. Be brief:<br><br>He or she said: _____<br><br>_____<br><br>_____<br><br>_____ | **Step 2:** Write down *exactly* what you said next. Be brief:<br><br>I said: _____<br><br>_____<br><br>_____<br><br>_____ |
|---|---|
| Circle the emotions *he or she* might have been feeling | Circle the emotions *you* were feeling |
| **Sad**, blue, depressed, down, unhappy | **Sad**, blue, depressed, down, unhappy |
| **Anxious**, worried, panicky, nervous, frightened | **Anxious**, worried, panicky, nervous, frightened |
| **Guilty**, remorseful, bad, ashamed | **Guilty**, remorseful, bad, ashamed |
| **Inferior**, worthless, inadequate, defective, incompetent | **Inferior**, worthless, inadequate, defective, incompetent |
| **Lonely**, unloved, unwanted, rejected, alone, abandoned | **Lonely**, unloved, unwanted, rejected, alone, abandoned |
| **Embarrassed**, foolish, humiliated, self-conscious | **Embarrassed**, foolish, humiliated, self-conscious |
| **Hopeless**, discouraged, pessimistic, despairing | **Hopeless**, discouraged, pessimistic, despairing |
| **Frustrated**, stuck, thwarted, defeated | **Frustrated**, stuck, thwarted, defeated |
| **Angry**, mad, resentful, annoyed, irritated, upset, furious | **Angry**, mad, resentful, annoyed, irritated, upset, furious |
| **Other** (specify) | **Other** (specify) |

---

**Step 3: Good Versus Bad Communication:** Was your response an example of good or bad communication? Use the EAR Checklist to analyze what you wrote down in Step 2.

### EAR Checklist

| 👂 | Good Communication | ✓ | Bad Communication | ✓ |
|---|---|---|---|---|
| **E =**<br>**Empathy** | 1. You acknowledge the other person's feelings and find some truth in what he or she said. | | 1. You ignore the other person's feelings or argue and insist he or she is "wrong." | |
| **A =**<br>**Assertiveness** | 2. You express your feelings openly and directly. | | 2. You fail to express your feelings or express them aggressively. | |
| **R =**<br>**Respect** | 3. Your attitude is respectful and caring. | | 3. Your attitude is not respectful or caring. | |

**Step 4: Consequences:** Did your response in Step 2 make the problem better or worse? Why?

_____

_____

_____

_____

**Step 5: Revised Version:** Revise what you wrote down in Step 2. Use the five secrets of effective communication. If your revised response is ineffective, try again.

_____

_____

_____

_____

_____

# 18 | Magnification and Minimization

I recently treated a single man named Keeshawn who was caring for his elderly mother, who was in her 80s. Keeshawn loved his mother dearly and was concerned about her health and what would happen if she died. He told me he was waking up in the middle of the night in a panic and having a lot of trouble getting back to sleep.

Here are some of the catastrophic messages Keeshawn was giving himself that were contributing to his panic:

1. My mother is going to die, and I am going to be alone.
2. There will be no one to help me when she's gone.
3. I will be alone in the universe. I will be lonely.
4. If I don't stop this panic, then it will be more difficult to do my job.
5. I may never sleep again.
6. I won't be able to handle going through life alone with no family.
7. I'll wake up in the middle of the night with a panic attack and won't be able to calm myself down.

Keeshawn's problems were real—his mother was frail, and he had been struggling with insomnia for two months—so my heart went out to him. Still, his intense anxiety was not a result of his problems, but of the distorted way he was thinking about them.

Specifically, Keeshawn was engaging in a common set of cognitive distortions called **magnification** and **minimization**. Here's the definition:

- You blow things up (magnification) or shrink them (minimization) way out of proportion. For example, you may magnify your flaws or minimize your strengths. I also call this the binocular trick because it's like looking at things through a set of binoculars. From one end, your problems seem much bigger and more terrifying. But if you look through the opposite end, your positive qualities look small and insignificant.

Some people use the term *catastrophizing* to describe magnification. You imagine you are on the verge of a terrible catastrophe—when you aren't—and this triggers feelings of anxiety and panic.

Keeshawn was clearly engaging in magnification. Although his mother was quite old, she wasn't on the verge of death, and she wasn't even sick. He was also magnifying the danger he was in. Panic attacks and insomnia are intensely uncomfortable, but they're not dangerous, and they wouldn't cause Keeshawn to "never sleep again."

Keeshawn was also engaging in minimization because it wasn't true that he'd be entirely alone in the universe after his mother died. In fact, he had a strong network of friends who loved him and would support him after her death. He was also minimizing his own strengths, as he was functioning superbly at work in spite of his insomnia, and he was extremely capable and self-reliant.

I don't mean to criticize Keeshawn or anyone who's struggling with feelings of panic and insecurity. Keeshawn's symptoms were clearly an expression of his core values and his love for his mother, and I admired him greatly.

But much, if not all, of his pain resulted from the distortions in his thoughts, especially magnification and minimization. Magnification and minimization play key roles in:

- **Anxiety Disorders.** You magnify the dangerousness of the thing you fear. This is obvious with phobias. A student came to my house with several other students for some training in statistics. When she saw our sweet little cat, named Happy, she screamed at the top of her lungs and ran out of the room in terror. Apparently, she had a cat phobia and was convinced Happy was about to jump on her and viciously attack her.

- **Anger.** You exaggerate the "badness" and awfulness of someone you dislike and minimize his or her positive qualities because you're so frustrated and annoyed.

- **Fear of Disapproval.** You magnify how awful it would be if even one person disapproved of you, judged you, or rejected you. You may tell yourself that these negative opinions about you will spread and that pretty soon you'll be cast out and ostracized by the entire human race. If you review my list of common self-defeating beliefs from the previous chapter, you'll see that this is also called the brushfire fallacy.

- **Feelings of Worthlessness, Inferiority, or Defectiveness.** You magnify your flaws and minimize your positive qualities, and you conclude there's nothing very special, unique, or likable about you.

- **Procrastination.** You magnify how hard and time-consuming some task you're putting off will be, and you catastrophize how incredibly anxious and awful you're going to feel if you try to get started.

- **Perfectionism.** You tell yourself that you shouldn't have made some mistake that's eating away at you. You magnify its importance and tell yourself that failure is shameful and awful.

- **Habits and Addictions.** When you're feeling tempted to eat some forbidden but delicious fattening food, you tell yourself that it's going to taste so good and that it's going to make you feel wonderful!

- **Panic Attacks.** This is probably the most extreme version of magnification. During a panic attack, you may have many physical symptoms of anxiety, such as tightness in your chest, dizziness, or tingling fingers. Then you may tell yourself that these symptoms are dangerous and conclude that you're on the verge of dying, passing out, suffocating, or going crazy. And you *feel* terrified, so you conclude that your symptoms *are* incredibly dangerous.

I'm sure we could add to that list, but the practical question is—what can you do if you spot magnification and minimization in your own negative thoughts? Lots of techniques can be helpful, so let's circle back to Keeshawn, and I can show you how they work.

**Positive reframing** is one of the most powerful techniques and is definitely the first tool I used when working with Keeshawn. That's because I needed to reduce his stuckness, or possible resistance to letting go of his intense anxiety, before I could help him change the way he'd been thinking and feeling.

Keeshawn reported a variety of negative feelings, which I've listed on the following chart. Go through each feeling and ask yourself what some benefits of this feeling might be and what it might say about Keeshawn's core values that's positive and awesome.

Don't worry about getting it "right." There is no right answer as long as the list rings true for Keeshawn and doesn't simply consist of buzzwords, false compliments, or efforts to cheer him up. In fact, the goal at this point is *not* to encourage change. The goal is the opposite: to bring out what's beautiful

and positive about his struggles and feelings of depression, panic, hopelessness, and despair.

In case you're wondering, we could also do positive reframing with
Keeshawn's negative thoughts, but to keep things simple, we'll just focus on
his negative feelings.

When you're done, you can check the list that Keeshawn and I came up
with on the next page.

| Feeling | Advantages and Core Values |
|---|---|
| Sad | |
| Anxious | |
| Ashamed | |
| Defective | |
| Lonely | |
| Embarrassed | |
| Hopeless | |
| Frustrated | |
| Angry | |

## Keeshawn's Positive Reframing List

| Feeling | Advantages and Core Values |
|---|---|
| Sad | My sadness shows:<br>• How much I love my mother.<br>• That I want something better for her and for me.<br>• How much passion and appreciation I have for life. |
| Anxious | My anxiety has motivated me to:<br>• Prepare and do many loving things for my mother so she'll feel comfortable, safe, and cared about in her old age.<br>• Get close to others so I'll have a network of friends when she dies.<br>• Be vigilant. |
| Ashamed | My shame shows that:<br>• I have a moral compass.<br>• I have high standards for myself. |
| Defective | This feeling shows that:<br>• I'm honest and realistic since I have many flaws and defects.<br>• I have high standards. My high standards have motivated me to work hard and accomplish a lot throughout my entire life.<br>• I'm compassionate for others who are suffering and who feel inadequate since I can connect with their struggles and feelings of self-doubt.<br>• I'm humble and modest. Humility is a spiritual value, and my religious beliefs are very important to me. |
| Lonely | My loneliness:<br>• Shows that I want to connect more deeply with others.<br>• Shows that I value meaningful relationships with people I care about.<br>• Has motivated me to reach out to others. |
| Embarrassed | This feeling sometimes keeps me in check! |
| Hopeless | My feelings of hopelessness and discouragement:<br>• Show how incredibly important hope is to me.<br>• Protect me from disappointment.<br>• Show that I'm facing the facts and have a sense of integrity since my mother *is* old and since I have been struggling unsuccessfully with panic, anxiety, and insomnia.<br>• Show the depth of my feelings. |
| Frustrated | My frustration shows that I haven't given up! |
| Angry | My anger:<br>• Shows that I have high standards.<br>• Motivates me to take action.<br>• Shows how much I care. |

Keeshawn was surprised to see so much beauty in his so-called "negative" emotions! I suggested we might use the magic dial to dial each type of feeling down to some lower level that would allow him to feel better without losing any of the positives we'd listed.

He agreed and was eager to use several techniques to crush his negative thoughts, and he was able to do so pretty rapidly. Here are some of the techniques that were especially helpful to him:

- **Examine the Evidence.** Although you may feel extremely upset because of a negative thought, you can examine the actual evidence for what you're telling yourself.
- **The Acceptance Paradox.** Instead of arguing with a negative thought, you can simply accept it in the spirit of dignity and self-respect.

Examine the evidence was helpful in evaluating the validity of Keeshawn's first two negative thoughts: "My mother is going to die, and I am going to be alone" and "There will be no one to help me when she's gone."

Keeshawn reminded himself that his mother was not on the verge of death but was in good health. In addition, he had many friends who loved and supported him. Furthermore, he had been a strong and self-reliant individual his entire life. This caused his belief in the first two negative thoughts to drop dramatically.

Keeshawn also used examine the evidence and the acceptance paradox to challenge his third negative thought: "I will be alone in the universe. I will be lonely." He reminded himself that he had many friends and could always connect with others through the volunteer work he did. At the same time, he often enjoyed his solitude too. He also pointed out that some loneliness was appropriate, and maybe even a good thing, since it reflected his intense loyalty and love for his mother.

Examine the evidence also helped with his fourth negative thought: "If I don't stop this panic, then it will be more difficult to do my job." Although there was some truth in this thought—it can suck having to go to work when you're exhausted—he had to admit that he'd always done good or even superb work on the days following a night of poor sleep.

As you can see, examine the evidence and the acceptance paradox were very helpful to Keeshawn, and his belief in all of his frightening negative thoughts went down dramatically. I'm convinced that the positive reframing we did first was the key to his remarkably rapid improvement. When your resistance or stuckness disappears, a healing and loving voice can emerge.

Keeshawn's negative feelings also went down dramatically, confirming once again that when you change the way you *think*, you can change the way you *feel*.

Now that you have a feel for these two techniques, review your list of negative thoughts from your Daily Mood Journal, and see if any of your thoughts are examples of magnification or minimization. Select one thought and record it here.

_____

_____

_____

_____

_____

Now see if you can explain *why* this thought is an example of magnification or minimization. For example, maybe you are blowing something out of proportion or overlooking its importance. Write your answer here.

_____

_____

_____

_____

_____

Finally, try using examine the evidence or the acceptance paradox to come up with a positive thought that's 100% true and that crushes your belief in the negative thought.

_____

_____

_____

_____

_____

## OTHER TECHNIQUES

There are a couple of additional methods that you might want to consider if you've got some negative thoughts with magnification that plague you over and over again. This is especially common in people with OCD who have anxious thoughts that haunt them all day long. They attempt to neutralize the anxiety by performing some ritualistic, compulsive behavior, and although this provides some temporary relief, the obsessive thought and anxiety inevitably come back, so they repeat the compulsive behavior again and again.

That's classic OCD, and it can really interfere with your life and your emotional well-being. And in severe cases, it can be crippling.

In a case like this, reattribution and self-monitoring can be helpful, as well as exposure.

- **Reattribution/Self-Monitoring.** When you have a recurring negative thought that you have already crushed, and it pops back in your mind, you can simply count it on an index card or a wrist counter. This is called self-monitoring. In addition, you can tell yourself, "Oh, there's that negative thought again." This is called reattribution because you're reminding yourself that the negative thought is just a bad habit and that you don't have to dwell on it.

  You just let it go and focus on what you were doing so you can get back to your life instead of dwelling endlessly on repetitive negative thoughts that are not valid. I also call this strategy "mindfulness in daily life" because it is very similar to what people try to learn through meditation, but it's a whole lot faster. It's really the art of letting go.

  If you'd like to give it a try, I'd suggest that you count your negative thoughts every day for four weeks and record the daily total on your calendar. For many people, the daily total will go down after three weeks or so and may disappear completely. Like any technique, it works for some people, but not for everybody, but it's easy and worth a shot.

- **Exposure/Cognitive Flooding.** This is the opposite strategy, but it can also be incredibly effective if you have a little courage. If you're feeling terrified because you're magnifying some danger, then you can imagine the very thing you're afraid of and try to make yourself as anxious as possible.

  For example, Keeshawn could close his eyes and imagine that his mother has died and that he's entirely alone and abandoned by the universe. He could visualize the most frightening possible scenario and record his negative thoughts and feelings every minute or two until his anxiety diminishes and disappears completely.

This may take an hour or more, or it may only take a few minutes. We're all different. The key is *not* to try to avoid the anxiety, distract yourself, or calm yourself down. Instead, try to freak out and see if you can bring your anxiety all the way up to 100. You'll discover that over time, it will diminish and disappear on its own—and then you'll have defeated your fears!

It takes guts, and it can feel incredibly uncomfortable—even terrifying—but it's one of the most powerful antianxiety, anti-magnification techniques of all. If you want to give this one a try, I've included a flooding flowsheet at the end of this chapter where you can record your observations.

Remember that there are tons of ways to challenge and smash your negative thoughts and overcome your feelings of depression and anxiety. If the techniques we discussed in this chapter are not effective for you, no problem. We've got *lots* of ways to slay any dragons that have been haunting you!

## Flooding Flowsheet

**Instructions:** Close your eyes and visualize something you fear, making yourself as anxious as possible. Every couple of minutes, record the time in the first column, and then record how anxious you are on a scale from 0 (not at all) to 100 (the worst imaginable panic) in the second column. In the third column, describe the frightening images, pictures, or fantasies in your mind, and in the fourth column, record your negative thoughts.

Try to make yourself as anxious as possible for as long as possible. Do *not* try to control or avoid the anxiety. Instead, try to intensify it. Eventually, it will diminish and disappear completely. You can do the exposure all at once (flooding) or in 10- to 20-minute periods over a period of days (gradual exposure).

| Time Every 2 or 3 Minutes | Anxiety 0 to 100 | Frightening Images/Fantasies | Frightening Negative Thoughts |
|---|---|---|---|
| | | | |
| | | | |
| | | | |
| | | | |
| | | | |
| | | | |
| | | | |

# 19 | Emotional Reasoning

In case you have a short attention span, here's the condensed version of this chapter: It's great to get in touch with your feelings—no doubt about it. But it can also be a deep pitfall.

Getting in touch with your feelings is a time-honored focus of an awful lot of psychotherapy. For years, therapists have claimed that the secret of mental health and happiness is learning to feel (or lean into) your feelings or learning to express them.

Sounds appealing! But is this formula too good to be true?

I decided to check it out when I was a Stanford medical student. I decided to express all my feelings—no matter how I felt—to everyone I interacted with for a full week. I skipped all my medical school classes and just wandered around Palo Alto and San Francisco with a tape recorder so I could record everything that happened.

To be honest, nothing very wonderful or exciting happened until the seventh day of my experiment, when I was sitting in the Stanford Student Union eating lunch. I'd spotted a fellow eating alone and had a strong negative feeling about him for no particular reason. So according to my plan, I approached him with my tape recorder in hand and said, "I just want to let you know that I don't like you."

He said, "I'm not surprised."

I asked him why. He asked if I'd read the morning newspaper. I said I hadn't seen it and had no idea what he was referring to.

He explained that he'd been planning to blow up a building on the Stanford campus but had just been arrested, and his picture was on the front page of the *San Francisco Chronicle*.

This really took me by surprise! Then I noticed he was wearing a handsome Navajo turquoise ring. Since I'd grown up in Phoenix, I had a feeling for Navajo jewelry, so I said, "I really like your ring."

He said, "I'll tell you what. I'm going to give it to you because where I'm going, I won't need my ring."

So he gave me his Navajo ring!

That was pretty cool, but it was the only cool thing that happened in a week of expressing my feelings. I discovered that magic doesn't actually happen just because you get in touch with the way you feel.

And since I've been a shrink, I've also learned that your feelings can sometimes be very misleading. That's why I've included emotional reasoning on my list of cognitive distortions. Here's the definition:

- **Emotional Reasoning.** You reason from how you feel. For example, if you *feel* like a loser, then you conclude that you really *are* a loser. Or if you *feel* unlovable, then you conclude that you really *are* unlovable. Or if you *feel* hopeless, then you conclude that you really *are* hopeless and will never recover from your depression.

The consequences of emotional reasoning can sometimes be disastrous. Some depressed individuals who feel hopeless are so convinced that they *really are* hopeless that they take their own lives. Hopelessness is probably the most common cause of suicide, and it's a devastating tragedy for the patient, the family, and the therapist who was treating the patient.

The tragedy is made even worse by the fact that the feelings of desperation and hopelessness that trigger suicide do not result from the truth but from negative thoughts that are massively distorted. I've often said that depression is the world's oldest con, and this con artist can sometimes try to steal your life.

Why did I include emotional reasoning on my list of cognitive distortions? It's because all of your emotions result entirely from your thoughts. But if your thoughts are distorted, then your feelings will be just as misleading as the curved mirrors in amusement parks that make you look grotesque and bizarre. This phenomenon of being fooled by your emotions can occur with *any* emotion.

This does not mean that listening to your emotions is bad. It's only harmful when you use your emotions, without additional evidence, to draw conclusions about yourself or the people and situations around you. Fortunately, there are good solutions to this problem!

Early in my career, I was doing research on the so-called "chemical imbalance" theory of depression and was giving out antidepressants by the bushel, but very few of my patients truly recovered from depression. Some got a little better, some got worse, and many stayed the same, but very few became joyous and completely free of depression. This bothered me, so I started looking for some kind of psychotherapy that might boost my therapeutic effectiveness.

I heard that a colleague named Dr. Aaron Beck was developing a new treatment for depression called "cognitive therapy." Dr. Beck believed that depression was caused by negative thoughts and that you could overcome depression by learning to think more positively.

I was very skeptical. It seemed too simple. To be totally honest, I thought it was a lot of BS.

I decided to attend some of Dr. Beck's weekly seminars so I could try out his techniques on a few severely depressed patients and satisfy myself that they didn't work. But my experiment didn't work as anticipated.

One of my patients was an elderly Latvian woman named Katrina who had been referred to me from the intensive care unit of our hospital following a serious suicide attempt. I had been treating Katrina with antidepressants and traditional talk therapy, but she wasn't making much progress, if any. This was typical of most of the people I was treating.

I asked Dr. Beck how I might help Katrina using cognitive therapy. He reminded me that our thoughts create all of our feelings and said I should ask Katrina what she was thinking at the moment she decided to commit suicide. What was she telling herself?

I asked her at our next therapy session, and she explained she was telling herself she was a totally worthless human being because she'd never accomplished anything meaningful in her life. She asked what she could do about that.

I told her I didn't know, but if she'd wait another week, I would ask Dr. Beck and tell her what he said at our next session.

Dr. Beck told me to ask Katrina to list a few things that she *had* accomplished. You might recognize that technique as examine the evidence. The idea is that Katrina *felt* like a failure, so she concluded that she'd never accomplished anything meaningful. But what's the evidence for this? Just because you feel something very strongly, it doesn't mean it's true.

At our next session, I told Katrina that she was supposed to list several things that she *had* accomplished. She said:

*Well, that's my problem. I can't think of anything worthwhile that I've ever accomplished. That's why I decided to kill myself. I just feel totally worthless.*

I was stumped, so I told Katrina that perhaps she could take it as a homework assignment and see if she could think of a few things she had accomplished during her life.

At our next session, I forgot to ask her about the homework assignment and did my usual thing—I checked on the side effects of her antidepressant and encouraged her to share her negative feelings. About halfway through the session, she said, "Aren't you going to ask about my homework?"

I apologized for forgetting and asked if she'd come up with anything.

She handed me a list of ten things she had accomplished in her life. The first thing was the fact that she'd smuggled her children out of Nazi Germany and managed to get them to the United States during World War II. She explained that her husband and all of her relatives perished in the concentration camps and that she and her two boys were the only ones who survived.

She said, "That might be considered an accomplishment." To say I agreed would be an understatement—wow!

Second on her list was the fact that once she got to the United States, she worked cleaning houses and scrubbing floors to support herself and her boys so they'd have food to eat and a place to sleep at night. She said that might also be an accomplishment of sorts. She added that her oldest son had just graduated first in his class from the Harvard Business School and that she was very proud of him!

The third thing on her list was that she spoke five languages fluently.

The next thing was that she was a gourmet chef.

The other accomplishments on her list were equally impressive.

Then I asked, "How do you reconcile this list with the idea that you're a worthless human being who's never accomplished anything?"

She said, "I can't! My negative thought suddenly doesn't seem to make sense. It felt completely true when I tried to kill myself, but now I don't believe it anymore."

I asked, "How are you feeling at this moment?"

Katrina said, "I'm suddenly feeling a whole lot better. This has been *so* helpful! Do you have any more of these techniques?"

I said, "This is the only technique I've learned so far, but I'll learn another technique at Dr. Beck's seminar this week, and we can use it at our next session." She was fine with that.

Three weeks later, Katrina was free of depression and bursting with happiness and self-esteem.

Katrina almost lost her life because of emotional reasoning. She *felt* worthless, so she concluded she *was* worthless. She *felt* hopeless, so she concluded she *was* hopeless.

Emotional reasoning is incredibly common, and you'll find this distortion in the negative thoughts of just about every person in this book. When you *feel* something so strongly, it's natural to conclude that it simply *must* be true.

Like any distortion, there are negative and positive versions of emotional reasoning. Here are some examples of **negative emotional reasoning**:

- "I'm feeling really anxious and scared, so I must be in danger."
- "I feel guilty, so I must be bad."
- "I feel angry, so this must be your fault."
- "I feel ashamed, so these people are probably judging me."
- "I'm feeling shy and insecure, so she probably notices my anxiety and doesn't like me."
- "I feel like he is a total jerk, so he must be a jerk!"
- During a panic attack, you may feel like you are about to die or are on the verge of going crazy, so you conclude that you really are about to die or about to have a psychotic break.

**Positive emotional reasoning** is just the opposite. You feel so happy and worthwhile that you're absolutely certain good things are about to happen. Here are some examples:

- "He's so cute, so he must be really nice!" (He could be someone you just met who turns out to be extremely controlling, narcissistic, abusive, or self-centered.)
- "She says such inspiring and visionary things. I feel wonderful when I'm around her, so she must be wonderful!" (This person could be a cult leader or con artist.)
- You just won your bet at the casino and tell yourself, "I'm feeling lucky, so I think I'll raise my bet!"

- You feel superior to people from certain ethnic, political, or religious groups, or people with a different sexual orientation, so you conclude that they really are bad, wrong, or inferior.

What can you do about emotional reasoning? Many techniques can be helpful, but examining the evidence is a good place to start. It was helpful for Katrina and it might be helpful for you too.

## EXAMINE THE EVIDENCE

You are already familiar with this technique, but we can revisit it briefly here. Instead of jumping to conclusions based on the way you feel, you can look at the actual evidence for and against your negative thought or belief.

First, look at your Daily Mood Journal and see if you can find a thought that is an example of emotional reasoning, such as:

- "I've never accomplished anything meaningful."
- "I feel like a failure (or a loser), so I must be one."
- "I feel unlovable, so I must be unlovable."
- "I feel hopeless, so I must be hopeless."
- "I have an intense fear of flying, so flying must be very dangerous."

If so, put the thought at the top of the examine the evidence chart on the next page. Then list all the evidence you can think of that supports the thought, as well as the evidence indicating that the thought might not be true.

When you've listed all the evidence you can think of, put two numbers adding up to 100 in the circles at the bottom of the chart to indicate whether the evidence for or against your negative thought is more compelling.

## Examine the Evidence Chart

**List your negative thought here:** _____

_____

| Evidence That This Negative Thought Might Be True | Evidence That This Negative Thought Might Not Be True |
|---|---|
| | |

## BE SPECIFIC

Another technique you can use to combat emotional reasoning is called **be specific**. This technique is pretty basic, but it can be incredibly powerful. If you're upset because you're feeling a certain way, ask for the specifics. For example, from time to time I get a lower-than-expected rating in a workshop or therapy session, and I usually feel like a failure. It's a very global kind of feeling, and it includes shame.

But then I say, "What *specific* errors did I make in the workshop? And how can I correct those errors?" This is always a relief because specific errors can nearly always be corrected. But when you feel like a failure, it feels like you really are some kind of globally and irreversibly defective failure, so you feel doomed!

This technique is especially useful for emotional reasoning that involves guilt, especially thoughts like "I feel guilty, so I must have done something wrong." This is an extremely common thought, but it can get you into trouble.

Sometimes I feel plagued by guilt, even when I'm pretty sure I'm doing the right thing. For example, early in my career, I was treating a severely depressed teenager who was quite angry and oppositional, and she refused to do any psychotherapy homework. I confronted her and told her that she wouldn't recover unless she did the homework. She said she didn't give a "damn" about homework or recovery and intended to kill herself after the session.

I told her I would not permit her to do that.

She said, "You can't stop me!" and bolted for the door. I jumped up to block her and said I *could* stop her! She started screaming, hitting me, and trying to get out, insisting she was going to kill herself.

I restrained her with one hand and managed to pick up the phone with my other hand, dialed the operator (this was before 911), and said I needed the police immediately.

The police arrived in less than three minutes and said they would take her to the university hospital's emergency room for evaluation. They had to drag her from my office, kicking and screaming that Burns was a horrible fraud and the worst psychiatrist in the world.

Since I'd just started my practice, this didn't seem like the best advertising in the world, and I felt really guilty and inadequate, like I'd done something wrong.

But then I said, "What exactly, did you do, David, that was so wrong or so bad? Be specific."

And when I thought about it, I could not think of any specific thing I'd done wrong. Logically, I thought I might have actually saved her life, and I felt the message I gave her about homework was the exact message she needed to hear.

That helped a fair amount, and I never saw her again. I knew I wouldn't.

Years later, I got a call from the chief of the National Institutes of Health in Bethesda, Maryland, which freaked me out. He asked if I'd ever treated a young woman named so and so. It was the teenage girl I'd treated years earlier, and I felt terrified he was going to be critical of me. He was one of the biggest names in psychiatric research and was actually one of my heroes, but I'd never met him.

I awkwardly confessed that I'd treated her for a few sessions, but it hadn't worked out terribly well and wondered why he was calling. I thought he might be planning to complain about me to the ethics board or something.

He then explained:

*After she was hospitalized in Philadelphia for her suicide threat, she was treated by more than a dozen psychiatrists, and now she's on our treatment unit. I asked her if any of her psychiatrists had been helpful to her, and she said only one, and that was Dr. David Burns. So I'm just calling to find out what approach you were using that was so helpful to her.*

So much for emotional reasoning!

## POSITIVE REFRAMING

Just this week, I treated a woman named Berna who tearfully confided something she'd kept secret ever since she was 12—that her brother had sexually abused her and done many other things that seemed incredibly insensitive and cruel. She was upset and felt intensely sad, guilty, unloved, embarrassed, discouraged, frustrated, angry, and resentful. One of her negative thoughts was, "I'm damaged."

This is a classic example of emotional reasoning. Berna *felt* damaged, so she concluded she really *was* damaged. She was also convinced that I was judging her and that the others in the therapy group were judging her too.

When I offered the magic button, she instantly said she'd press it!

But before trying to help her change the way she was thinking and feeling, I suggested we might first make a list of the benefits of each negative thought and feeling, as well as what each negative thought and feeling showed about her that was positive and awesome.

Here's the list of positives that we came up with:

1. Feeling damaged has motivated me to accomplish a great deal in my career.

2. My intensely negative feelings highlight the importance of what happened to me. If my negative feelings suddenly disappeared, it might trivialize the abuse and the other cruel things my brother did.

3. My anger protects me from others who could hurt me and keeps them away.

4. My anger shows that I have a moral compass and a strong sense of what's right and wrong.

5. My feelings of sadness and guilt have given me greater empathy and compassion for others.

6. They have also made me a better mother.

7. My self-criticisms show that I have high standards.

8. My concerns about being judged show how much I care about relationships.

9. My strong negative feelings show that I'm willing to feel things rather than denying my feelings.

10. My negative feelings are appropriate and realistic since a lot of genuinely abusive things have happened.

This list was a surprise to Berna and a relief. She'd never thought of her negative thoughts and feelings as being positive—in fact, she'd hidden them in shame until the moment she opened up in our group that week.

Despite these positives, Berna said she *did* want to change the way she was thinking and feeling. She was tired of feeling so incredibly upset and damaged. Because she was convinced the other people in the group were judging her, I thought the survey technique would be a good place to start.

## SURVEY TECHNIQUE/EXPERIMENTAL TECHNIQUE

You may recall that when you use the **survey technique**, you ask others if they've ever felt the way you do, or you ask how they think and feel about you. For example, since Berna was convinced people in the therapy group (including myself) were judging her, I suggested she take a survey of what the other members thought about her.

She said she was afraid to do this and was convinced people wouldn't be honest with her. I pushed her to ask them anyway, and I said we could cross-examine them if they didn't sound honest.

She first asked a woman named Regina. Regina burst into tears and confided—while sobbing—that she'd had a similar experience as Berna and that she felt enormously close to her and grateful that she'd opened up.

Berna could see she was being entirely honest and seemed touched.

Then two men expressed their intense respect and admiration for Berna, with tears streaming down their cheeks as well, and everyone in the group said they felt the same way.

The experience blew her mind, and I just got an email from Berna that she's been on cloud nine ever since that experience!

After the group, I summarized about a dozen teaching points in an email to those who participated, and this was part of what I wrote. I hope it will be interesting or helpful to you.

*Most of us, and perhaps nearly all of us, have parts of ourselves that we keep hidden from others, fearing rejection or judgment, thinking we are broken, not good enough, flawed, defective, or whatever.*

*When you share and accept that hidden and suppressed part of yourself, the part you think of as your "worst," it can often get transformed into your "best." I've seen that hundreds of times, maybe thousands of times, in therapy.*

*We saw it dramatically in our group. When Berna courageously stepped up to the plate, faced her worst fears, and opened up about what happened, the group became amazingly inspiring and transformative, not just for her but for all of us.*

*This is the spiritual or mystical aspect of my work with TEAM-CBT. It involves the death of the "self" and also the concept of rebirth, suddenly seeing and experiencing things in a radically different way. This involves the acceptance paradox, first described by the Buddha 2,500 years ago. Someone once said that self-acceptance is actually the greatest change a person can make.*

*The goal of therapy is not to become whole, undamaged, worthwhile, special, or anything like that. "Self-improvement" is arguably the wrong direction, a kind of endless trap. We saw a glorious acceptance last night.*

*Words like the ones I just wrote can only point in a particular direction, can only hint at the process of enlightenment. I'm pretty sure you have to "see" and experience this before you can "get it."*

*So thanks again to our beautiful and incredible "patient" who provided such great insight, support, and openness, including your own tears at times.*

I've only touched on a few techniques that can be helpful for emotional reasoning, and there are a great many more, including:

- **The Double Standard Technique.** Would you talk to a dear friend who had the same problem in the same way that you're talking to yourself? What would you say to him or her?

- **Thinking in Shades of Gray.** Instead of thinking about your flaws and errors in a black-or-white, all-or-nothing manner, can you think in shades of gray? Few of us are ever 0% or 100% at anything.

- **Let's Define Terms.** If you think you are worthless, hopeless, or unlovable because you *feel* worthless, hopeless, or unlovable—or if you're feeling like a failure—ask yourself what these terms actually mean. What's the definition of a human being who's worthless, hopeless, or unlovable? What's the definition of a failure?

You'll find that no matter how you define these terms, there will be a fatal flaw with your definition because:

1. Your definition will apply to all human beings.

2. Your definition will apply to no human beings.

3. Your definition will be meaningless, nonsensical, or just plain wrong.

4. Your definition will not apply to you.

I'll give you many examples of let's define terms in section III of this book on the philosophy and spirituality in TEAM-CBT.

Finally, remember that any negative thought with emotional reasoning will have many more distortions, so there will be lots of ways to challenge and crush the thought if you look at the cheat sheet for other promising methods.

# 20 | Should Statements

On one of my recent Sunday hikes, a software engineer named Julia confided that she was feeling discouraged about her 9-year-old son, Jacob, who was a child with special needs. Although he was a loving and gentle boy, he had significant difficulties with speech, coordination, and learning that were causing struggles at home and at school.

Julia and her husband had showered Jacob with love, extra tutoring, counseling, and a wide variety of enrichment activities, but he was still falling far behind the other children his age.

When Julia visited Jacob's school for parents' night, she saw the children's art proudly displayed on the wall. But Jacob's artwork stood out as vastly more primitive than that of the other children in his class. Julia felt embarrassed and worried the other parents might look down on her because of her son's difficulties.

She also felt ashamed because she was telling herself, "A loving mother *shouldn't* feel ashamed of her son." This is a classic should statement.

Julia told me she sometimes felt frustrated with Jacob as well since he often gave up on things without much effort, and he sometimes had temper tantrums when trying to finish his homework. She told herself, "Jacob *shouldn't* give up so easily. He *should* try harder."

These should statements triggered feelings of annoyance and frustration. She then told herself, "I *shouldn't* feel annoyed with Jacob. I *should* be more patient with him." This thought triggered even more shame.

As you can see, Julia's negative feelings resulted from should statements. Here is the definition:

- **Should Statements.** You beat up on yourself, other people, or the world with *should*s, *shouldn't*s, *must*s, *ought to*s, and *have to*s.

There are several types of should statements:

- **Self-Directed Shoulds.** You tell yourself, "I shouldn't have made that mistake" or "I shouldn't have been so irritable." Or in Julia's case, "I shouldn't feel so ashamed and frustrated with my son." These kinds of should statements create feelings of guilt, shame, anxiety, depression, and inadequacy.

- **Other-Directed Shoulds.** When you're annoyed with someone, you may tell yourself, "She's got no right to say that" or "He shouldn't feel (or think) that way!" These kinds of should statements cause feelings of anger and resentment, and they trigger conflicts in your relationships.

- **World-Directed Shoulds.** For example, "It shouldn't rain today because I was planning a picnic" or "This software program shouldn't be so buggy." These kinds of should statements create feelings of frustration and exasperation.

In addition, you can have **hidden should statements**. This is where a should statement is implied in the negative thought even though words like *should*, *must*, or *ought* do not appear.

For example, if you think back to Marilyn's example from chapter 8, one of her negative thoughts after being diagnosed with stage 4 lung cancer was "I'm not spiritual enough." This is a hidden should statement because Marilyn was really telling herself, "I should be more spiritual. My faith should be stronger. I should not doubt the afterlife or the existence of God."

Hidden should statements can also hide behind negative thoughts that take the form of rhetorical questions. A young man named Johan was extremely shy because he sweated a great deal in social situations. He was ashamed and told himself, "Why am I like this? What's wrong with me?"

Rhetorical questions can't be easily challenged because they don't make claims of any sort. But you can easily convert them into should statements. Johan really is telling himself, "I shouldn't sweat so much!"

Should statements can cause tremendous damage. They trigger internal suffering in terms of depression and anxiety, as well as hostility between individuals, nations, races, religions, and ethnic groups. In fact, throughout human history, people have been willing to kill themselves or others to defend their shoulds and shouldn'ts.

Although should statements are at the root of most emotional distress, they can be incredibly difficult to let go of because they're addictive. That's because they create feelings of moral superiority. Sometimes it feels good to get angry and look down on other people. Or even ourselves!

Do you know what I mean? I have to admit that I sometimes enjoy looking down on certain people. In fact, all I have to do is watch the news on television, and I'm instantly flooded with should statements and feelings of intense annoyance. I wouldn't be surprised if you've had that experience too.

Before I show you how to get rid of your should statements, I want to emphasize that some should statements are actually helpful and valid. In my first book, *Feeling Good*, I pointed out there are three valid uses for the word *should* in the English language:

1. **The laws of the universe should.** When I drop a pen, it should fall to the ground because of the law of gravity. It's simply doing what it should do: obeying the laws of the universe. It has to fall because of the force of gravity.

2. **The legal should.** When you are driving down the freeway, you should not drive 90 miles an hour because it's against the law. You'll probably get a ticket and may even cause an accident.

3. **The moral should.** You should not do things that are immoral, such as committing murder, lying, or cheating. The Ten Commandments are perhaps the earliest source of moral shoulds.

Now let's consider Julia's should statements.

1. I shouldn't feel ashamed of my son. A loving mother shouldn't feel that way.

2. Jacob shouldn't give up so quickly and throw temper tantrums when he gets frustrated with his homework.

3. I shouldn't get so frustrated with him when he's having temper tantrums. I should support him and be more patient with him.

Are these laws of the universe shoulds? Julia isn't violating any scientific laws since practically all human beings feel ashamed or get frustrated at times. So these clearly aren't laws of the universe shoulds.

Are these legal shoulds? It isn't against the law to feel frustrated or ashamed of your son, and temper tantrums also aren't against the law, so these aren't legal shoulds either.

Are these moral shoulds? Nearly all parents feel ashamed or frustrated with their children at times. These feelings can be intensely uncomfortable, but they aren't immoral. So these don't appear to be moral shoulds either.

What kinds of shoulds are they? Put your answer in the chart here. There could be one or more correct answers:

| Should Statements | Yes (✓) | No (✓) |
|---|---|---|
| Self-directed | | |
| Other-directed | | |
| World-directed | | |
| Hidden shoulds | | |

When you're done, you can keep reading for the answer.

## My Answer

Julia is involved in self-directed shoulds ("A mother shouldn't feel ashamed of her son") and other-directed shoulds ("Jacob shouldn't give up so easily"). She does not seem to be involved in world-directed shoulds.

Can you think of a should statement against the world that a mother might easily have if her child had developmental challenges?

If Julia told herself it was *unfair* that she had a son with developmental problems, then it would be a hidden should statement against the world. That would probably make her feel angry with fate.

If you look up the origin of the word *should*, you'll see that it traces back to the Anglo-Saxon word *scolde*. So you might say that Julia is scolding herself and her son when she uses should statements.

While Julia has every right to scold herself and her son with should statements, doing so might actually make things worse. In the first place, Julia feels frustrated and ashamed of her son, whom she loves tremendously, and at the same time, she starts beating up on herself. So she's doubled her troubles.

What's the best way to get rid of should statements?

## POSITIVE REFRAMING

I have many helpful techniques for challenging should statements, but **positive reframing** is a great place to start. Before we help Julia overcome her should statements, we'll definitely have to melt away her resistance. Otherwise, she'll probably fight us.

To do positive reframing, remember to ask yourself two things: What are some advantages of Julia's should statements, and what might they reveal about her core values that's positive and awesome?

Record your ideas here:

| Negative Thoughts | Advantages and Core Values |
|---|---|
| "A loving mother shouldn't feel ashamed of her son." | |
| "Jacob shouldn't give up so easily. He should try harder." | |
| "I shouldn't feel frustrated with Jacob. I should be more patient with him." | |

When you're done, you can review what Julia and I came up with on the next page.

Here's what Julia and I came up with. Although I've divided this list into two categories for you, you don't need to do this when you do positive reframing. One column is usually enough for the list of positives.

| Negative Thoughts | Advantages | Core Values |
|---|---|---|
| "A loving mother shouldn't feel ashamed of her son." | Julia's feelings of shame may prompt her to focus more on her son's positive behaviors. Julia's high standards have motivated her to accomplish a great deal for herself and for her family. | This thought shows:<br>• That Julia has a moral compass.<br>• How much she loves her son.<br>• That she has high standards.<br>• That she wants to have unconditional acceptance of her child. |
| "Jacob shouldn't give up so easily. He should try harder." | This thought may motivate Julia to find more creative ways of helping her son. Her love and support will be crucial to his growth and development in spite of his limitations. | This thought shows that Julia:<br>• Believes in her son and wants him to fulfill his potential.<br>• Isn't giving up on him.<br>• Is willing to hold him accountable. |
| "I shouldn't feel frustrated with Jacob. I should be more patient with him." | Same as the advantages of the previous thought. | This thought:<br>• Shows how much Julia loves her son.<br>• Reminds Julia of the importance of patience and compassion in parenting. |

After we completed the positive reframing chart, Julia felt a lot more relaxed and self-accepting. She could see that there were some really good things about her should statements, as well as the anxiety, shame, frustration, and anger she sometimes felt. And paradoxically, she felt more strongly motivated to talk back to the should statements.

Positive reframing could be really helpful for you too. It will be a lot easier for you to modify your own should statements once you realize that they are helping you in many ways and that they reveal some really great things about you and your core values as a human being.

And of course, you might decide that you *don't* want to give up your should statements because that would involve a really major shift in your personal philosophy and view of yourself and the world.

## THE SEMANTIC METHOD

Once of the easiest ways to tackle should statements is by using the **semantic method**. You simply substitute an expression like "it would be preferable if" or "it would be great if" in place of the should statement. For example, instead of telling yourself that you *shouldn't* feel the way you do, you tell yourself that it would be *preferable* if you didn't feel that way. This simple change can reduce the scolding quality of the should statement because you're using less judgmental language.

For example, instead of telling herself, "I shouldn't feel ashamed of my son," Julia could tell herself:

> *I love Jacob tremendously, and* it would be preferable if *I didn't feel ashamed of him, but it's probably pretty human to feel that way at times. And I often feel proud of his accomplishments too.*

Notice the simple substitution of *it would be preferable if* in place of *should* or *shouldn't.* Julia doesn't have to like feeling ashamed of Jacob, but she doesn't have to punish herself for feeling the way she does.

Similarly, instead of telling herself, "I shouldn't get frustrated with him when he's having temper tantrums," she could tell herself:

> It would be wonderful *to be a saint and never get frustrated with my son, but Jacob can be very challenging at times. Most parents probably get frustrated when their kids are acting out or throwing temper tantrums.*

Finally, instead of telling herself, "Jacob shouldn't give up so quickly and throw temper tantrums when he gets frustrated," she could say:

> I wish *Jacob didn't get so frustrated because his behavior is disruptive and upsetting to everybody. But he's immature, and he's having a tough time socially and academically. He feels lonely and inadequate because learning is so hard for him. He can't keep up with the other kids, so it's totally understandable that he's frustrated. My husband and I can continue to work together to try to shape his behavior in a more positive direction, and he is making lots of progress.*

Julia told me that these changes in her thinking replaced her feelings of intense shame, anger, and frustration with gentler feelings of grief and sadness about her son's severe challenges.

The semantic technique isn't flashy, but it takes the moral sting out of the should statements while still acknowledging that there's a problem that needs to be solved.

That's all there is to it!

## SOCRATIC METHOD

The **Socratic method** can help you challenge should statements by allowing you to see the illogic behind them. You ask yourself a series of questions
that show the irrationality or absurdity of what you're telling yourself. This
method was first developed by Socrates, the classical Greek philosopher, and
was popularized in the twentieth century by Dr. Aaron Beck, one of the cre-
ators of cognitive therapy.

Let's see if we can use the Socratic method to help Julia. Remember, she
was telling herself that she *should not* feel frustrated with Jacob. Perhaps you've
also told yourself that you shouldn't feel the way you do.

We could ask Julia questions like these:

1. Do parents sometimes feel frustrated with their children?

   **Answer:** "Yes."

2. And what are you?

   **Answer:** "I'm a parent."

3. What follows?

   **Answer:** "Sometimes I will feel frustrated with my son."

Once again, this is a pretty humble method, but it may help you accept
your failures and limitations—which are real—instead of berating yourself
with endless *should*s and *shouldn't*s, such as punishing yourself and insisting
that you *should* be way better than you are.

But once again, this will be a decision for you. Do you want to accept
yourself just as you are, or would you prefer to keep beating yourself up with
should statements? This is by no means an easy decision!

## DOUBLE STANDARD TECHNIQUE

As you may recall, the idea behind the **double standard technique** is that
many of us operate on a double standard. When we fall short, we beat up on
ourselves mercilessly with harsh, critical statements. Those statements are the
voice of a bully. We are essentially bullying ourselves. But if we were talking to
a dear friend who was upset over the same kind of problem, we'd talk to him
or her in a warm, compassionate, and more realistic way.

When you use the double standard technique, you ask yourself, "What would I say to a dear friend with the exact same problem?" Then you ask yourself if you'd be willing to talk to yourself in the same compassionate way.

Like the other techniques I've mentioned in this chapter, using the double standard technique involves deciding whether you want to give up your inner critic or whether you'd prefer to continue bullying yourself. Remember that your self-critical voice can have many benefits and reflects an expression of your high standards.

So it's entirely understandable if you *don't* want to talk to yourself in the same compassionate way you'd talk to a dear friend who was hurting. It's a decision only you can make!

## THE SELF-DEFENSE PARADIGM/THE ACCEPTANCE PARADOX

The **self-defense paradigm** and the **acceptance paradox** are two opposite ways to defeat negative thoughts. When you use the self-defense paradigm, you argue with the negative thought and point out that it isn't true. The self-defense paradigm is based on the idea you should defend yourself from attack—even when the attack comes from within. When you use the acceptance paradox, you defeat the negative thought by agreeing with it with a sense of humor or inner peace.

Nearly everyone gravitates to the self-defense paradigm, and it can be helpful for certain kinds of negative thoughts, like "I'm always screwing up." It is pretty easy to show this negative thought isn't really true because you aren't *always* screwing up.

But sometimes the acceptance paradox is vastly more powerful. In fact, the acceptance paradox can catapult you into spiritual enlightenment. You can experience joy, inner peace, and liberation from your feelings of depression, anxiety, and self-doubt.

The acceptance paradox has always been one of my favorite techniques, and it's been extremely helpful for me personally. However, it can be difficult to grasp at first, even though it becomes totally obvious once you "see" it.

Here's the essence of how it works: Instead of criticizing yourself when you fail or fall short, you simply accept yourself as you are, warts and all. Paradoxically, *acceptance is often the greatest change a human being can make.* In fact, you may suddenly discover that self-acceptance and profound change are the same thing. This is a paradox, but once you understand it, it can be pretty awesome.

The acceptance paradox involves the death of the "self" or ego. Buddhists call this the "Great Death." The moment your ego dies, you will experience peace, joy, and renewal. And although *nothing* has changed, *everything* becomes different in a joyous and celebratory way. In chapter 27, you'll learn more about four "Great Deaths" that are involved in recovery from depression, anxiety, relationship problems, and habits and addictions.

To illustrate how the acceptance paradox works, let's take the thought "I should be better than I am" or "I shouldn't be so screwed up." Using the acceptance paradox, you could talk back to these thoughts along these lines:

*Yes, it would be wonderful to be better than I am. In fact, I have tons of flaws, and there's almost nothing about me that couldn't be improved!*

Do you see how that works? You learn to accept your flaws without hating yourself. When you use the acceptance paradox, you lower your standards. In fact, you might even lower them all the way to zero! That's what I've done. However, that's not easy to do, and for many years, I did not want to lower my perfectionistic standards.

You may feel the same way. You may think that as long as you berate yourself and punish yourself for your failures, you'll evolve into a better or even superior human being. This idea is woven into the very fabric of our culture and reflects the high standards you have for yourself.

There's another big reason why you may resist self-acceptance: You may not understand the difference between healthy versus unhealthy acceptance.

At my workshops for mental health professionals, I often ask how many of the therapists in the audience believe the thought "I'm defective." Nearly all the hands go up, and there's usually quite a bit of nervous laughter too.

Then I ask whether our defectiveness is a reason for celebration or suicide. I point out that one big advantage is that if we have a party tonight and invite all the "defective" people, we'll have a huge turnout. And we'll all have loads of fun because we won't have to try to impress anyone!

But people who are depressed can't easily get it at first. They think that because they're defective, they should kill themselves. They can't distinguish between healthy acceptance and unhealthy acceptance when it comes to the belief that they are defective. But what is the difference?

The following chart contrasts these two different ways of accepting the thought "I'm defective."

## Healthy Versus Unhealthy Acceptance: "I'm Defective."

| Unhealthy Acceptance | Healthy Acceptance |
|---|---|
| Self-hatred | Self-esteem |
| Despair | Joy |
| Paralysis | Productivity |
| Hopelessness | Hope |
| Isolation | Intimacy |
| Atrophy | Growth |
| Cynicism | Laughter |
| Confusion | Enlightenment |
| Death | Life |
| Antisocial behavior | Respect for others |

Unhealthy acceptance involves the belief that you really have accepted the horrible truth about yourself. That is, that you really are a defective or worthless person. Unhealthy acceptance is done in the spirit of bitterness and resignation, and it leads to feelings of despair, hopelessness, isolation, and even suicidal urges. I've had thousands of hours of therapy sessions with individuals who felt like this. Many were determined to kill or mutilate themselves because they felt so hopelessly defective.

In contrast, healthy acceptance leads to joy, intimacy, growth, hope, and unconditional self-esteem. In fact, you'll discover that you don't even need unconditional self-esteem. You can just get rid of it! Healthy acceptance leads to something far more precious than self-esteem: a robust appreciation of the miracle of life at every moment.

So now you've got lots of tools for challenging should statements. Review the negative thoughts in your Daily Mood Journal, and see if some of them contain should statements. If so, see if you can challenge them with some of the techniques you've learned about in this chapter:

- Positive reframing
- Semantic method
- Socratic method
- Double standard technique
- Self-defense paradigm
- Acceptance paradox

Your goal is to challenge the should statement with a positive thought that is 100% true and that substantially reduces your belief in the negative thought. However, your belief in the should statement does not have to go all the way to zero since should statements do contain some truth.

Record one of your negative thoughts here, and explain why it's a should statement:

_____

_____

_____

_____

_____

Now record your positive thought here:

_____

_____

_____

_____

_____

Were you able to reduce your belief in the negative thought? If not, don't worry! There are still many more techniques that you can use.

# 21 | Labeling

So far, you've learned about some helpful tools to combat all-or-nothing think-ing, overgeneralization, mental filtering, discounting the positive, jumping to conclusions, magnification and minimization, emotional reasoning, and should statements. Now we're going to focus on the ninth distortion: labeling.

In chapter 4, you read about Karen, the woman who thought she was a "bad mom" because of her daughter's trauma, and in chapter 7, you learned about Mark, who was convinced he was a "failure as a father" because he hadn't been able to form a close relationship with his oldest son. These are classic examples of labeling. There are negative and positive versions of this distortion:

- **Negative Labeling.** You attach a pejorative label to yourself or others. For example, you might think of yourself (or someone you don't like) as a "loser," "jerk," or worse. Labeling is simply an extreme form of overgener-alization because you view your (or someone else's) entire "self" as bad.

- **Positive Labeling.** You call yourself or someone else a "winner" because of some success you've had. For example, motivational speakers often inspire their audiences by promising that if you set goals and work hard, you can be a "winner" and achieve *anything*. Hey, that sounds pretty good, and it might motivate you to work really hard!

  The danger is that when you lose or fail, you might conclude that you're not a "winner" after all, and you might feel like a "loser" again. No one can win or succeed all the time. Failing is an inevitable part of the human experience and can be a vitally important source of growth and learning.

What's the best way to combat labeling? Two helpful techniques, among many others, are the Socratic method, which you learned about in the last chapter, and a new technique called worst, best, average, which is actually a combination of two techniques: be specific and thinking in shades of gray.

## THE SOCRATIC METHOD

Recall that the **Socratic method** involves asking yourself a series of questions that lead to the illogic of a negative thought. On one of my Sunday hikes, a high school teacher named Don confided to me that he felt like a "bad father" because he'd gotten impatient and shouted at his two sons when they weren't doing their chores around the house. He seemed on the verge of tears.

I asked Don if he felt like a "bad father" because he sometimes screwed up or treated his sons in a negative manner.

He said, "Exactly. That's why I feel like a bad father."

I then asked Don if he sometimes did positive things for his sons and treated them well. He said this was definitely the case and explained that he and his wife had bent over backward doing all kinds of positive things for them, like sending them to costly private schools, going on vacation to fun places, helping them with their homework, and doing tons of activities together as a family. In fact, that's why he felt hurt and angry when they were sluffing off—because they seemed ungrateful.

I asked Don if he was a "good father" when he was doing these "good things" for his sons.

He said, "Oh definitely!"

Then I asked, "So it sounds like you are a good father and a bad father at the same time? Is that what you're saying?"

Don laughed and suddenly got it. Instead of focusing on his screwup—shouting at his two sons—he was labeling himself in a vague, global way as a "bad father." You could argue that it's impossible to feel depressed without labeling and overgeneralizing. Depression exists in the clouds of abstraction. When you focus on what's real and make a specific plan for dealing with your error, the depression usually disappears.

Don and I focused on how he might share his feelings and concerns with his sons in a more effective manner using the five secrets of effective communication, which you learned about in chapter 17. He did a great job. When he returned for the Sunday hike a week later, he was feeling terrific and said that his chat with his sons had worked really well.

What happened was so simple and basic that it might not have been clear. Don gave up labeling, which triggered feelings of shame and worthlessness, and focused instead on solving the problem, which led to growth, joy, and a more loving relationship with his sons.

There's really no such thing as a good or bad father, a good or bad mother, or a good or bad anything. We're all pretty much somewhere in between all the time. But when you label your "self" in a global way because of some screwup, it hurts and distracts you from focusing on the specific error you made. Focusing on the specific error allows you to learn from it and grow.

If you find that any of the negative thoughts in your Daily Mood Journal are an example of labeling, write it down here and explain why it involves labeling.

_____

_____

_____

_____

_____

Now see if you can come up with a positive thought that helps you accept your specific failures and limitations without applying a global, negative label to yourself. Remember, you have to believe the thought 100%, and it must crush your belief in the negative thought.

_____

_____

_____

_____

_____

## WORST, BEST, AVERAGE

To use this technique, first select a negative thought that's been bothering you, like "I'm a bad father" (or a bad teacher, mother, spouse, daughter, salesperson, and so forth—it can be any negative label at all). To make it simple, let's take "I'm a bad teacher." Sometimes I think of myself that way, and it can be quite painful.

Next, make a list of some characteristics of a "good teacher." We might say that a good teacher has these qualities:

1. Presents interesting material

2. Prepares classes ahead of time

3. Explains things clearly

4. Makes the learning fun

5. Is patient with students who aren't getting it

6. Encourages students

7. Praises students for their strengths and points out errors in a kind way

8. Gives and reviews homework

9. Answers questions and challenges from students in a nondefensive, supportive way

10. Is a good listener and doesn't talk too much

Then rate yourself in each category on a scale from 0 (terrible) to 100 (outstanding) when you're at your worst, at your best, and on average. Your ratings don't have to be perfect, just take a stab at it.

I'll rate myself on a few of them to show you how it works.

| Some Qualities of a "Good Teacher" | At My Worst (0–100) | At My Best (0–100) | On Average (0–100) |
|---|---|---|---|
| 1. Presents interesting material | 25 | 95 | 75 |
| 2. Praises students for their strengths and points out errors in a kind way | 10 | 99 | 60 |
| 3. Makes the learning fun | 0 | 99 | 75 |
| 4. Answers questions and challenges in a nondefensive, supportive way | 0 | 99 | 50 |
| 5. Is a good listener and doesn't talk too much | 0 | 90 | 50 |

Once you've rated all the categories, you can choose some of the areas where you rated yourself poorly and make a plan to improve. For example, I think I'm usually okay on presenting interesting material, but sometimes I talk too much when explaining things or answering questions. And sometimes

I intimidate students and have a tendency to interrupt and talk over people who are asking questions.

My plan to improve would be:

1. Come to the point more quickly when explaining things, answering questions, or telling stories.
2. Get written feedback from students after every class so they can write down what they liked the least and the most.
3. Process their negative feedback in a warm and nondefensive manner so they'll feel that it's safe to be honest and open with me.
4. Resist the impulse to jump in when the other person is still talking.

Does this work? Or is it just nice words on paper?

Well, I actually focused on making those changes this summer at two intensive workshops. I made absolutely certain I treated every participant with warmth and respect, and although I didn't do this perfectly, it made a huge difference. In fact, my workshop evaluations were the highest I've received, by far, in the past twenty-five years. I was even delighted to receive enthusiastic standing ovations at both workshops.

How might worst, best, average help you?

When you label yourself as a "bad father" or "bad teacher" or whatever, you view yourself as some globally bad glob. You'll probably feel ashamed and demoralized, and you may even give up. In addition, because these labels do not provide you with any specific information on what you did or said that didn't work very well, you may end up feeling stuck, defective, defeated, and hopeless.

In contrast, when you list the characteristics of a "good" father, teacher, or whatever, you're focusing on *specific* skills or behaviors rather than judging your entire "self" in a global, mean-spirited way.

Then when you rate yourself on these characteristics at your worst, at your best, and on average, you are thinking in shades of gray, and you can see that you have a range on all these qualities. Nothing is black or white. Sometimes you're doing better, and sometimes you're doing worse. And most of the time, you're somewhere in between. But you may never be at 0 or 100 because it could always be worse, and it could always be better.

And finally, when you make a plan for improvement, you focus on positive things that can result in change. So instead of feeling depressed, anxious, ashamed, defective, or hopeless, you're involved in the experience of self-acceptance, growth, and learning.

It's a fairly humble method, but it can be surprisingly helpful. If you've had any negative thoughts that involve labeling, and you'd like to give it a try, you can use the worst, best, average form on the next page.

# WORST, BEST, AVERAGE*

Choose a statement in which you apply a harsh critical label to yourself, like "I'm a loser," "I'm a bad mother," or "I'm a failure." Then write down the opposite of the label that you have applied to yourself. For instance, the opposite of a "bad mother" may be an "adequate mother," a "good mother," a "good-enough mother," or a "great mother."

Write the label here: _____

| List at Least Five Qualities That Are the Opposite of the Negative Label (e.g., a "good" husband, wife, partner, therapist, parent, human) | At Your Worst (0–100) | At Your Best (0–100) | On Average (0–100) |
|---|---|---|---|
| 1. | | | |
| 2. | | | |
| 3. | | | |
| 4. | | | |
| 5. | | | |
| 6. | | | |
| 7. | | | |
| 8. | | | |
| 9. | | | |
| 10. | | | |

Now focus on one specific quality or characteristic that you'd like to improve, and list a few specific steps that you could take to improve in that area:

1. _____

2. _____

3. _____

4. _____

5. _____

# 22 | Self-Blame and Other-Blame

In my first book, *Feeling Good*, I wrote about a young physician named Nadine who became suicidal after her younger brother, Nick, tragically died by suicide. Nick had struggled with heroin addiction and severe depression after coming home from the Vietnam War, but Nadine loved him tremendously and was totally devoted to him. She felt her parents had loved her more when they were growing up, so she felt to blame for Nick's depression and did everything she could to help him. She encouraged him to go to school to become a respiratory therapist and even paid for his psychiatric treatment.

One evening, Nick called Nadine to ask about the effects of carbon monoxide on the blood. He said he needed the information for a report he was writing for his respiratory therapy class. She was annoyed he was calling so often because she was busy preparing a presentation for the next day, so she gave him a brief answer and got off the phone.

Nick parked his car under the window of Nadine's apartment and connected a hose from the exhaust pipe into the passenger compartment. He turned on the engine, and the police found him slumped over in the driver's seat a couple of hours later. They rushed him to the hospital where he was pronounced dead on arrival.

Nadine was stunned and told herself, "I *should* have known he was suicidal when he called. His death was my fault, so I deserve to die too."

As you can imagine, Nadine's self-blame triggered unbearable pain and nearly cost Nadine her life. In my opinion, the suicide of a loved one is one of the most devastating shocks a human being can experience. Many people who've experienced this type of loss suffer from depression, shame, guilt, and anger for years or even decades.

People behave very differently when they're depressed. Many give up on their normal activities and don't even want to get out of bed because they're convinced that nothing could be rewarding or worth doing. And, like Nadine, many give up on life itself. In fact, most people with depression as severe as Nadine's would end up in the hospital.

Nadine was different. In spite of her extreme depression, she'd been working 18 hours a day as a compassionate and dedicated pediatrician, working with severely ill children in the hospital and bringing them hope and cheer in spite of how devastated she felt. If you had interacted with her, you would not have guessed that she was dying inside.

You learned about the Socratic method in the last couple of chapters, so it might not be surprising that it can sometimes be helpful for self-blame as well since shoulds and blame often go together. You may recall that when you use the Socratic method, you ask yourself a series of questions that will lead you to the illogic and unfairness of what you're telling yourself.

Around the fifth or sixth therapy session, I asked Nadine, "If you had known your brother was suicidal that day, would you have intervened to save his life?"

She immediately agreed that she *definitely* would have done that. She said she loved him tremendously and would have done anything to save his life.

Next, I asked if she was aware that he was suicidal that day. She said she didn't realize he was feeling desperate and just thought he was preparing for his class.

Then I asked if the world's best psychiatrists could consistently predict and prevent suicides. She said that they couldn't since almost all psychiatrists have patients who die by suicide.

I followed up by asking Nadine if *anyone* could consistently predict the future, and she said, "Only God can predict the future."

So I said:

*You've been blaming yourself for your brother's death and telling yourself that you* should *have known he was suicidal that day. This shows how much you loved him and how committed you were to him. But are you saying you're like God? Can you predict the future?*

Nadine began to cry and admitted she couldn't. This realization helped her let go of the intense shame and guilt she was struggling with, and after a few additional sessions, she was no longer depressed. The key to her recovery was learning how to talk back to the should statements and self-blame that were causing such unbearable feelings of failure, guilt, despair, and hopelessness.

And once she was no longer depressed, she was able to grieve her brother's tragic loss and move ahead with her own life. Paradoxically, she'd been stuck and unable to grieve because of her depression.

There are two common forms of blame:

- **Self-Blame.** You find fault and blame yourself for some shortcoming, flaw, error, or screwup, so you use up all your energy feeling guilty or frustrated instead of pinpointing the actual cause of the problem and making a plan to grow and learn from it.

  Self-blame nearly always goes hand in hand with should statements directed against yourself. Nadine was also telling herself, "I *should* have known he was suicidal."

- **Other-Blame.** You find fault with someone else or the world and convince yourself that you're the innocent victim of the other person's badness. Other-blame nearly always goes hand in hand with should statements directed against other people or the world.

Some people struggle with self-blame and other-blame at the same time. I call this particularly toxic combination the "blame beacon" because the blame goes round and round, just like the beacon on a lighthouse. Part of the time you're telling yourself that you're no good, and part of the time you're telling yourself that someone else is no good, so you oscillate between feelings of guilt ("I'm no good") and rage ("You're no good").

A psychiatrist colleague named Megan found herself in this trap. She felt intensely ashamed, anxious, inadequate, and demoralized because one of her patients—a chronically depressed woman named Helga—had been hospitalized following an unexpected and severe suicide attempt. Megan was greatly relieved Helga had survived but blamed herself for the suicide attempt. She'd struggled with Helga for nearly a year with little or no progress and was telling herself that she *should* have been more skillful and able to help more.

Megan told me:

*The suicide attempt was extremely upsetting to me, one of the worst events of my career. It was devastating and kept me up at night. I had a whole host of negative emotions and kept reviewing the situation in my mind, over and over again, wondering if I should have done something differently.*

*I felt extremely worried about her and her family and was so relieved she was not successful in the suicide attempt. She jumped off a bridge, so it was a very serious attempt and she required a long recovery.*

Megan was also angry and blamed Helga for the lack of therapeutic progress. Helga had complained endlessly about her husband, her children, and

her fate during psychotherapy sessions but seemed to have little or no interest in learning any tools for change, and she rarely completed her homework
assignments between sessions. She'd complain that she'd been "too tired" or
"forgot" and seemed addicted to self-pity, bitterness, and unhappiness.

I don't mean to be overly critical of Helga and apologize if it sounds that
way. We all have times when we feel sorry for ourselves and want to complain
about things. At least I know I do!

Nor do I mean to be critical of Megan. Seemingly endless complaining
is rarely or never helpful and can be pretty darn frustrating to the therapist
who's trying to help.

You can see the self-blame and other-blame in Megan's negative thoughts,
along with self-directed and other-directed should statements. She was telling
herself:

1. I should have treated Helga more effectively.

2. Her suicide attempt was my fault.

3. She shouldn't have been so resistant and rigid.

4. She should have worked harder to overcome her depression. She should
   have done her psychotherapy homework.

5. She shouldn't complain so much.

6. She should have told me she was feeling suicidal.

I'm a little worried that you might be taken aback by the fact that a highly
trained, highly regarded mental health professional could have such strong
negative feelings about a patient. But I have to confess that we are quite
human in spite of the fact that we are presumably "experts," and we are definitely not exempt from the same kinds of negative feelings that our patients
experience.

That's why personal healing is so incredibly important for mental health
professionals. The rewards of our profession can be enormous—when you
see a patient suddenly recover, the joy is incredible. But the stresses of working with seriously depressed and unstable individuals can also be enormous.
There's a dark side to our profession.

That's one of the reasons I do free weekly psychotherapy training, including personal work, at Stanford for local mental health professionals. We all
need a little tune-up from time to time—a chance to get unburdened and

develop a more positive lease on life again. I believe the therapist's inner feelings of joy and peace can have a profound impact on the therapist's effectiveness and that no therapist should have to work in the trenches alone without ongoing support and learning.

## POSITIVE REFRAMING

Now let's see if we can help Megan. Remember the basic premise of cognitive therapy: Your thoughts, and not external events, create your feelings. So although Helga's suicide attempt was understandably disturbing, Megan's negative feelings resulted from her negative thoughts about herself and her patient.

But before we try to change the way Megan is thinking, let's step back and ask ourselves: What do these negative thoughts and feelings show about her that's positive and awesome? And what are some benefits of thinking and feeling this way?

Please list as many positives as you can think for both self-blame and other-blame before you continue reading.

### Positives of Self-Blame

1. _____
2. _____
3. _____
4. _____
5. _____

### Positives of Other-Blame

1. _____
2. _____
3. _____
4. _____
5. _____

When you're done, turn the page to see the lists Megan and I came up with. But please don't look until you've written something down!

These are the positives Megan and I came up with. Your list is likely to be different, which is fine, and you may have thought of a number of positives that did not cross our minds.

### Positives of Self-Blame

1. The self-blame shows that Megan holds herself accountable and is willing to examine her own errors.

2. The self-blame shows that Megan has high standards.

3. Megan's high standards have helped her and motivated her. In spite of this shocking event, Megan is actually an extraordinarily skilled and compassionate psychiatrist.

4. The self-blame shows that Megan wants to learn and grow so she can improve her therapy skills with extremely challenging patients.

5. The self-blame shows humility.

6. The self-blame is realistic since she could have treated her patient differently and perhaps more effectively.

7. The self-blame is a reflection of her strong commitment to an extremely difficult, resistant patient.

### Positives of Other-Blame

1. Megan's other-blame and feelings of anger show that she has a moral compass.

2. Megan's other-blame and feelings of anger show that she holds her patient accountable since her patient has been acting irresponsibly.

3. Sharing her anger and frustration in a kind, respectful way could be helpful to her patient and might break the therapeutic logjam. This is contrary to the philosophy held by many mental health professionals, who are taught to hide their feelings. A frank dialogue with a patient about a therapeutic logjam can often lead to a therapeutic breakthrough.

4. Megan's anger shows that she is human and vulnerable and that she cares deeply about her patients.

After we listed all the positives, Megan decided she wanted to dial down her negative thoughts and feelings without getting rid of them entirely. It was also helpful and a bit surprising for her to see that what she thought of as negative feelings were actually reflections of her tremendous strengths, compassion, and high standards.

## SEMANTIC TECHNIQUE

One technique that is particularly helpful in challenging thoughts that involve self-blame and other-blame is the **semantic technique**. If you recall from chapter 20, the semantic technique simply involves substituting your blaming statements with language that is softer and less demanding. It works the same way as it did for should statements. For example, instead of saying "I should have" or "She should have," you use phrases like "it would be preferable if," or something along those lines.

Megan was able to successfully use this technique to replace her blaming statements with language that was less critical. But before I show you how she did this, try putting yourself in Megan's shoes first and see if you can challenge her negative thoughts using the semantic technique (or any other techniques that appeal to you). To the right of each negative thought listed here, see if you can come up with a positive thought that is 100% true and that can crush the negative thought.

When you do this exercise, keep in mind that Megan is, in fact, a very skillful and compassionate therapist. Her error (if any) in working with Helga was failing to set limits when Helga consistently failed to follow through on psychotherapy homework. This was arguably an error of simply having too much compassion or niceness.

Sometimes it's easier to see through someone else's negative thoughts than your own, so this will give you a chance to practice. Give it a shot! When you're done, continue reading to see what Megan and I came up with.

| Negative Thoughts | Positive Thoughts |
|---|---|
| 1. I should have treated Helga more effectively. | |
| 2. Her suicide attempt was my fault. | |
| 3. She shouldn't have been so resistant and rigid. | |

| | |
|---|---|
| 4. She should have worked harder to overcome her depression. She should have done her psychotherapy homework. | |
| 5. She shouldn't complain so much. | |
| 6. She should have told me she was feeling suicidal. | |

## My Answer

Here is what Megan and I came up with:

| Negative Thoughts | Positive Thoughts |
|---|---|
| 1. I should have treated Helga more effectively. | *I definitely wish* I had treated her more effectively, but I did my best, and telling myself that I should have known what to do just doesn't seem very helpful or compassionate. |
| 2. Her suicide attempt was my fault. | *I wish I'd known* how hopeless she was feeling so I could have intervened, but she had a lot to do with it. I can be responsible for the treatment I offer, but I cannot be totally responsible for what she does or doesn't do. |
| 3. She shouldn't have been so resistant and rigid. | *I really wish* she weren't so resistant and that she'd be more open to working together as a team. But her rigidity is one of her main problems. If she weren't resistant and rigid, then she probably wouldn't need treatment! |
| 4. She should have worked harder to overcome her depression. She should have done her psychotherapy homework. | *I really would have liked* for her to work harder, but it makes no sense to say she *should* have done these things. That sounds like she's breaking some kind of law, which is ridiculous. If she returns for therapy, I can require homework as a condition for us to work together again. |
| 5. She shouldn't complain so much. | *It would be terrific if* she didn't complain so much, and it's one of the therapy goals. But she will probably continue to complain until she has recovered because that's the pattern she's trapped in right now, and that's why she's coming for treatment. |
| 6. She should have told me she was feeling suicidal. | *While I wish* she would have told me, she may have been feeling ashamed or afraid that I would intervene and hospitalize her involuntarily. If we work together again, I can encourage her to talk about this problem and provide support for her. |

Megan said that talking back to her negative thoughts was exceptionally helpful, and she felt at peace and confident in her skills again. But she said it was also really interesting to "discover," once again, that her angst was not the result of her patient's horrifying suicide attempt but from the way she was thinking about it.

Even those of us who are highly experienced mental health professionals, like Megan, fall into black holes from time to time. It's just a part of being human. But once we do our own personal healing, it can also help us do more effective therapy because we can say, "I know how horrible it is to feel anxious, worthless, and angry—because I've been there myself! And what a joy it's going to be when I show you how to find your way out of the woods!"

## REATTRIBUTION

With the **reattribution** technique, instead of blaming yourself (or someone else) entirely for something bad that happened, you examine all the possible factors that contributed to it. For example, an extremely shy young man named Nathaniel was standing in the checkout line at the grocery store one Saturday morning. He thought the checkout woman might have been eyeing him up, and he wanted to flirt with her but was terrified that she'd turn him down and that he'd make a fool of himself.

When he got to the front of the line, he was so nervous that he simply stared at the counter while she checked his groceries. She said, "That will be $9.96." He handed her $10 and kept staring at the counter while she gave him his change. He walked out of the store feeling humiliated and told himself he'd wimped out again.

Nathaniel's negative thought—"If she rejects me, it will mean that I'm a loser"—was a classic example of self-blame, as well as many additional distortions, including:

- **All-or-Nothing Thinking.** He thinks he's either a "winner" or a "loser."
- **Overgeneralization.** He's generalizing from one experience to his entire "self."
- **Mind Reading.** He's assuming, without evidence, that she wouldn't be interested in him.
- **Magnification.** He thinks it's a *really* big deal to flirt with someone who's not interested.

- **Emotional Reasoning.** He felt like a loser, so he assumed she'd see him the same way.
- **Labeling.** He felt like rejection would make him a "loser."
- **Hidden Should Statement.** "I should never get rejected" and "I should be able to sweep her off her feet."

To use reattribution with Nathaniel, I asked him to list all the possible reasons why a young woman checking groceries might not respond positively to a young man's attempts to flirt with her. See what you can come up with. I think you'll have fun with this exercise, and it's not terribly difficult. When you're done, continue reading to see what Nathaniel and I came up with.

1. _____

2. _____

3. _____

4. _____

5. _____

6. _____

7. _____

8. _____

9. _____

10. _____

## My Answer

Here is the list that Nathaniel and I came up with:

1. It might be against store policy.

2. She may be married or have a boyfriend.

3. The grocery store manager may be watching.

4. She may get tired of guys hitting on her all the time.

5. I may not be her cup of tea. She might prefer guys who are older, younger, or of some different ethnic group.

6. She may be shy.

7. She may be in a bad mood.

8. She may be gay.

9. She may be feeling sick.

10. She may be turned off because I'm not very good at flirting yet.

The list was a great relief to Nathaniel, and he made two important decisions. First, he decided it was okay to try flirting (and potentially get rejected) since he was just learning the ropes of how to flirt and talk to women. Second, he decided that he did not need to say anything terribly clever or awesome when he approached attractive women. Instead, he could just smile and say hello, and that would be a huge first step whether or not they responded positively.

I also told Nathaniel that I wanted him to use a number of interpersonal exposure techniques to help him overcome his shyness, including:

1. **Smile and Hello Practice.** Smile and say hello to at least five strangers every day even if it makes you intensely anxious.

2. **Talk Show Host.** Shy individuals typically believe they have to talk about themselves or say something terribly clever to impress people. This typically turns people off. Instead, I asked Nathaniel to study talk show hosts, like Jimmy Fallon, who make a living talking to strangers on national television. What techniques do they use?

    For the most part, they use other-centered conversational techniques and rarely talk about themselves or try to say anything impressive. They encourage their guests to talk about themselves, compliment them, and ask them questions so they'll open up even more. Most people really like it when you express a genuine interest in them.

    I encouraged Nathaniel to do the same, wherever he was, every day.

3. **Self-Disclosure.** Every day, tell at least one person (either strangers or people you know) that you've been struggling with shyness and that you've been incredibly ashamed and hiding it, but you're not hiding it anymore, and that's why you're telling them.

4. **Survey Technique.** Ask people if they've ever felt shy or awkward in social situations, if they sometimes look down on people who are shy, or if they think less of you for being shy.

5. **Shame-Attacking Exercises.** Do something crazy or bizarre in public to get over your fear of people looking down on you or thinking that you're weird. For example, approach a group of strangers in a mall and tell them, "I wish to entertain you with a song." Then ask what song they'd like to hear, and belt it out!

6. **Rejection Practice.** When you talk to women (or men) you're attracted to, ask them out in a friendly and respectful way even if you think they might reject you. Try to collect at least five rejections per week. If you get a date, you don't get a point. You only get points for rejections. The goal is to collect as many rejections as possible!

Nathaniel found the assignment frightening but exciting, and although he had his share of rejections, he had quite a few successes as well, and before long, his social life was blossoming.

One final note about reattribution before moving on to the next technique. This technique, like any, can be abused. Sometimes people use reattribution as a defense against feeling worthless when they're criticized or rejected by someone they care about. They tell themselves that the other person is a jerk or a loser.

This is just switching from self-blame to other-blame. To me, this isn't very realistic or productive because the people who criticize us or feel annoyed with us aren't, in fact, "jerks" or "losers."

So how can you deal with other-blame when you're feeling really annoyed with someone? Do a cost-benefit analysis!

## COST-BENEFIT ANALYSIS

The **cost-benefit analysis** is one of the easiest and most useful techniques when you are feeling angry and blaming someone for a conflict or problem in your relationship. You simply list the advantages and disadvantages of blaming the other person and then balance them against each other on a 100-point scale. You may discover that you don't want to stop blaming others, which is fine, but the cost-benefit analysis will definitely help you decide.

Below, you will see a cost-benefit analysis from my book, *Feeling Good Together*. As you can see, there are *lots* of compelling advantages of blame. For example, it's super easy, and you can feel superior to the person you're blaming. In addition, you don't have to examine your own role in the problem, and you can tell yourself that you're right and that the other person is wrong. We all like to feel like we're on the side of "truth"! There are at least twenty more advantages as well.

But there are also some possible disadvantages. One big problem is that you'll be totally stuck because there's simply no way to get close to someone you're blaming. In addition, the other person will nearly always get defensive and blame you back, which can be exasperating. You'll also be embroiled in anger and hostility, which can be pretty exhausting.

## Blame Cost-Benefit Analysis*

| Advantages of Blaming the Other Person | Disadvantages of Blaming the Other Person |
|---|---|
| 1. It's easy. I won't have to change. | 1. Nothing will change. |
| 2. I can feel self-righteous and morally superior. | 2. This attitude will turn the other person off. |
| 3. I won't have to get close to the other person. I can keep him or her at a distance. | 3. We won't be able to develop a better relationship. |
| 4. I'll feel powerful. | 4. I'll be powerless to resolve the conflict. |
| 5. I'll be convinced that the problem really *is* the other person's fault. This lets me off the hook. | 5. The other person will be equally convinced that the problem is all my fault. We'll blame each other endlessly, and no one will give in. |
| 6. Truth will be on my side. I'll feel like I'm right and the other person is wrong. | 6. The other person will be equally convinced that I'm wrong and that he or she is right. |
| 7. I can play the role of victim. | 7. The role of victim can get tiresome. I may get addicted to self-pity. |
| 8. I won't have to feel vulnerable. It feels safe. | 8. I'll hide my feelings, and the other person won't see how I really feel inside. |
| 9. Blaming the other person will protect my self-esteem and pride. | 9. I'll deprive myself of any chance for love or intimacy. |
| 10. I won't have to feel guilty. | 10. I may feel guilty anyway. |

* Copyright © 2019 by David D. Burns, MD.

| | |
|---|---|
| 11. I can hide my faults and deny my own role in the problem. | 11. I'll be blind to my role in the problem and may have an overly positive view of myself. |
| 12. I won't have to experience the pain and humiliation of self-examination. I won't have to feel ashamed. | 12. I won't grow or learn anything new. |
| 13. I'll show that I can't be pushed around or taken advantage of. | 13. I'll give the other person the power to control me by pushing my buttons. |
| 14. I can fantasize about getting revenge on the other person. | 14. The other person may fantasize about getting revenge on me. |
| 15. I can do mean and petty things and tell myself that he or she deserves it. | 15. The other person may retaliate. |
| 16. I can get back at the other person and do nasty things behind his or her back. | 16. I may hurt him or her. |
| 17. I can tell myself that I have *every right* to be angry. | 17. I also have the right to feel happy. |
| 18. The anger will give my life purpose and meaning. | 18. I may get trapped in my anger. |
| 19. Life will seem dramatic and exciting. The conflict will make me feel special and important. | 19. The constant fighting can be exhausting, demoralizing, and a waste of time. |
| 20. I can gossip about what a loser the other person is and get sympathy from others. | 20. People may get tired of my complaining. |
| 21. I can scapegoat the other person and look down on him or her. | 21. This may set a bad example for friends and family members. |
| 22. I can tell myself that the other person is a jerk and that he or she is not worth the effort. | 22. This mindset may function as a self-fulfilling prophecy. |
| 23. I can put up a wall and take pot shots at the other person. | 23. I may keep smashing into the wall that I've created. |
| 24. I can reject the other person. | 24. I'll lose the chance to solve the problem and get close to him or her. |
| 25. I can comfort myself by overeating, drinking, or using drugs. | 25. The constant resentment may lead to headaches, fatigue, or high blood pressure. |

Now that you have a sense of how a blame cost-benefit analysis works, try it out yourself. Look through your Daily Mood Journal and see if any of your negative thoughts involve blaming others. If so, list the advantages and disadvantages of continuing to blame the other person using the chart here.

Once you've listed all the advantages and disadvantages you can think of, balance them against each other on a 100-point scale. Ask yourself whether the advantages or disadvantages are greater, and put two numbers adding up to 100 in the circles at the bottom of this chart that reflect your evaluation.

Don't worry about how many things you've listed in each column because sometimes one big advantage can outweigh many disadvantages and vice versa. Instead, evaluate how the two lists compare overall.

## Blame Cost-Benefit Analysis

| Advantages of Blaming the Other Person | Disadvantages of Blaming the Other Person |
|---|---|
| | |

What should you do if the advantages of blame are greater? You don't actually have to do anything! You can just keep blaming the other person. Go for it! There's no reason to change if something is working for you.

What should you do if you put 50 in both circles? I would give you the same advice. Change can be hard, and relationship conflicts can be especially challenging, and there's really no reason to put out all that energy when there's a standoff without any clear-cut reason to change.

And if the disadvantages of blame are greater, what then? Well, you can try talking back to your other-blaming statements with the semantic technique, just as you did in the exercise with Megan. But if you're feeling really ambitious, you might want to try a really cool and illuminating method called forced empathy.

## FORCED EMPATHY

I created the **forced empathy** technique more than twenty years ago, but it was kind of dormant for a while because I didn't promote it very much, and it only worked part of the time. However, I recently figured out why this technique sometimes works fantastically well and sometimes falls flat. It all depends on whether you really want to get close to someone you're at odds with. If you do, this technique can work like magic. If you don't, then no technique in the world will be helpful to you, including forced empathy.

Here's how it works. Let's imagine that you're really annoyed with someone and you're blaming him or her for something. Because you don't really know how that person is thinking or feeling, you'll make up all kinds of explanations for his or her behavior. For example, you may tell yourself that the other person is a "jerk" or "bitch." Or you may tell yourself that he or she always has to be right, never listens, or simply doesn't understand or care about you.

These thoughts nearly always involve many cognitive distortions, including other-blame, and they will trigger you to feel and act in negative ways. For example, because you feel angry, frustrated, or hurt, you may treat the other person in a defensive, adversarial, or hostile manner. Then the other person will inevitably get defensive and nasty, and you'll tell yourself, "See, I was right! He really is a total jerk!"

Now you've trapped yourself in a self-fulfilling prophecy. You feel like a victim because you're not aware of how you might be triggering and reinforcing the other person's nasty behavior.

Of course, there's no reason for you to change unless you want a better relationship. There's no rule that says we have to try to get along with everybody. But if you want a better relationship and you'd prefer to get close to that person again, then forced empathy might be very helpful to you.

The goal of forced empathy is to see if you can develop a deeper form of understanding with the person you're not getting along with. When you suddenly see the conflict through the eyes of the person you're mad at, things can sometimes fall into a radically different perspective.

To do so, you play the role of the person you're annoyed with while someone else plays the role of a good friend of that person. In the role play, you have to agree to the following rules:

1. When you are playing the role of the person you're annoyed with, you have to agree to tell the truth, the whole truth, and nothing but the

truth. In fact, we can pretend you've taken truth serum, so you have to speak the truth.

2. You are not allowed to be defensive, to rationalize, or to deny anything.

3. You have to agree to speak, as best you can, on behalf of the other person's conscious and subconscious mind.

Here's an example of how it works.

During a consultation group two years ago, a dear colleague, Dr. Jill Levitt, mentioned that she'd been feeling sad, annoyed, and frustrated because of an ongoing conflict with her oldest son, Alex, who was 12 and in the sixth grade. Alex was wanting more freedom and was picking fights on anything that involved setting limits. For example, he complained about his bedtime, he wanted more time to play video games, and he rolled his eyes when Jill would remind him to put his things away or to do his homework.

Jill understood Alex's need for greater independence but was hurt and upset over how argumentative he'd become. Although she had given him more freedom—including later bedtimes, the right to ride his bike to his friends' houses, and his first cell phone—he was still snapping at her for babying him. She wondered what was happening with her child and didn't understand why he was so annoyed with her.

Richard Lam, a colleague in the group, suggested she try the forced empathy technique. All the therapists in TEAM-CBT try to practice what we preach. We use the tools we've developed on ourselves when we fall into a black hole of self-doubt or, in this case, a painful conflict with a loved one. That way, we can refine our skills and find out if our tools actually work. After all, we are sometimes our most challenging patients!

Richard asked Jill to play the role of Alex, while he played one of Alex's friends. He asked Jill to close her eyes, imagine she was Alex, and tell him about his relationship with his mother. Jill explained that the moment she closed her eyes, she could see Alex and began to feel tearful.

Here's how the forced empathy dialogue unfolded:

**Richard (playing the role of a friend of Alex):** I've heard that you're ticked off at your mom. Tell me about it. What's it all about?

**Jill (playing the role of Alex):** She's always bugging me and reminding me to do this or do that. I'm a bright kid, and I'm really responsible. I have friends who like me, and I'm good at taking care of myself. I do my homework on time without being asked. I have a great relationship with my mom, and I love her a lot, but she's on top of me *all the time*. She's always reminding me to do things that I would remember to do on my own. She's always checking up on me.

**Richard (playing the role of a friend of Alex):** How does that make you feel?

**Jill (playing the role of Alex):** I feel like she doesn't trust me or think I'm capable of taking care of myself.

**Richard (playing the role of a friend of Alex):** What do you want to tell your mom?

**Jill (playing the role of Alex):** I want to tell my mom that I'm a really good kid, that I can make good choices, and that she doesn't have to watch me all the time. I want to tell her that she should trust me and believe in me more than she does.

Jill immediately began bawling and described the impact of what had just occurred. She explained that she suddenly realized she had not been aware of Alex's more tender feelings, only his annoyance and combativeness. She hadn't seen his vulnerable side since she usually thought of him as so competent.

She could also see that she was treating him like a little kid and that he did not deserve that treatment. She said he had earned his independence, and she was making him feel like she didn't trust him. She had not told Alex how proud she was of him and how mature and responsible he was, and it was painful to see that those were the very things she was undermining.

After that, she went back and told Alex that she realized he was growing up and that letting go was *her* struggle. She explained that her role had always been to be the caretaker and organizer but that she sometimes overdid it, and that was *her* struggle and not his fault in any way. She told Alex that she saw him as incredibly responsible, and she realized she was making him feel like she didn't believe in him. She explained that learning to let go was a project she was working on.

He definitely liked that and totally understood!

I hope you found that example of forced empathy interesting. It can be powerful and helpful, especially if you have a strong desire for a more loving relationship with a friend, family member, or colleague you've been feuding with.

If you find self-blame or other-blame in your negative thoughts, remember that many of the techniques discussed in this chapter can be helpful for these distortions, including positive reframing, reattribution, cost-benefit analysis, and forced empathy.

Be aware, though, that resistance to change can be intense when you're blaming yourself or someone else. Blame is extremely addictive. If you're blaming yourself, then your high standards may be keeping you stuck, and if you're blaming someone else, then your anger and feelings of moral superiority may be keeping you stuck. That's why blame is usually the toughest distortion to challenge, by far, and why anger is usually the toughest emotion to overcome.

That's also why it's always a good idea to start out with a motivational technique, like positive reframing or a cost-benefit analysis, if you're trying to crush a negative thought that involves self-blame or other-blame. If you decide that you're tired of beating up on yourself or others, then the techniques in this chapter, as well as many others I've described in this book, can be very helpful to you!

Now you have several tools under your belt to crush every type of cognitive distortion. But keep in mind that I've only given you a starter kit and that there are many more amazing techniques. If you review the list in chapter 33, you'll see that there are actually fifty techniques to help you change the way you think and feel so you can start to feel great again!

# The Spiritual/Philosophical Dimension: The Four "Great Deaths" of the Self

# 23 | Do You Have a Self? Do You Need One?

Are you afraid of being judged? Do you sometimes feel inferior or worry that others will look down on you if they find out about your flaws or how you really feel inside?

If you're like most people, you're convinced that you have a "self" or "identity" that can be measured or judged based on your income, intelligence, talent, success, appearance, race, social status, or some other criterion. And when you're feeling down or insecure, you may feel like your "self" is flawed or just not good enough. This belief triggers feelings of depression, anxiety, shame, worthlessness, loneliness, hopelessness, and more.

As you can see, you sometimes have to pay a pretty heavy price for believing that you have a "self."

The other night, I had pizza with a friend named Jonathan, who told me he's struggled with an inner bully for the past nine years. This relentless, self-critical voice tells him that he is a "failure" because he does not have a sufficiently high-paying, prestigious career and because he has not yet found the love of his life. These thoughts create intense feelings of inadequacy that don't wear off until the end of the day, only to resurface with renewed ferociousness the next morning.

Of course, there is always some truth to our self-criticisms. Jonathan recently lost out on a bid for an important commercial painting job he'd put a lot of work into. Although his bid was the second best, he did not get the contract and the much-needed income.

In addition, his relationship with his former girlfriend has been rocky at times. Although they're no longer romantically involved, she's the mother of his child, so they have a co-parenting arrangement. When he visits, she's often critical of Jonathan, and the conflicts typically escalate. Jonathan told me,

"They're just like the arguments my parents had when I was growing up. It's something I was determined to avoid in my own life."

Jonathan is not alone. Many people feel like they aren't good enough because their careers have fallen short or because they haven't found the loving relationship they've always dreamed about. Still, Jonathan has supported himself and two other employees with his commercial painting business. And while his relationship with his ex is rocky, he's had good relationships with many women in the past, and he's the proud and loving father of an adorable, 1-year-old son. But when he tells himself that he's a "failure," the thought appears to be the absolute truth, and his pain is palpable.

Jonathan believes he has a "self" that isn't good enough. And that's the root cause of his emotional pain.

Feelings of inadequacy seem almost universal, at least among the people I know. Last week, I met a young Jamaican woman named Janelle who confessed that she has also been plagued by chronic feelings of depression, anxiety, and shame ever since she was a child.

When Janelle was growing up, her mother and older sister told her that her brown skin was inferior and that she had to try to act "white" in order to be accepted. They also told her that she was not interesting and that no one would really want to get to know her.

To this day, Janelle continues to struggle with low self-esteem and still believes people won't find her interesting. Yet she has a loving husband, a PhD from a top university, and is doing important research at a prestigious medical center. But her inner voice insists that she's still "not good enough."

Even people with few assets struggle with the same feelings of self-doubt and inadequacy. When I lived in Philadelphia, I developed a ten-step therapy program for the people our hospital served, which was based on my book, *Ten Days to Self-Esteem*. The hospital was in a pretty rough neighborhood with lots of drug use, crime, and gang activity. Many patients had severe mental health problems with limited resources, and quite a few couldn't read or write. Some were homeless.

One afternoon, I was leading a therapy group and asked the patients if they could describe a specific time when they felt a loss of self-esteem. A homeless man named Juan explained how he felt whenever he saw someone wearing a suit and tie walk past him on the sidewalk:

*I tell myself that he has a job, that he has a bed to sleep on at night and a family who loves him. I sleep on the sidewalk. I didn't even make it through the*

*fifth grade. I've never had a job. I've never contributed anything to anybody.*
*I'm just a leech on society. I feel like a totally worthless human being.*

There were tears rolling down his cheeks. As you can see, Juan's concerns
were surprisingly similar to the concerns of Jonathan and Janelle—he also
believed that his "self" wasn't good enough.

Maybe you've sometimes felt that way too. Have you? Have you ever felt:

- Inferior to friends or colleagues who seem more successful, attractive, or
  popular?
- Defective or ashamed because of some flaw you've been hiding?
- Afraid that others will look down on you if they see you as you really are,
  warts and all?
- Shy or awkward in social settings, fearing that others will judge you if you
  say something foolish or look nervous and insecure?
- Afraid of public speaking, worrying that your mind might go blank or that
  you'll mumble and make a complete fool of yourself?
- Inadequate or ashamed because you think you aren't smart or successful
  enough?
- Worthless or unlovable because you were rejected by someone you care
  about or because you don't have a meaningful relationship with someone
  you love?

Although there probably are some lucky individuals who feel happy and
confident nearly all the time, I'm convinced most of us struggle with insecurity and self-doubt at times. Even though I'm generally a pretty happy guy,
I've struggled with these same feelings too, so I know how intensely painful—
even agonizing—it can be.

For example, I had the opportunity to present at the 2017 Evolution of
Psychotherapy Conference in Anaheim, California. This event has been called
the "Woodstock of Psychotherapy" because it features dozens of the biggest
names in the world of psychotherapy and draws thousands of therapists from
all over the world. You'd think I'd have been happy and excited to be included
in such a prestigious event, but that wasn't how I felt inside.

My first two presentations drew approximately 1,000 people and seemed
to go reasonably well or perhaps even very well. But afterward, I began obsess-
ing about the errors I'd made and felt deflated because I didn't hit it out of

the park at one of my presentations. It was decent but perhaps not amazing or awesome. I started feeling down and noticed I was telling myself:

- I don't belong here.
- I'm out of my league.
- I should have done better.
- I'm just a has-been. My best days are in the past.
- The field has moved on without me and has left me in the dust.

It was painful, but these thoughts seemed absolutely valid. I felt like I was facing some awful but inevitable "truth" about myself.

Can you find any cognitive distortions in my thoughts? Check them off on this quiz. There are no strictly right or wrong answers, so just take your best guesses.

| Cognitive Distortions Quiz | (✓) |
|---|---|
| 1. **All-or-Nothing Thinking.** You think about yourself or the world in black-or-white, all-or-nothing categories. Shades of gray do not exist. | |
| 2. **Overgeneralization.** You think about a negative event as a never-ending pattern of defeat by using words like *always* or *never*. | |
| 3. **Mental Filter.** You dwell on something negative and filter out or ignore things that are positive. This is like a drop of ink that discolors the beaker of water. | |
| 4. **Discounting the Positive.** This is an even more spectacular mental error. You tell yourself that your positives don't count. This way, you can maintain a universally negative view of yourself. | |
| 5. **Jumping to Conclusions.** You jump to conclusions that aren't warranted by the facts.<br>• **Mind Reading.** You assume you know what other people are thinking and feeling.<br>• **Fortune Telling.** You make negative predictions about the future. | |
| 6. **Magnification and Minimization.** You blow things out of proportion or shrink their importance inappropriately. I call this the "binocular trick" because things either look much bigger or much smaller depending on what end of the binoculars you look through. | |
| 7. **Emotional Reasoning.** You reason from how you feel. For example, you may *feel* like a loser, so you assume you really *are* a loser. Or you *feel* hopeless and conclude you really *are* hopeless. | |

| | |
|---|---|
| 8. **Should Statements.** You make yourself (or others) miserable with *shoulds*, *musts*, or *ought tos*. Self-directed shoulds cause feelings of guilt, shame, depression, and worthlessness. Other-directed shoulds trigger feelings of anger and relationship problems. World-directed shoulds cause feelings of frustration and entitlement. | |
| 9. **Labeling.** You label yourself or others instead of focusing on the specific problem. Labeling is an extreme form of overgeneralization because you see your entire self or someone else as totally defective or bad. | |
| 10. **Blame.** You find fault with yourself (self-blame) or others (other-blame). | |

Are you done? Did you give it a try? If so, you can keep reading to find out my answers. But please don't peek until you've completed the quiz!

## My Answer

How many distortions did you find? I was clearly involved in quite a few and arguably all ten! Here's why:

1. **All-or-Nothing Thinking.** I was telling myself that since I hadn't hit a home run, I'd struck out.

2. **Overgeneralization.** I was thinking I was a "has-been" whose best days were in the past.

3. **Mental Filter.** I was ruminating about the presentation that was the less effective of the two and entirely forgot about the other presentation, which was actually very strong.

4. **Discounting the Positive.** I was overlooking the standing ovations I'd gotten at many of my recent workshops, as well as the large numbers of glowing emails I get from fans every day.

5. **Jumping to Conclusions.** I was assuming people were no longer interested in what I had to say (mind reading) and was predicting that there wouldn't be much interest in the rest of my presentations and that my career was pretty much over (fortune telling).

6. **Magnification and Minimization.** This is perhaps a reach, but you could argue that I was magnifying the importance of every error I made in my presentations and minimizing the potential impact of what I was teaching.

7. **Emotional Reasoning.** I *felt* like a failure, so I concluded that I *was* a failure.

8. **Labeling.** I was calling myself a "has-been."

9. **Should Statements.** I was telling myself that I *should have* been more charismatic and blown people away.

10. **Self-Blame.** I was criticizing and blaming myself for not being "good enough."

As you can see, there were *lots* of distortions in my negative thoughts, but at the time, I didn't realize it, so they mushroomed and I got more and more anxious. In fact, I got so nervous and demoralized that I showed for my next presentation 90 minutes early. The ballroom was enormous, with seating for 2,400 people, but there was only *one* other person in the room, a woman sitting near the back. My heart sank!

I asked her if she had a program so I could make sure I was in the right place. She looked up the program on her cell phone, and it turned out *she* was in the wrong lecture hall, so she left. I was left totally alone in that cavernous room feeling humiliated, thinking only a small number of people would show up for my talk.

I dejectedly went up on the stage to set up my computer and sat down to wait. I was so anxious that I fell asleep. For me, sudden sleepiness is an occasional odd symptom of intense anxiety.

I woke up a few minutes before my talk was scheduled to begin and was shocked to see that the room was packed to capacity. When I began speaking, the audience became extremely enthusiastic and broke into spontaneous applause and cheering at times. It was the largest and most enthusiastic crowd I've ever had!

It became obvious that my negative thoughts were pretty distorted, and that was a huge relief. This type of recovery is what Dr. Albert Ellis has called the "low-level solution." You suddenly feel better because you discover that your negative thoughts simply aren't true.

A "high-level solution" is different: That's where you discover that you can feel happy even if your negative thoughts *are* true.

How does that work? Suppose, for example, that the crowd in Anaheim had been much smaller and less enthusiastic. What then? Would that have meant that my "self" really wasn't "good enough"?

I learned the answer to this question at the end of my Tuesday group at Stanford last week. Just as I was about to leave the group, a psychologist named Robert turned to me with tears in his eyes. This was surprising because I've felt a bit intimidated by him.

Robert said he wanted to thank me for creating the Tuesday group and for devoting so much time and effort to it. He said it meant a great deal to him, and he seemed a bit choked up.

I deeply appreciated his comments. I told Robert that the sessions meant a lot to me too and that the group was also one of the highlights of my week.

So whenever my ego tries to tell me that I'm "over the hill" or not quite "good enough," I try to remember what Robert said. That reminds me of what's really important in my life and what gives me the deepest feelings of satisfaction and joy—it's not being "special" but hanging out with other flawed people who share their failures and vulnerabilities, as well as their successes, so we can all learn and grow together. That's my "high-level" solution!

In the next few chapters, we're going to examine the idea that you, or any human being, might not be "good enough," and I will raise several questions:

1. Is it possible to be more worthwhile or less worthwhile as a human being?

2. People can criticize the specific things we think, feel, do, or say. But is it possible for them to judge our "self"?

3. Do you have, or even need, a "self"?

4. If you do have a "self," what's the best way to get rid of it?

The answers to these questions all turn out to be pretty simple, but they may be hard to comprehend at first. You'll have to be patient with yourself until you suddenly get it.

Have you ever seen one of those pictures that can be seen in two different ways? For example, when viewed one way, the picture on the next page appears to be a rabbit. But when viewed another way, it looks like a duck.

It's the same when we think about our flaws and shortcomings. Looked at from the perspective of having a "self," we think that our flaws and failures mean we have a "self" that's flawed, inferior, bad, or even worthless. This perspective triggers feelings of anxiety, despair, inferiority, shame, and hopelessness—and sometimes even suicidal urges.

*(Source: Wikimedia Commons)*

But from another perspective, we can view our flaws and shortcomings as opportunities to learn and grow or to get closer to the people we care about. It all depends on the way you look at it.

What I'm really referring to is what Buddhists call the "Great Death." If you allow your "self" to "die," you can suddenly experience profound growth, freedom, and joy. This may sound nonsensical or even frightening, but it can be profoundly liberating. In fact, in the last chapter in this section, I'll talk about not one but four "Great Deaths" of the self and four incredible ways to achieve enlightenment.

# 24 | Are Some People *More* Worthwhile? Are You One of Them?

It is clear that people can be better—in fact way better—at certain things. They may be smarter, more talented, and more successful. But does this make them superior or more worthwhile human beings?

Sometimes it seems like tremendous success really does make people superior or more worthwhile! For example, I turned on the TV a few years ago and discovered that one of my college roommates, Joe Stiglitz, had just won the Nobel Prize in economics. I looked him up online and learned that he has received more than forty honorary degrees from prestigious universities like Cambridge and Harvard, and he was named by *Time* magazine as one of the 100 most influential people in the world.

Yikes! How can the rest of us compete with that?

To find out if it's possible to be more worthwhile than other people, we'll have to answer this question: What's the definition of a more worthwhile human being? If we can't define this concept in a meaningful way, then the concept is meaningless. There won't be any such thing as a more worthwhile human being, so we won't have to worry about it.

Why might this be useful to you? It's because inferiority and worthlessness—two of the most common symptoms of depression and anxiety—often result from the belief that we're not good enough and that others are somehow "better."

Let's examine some popular definitions of a more worthwhile human being and see if any of them make sense. You could say that a more worthwhile human being is someone who:

- Is successful or works hard and achieves a lot.
- Is intelligent or talented.

- Is happy.
- Is loved or very loving toward others.
- Is famous or powerful.
- Is attractive, charming, or popular.
- Is rich.
- Believes in God.
- Is exceptionally kind and compassionate.
- Helps others.

You may have your own definition, which is fine. If you like, you can write it down here:

_____

_____

_____

_____

Let's examine the first definition. Is it true that a more worthwhile human being is someone who works hard and is very successful?

This common way of thinking is the embodiment of the Calvinist work ethic: You *are* what you *do*. If you do good work, then you are a good human being. But if you're lazy and achieve very little, or if you do bad things, then you are a bad, worthless, and inferior human being. This way of thinking is arguably the foundation of Western civilization, and most people buy into it.

Can you see any problems with defining a worthwhile human being as someone who is very successful?

Write down your ideas here before you continue reading. If you aren't clear, just take a guess. Even a wrong guess can lead to new insights. The goal is not to be "right" or "wrong" but to learn how to challenge the negative thoughts and beliefs that create emotional pain.

_____

_____

_____

_____

## My Answer

If you define a worthwhile human being as someone who is very successful, then you'll have to answer this question: *How* successful do you have to be to be worthwhile? Do you have to be successful at everything all the time? Or some things some of the time?

If you say, "everything all the time," then no one is worthwhile because nobody is successful at everything all the time. We all fail at many things over the course of our lives. In fact, failing is essential to learning and growth.

If you now say, "at some things some of the time," then all human beings are worthwhile because we all succeed at many things over the course of our lives. For example, you learned to walk, talk, read and write, and add and subtract numbers. In fact, at this very moment, you are successfully reading this book, and you may be thinking about a few new ideas that you've never thought about before. So according to this definition, we're *all* worthwhile.

So if we're *all* worthwhile, or if *no one* is worthwhile, then we're all in the same boat.

You may still be convinced that some people really *are* more worthwhile than others, which is fine, and you may still believe that success is the key to being worthwhile. These beliefs don't die easily.

So let's define a worthwhile human being a little differently. For example, you could define a worthwhile human being as someone who is successful more than 50% of the time.

Can you see any problems with this definition? Write down your ideas here before you continue reading. If you aren't clear, just take a guess.

---

---

---

---

## My Answer

With this new definition, we'll run into the logical problem of arbitrary cutoff points. For example, if we now claim that someone who is successful 50% of the time is worthwhile, then someone who is successful 49% of the time is not. That doesn't make sense because these two people have almost the same level of success. We'll run into this problem no matter what cutoff point we choose.

But let's assume that you still believe some highly successful people, like my college roommate—or some other person you idolize, like a famous athlete, singer, or movie star—really are more worthwhile. These notions are seductive. It may seem like it just *has* to be true because it *feels* true.

Is that the way you think?

Let's try a new definition that might work better. We could say that the more successful you are, the more worthwhile you are. Let's see if this new definition makes sense. Imagine that we have a sliding scale of success that ranges from 0 to 1,000. An unfortunate homeless person might have a very low rating, maybe around 25, whereas someone like Bill Gates or Albert Einstein might have a super high rating of more than 950. So if your success rating is 650, your worthwhileness rating is also 650.

This definition of a worthwhile human being seems more compelling. Can you see any problems with the claim that the more success you have, the more worthwhile you are? Think about it and jot down your ideas here before you continue reading.

_____

_____

_____

_____

## My Answer

We are now claiming that the more successful you are, the more worthwhile you are.

Hmm, that *does* seem to make sense... Or does it?

Here's one potential problem: Our success constantly fluctuates. Sometimes we're more successful, and sometimes we're less successful. For example, fifth grade was my best year in school by far! I got all A's and had perfect attendance. I was so proud of my report card and just loved my teacher. Did that mean I was an especially "worthwhile child" that year?

In high school, I landed my first real job working for Abbey Rents, a party rental company. I worked in the warehouse and filled orders so the correct supplies could be delivered to the customers. I carefully and meticulously filled each order, but customers started complaining that they were getting the wrong orders. I tried really hard, but the manager kept getting complaints.

One day, when I reported to work, they said they'd hired someone else and that I'd been fired. I'd lasted less than two weeks! Clearly, I had failed in spite of my best efforts. Did this mean I was a "less worthwhile human being" at that time?

Do you really want to generalize from some specific flaw or skill to your "self"?

All famous people have had periods where they failed repeatedly, like Edison when he was trying to invent the incandescent light bulb. All the filaments he tested were unsatisfactory. Was he "worthless" at that time? And did he suddenly become "more worthwhile" when he finally found a filament that worked better?

Here's another problem with the sliding scale of success and human worthwhileness: The successes that any of us have are rather specific. If someone is a tennis star, then he or she will be very successful at tennis. But that person won't necessarily be successful at some other skill, like singing.

So is that person a more worthwhile and less worthwhile human being at the same time?

Do you get it yet? We can judge or rate a specific activity that someone performs, like singing or playing tennis, but we can't rate or judge the "worthwhileness" of a human being.

That's because there's no meaningful way to generalize from some specific skill or failure to your "self." Specific successes and failures exist, but more worthwhile or less worthwhile human beings do not.

Suppose you *still* feel certain that success and worthwhileness just *have* to be linked in some way. That's okay! Sometimes these notions can be really hard to let go of.

I also thought about this problem a great deal in the early days of my clinical work, and I wasn't convinced either. Like you, I was hooked on the notion that people who are more successful are more worthwhile. But now it seems crystal clear that great success at anything does not make you a more worthwhile human being.

Let's try another definition of a more worthwhile human being. We could say that you must be successful at *something* to be worthwhile. And the more successful you are at that specific thing, the more worthwhile you are.

What do you think about this new definition? Can you see any problems with it? Put your ideas here before you continue reading.

_____

_____

_____

_____

## My Answer

It's pretty easy to attack this new definition. You might be extremely successful at something illegal or immoral, like bank robbing or serial killing. Does this mean that you're an especially worthwhile human being? Clearly, that doesn't make sense!

Could we say, instead, that you have to be successful at something that's legal and moral to be worthwhile? This definition also falls apart for all the reasons we've pointed out in this chapter, like the problem of arbitrary cutoff points.

You will find similar contradictions and logical problems with any way you try to define a more worthwhile human being. It doesn't matter whether your definition has to do with love, happiness, intelligence, wealth, fame, or power. All these definitions will fall apart.

Why does this happen? Why is it so hard to define a more worthwhile human being?

It's because we're trying to define something that doesn't exist. There is no such thing as a more worthwhile human being!

You may not be willing to give up quite yet! Perhaps we could try a more humanistic or idealistic definition of a more worthwhile human being. For example, we could define a more worthwhile human being as someone who helps others.

Certainly, that definition seems like it should hold water. How could anyone argue with that?

Let's see what you think. Can you see any problems with this new definition? Put your ideas here before you look at the answer.

_____

_____

_____

_____

## My Answer

Let's take a close look at the idea that a worthwhile human being is someone who helps others. Would you have to help everybody all the time or some people some of the time?

If you say, "everybody all the time," then no one is worthwhile because no one helps everybody all the time. And if you say, "some people some of the time," then everyone is worthwhile since we've all helped someone at some point.

As you can see, we're going to run into the same blind alleys we ran into when we tried to define a more worthwhile human being based on productivity or success.

Of course, you could still try to argue that if you help "lots of people," then you are more worthwhile—and the _more_ people you help, the _more_ worthwhile you are.

This new definition seems innocent enough, and it seems pretty compelling! Are there any problems with it? Put your ideas here.

_____

_____

_____

_____

## My Answer

If we have to help "lots of people" to be worthwhile, then we could ask, "How many people do we have to help to become worthwhile?" Five people?

Thirty-five people? More than a hundred people? Clearly, this doesn't make sense because we have another arbitrary cutoff point.

And if you think that the more people you help, the "more worthwhile" you are, think about Dennis Rader, the BTK serial killer. He was a member of the Christ Lutheran Church and was even president of the church council. He did lots of helpful things for people when he wasn't doing his serial killing. Did that make him especially worthwhile?

Now you might be wondering about Mother Teresa, the Buddha, or other religious prophets, like Moses, Jesus, or Muhammad, who spent their lives trying to help people. Aren't they especially worthwhile?

Wow, this is getting a bit dicey. We are in sensitive territory! I want to free you from the mental trap of believing you're not good enough, but I don't want to challenge your religious faith. But if you're feeling brave, we can do a little thought experiment together and see if it's true that people who help lots and lots of people are especially worthwhile.

I'm going to invite you to participate in a kind of goofy technique I've developed called the **feared fantasy**, which you might remember from chapter 15. It's kind of a humor-based technique, but the goal is to make a pretty serious point.

Let's imagine that you won a $500 million lottery and decided to spend all of your time and resources helping others. You provide food, housing, education, and medical care to vast numbers of people all over the world.

In fact, you are pictured on the cover of *Time* magazine and named the most helpful and generous person in the world. Experts say that you have been even more helpful than the Pope or the Dalai Lama, whom you beat out for this year's Helpfulness Award.

Now let's pretend that you and I meet at a party, and we have an imaginary chat, but there's an unusual rule you must follow. The rule is that you *always* have to speak the truth, the whole truth, and nothing but the truth. You're not allowed to deny, rationalize, or minimize anything. You have to be 100% honest!

In fact, we can imagine that you've just been given a strong dose of truth serum. Do you agree?

Okay, good.

Let's see what happens. I might begin by saying this to you:

*Hey, I read about you in* Time *magazine and learned all about the fabulous charitable work you do to help people all over the world. I think that's great! But I'm wondering if I could ask you a somewhat personal question?*

Being a very helpful person, you generously agree, so I say:

*Thanks! I appreciate it! Here's my question: I heard something about you through the grapevine that sounded a little negative and was definitely surprising, and I wonder if I could mention it to you and find out what your thinking is. I don't want to spread any false rumors about you.*

You say sure, in your wonderfully helpful and friendly tone of voice, and ask me what I've heard. I say:

*Well, I'm a bit embarrassed to say this, but I heard that you believe that the more helpful you are, the more worthwhile you are as a human being… And since you've just won the award as the most helpful person in the world, I heard that you think you're the most worthwhile person in the world.*

*Do you feel like that? Do you feel like you're some kind of exceptionally worthwhile human being because of all the helping you do? I want you to be completely honest with me.*

Since you've agreed to be 100% honest—and you believe that worthwhileness can be measured by how many people someone has helped—you say something like:

*Of course! Doesn't that follow? After all, they say I'm a paragon of helpfulness! No one in the entire world is at my level of helpfulness! Not even the Pope or the Dalai Lama. I blew them both away with my incredible helpfulness.*

*So to be honest, I would have to say yes, I am an incredibly worthwhile human being. In fact, many people have concluded that I'm the most worthwhile human being in the world! Numero uno!*

Then I might ask:

*I certainly admire all the cool stuff you do to help poor people all over the world. But do you really think you're more worthwhile than other people?*

You might say:

*Well, doesn't it follow? Remember, human worthwhileness is based on helpfulness. And since I'm the most helpful person in the world, doesn't it follow that I'm the most worthwhile person in the world?*

Then I would ask:

*Well, I have one last awkward question. Do you think you're more worthwhile than I am? I help people here and there and enjoy it, but I'm not nearly as helpful as you, not by a long shot. Do you feel like you're a more worthwhile human being? Are you looking down on me as being some kind of less worthwhile human being?*

If you say no, then we've both agreed that helping others does *not* make you a more worthwhile human being. Helping others might be a wonderful thing to do, but it doesn't make you better than anyone else.

But if you stick to your guns and insist that you really *are* more the most worthwhile person in the world, then you kind of look like a jerk! We don't generally idolize people who go around judging others and thinking they're better than other people.

Do you see what I mean?

Don't misinterpret my argument. I believe that success and hard work are desirable and that helping others is very worthwhile. My entire focus is on jumping from any specific thing you say or do to the "self."

You can judge the specific things you say or do, but you cannot judge the "self." Once you grasp this, your suffering will disappear. Depression always exists in the clouds of abstraction, thinking that your "self" is not good enough or that you have a "self" that can be judged.

# 25 | Are Some People *Less* Worthwhile? Are You One of Them?

In the last chapter, we examined the idea that some people are more worthwhile because of their superior qualities, intelligence, status, or accomplishments, and we saw that these definitions of a more worthwhile human being don't make sense.

Now we'll look at the other side of the coin. Is it possible to be a less worthwhile, or worthless, human being because of your flaws and failures or because you don't measure up to your own or society's standards?

If you've struggled with depression, then you probably believe the answer to this question is yes. But in this chapter, I'm going to try to persuade you that the answer is no—there is no such thing as an inferior or worthless human being. However, I won't try to persuade you that you have no flaws. That would be crazy. We all have *lots* of flaws!

Instead, I'm going to show you that your suffering does *not* result from your flaws, failures, or deficiencies. You only suffer when you try to generalize from these flaws or failures to your "self." You can probably recognize this as a prime example of overgeneralization—one of the most common cognitive distortions.

In chapter 10, I described a computer programmer named Ben who felt crushed when he was rejected by an attractive man with whom he'd had a brief affair. He was disappointed when he learned that the man was not looking for an ongoing relationship but was simply enjoying a series of one-night stands.

I've often said that a rejection could never upset a human being—only a distorted thought about a rejection could upset you. Let's see if that's true. Here's what Ben was telling himself about the rejection:

1. I am worthless because I am sexually and physically inferior.

2. It's impossible to be happy without romance.

3. There is some deep, worthless thing about me that makes me unlovable.

Ben was convinced that all three negative thoughts were 100% valid. But are they? What do you think about Ben's thoughts?

There are really two separate issues. Is it true that Ben is sexually and physically inferior? And is it also true that his worthwhileness as a human being depends on his attractiveness?

See if you can identify any cognitive distortions in Ben's negative thoughts. Here are some facts that might help you. Although Ben is not a male model or movie star, he is definitely attractive, and many men have been attracted to him. In fact, he's very fit and works out a lot. He even came in second place in a stripper beauty contest in a gay bar in San Francisco, where he received tons of enthusiastic applause and cheering!

In addition, he's smart, personable, and articulate. He has a terrific sense of humor and an excellent career in a high-tech field. He's also very generous with friends and family members who are down and out. But he has his faults as well, including a temper that sometimes turns people off, and he can seem pretty self-centered and demanding at times. But he can also be exceptionally kind, thoughtful, and supportive.

Now see how many distortions you can find in Ben's negative thoughts. When you're done, keep reading to see the answers.

| Cognitive Distortions Quiz | (✓) |
|---|---|
| 1. **All-or-Nothing Thinking.** You think about yourself or the world in black-or-white, all-or-nothing categories. Shades of gray do not exist. | |
| 2. **Overgeneralization.** You think about a negative event as a never-ending pattern of defeat by using words like *always* or *never*. | |
| 3. **Mental Filter.** You dwell on something negative and filter out or ignore things that are positive. This is like a drop of ink that discolors the beaker of water. | |

| | |
|---|---|
| 4. **Discounting the Positive.** This is an even more spectacular mental error. You tell yourself that your positives don't count. This way, you can maintain a universally negative view of yourself. | |
| 5. **Jumping to Conclusions.** You jump to conclusions that aren't warranted by the facts.<br>• **Mind Reading.** You assume you know what other people are thinking and feeling.<br>• **Fortune Telling.** You make negative predictions about the future. | |
| 6. **Magnification and Minimization.** You blow things out of proportion or shrink their importance inappropriately. I call this the "binocular trick" because things either look much bigger or much smaller depending on what end of the binoculars you look through. | |
| 7. **Emotional Reasoning.** You reason from how you feel. For example, you may *feel* like a loser, so you assume you really *are* a loser. Or you *feel* hopeless and conclude you really *are* hopeless. | |
| 8. **Should Statements.** You make yourself (or others) miserable with *shoulds*, *musts*, or *ought tos*. Self-directed shoulds cause feelings of guilt, shame, depression, and worthlessness. Other-directed shoulds trigger feelings of anger and relationship problems. World-directed shoulds cause feelings of frustration and entitlement. | |
| 9. **Labeling.** You label yourself or others instead of focusing on the specific problem. Labeling is an extreme form of overgeneralization because you see your entire self or someone else as totally defective or bad. | |
| 10. **Blame.** You find fault with yourself (self-blame) or others (other-blame). | |

## My Answer

To my way of thinking, Ben's involved in all ten distortions:

1. **All-or-Nothing Thinking.** He's telling himself he's a worthless, unlovable loser if he's not 100% good-looking and if he isn't always successful at romance.

2. **Overgeneralization.** He's generalizing from this rejection to his "self." He's also telling himself that this rejection will be a never-ending pattern of defeat, rejection, and loneliness.

3. **Mental Filter.** He's thinking only about his flaws and romantic failures.

4. **Discounting the Positive.** He's discounting his many positive qualities, as well as the many men who have been attracted to him.

5. **Jumping to Conclusions.** He assumes that others will view him as negatively as he views himself (mind reading), and he tells himself that

he'll probably be alone, unloved, and unhappy for the rest of his life (fortune telling).

6. **Magnification and Minimization.** He's blowing the importance of this rejection way out of proportion and exaggerating his flaws. He's also minimizing his good qualities.

7. **Labeling.** He's labeling himself as inferior, unattractive, and unlovable.

8. **Emotional Reasoning.** He *feels* worthless and unattractive, so he concludes that he *is* worthless and unattractive.

9. **Should Statements.** He has lots of hidden shoulds because he's telling himself he *should* be better looking and *must* be loved by some hot guy before he can feel happy and fulfilled.

10. **Self-Blame.** He's telling himself the rejection was all his fault and that the lifestyle of the man who rejected him—having frequent one-night stands—has nothing to do with it.

Perhaps the most important distortion is Ben's gigantic overgeneralization. He is telling himself that he is worthless because he is sexually and physically inferior. Clearly, there are some incredibly handsome men who are physically and sexually superior to Ben. These men are physically and sexually superior to most men. And there are women with incredible looks too who are supermodels for a living.

Does this mean that the rest of us are worthless because we are less attractive or sexy? That would make for an awful lot of worthless human beings!

It may seem unrealistic that Ben is basing his self-esteem on his appearance, but he's not alone. Our culture places a super strong emphasis on attractiveness and physical perfection, and *many* people generalize from some physical flaw or defect—like being overweight, too thin, too short, too tall, not muscular enough, or not busty enough—to the "self." The pain can be severe, but it's always based on cognitive distortions in our negative thoughts about our (nonexistent) "self."

Even if the leap from one's appearance to the "self" doesn't make much sense to you, you may still be convinced that you really *are* inferior, worthless, or defective because of some flaw or inadequacy that you have.

So let's see if we can figure out if anybody—including you—really is an inferior, worthless, defective, or flawed human being. To find out, we'll have to know what we mean by those terms. Let's see if it's possible to define an inferior or worthless human being.

Most people think that an inferior or worthless human is someone who:

- Hasn't achieved anything significant or important.
- Doesn't live up to his or her personal standards or to society's standards.
- Is depressed and unhappy.
- Doesn't believe in God.
- Believes in the "wrong" religion.
- Bullies or hurts others.
- Isn't very smart.
- Isn't loved.
- Is selfish and lacking in compassion for others.
- Breaks the law, like rapists, robbers, or drug dealers.

Let's focus on the first definition. Let say we define an inferior or worthless human being as someone who hasn't achieved anything significant or important. Can you see any problems with this definition? Put your ideas here before you continue reading.

---

---

---

---

---

## My Answer

You probably noticed that we already debunked this definition in the last chapter. One problem with this definition is that we have all achieved many things that are important. For example, if you became paralyzed and couldn't walk, then you'd suddenly realize how incredibly important it is to be able to walk, which is something that we sometimes take for granted. So if an inferior or worthless human being is someone who hasn't accomplished anything of importance, then no one is inferior or worthless.

You could argue that almost everyone has learned to walk or talk, so these accomplishments "don't count." You could argue that if you haven't achieved something *really* important and unique, then you're inferior or worthless.

If that's your argument, then I'd want to know how important and unique your achievement would have to be on a scale of 0 to 100. Does this sound familiar too? This is the problem with arbitrary cutoff points.

We're all above average in some respects and below average in many other ways. You may be a reasonably good singer but a poor athlete or vice versa. But your strengths and weaknesses will never cause you to feel happy or depressed—it's only when you generalize from your flaws to your "self."

If you recall from earlier in the book, I go out jogging quite a few days a week, but I call it "slogging" because I have gotten really slow. (I'm 77 years old now!) The mailman came to the front door a few days ago and said, "Dr. Burns, I saw you out walking earlier. That's great! Good for you!"

I wanted to kill him! I had the urge to say, "I wasn't walking! I was *jogging* and darn fast too!"

But the truth is, I've gotten really slow, and many neighbors have also said that they saw me walking. In fact, an elderly, wobbly woman with a cane zoomed right past me today! I wouldn't be a very worthwhile member of your track team. My running speed *is* very inferior. But does that mean that I have a "self" that's inferior? To me, it doesn't really make sense!

If you think about it, you can compare any two individuals in terms of their careers, income, athletic or musical ability, charm, looks, height, or any other quality you can measure. And one of those individuals will have lower ratings in certain areas.

Does that mean the person with lower ratings in more areas is a "less worthwhile" human being? If you make that claim, I have to admit that I don't understand what you're talking about. It's nice to be tall. But are shorter people "less worthwhile" as human beings?

Can you see what I'm driving at yet? Or are you still entranced by the idea that we have "selves" that can be measured or judged based on our accomplishments or some other trait?

Not to worry if you're not quite there yet! What I'm saying is simple, but it can be hard to grasp at first.

We are easily seduced into thinking that people have "selves" that can be judged as "better than" or "less than." Part of the attraction to this type of thinking is that when you judge others based on their race, religion, gender, intelligence, status, or whatever, you may feel superior, which can feel really exhilarating! And we *all* do that, don't we?

But there's a downside—you might end up judging your own "self" as well.

You may still believe that some people really *are* worthless or inferior. If so, let's try some other definitions. We could define a worthless human being as someone who hurts and kills others intentionally, like Hitler and many other sadistic tyrants throughout history. Surely that definition makes sense!

Or does it?

Can you see any problems with this definition? Put your ideas here.

_____

_____

_____

_____

_____

## My Answer

There are lots of ways to challenge this definition. In the first place, if we define a worthless human being as someone who kills large numbers of innocent people, then the definition probably doesn't apply to you (unless you happen to be a serial killer). So if that's how you want to define a worthless human being, then you're not a worthless human being.

But isn't it true that we *all* have primal urges to get back at others at times? I know I sometimes get really angry, and when I reach a boiling point, I want to lash out and hurt the other person. Maybe you've felt that way too.

Do these impulses make us worthless? If so, I have to plead guilty!

But how about Hitler? Wasn't he *truly* worthless and evil? After all, the rest of us may have the occasional violent fantasy, but we don't act on our fantasies the way Hitler did.

Most people would agree that Hitler did horrific, unthinkable, and despicable things. And if we could go back in a time machine, I think most of us would justify killing Hitler before he came into power. This might have prevented World War II and the Holocaust, and it could have saved millions of lives and unimaginable suffering.

When you take the additional step of saying Hitler was a "worthless" human being, I think you are referring to all the unbelievably horrible things he did. I don't think you are referring to his "self." I think you are judging his actions, and that's totally appropriate.

Hitler also led a nation, conquered several countries, and got millions to embrace his views—so he was really high on the achievement scale. Did that mean he was especially worthwhile or superior? He and his followers certainly believed this!

To give you another example, I recently watched an incredibly sad and compelling television interview with the serial killer, Jeffrey Dahmer, and his father. It's called *Dahmer on Dahmer: A Serial Killer Speaks*, on NBC.

To be honest, when I saw his interview, I found him to be surprisingly likable—he was humble and incredibly honest. He confessed to all of his killings without making excuses or rationalizing. Although his parents got divorced when he was a kid, he didn't blame his upbringing, which he said was pretty average and similar to that of many of his classmates.

He explained that from the time he was a child, he'd had fantasies of dissecting bodies. It started with dead animals he found in the woods. Over time, his fantasies became more intense and sexually charged, and he wanted to have sex with men who were unconscious, in a zombie state. He said that the seventeen murders he committed were horrible and morally wrong, and he appeared to have genuine remorse.

Oddly, during the interview, his father said that he'd had the same kinds of fantasies as a child but did not act on them. This raises the possibility that Dahmer's sadistic urges were at least partially inherited and not the result of any traumatic childhood experiences. This definitely does not forgive or excuse Dahmer's behavior, but it provides an intriguing hypothesis about the causes of this type of atrocious behavior.

I understand that you may still want to label people like Dahmer or Hitler as "bad" or "worthless" human beings, and nearly everybody would agree with you. You can do that, but you are setting up the precedent of judging human beings—including yourself.

We can judge and rightfully condemn what others say, do, or believe as morally reprehensible, but we cannot meaningfully judge their "selves." The "self" is just an abstraction, whereas specific thoughts, feelings, and behaviors are real.

This may sound like a philosophical distinction, but the implications are practical and powerful because most, if not all, of our suffering results from the belief that we have a "self" that is not good enough, a "self" that others can judge.

# 26 | Let's Be Specific: What Are Your Flaws?

The last three chapters were based on philosophy and logic. I hope you found them interesting, but they may not have helped you with your own feelings of insecurity or the entrenched belief that you're not good enough.

So in this chapter, we'll focus on your specific flaws and failures rather than making global judgments about your "self." You will learn that most, if not all, of your emotional pain will disappear when you focus on what's real, as opposed to making abstract judgments about your "self."

To help me illustrate how this works, let me first introduce you to Alia, an attractive, loving, smart, and giving woman who has a tremendous amount to offer. Although she's in a serious relationship with her boyfriend, they've been arguing lately about seemingly trivial things. He's been complaining that she's too messy and that their apartment is too cluttered. He's also complained that she's often late when they have important things to do, like going to the airport to catch a flight.

In response to these criticisms, Alia has reacted by arguing back and saying, "That's not true!" Then the fight spirals out of control. Alia told me she was afraid they were on the verge of breaking up. She asked me, in tears, "Dr. Burns, am I unlovable?"

Before we move on, let's see if you can identify any cognitive distortions in Alia's thought that she's unlovable.

| **Cognitive Distortions Quiz** | (✓) |
|---|---|
| 1. **All-or-Nothing Thinking.** You think about yourself or the world in black-or-white, all-or-nothing categories. Shades of gray do not exist. | |
| 2. **Overgeneralization.** You think about a negative event as a never-ending pattern of defeat by using words like *always* or *never*. | |
| 3. **Mental Filter.** You dwell on something negative and filter out or ignore things that are positive. This is like a drop of ink that discolors the beaker of water. | |
| 4. **Discounting the Positive.** This is an even more spectacular mental error. You tell yourself that your positives don't count. This way, you can maintain a universally negative view of yourself. | |
| 5. **Jumping to Conclusions.** You jump to conclusions that aren't warranted by the facts.<br>• **Mind Reading.** You assume you know what other people are thinking and feeling.<br>• **Fortune Telling.** You make negative predictions about the future. | |
| 6. **Magnification and Minimization.** You blow things out of proportion or shrink their importance inappropriately. I call this the "binocular trick" because things either look much bigger or much smaller depending on what end of the binoculars you look through. | |
| 7. **Emotional Reasoning.** You reason from how you feel. For example, you may *feel* like a loser, so you assume you really *are* a loser. Or you *feel* hopeless and conclude you really *are* hopeless. | |
| 8. **Should Statements.** You make yourself (or others) miserable with *should*s, *must*s, or *ought to*s. Self-directed shoulds cause feelings of guilt, shame, depression, and worthlessness. Other-directed shoulds trigger feelings of anger and relationship problems. World-directed shoulds cause feelings of frustration and entitlement. | |
| 9. **Labeling.** You label yourself or others instead of focusing on the specific problem. Labeling is an extreme form of overgeneralization because you see your entire self or someone else as totally defective or bad. | |
| 10. **Blame.** You find fault with yourself (self-blame) or others (other-blame). | |

When you're done, you can review my answers on the next page.

## My Answer

If you found at least five distortions in Alia's thought, you can give yourself an A on this quiz. However, I think you could easily make a case for every single distortion:

1. **All-or-Nothing Thinking.** Alia is thinking about lovableness in black-or-white terms. She assumes she's either "lovable" or "unlovable," with no in between.

2. **Overgeneralization.** She's generalizing from a negative event—a conflict with her boyfriend—to her "self."

3. **Mental Filter.** She is dwelling on the conflict and all the recent arguments she's had with her boyfriend.

4. **Discounting the Positive.** Alia is ignoring her many positive qualities. She is a lovely, talented woman with a great career and many friends.

5. **Jumping to Conclusions.** Alia is mind reading when she assumes that her boyfriend, and men in general, will think she is "unlovable."

6. **Magnification and Minimization.** She is blowing things way out of proportion. Conflicts in relationships are painful but common. Most of us argue and fly off the handle at times.

7. **Emotional Reasoning.** She is reasoning from how she feels. Alia *feels* unlovable, so she assumes she *is* unlovable.

8. **Should Statements.** Alia is telling herself that she and her boyfriend *shouldn't* argue and that her relationship *should* be better than it is.

9. **Labeling.** She is clearly labeling herself.

10. **Blame.** She is using up all her energy blaming herself instead of pinpointing the specific errors she's making so she can correct them.

Overgeneralization is perhaps the most significant distortion. Alia is jumping from the recent conflict with her boyfriend to a judgment about her "self." You may think this difference is subtle, but there are several profound consequences.

First, this creates tremendous pain for Alia, as her unhappiness is not a result of the conflict with her boyfriend but her fear that her "self" is not lovable.

Second, she is wasting all her energy in the clouds of abstraction trying to figure out if she is "lovable." I don't mean to be critical, but this is a bit like the seventeenth-century theologians who argued about how many angels could dance on the head of a pin. You'll never figure it out because it's a nonsensical question.

Third, Alia is not doing anything to solve the real problem of escalating arguments with her boyfriend. If she is motivated, she can learn to respond to his criticisms much more effectively. However, she's not obligated to do that, and she may instead decide that this is not the right relationship for her. But either way, worrying about being "unlovable" is not going to help her or further her cause.

What would happen if Alia went in the opposite direction? Instead of worrying about an abstract concept like being "unlovable," she could focus on pinpointing and correcting the real problems in her relationship. If you recall from chapter 13, this technique is called **be specific**, and it's a really powerful tool for challenging overgeneralizations.

Alia has already told us what the problem is. When she responds defensively to her boyfriend's criticisms, things spiral out of control. Of course, Alia may or may not be open to changing the way she responds to her boyfriend's criticisms, but if she wants to improve their relationship, this is something specific she could work on. If so, perhaps Alia would benefit from using the **five secrets of effective communication** when they argue.

You may recall that the five secrets include:

- **The Disarming Technique.** She could find some truth in her boyfriend's criticisms instead of arguing defensively. This is an extremely powerful way of responding to criticism.

- **Thought and Feeling Empathy.** She could acknowledge that he probably feels angry, hurt, frustrated, and perhaps disrespected when she's messy or late.

- **"I Feel" Statements.** Instead of expressing her anger indirectly (by arguing and insisting he's "wrong"), she could let him know that she feels sad, hurt, and angry too.

- **Stroking.** She could let him know that even though they're fighting right now, she cares a lot about him and that her love for him is one of the reasons she feels so hurt.

- **Inquiry.** She could encourage him to tell her more about how he's been feeling and ask him whether there are other things she's done or said that were annoying to him.

Can you see that this approach might feel a whole lot different than arguing with him and wondering if she's "unlovable"? Learning to use the five secrets is not easy—in fact it's darn hard, and it requires lots of practice and determination. But these skills can transform a troubled relationship if they come from the heart.

Now you might be thinking that Alia shouldn't have to make all these changes in the way she communicates with her boyfriend. You could also point out that he has some changing to do too. And you might even suggest that she should break up with him and look for someone better.

I agree with you. Alia *doesn't* have to change, and her boyfriend clearly contributes to their dance of anger and bickering as well. But *he's* not asking for help. *She* is. So if she wants their relationship to improve, she'll have to focus on her own role in the problem. She'll have to work on changing herself rather than arguing and insisting that his criticisms are "wrong."

And, as you say, she has every right to break up with him. All I'm saying is that solutions exist for most real problems. But no solutions exist for the "problem" of being "unlovable" because it has no meaning. It's just a mean-spirited label, a put-down, and a way of being mean to yourself.

Be specific has been an extremely helpful technique for me on a personal level too. Here's how I use it: As you know, I do a lot of teaching, and I've always been interested in improving my teaching skills, so I get ratings from my students every time I teach. In fact, I get immediate feedback at the end of every class. Some people think students won't be honest when they give feedback, but that doesn't seem to be the case. They are *very* honest. Sometimes I've wished they weren't so honest!

My teaching errors become crystal clear when I review the feedback forms because I can see exactly what people liked and disliked about each seminar or workshop. The information can be incredibly illuminating, but it can also be painful.

I've learned there are several specific things I sometimes say when I teach that get some people upset:

1. When people ask challenging or critical questions in a kind of pompous way, I sometimes get irritated and answer them in a dismissive way that can be off-putting. Then other students become cautious or fearful, thinking it is not safe to ask questions because I might slam them too.

2. Sometimes I become overly critical of other schools of therapy. I often say that it's time to give up all the schools of therapy so we can develop a science-based, data-driven form of psychotherapy, which is what TEAM-CBT is. And I do believe that. But some people don't want to hear criticisms of their own school of therapy because they believe in what they're doing so strongly. They feel threatened and get angry and sometimes say that I seem arrogant. That really hurts!

3. Sometimes I get overly enthusiastic about TEAM-CBT and do too much "selling," which also turns some people off.

When I realize that I've made these mistakes, I sometimes tell myself that I'm a "bad teacher" or that I have some kind of character flaw. That makes me feel down, ashamed, defensive, frustrated, and anxious. Those are the moments when I think I have a "self" that's "not good enough."

But when I step back and get specific, I remind myself that these criticisms are specific errors rather than flaws in my "self." When I think this way, I can easily come up with ways to correct these errors. For example, I've discovered that if I just write the word "nice" on the handout I have in front of me at the start of every workshop, it reminds me to treat each audience member with warmth and respect and to find some truth in what that person is saying even if I find the comment or question a bit whacky or annoying. This always works well.

In addition, on the second morning of every workshop, I read out at least five of the worst things people said about me on the feedback forms, as well as five of the things they said they liked the most about the workshop. The audience loves this because I always find truth in their criticisms!

In fact, when I read the absolute worst comments out loud, they all seem happy and laugh in a really supportive way. This seems to bring us all together and greatly boosts the group's morale. I sometimes even get a standing ovation at the end. It's always a huge relief for me to discover that I don't have to be perfect.

And you don't have to be perfect either! Whenever you find yourself feeling down, list all your negative thoughts in a Daily Mood Journal so you can see exactly what you're telling yourself. If you're telling yourself that you're not good enough, see if you can focus instead on identifying some specific flaw you have or some error you've made. Then you can work on correcting the error or simply accepting your flaw.

Here's the idea: Only *specific* flaws, errors, and shortcomings exist. We can make specific errors at specific times, on specific days, and at specific locations—and we can either work to correct these errors or accept them. We only suffer when we overgeneralize and tell ourselves "I'm a screwup" or "I shouldn't have made that mistake" or "This shows what a bad father (or mother or teacher) I am." In other words, the belief that we have a "self" that can be judged is almost always the source of our misery.

This may sound overly philosophical, and philosophy may not be your "thing," but the emotional implications are tremendous. What we're talking about is transforming feelings of shame, worry, and self-doubt into golden opportunities for growth, liberation, and joy.

# 27 | How to Join the Grateful Dead!

The Buddha believed that we could experience liberation from suffering when we escape from the trap of thinking that we have a "self." Most religions, including Christianity, have also talked about the notion of death and rebirth, or being "born again."

In this chapter, you'll learn that when you let your "self" die, you can experience joy, peace, love, and liberation from your suffering. In fact, there are actually four Great Deaths—not just one—and they correspond to recovery from depression, anxiety, relationship conflicts, and habits and addictions. In each case, when you "die," you will experience an incredible and instantaneous rebirth. You will lose nothing but your suffering and your "self," and you will gain the world.

## THE FIRST GREAT DEATH:
## THE DEATH OF THE SPECIAL SELF

The first Great Death is involved in recovery from feelings of depression, inadequacy, guilt, shame, inferiority, and worthlessness. It requires the painful acceptance of the fact that you're not actually special and the fantastically liberating discovery that you don't need to be.

On the next page you'll see a photo of my beloved cat, Obie. My relationship with Obie had a rocky start, to say the least, but over time, he became my best friend in the world. My wife and I shared eight wonderful years with him until he vanished in the middle of the night several years ago. We had all the neighbors from miles around looking for him, but we never found the little guy. He was probably eaten by one of the many predators living in the woods behind our house.

I'm still grieving his loss and frequently go to the glass kitchen door where he first appeared, hoping to see him again. And when I jog, I still call out his name, hoping he'll suddenly appear from behind a bush. But I know he never will. His loss was heartbreaking for my wife and me.

I've often talked about Obie during workshops, and you may have noticed that this book is dedicated to him. Although he was a feral cat (meaning totally wild), he taught me some invaluable lessons that have helped me personally and professionally.

Obie had been living in the woods behind our house and had never had any contact with humans. He'd often wander into our backyard, and I chased him out many times because he seemed aggressive. My wife and I were afraid he would tyrannize our other more highly domesticated cats that we'd adopted as kittens.

Although he was afraid of me, Obie kept coming back. In retrospect, I think he saw that we had other cats and perhaps was hoping that we'd adopt him one day or at least give him some food from time to time. He may also have been looking for some cat romance.

One day, Obie appeared at our kitchen door. This was surprising since he was afraid of me. But he caught my eye and held up his left front paw. I was shocked to see that it was swollen almost to the size of his head. I was also saddened to see that he was not the same muscular animal I'd chased out of the yard on so many occasions—he'd become skinny and emaciated. Clearly, he'd had a serious injury and could not hunt, and he was desperate.

It was our cold and rainy season, so my wife and I put out some food for him and put a box under the table on the back deck so he'd have a place to sleep at night that was somewhat protected from the rain and wind. He hung around and gladly slept in it each night.

We hoped his paw would heal up, but after three weeks he was still going downhill and seemed on the verge of death. My wife and I decided to capture him and bring him to the local vet. He was covered with scars, fleas, and ticks. He also had worms. He'd clearly had a hard life. They said he'd need surgery to save his life. During the surgery, the vet cleaned up the puncture wound on his paw and said he had to stay indoors for ten days to receive antibiotics mixed with his food.

We put Obie in our guest room, but the poor guy was terrified and threw himself against the windows, hoping to break out and get free. When we came in the room, he hid under the bed, snarling and swatting at us if we reached in to try to pet him. We put a litter box in the room, but he was totally uninterested. He used the carpet for peeing and the heating vents on the floor for pooing. Within a week, the carpets were ruined, and the room smelled terrible. Eventually, we had to replace all the carpets and have the room repainted.

After ten days, we opened the door, and Obie shot out of the house like a rocket, but he never went far and spent most of his time hanging around on the deck near the kitchen door, like it was his kingdom. It seemed like he wanted to be a part of our family, but he was still so fearful that you couldn't get within ten feet of him. The first time my wife tried to pick him up, he bit her hard on the cheek.

One day, my wife accidentally touched him on the head, and he started purring instantly. We discovered that he *loved* to be petted on the head. We used that tiny bit of reinforcement to gradually shape his behavior. And little by little, things began to change.

We decided to put his food right inside the kitchen door so he had to put his head inside the house to eat. Once he got used to that, we moved it an inch further inside so he had to put his front paws inside to eat. Eventually, he was entirely inside the kitchen when he ate.

Encouraged by that little bit of progress, my wife and I continued to set goals that seemed impossible at first. Could he trust us enough to roam about inside the house? One day, that happened! Could he ever trust us enough to jump up on our laps for petsies and love? One day, when my wife was watching TV, that happened too!

But could he ever learn to use a litter box? Would he ever sleep on the bed with us and our two other cats? Could he ever learn to trust strangers, like my colleagues and students who come to our house every Sunday morning for a hike?

One by one, he accomplished all those goals. The neighbors called him the miracle cat.

Over time, Obie became the sweetest little guy you can imagine. He would get up on my chest in the middle of the night and purr and drool excitedly while I petted him. Then he'd shake his head, and it was like being in a drool shower. If you don't love cats, I'm sure that sounds gross, but if you love cats, you'll understand—it's like being in heaven.

And whenever I was outside, Obie would follow me around like a puppy and nudge my legs every few feet to get me to stop. Then he'd roll over so I could pet his tummy. Touching his stomach was another huge milestone. Initially, he was so paranoid that he wouldn't even let us touch his back.

Although my wife and I had heard that feral cats can only learn to trust one person at most, this turned out not to be true. When my colleagues and students came to our house on Sundays, Obie worked the crowd and schmoozed with everybody. Obie really *was* a miracle cat. He became my best friend, and I came to love him more than life itself.

Now I don't want you to think that Obie was a saint. He was very flawed, just like the rest of us. Several years ago, my wife and I were honored to have Dr. Jeffrey Zeig stay with us during a visit. Dr. Zeig is the head of the Milton H. Erickson Foundation, the group that puts on the wonderful Evolution of Psychotherapy Conference I talked about previously. Dr. Zeig stayed overnight at our house and did a dramatic demonstration of indirect hypnosis for my training group at Stanford the next day.

At one point, Dr. Zeig and I were sitting at my computer checking something on the internet. I think Obie felt jealous and a bit threatened that Dr. Zeig was spending too much time with me. To let me know how he was feeling, Obie peed on the modem right in front of us and shut the internet down, as if he were saying, "Take that, Daddy. I'll teach you not to spend time with male visitors!"

I had to replace the modem. But I have to admit that I was kind of proud of the little guy. And I still am.

So what were the lessons I learned from Obie? And what does this have to do with the treatment of depression, or the first Great Death?

First, he taught me about the incredible importance of patience, kindness, optimism, and compassion. Although TEAM-CBT is incredibly powerful, this treatment method alone will not be enough if you're hoping for the miracle of recovery. Gentleness, warmth, and compassion have to be part of the mix. That's because depression results from the belief that you're defective, a "failure," or a "loser." Recovery results from the decision to treat yourself with love and compassion instead.

Second, Obie taught me that when you no longer have to be special, life becomes special. One of the most common themes I hear from my patients is "I'm a failure" or "I'm not good enough." During moments of self-doubt, you may also be convinced that you can never feel truly happy and fulfilled because you aren't "special." Or you may feel inferior because you aren't married, because you have a rather ordinary career, or because you have never been really outstanding at anything. I've also sometimes felt that I'm not "special" or "good enough."

Well, Obie taught me a lot about the need to be "special." Clearly, Obie was not special. He was just an ordinary, homeless, desperate cat who appeared at our kitchen door on the verge of death, hoping for some food. And although he became a healthy, proud, and gorgeous boy, he was not a purebred and couldn't win any cat shows.

And I'm not special either. I'm just an old fart now. But when I was with my buddy, Obie—just hanging out and not doing much—that was the greatest experience in the world. Obie taught me that when you no longer need to be "special," life becomes special. And that's the first of the four Great Deaths.

I have to admit that I've sometimes encouraged the Great Death of my colleagues and students too. Over the years, I've had the privilege of training many gifted young therapists, including Dr. Matthew May when he was a psychiatric resident. Matt was exceptionally skillful and a joy to work with.

One night, we were driving back to my house from a supervision session when we came to a stop sign. Matt looked at me with a very sincere look in his eyes and said, "Dr. Burns, I just want you to know that every day I'm trying *really* hard to become a better person."

I gave him an equally sincere look and said, "Matt, I really hope you get over that pretty soon!"

He suddenly got it and broke into laughter. That was *his* moment of enlightenment.

I hope you also get it now or perhaps soon. Because when your ego dies—and you discover that you are not "special" and that you no longer need to be special—life can become pretty incredible.

Thanks for listening! And thank you, Obie, for loving me and teaching me so much. I will love and miss you forever.

## THE SECOND GREAT DEATH: THE DEATH OF THE FEARFUL SELF

The second Great Death involves recovery from anxiety. When you surrender to the terrifying monster you fear the most instead of running away, you will make the incredible and startling discovery that the monster has no teeth. You might recall that this technique is called exposure. It's been around for 2,500 years, and it's absolutely necessary in the treatment of anxiety disorders.

For example, a young man named Luther recently emailed me to ask if he could attend one of my Sunday hikes. He explained that he was a college student majoring in psychology. Usually, the hikes are limited to folks in my training groups, but I decided to make an exception since he seemed very sincere and said he might be heading for a mental health career.

Luther showed up at my front door last Sunday morning after having driven several hundred miles. That's what I call motivation!

Luther explained that he sweated a great deal, especially when he felt anxious, and was intensely ashamed of this. He believed others would look down on him if they discovered his secret flaw, so he constantly struggled to hide the fact that he was sweaty.

To make matters worse, he was quite handsome and a member of a prestigious fraternity at his university, so he felt that appearance was exceptionally important. You've learned that emotional problems often result from our self-defeating beliefs, like perfectionism or addictions to achievement, love, or approval. These beliefs are a part of our personal value system, and they can motivate us to work hard and achieve. But the very same beliefs can also trigger emotional distress.

Perceived perfectionism was one of Luther's self-defeating beliefs. This is the belief that others expect you to be perfect and that they won't love or accept you if they find out about your flaws.

Luther had received lots of treatment, but apparently nothing had been effective. He said his previous therapist had given up on him and referred him to a psychiatrist for drug treatment. Luther was reluctant to take medications for anxiety, something I applaud. Although medications can sometimes be helpful or even lifesaving for people with severe psychiatric problems, most anxiety can now be treated effectively without drugs.

My colleague, Sunny Choi, also attended the hike and did some excellent TEAM-CBT with Luther as we hiked along some gorgeous trails for about seven miles. After the hike, we went out for lunch at our favorite dim sum restaurant.

After lunch, I suggested that Luther could do some shame-attacking exercises as an experiment to test his belief that others expected him to be perfect. Specifically, I urged him to go up to strangers and say something like:

*Hi, I'd like to talk to you for just a moment if I can. I want you to know that I have a tendency to sweat way more than most people, and I try to hide it because I'm really ashamed and afraid that people will judge me or be turned off if they notice. In fact, I'm sweating quite a bit right now. You can probably see the sweat on my face. But I've decided to stop hiding it and stop being ashamed. So that's why I'm telling you!*

Well, as you can imagine, this assignment freaked him out, but being brave and strongly motivated, he (rather reluctantly) agreed.

The first group of strangers we approached happened to be three young Asian guys who looked pretty tough. I stopped them and told them that my friend had something he needed to tell them. They looked rather angry and impatient while Luther was talking, so the tensions and feelings of anxiety were definitely on the rise. When he finished, the middle fellow reached forward and put his hands on Luther's shoulders. Were we about to see a fight?

I was surprised to see that the fellow had tears in his eyes. He said, "I'm gay, and I've been hiding it, and what you just said meant so much to me! I'm going to stop hiding the fact that I'm gay!" Then he hugged Luther, and we were on our way.

So much for the monster!

## THE THIRD GREAT DEATH: THE DEATH OF THE ANGRY, BLAMING SELF

The third Great Death involves the transformation of conflicted, hostile relationships into ones that are far more loving and trusting. This death involves the intensely painful but liberating discovery that we are not actually innocent victims of the other person's "badness." Although we may tell ourselves that the problem is the other person's fault, we are almost always creating the very problem we are complaining about. You could even say that we are almost *forcing* the other person to treat us badly and then pointing the finger of blame at him or her.

I understand this may not sound politically correct and may even be offensive. But before you throw the book away in disgust, let me give you an example of what I'm talking about.

A colleague named Lee told me that he wanted help with a marital problem. He explained that his wife, Liza, was overly controlling and critical of him, and he attributed this to the fact that she had an overly controlling mother. This is very typical of how most people with troubled relationships feel—we tend to blame the other person, and Lee was no exception. He was firmly convinced Liza was the one who needed to change.

Lee initially thought I'd offer couples therapy, but I prefer to treat just one person in a troubled relationship—and that's the person who's asking for help. That's because I can make that person accountable, and the moment he or she changes, the partner will nearly always change as well.

Whenever I'm working with someone with a relationship problem, I use a powerful tool called the relationship journal, which you may remember from chapter 17. The relationship journal helps you understand why you're having conflicts with the person you're not getting along with. It allows you to pinpoint your own role in the problem so you can suddenly "see" how you are triggering the exact problem you've been complaining about.

For example:

- If your complaint is that the other person won't express his or her feelings, you will discover that you are *preventing* that person from expressing these feelings.

- Or if your complaint is that the other person won't listen, you will discover that you are *preventing* him or her from listening.

- Or if you are convinced that the other person isn't interested in your feelings, you will see that you are *forcing* him or her to react negatively when you try to express your feelings.

- Or if you are frustrated and annoyed because the other person is relentlessly critical or controlling, you will discover that you are *forcing* him or her to be critical and controlling.

These insights can be humiliating and shocking, but if you have the courage to examine your own role in the problem, you will discover that this Great Death of your angry, blaming "self" can be tremendously empowering.

Now let's get down to specifics and see if this is really true for Lee! I asked Lee to focus on one unpleasant exchange he'd had with Liza and to complete the first two steps of the relationship journal. In Step 1, you write down exactly what the other person said to you, and in Step 2, you write down exactly what you said next. You also indicate how you think the other person was feeling, as well as the way you were feeling.

For these first two steps, Lee described an incident when he was trying to convince their 18-month-old daughter to put her pajamas on. She didn't respond, so Lee raised his voice and spoke to her in a stern manner. This is what his relationship journal looked like at this point:

| Step 1: Write down *exactly* what the other person said. Be brief: | Step 2: Write down *exactly* what you said next. Be brief: |
|---|---|
| Liza said, "I don't think you need to use that tone with a small child." | I said, "I don't think there was anything wrong with what I did. You can be stern without losing your shit. There are times when she needs to know I am serious and not messing around anymore." |
| Circle the emotions *he or she* might have been feeling | Circle the emotions *you* were feeling |
| **Sad,** blue, depressed, down, unhappy | **Sad,** blue, depressed, down, unhappy |
| **Anxious,** worried, panicky, nervous, frightened | **Anxious,** worried, panicky, nervous, frightened |
| **Guilty,** remorseful, bad, ashamed | **Guilty,** remorseful, bad, ashamed |
| **Inferior,** worthless, inadequate, defective, incompetent | **Inferior,** worthless, inadequate, defective, incompetent |
| **Lonely,** unloved, unwanted, rejected, alone, abandoned | **Lonely,** unloved, unwanted, rejected, alone, abandoned |
| **Embarrassed,** foolish, humiliated, self-conscious | **Embarrassed,** foolish, humiliated, self-conscious |
| **Hopeless,** discouraged, pessimistic, despairing | **Hopeless,** discouraged, pessimistic, despairing |
| **Frustrated,** stuck, thwarted, defeated | **Frustrated,** stuck, thwarted, defeated |
| **Angry,** mad, resentful, annoyed, irritated, upset, furious | **Angry,** mad, resentful, annoyed, irritated, upset, furious |
| **Other** (specify) Troubled, defensive, dismayed, downhearted, disconnected | **Other** (specify) Agitated, defensive, stubborn, exasperated, sarcastic, powerless, diminished, low, resistant, confused, judgmental, vulnerable, inept |

As you can see, Lee responded to Liza by arguing and defending himself. Then the conflict escalated into a heated debate about how to raise their daughter, the exact argument that seemed to be happening over and over.

Now for the hard part!

In Step 3 of the relationship journal, you examine what you wrote down in Step 2 and ask yourself if it was an example of good communication or bad communication using the EAR checklist. In particular, you ask yourself if you acknowledged the other person's feelings (empathy), shared your own feelings (assertiveness), and conveyed a warm and loving attitude (respect).

In Lee's case, the analysis was a no-brainer. Clearly, Lee hadn't acknowledged *any* of his wife's feelings, and he didn't find any truth in her criticism either. Instead, he defended himself (no E = Empathy). He also didn't share his own feelings openly and directly (no A = Assertiveness). Finally, he didn't convey any warmth, love, or caring (no R = respect).

Yikes! Looks like we'll have to give Lee three check marks in the bad communication column.

## EAR Checklist*

| ☞ | Good Communication | ✓ | Bad Communication | ✓ |
|---|---|---|---|---|
| E = Empathy | 1. You acknowledge the other person's feelings and find some truth in what he or she said. | | 1. You ignore the other person's feelings or argue and insist he or she is "wrong." | ✓ |
| A = Assertiveness | 2. You share your feelings openly and directly. | | 2. You express your feelings aggressively or not at all. | ✓ |
| R = Respect | 3. Your attitude is respectful and caring. | | 3. Your attitude is not respectful or caring. | ✓ |

Step 3 is painful, and intentionally so, because you have to stop blaming the other person and look at your own role in the problem. Remember, Lee felt like his wife was being overly controlling and overly critical. In his mind, the finger of blame was pointing directly at her. But when he was forced to examine his own role in the problem, the finger of blame rotated 180 degrees and seemed to be pointing directly at him!

If this realization isn't painful enough, it's about to get even more painful. In Step 4, you ask yourself about the impact of your response on the person you're in conflict with. Lee can ask himself questions like this:

*How will my response impact Liza? What will she conclude? How will she think, feel, and behave? What will happen next? Will my response make the problem better or worse?*

Think about it for a moment before you continue reading.

Lee had been complaining that Liza was constantly criticizing him and trying to control him. But when she expressed her concerns, Lee ignored her feelings and argued with her. As a result, she continued to criticize him because she wanted him to get it. In other words, Lee was *forcing* her to be critical of him.

In addition, he wasn't showing any respect for Liza's concerns about their daughter, so her worrying just intensified. She was afraid that his excessive sternness would frighten their daughter and make her feel unloved and unsafe. And because Liza loved their daughter intensely, she kept trying to persuade him to change his behavior. And that's exactly what he was complaining about!

Can you see that now?

When Lee suddenly "saw" this during the session, he broke down and began to cry. It was shocking to him, but he could not deny what he saw in the relationship journal. This was the Great Death of Lee's ego, and I have to admit that when he broke down, I felt tremendously close to him!

Finally, in Step 5, you revise what you wrote down in Step 2 using the five secrets of effective communication. Once you get an excellent response on paper, you can role-play with a therapist or friend so you can learn to respond more effectively in real time.

## Five Secrets of Effective Communication (EAR)*

| E = Empathy |
| --- |
| 1. **The Disarming Technique.** Find some truth in what the other person is saying, even if it seems totally unreasonable or unfair.<br>2. **Empathy.** Put yourself in the other person's shoes and try to see the world through his or her eyes.<br> • **Thought Empathy.** Paraphrase the other person's words.<br> • **Feeling Empathy.** Acknowledge how the other person is probably feeling based on what he or she said.<br>3. **Inquiry.** Ask gentle, probing questions to learn more about what the other person is thinking and feeling. |
| **A = Assertiveness** |
| 4. **"I Feel" Statements.** Express your own ideas and feelings in a direct, tactful manner. Use "I feel" statements (such as "I feel upset") rather than "you" statements (such as "You're wrong!" or "You're making me furious!") |
| **R = Respect** |
| 5. **Stroking.** Convey an attitude of respect even if you feel frustrated or angry with the other person. Find something genuinely positive to say to the other person even in the heat of battle. |

Using the five secrets of effective communication, here is how Lee could revise his response to Liza:

> *You're right—I was frustrated and got overly aggressive with her* (disarming technique). *I'm feeling guilty, inadequate, and ashamed right now* ("I feel" statement). *I really love you and our daughter more than anything in the world, and I imagine that you might be feeling really unhappy with me* (stroking, feeling empathy). *You might be feeling worried and maybe even a bit angry with me too* (feeling empathy). *Can you tell me more about how you are feeling?* (inquiry)

Perhaps you can see that a response along these lines would lead to greater trust because Lee is opening the door to communication and conveying love and respect rather than arguing and slamming the door shut.

---

* Copyright © 1991 by David D. Burns, MD. Revised 2006.

But is that what actually happened in Lee's case? After the session, Lee sent this beautiful follow-up note:

*I had a lightbulb moment this week, and I wanted to share it with you.*

*I have been communicating with Liza as coached, but something happened I wasn't expecting. Liza began giving me little passive-aggressive digs. I didn't handle them very well and found myself back in a conflict situation with her laying the blame squarely back to me.*

*I told her that the session didn't work because I needed her also to understand her part in this problem and that I wouldn't accept these little digs. Then it hit me that she was throwing punches because she was unhappy.*

*Once I realized this, I began expressing empathy instead of angst. I dropped the need to be a man "as society defines it" and became the man I wanted to be. Once I flipped and was able to rise above my ego, her demeanor changed, and she fell in love with me again.*

*I wanted to share that with you. I was close to emailing you to tell you I had failed before this happened.*

*Thanks for everything!*

The session with Lee was recorded and published as a series of three *Feeling Good* podcasts. They are entirely free of charge, and you can find them on my website (Podcasts 096–098).

So what does the session with Lee have to do with the third Great Death of the "self"? Mystics and philosophers through the ages have talked about self-examination. They say we have to look within to find the "answer."

But what is this "answer" we're supposed to be looking for, and how do we look within? I never knew what that meant until I started working with individuals with troubled relationships.

Now the answer is crystal clear. The relationship journal gives you the opportunity to "look within" and discover how you create your own interpersonal reality at every minute of every day—*if* you're willing to do that!

It also allows you to examine the Buddhist concept of "oneness." According to Buddhists, the universe is "one" and our suffering—as well as evil—result from the illusion that we're separate from the rest of the universe. But there is no "external reality" and no separate "self."

You could think of Step 4 of the relationship journal as practical Buddhism because it allows you to discover that you and the person you're not getting along with are not separate from each other. Instead, you are both enmeshed in a system of circular causality. You're constantly provoking and reinforcing each other's negative behavior. The other person is not a "separate" and malignant entity that's doing something *to* you but is the manifestation of the interpersonal reality that you create every time you interact with him or her.

You are both "one." This discovery can be extraordinarily liberating and empowering, but it comes at a steep price—the death of the ego. Looking at your own role in the problem can be extremely shocking, painful, and even humiliating.

Although this third "death" of your ego may not sound terribly appealing, it can also be tremendously empowering. When you let go of your own defensiveness, convey genuine humility and respect, and find the truth in the other person's criticisms, he or she will nearly always do the same.

Now I have to issue a disclaimer because I don't want you to get the wrong idea. Some people may be trapped in abusive and violent relationships. If so, it may be extremely difficult or impossible to create a loving and trusting relationship with that person no matter how skillfully you use the five secrets of effective communication.

In these cases, you may be far better off cutting ties rather than investing further in a relationship that is destined for more abuse. However, if you decide to leave, then the five secrets may be even more important so you can leave the relationship safely.

## THE FOURTH GREAT DEATH: THE DEATH OF THE ENTITLED, PLEASURE-SEEKING SELF

The final Great Death is involved in the recovery from habits and addictions. This includes all the typical addictions, like overeating, drinking, gambling, using drugs, shopping, sex and porn, and procrastination. But it also includes recovery from psychological addictions to love, approval, achievement, power, and wealth.

Lots of people believe that habits and addictions result from emotional problems, like depression, anxiety, loneliness, or troubled relationships. The idea is that you may be "treating" your loneliness or depression with food, alcohol, or drugs. A few years ago, I had a chance to test this theory in patients who had been newly admitted to the psychiatric inpatient unit of Stanford University Hospital.

I examined whether habits and addictions—such as binge eating and anorexia, as well as alcohol and drug abuse—in these patients resulted from emotional problems, like depression, anxiety, loneliness, relationships conflicts, and personality disorders.

What kinds of personal and emotional problems do you think were the most strongly associated with these habits and addictions?

I was shocked to discover that there were few, if any, significant relationships between addictions and emotional problems. In fact, depression was associated with eating, but the correlation was in the wrong direction. The more depressed you were, the less you ate!

The only variable that was significantly associated with habits and addictions was patients' scores on my Temptations Test, which you also completed in chapter 1, and that association was incredibly strong.

The data strongly suggested that habits and addictions primarily result from the intense human desire to gratify our cravings and not because of the problems in our lives. In other words, habits and addictions result from the belief that we need our fix, and we need it now, and that life without our favorite yummy food, or another drink or two, would be drab and unrewarding. The Great Death of this entitled, pleasure-seeking self leads to the liberating discovery that you *don't* actually need these things to feel happy and fulfilled. But the death of our pleasure-seeking "self" is not so easy because none of us wants to give up our favorite "fix."

In the original draft of this book, I created two chapters on the treatment of habits and addictions, including some amazing new techniques to deal with the powerful cravings and urges that trigger habits and addictions. The bad news is the book was too long, so I removed them.

But here's the good news: You can download those two chapters for *free* on my website right on the bottom of the homepage. If you're struggling with habits or addictions, check out these chapters, and let me know what you think!

## JOIN THE GRATEFUL DEAD

In this chapter, we've talked about four Great Deaths of the self. Most of us are afraid to die because we think we will lose something that's incredibly valuable and important. But when your ego "dies," it's not like going to a funeral. It's more like getting out of prison or going to a fantastic celebration. When you lose your "self," you inherit the world, along with the freedom to explore and enjoy it. In fact, once your "self" has "died," you can join the Grateful Dead.

You will discover that the Great Death is actually the Great Rebirth. It's one of the most amazing and helpful things I've learned in my career and in my life. And I hope it's been helpful to you too.

If you're still afraid of your own Great Death, you might like this poem by Rumi (translated by Coleman Barks). One of my dear colleagues, Dr. Brandon Vance, kindly sent the poem to me when he was reviewing a draft of this book. He said he loved this poem because it reminded him of the death of the ego. It might inspire you too!

*Into this new love, die.*

*Your way begins on the other side.*

*Become the sky.*

*Take an axe to the prison wall.*

*Escape.*

*Walk out like someone suddenly born into color—*

*Do it now.*

# Section IV

## *Relapse Prevention Training*

# 28 | How Are You Feeling Now?

This book has been all about changing the way you feel, so let's see if there have been any changes! You took these tests in chapter 1 based on how you were feeling then, and I'd like you to take them again based on how you're feeling now. Once you've checked off how you feel, make sure you put the totals for each test in the box at the bottom. This should only take a couple of minutes.

## Part 1. Your Moods*

**Instructions:** Use checks (✓) to indicate how you're feeling *right now*.
**Answer all items.**

| Depression | 0—Not at all | 1—Somewhat | 2—Moderately | 3—A lot | 4—Extremely |
|---|---|---|---|---|---|
| 1. Sad or down in the dumps | | | | | |
| 2. Discouraged or hopeless | | | | | |
| 3. Low in self-esteem, inferior, or worthless | | | | | |
| 4. Unmotivated to do things | | | | | |
| 5. Decreased pleasure or satisfaction in life | | | | | |

Total Items 1 to 5 ➔

| Anxiety | | | | | |
|---|---|---|---|---|---|
| 1. Anxious | | | | | |
| 2. Frightened | | | | | |
| 3. Worrying about things | | | | | |
| 4. Tense or on edge | | | | | |
| 5. Nervous | | | | | |

Total Items 1 to 5 ➔

## Part 2. Your Relationships*

**Instructions:** Use checks (✓) to indicate how you're feeling *right now*.
**Answer all items.**

| Anger | 0—Not at all | 1—Somewhat | 2—Moderately | 3—A lot | 4—Extremely |
|---|---|---|---|---|---|
| 1. Frustrated | | | | | |
| 2. Annoyed | | | | | |
| 3. Resentful | | | | | |
| 4. Angry | | | | | |
| 5. Irritated | | | | | |

Total Items 1 to 5 ➜

## Relationship Satisfaction Scale*

Think about an important relationship, like your spouse, partner, friend, colleague, or family member. Use checks (✓) to indicate how you feel about this relationship.

**Answer all items.**

| | 0—Very dissatisfied | 1—Moderately dissatisfied | 2—Somewhat dissatisfied | 3—Neutral | 4—Somewhat satisfied | 5—Moderately satisfied | 6—Very satisfied |
|---|---|---|---|---|---|---|---|
| 1. Communication and openness | | | | | | | |
| 2. Resolving conflicts | | | | | | | |
| 3. Degree of affection and caring | | | | | | | |
| 4. Intimacy and closeness | | | | | | | |
| 5. Overall satisfaction | | | | | | | |

Total Items 1 to 5 ➜

## You're doing great. You're almost done!

## Part 3. Temptations Test*

**Instructions:** Use checks (✓) to indicate how much each statement describes how you have been feeling in the past week, including today.

**Answer all items.**

| | 0—Not at all true | 1—Slightly true | 2—Moderately true | 3—Very true | 4—Completely true |
|---|---|---|---|---|---|
| 1. Sometimes I crave drugs or alcohol. | | | | | |
| 2. Sometimes I have the urge to use drugs or alcohol. | | | | | |
| 3. Sometimes I really want to use drugs or alcohol. | | | | | |
| 4. Sometimes it's hard to resist the urge to use drugs or alcohol. | | | | | |
| 5. Sometimes I struggle with the temptation to use drugs or alcohol. | | | | | |
| Total Items 1 to 5 ➔ | | | | | |

## Part 4. Happiness Test

**Instructions:** Use checks (✓) to indicate how you're feeling *right now.*

**Answer all items.**

| | 0—Not at all | 1—Somewhat | 2—Moderately | 3—A lot | 4—Extremely |
|---|---|---|---|---|---|
| 1. Happy and joyful | | | | | |
| 2. Hopeful and optimistic | | | | | |
| 3. Worthwhile, high self-esteem | | | | | |
| 4. Motivated, productive | | | | | |
| 5. Pleased and satisfied with life | | | | | |
| Total Items 1 to 5 ➔ | | | | | |

What can we learn from the tests you took in chapter 1 and in this chapter? If you compare your initial scores on the mood, relationship, temptations, and happiness scales with how you're feeling now, you'll see how much your thoughts and feelings have changed while you've been reading this book.

---

You can calculate your before-and-after scores using this chart:

| | Total Score | | |
|---|---|---|---|
| **Test** | **Chapter 1** | **Now** | **Change** |
| Depression | | | |
| Anxiety | | | |
| Anger | | | |
| Relationship Satisfaction | | | |
| Temptations | | | |
| Happiness | | | |

Hopefully that wasn't too tough, assuming you completed the scales and totaled your scores at both times. What can we conclude from these scores? What do the changes or lack of changes mean?

Here's how you might think about it: If your scores on the depression and anxiety scales have fallen all the way to 0 (or close to 0), and if your happiness score has increased and is close to 20, then it means that you're probably feeling great, so you're ready for relapse prevention training in the next chapter.

Congratulations! That's really cool! I'm proud of you and incredibly happy that my book seems to have been helpful to you. That's what I was hoping when I wrote it.

But if your scores on the depression and anxiety tests have not improved as much as you'd like, what can you do?

First, there's no shame in getting help from a professional. You can check out the referral suggestions on my website or simply google therapists in your area. I'm sure you'll find tons of resources.

Second, there are many free resources for support throughout the United States, as well as throughout the world, such as Recovery International, which is a little bit like Alcoholics Anonymous, but this group focuses on recovery from depression and anxiety: www.recoveryinternational.org.

Third, I have created tons of additional resources for you as well, and most of them are also absolutely free. I've listed them in chapter 32.

But if you think you're ready to move on to relapse prevention training, then keep on reading so we can get you feeling great for good!

# 29 | Feeling Great for Good!

Once you're free of depression and anxiety, it's time for relapse prevention training. Relapse prevention training is super important because negative thoughts and feelings have a way of coming back. Very few people—perhaps no one—can feel happy all the time. We all hit occasional bumps in the road. But if you know how to deal with relapses, they don't have to be disasters.

As I mentioned in the introduction, Dr. Forrest Scogin and his colleagues found that individuals with moderate to severe depression who recovered after reading a copy of my first book, *Feeling Good,* continued to improve on their own two and three years later.

These patients said they weren't happy all the time but had the same ups and downs that anyone experiences. However, when they started to feel down, they just took *Feeling Good* off the shelf and reread the sections that had been the most helpful to them the first time around. And then they recovered again. You might want to do the same thing.

The relapse prevention training I do requires just a little more work on your part, but it will definitely be worth the effort because you'll learn how to nip relapses in the bud.

I don't do relapse prevention training until my patients' scores have fallen all the way to 0 or very close to 0. That's why the testing in the previous chapter is so important. It allows you to see exactly how much you've improved and whether you're completely recovered or need more work using the tools in this book.

There are three important steps in relapse prevention training. You must:

1. Accept the fact that relapses are *inevitable* and cannot be avoided.

2. Understand that the tool(s) that helped you recover the first time will probably *always* work for you.

3. Practice talking back ahead of time to the negative thoughts you'll have when you relapse.

## STEP 1

First, it's crucial for you to know that you *will* relapse. It's not a matter of if, but when. It's impossible to feel happy all the time. But don't panic! I'll show you exactly how to handle relapses so you won't need to be afraid of them.

I emphasize this because lots of people I've treated have gone from the "nothing" side of all-or-nothing thinking when they were depressed to the "all" side when they recover, as I mentioned in chapter 12. In other words, when they're depressed, they think they're worthless and hopeless. That's the "nothing" side. Then when they recover, they feel *so* good and think, "Wow— I've got it! I'm worthwhile after all! My problems are solved! I'll feel terrific forever. And it's so easy!" That's the dangerous "all" side of all-or-nothing thinking.

The "all" side is a problem because it's a positive distortion, and if you believe those thoughts, then you set yourself up for failure when you relapse. You'll feel shocked and devastated, and you may conclude that your "recovery" was just a hoax and that you were just fooling yourself. But if you accept the fact that we all feel down from time to time, then you won't make this mistake.

But what exactly is a relapse? I define a relapse as one minute or more of feeling crummy—down, anxious, irritable, or upset. According to that definition, we all relapse all the time. As long as you know that you can pop out of a bad mood fairly quickly, a "relapse" doesn't have to be a big thing. In fact, you can learn and grow during relapses, even though they can be painful and discouraging.

I'm actually in a bit of a "relapse" right now. I'm feeling pretty upset because one of my former students is working on an app based on my recent work without my permission and without collaboration. It hurts me that she's trying to commercialize my work without including me. I feel sad, anxious, confused, and a bit angry too.

But I know I will find a solution even though I have no idea what the solution will be. As they say, "This too shall pass," and I'll get back to feeling good—or even great—again.

So if relapses are inevitable, what can you expect? How much happiness is normal?

Here's my rule of thumb: We're all entitled to an average of five happy days per week and two lousy days. If you're not having your five good days, then you're being cheated, and you need a little tune-up. And if you don't have your two bad days per week, then you may be getting a little *too* happy, and we may have to put you on lithium!

## STEP 2

The second step in relapse prevention training is knowing that the techniques that worked for you initially will probably *always* work for you. When you get upset in the future, your negative thoughts will be similar, if not identical, to the negative thoughts you worked on in this book.

Most of us have just one pattern of suffering that gets repeated over and over again every time we get upset. That's why the same techniques that were helpful to you the first time you recovered will nearly always be effective in the future too.

So whenever you find yourself slipping back into negative moods, return to the methods that worked for you the first time. For example, you might have been helped by positive reframing, the double standard technique, or the acceptance paradox. You'll find that your job will be much easier the second time around because you can just use the same technique.

## STEP 3

The third step in relapse prevention training is practicing how you'll talk back to the negative thoughts you'll have when you relapse. I mentioned that when you relapse, your own negative thoughts will return. That's because we're all different, and we'll all have our own, unique negative thoughts when we relapse.

But nearly everyone will also have several additional negative thoughts when they relapse, and those thoughts are almost always the same for all of us. You'll have thoughts like these:

- The therapy didn't really work. I knew it couldn't last!
- I really am a hopeless case.
- My improvement was just a fluke.
- I wasn't really better. I just *thought* I was.
- My problems are too deep.
- I'm a worthless case after all.

If you haven't prepared for these thoughts, then they will be *totally* believable and devastating. But if you practice smashing those distorted thoughts ahead of time when you're feeling good, then it will be much easier for you to crush them when you relapse.

You can practice smashing these negative thoughts by preparing a Relapse Prevention Journal—like the one on the next page—today, *before* you relapse. So let's smash those negative thoughts right now!

Let's first imagine that you've recovered from a long bout with depression and anxiety, and you've had three really happy weeks. Then, on a Friday night, you have a fight with your spouse and forget to use the five secrets of effective communication. You go to bed angry and wake up on Saturday feeling incredibly depressed and anxious again.

## My Answer

Here are the distortions I spotted:

1. **All-or-Nothing Thinking.** You're thinking about the therapy in black-or-white terms. If you improved, then the treatment was helpful, which means you can't be "hopeless." All human beings get upset from time to time.

2. **Overgeneralization.** You're generalizing from the present moment—you're upset right now—to the future in thinking you're a hopeless case.

3. **Mental Filter.** You are focusing on how upset you feel right now and overlooking the significant progress you made in therapy.

4. **Discounting the Positive.** You're telling yourself that the methods you learned in therapy or in this book weren't helpful—but they were!

5. **Jumping to Conclusions.** You're engaging in fortune telling by predicting that you'll be depressed forever.

6. **Magnification or Minimization.** Although a relapse is upsetting, you may be blowing it out of proportion and minimizing the skills you've acquired. It might be more productive to focus on why you're upset and to make a plan for dealing with the problem.

7. **Emotional Reasoning.** You feel hopeless, so you conclude that you are hopeless.

8. **Labeling.** You're labeling yourself as "a hopeless case."

9. **Should Statement.** There may be some hidden shoulds here. You may be thinking that you shouldn't ever get upset and that you should feel happy all the time.

10. **Blame.** Calling yourself hopeless is a classic case of self-blame, and insisting that therapy didn't work is a classic example of other-blame.

As you can see, this negative thought is loaded with distortions.

Now ask yourself how you could talk back to that thought. See if you can come up with a convincing positive thought that satisfies the two conditions for emotional change: It has to be 100% true (necessary condition), and it has to reduce your belief in the negative thought dramatically (sufficient condition).

Write this new thought in the positive thought column of your Relapse Prevention Journal. Then indicate how strongly you believe it on a scale of 0 to 100 in the "% Belief" column. Next, re-estimate your belief in the negative thought in the "% After" column.

If you're having trouble coming up with a positive thought that satisfies the two conditions for emotional change, here's something I came up with:

*The therapy was very effective because I improved a lot. I had a fight with my spouse, so it's not surprising that I'd be upset. This doesn't mean I'm "hopeless." It just means that I need to pick up the tools and use them again.*

This is usually pretty easy if you do it *before* you relapse when you're feeling happy and confident. If you wait until *after* you've relapsed, you'll find that you'll be climbing out of a pretty deep hole. This is one case where an ounce of prevention is definitely worth a pound of cure.

In case that paragraph went in one ear and out the other, I suggest that you read it again! I don't mean to be insulting—but that paragraph could protect you from enormous grief and might possibly even save your life. I can't emphasize three facts enough:

1. The negative thoughts you have when you relapse will be massively distorted.

2. If you wait until you relapse to challenge them, your belief in the thoughts will be overwhelming, and it will be extremely difficult to crush them.

3. If you crush them ahead of time, it will be vastly easier to crush them when you relapse!

After you've smashed all of your negative thoughts on paper, you can try the **externalization of voices** technique to help solidify your learning on an emotional level. You and another person, such as a friend, family member, or therapist, take turns playing the role of your negative self and your positive self.

In particular, your partner will play the role of your negative self and speak in the second person ("you"), while you play the role of your positive self and speak in the first person ("I"). Your partner will read your negative thoughts to you, one at a time, while you will try to defend yourself.

Make sure you and your partner both understand that you are imagining you have experienced a relapse several weeks after your initial recovery. It's also important that you record the role-play so you can listen and review it later on when you relapse.

Finally, make sure that you and the other person realize you are both the same person in the role-play. One of you will be playing the role of your negative self, and the other will be playing the role of your positive self.

The dialogue might go like this:

**Partner (as your negative self):** This relapse proves that you'll *never* get better. You're a hopeless case.

**You (as your positive self):** No, this relapse is understandable. I had a fight with my spouse last night, and it's time to pick up the tools that were so helpful to me several weeks ago, like the five secrets of effective communication. I'm sure if we talk things over, we'll be able to resolve this conflict, just as we've done in the past. And then I'll feel really good again!

**Partner (as your negative self):** The therapy didn't work.

**You (as your positive self):** No, the therapy was very helpful. My problem isn't that the therapy didn't work. My problem is that I'm listening to your BS instead of figuring out how I can talk things over with my spouse.

**Partner (as your negative self):** Your improvement was just a fluke.

**You (as your positive self):** No, my improvement was the result of what I learned and the effort I put in.

**Partner (as your negative self):** You weren't really better. You just *thought* you were.

**You (as your positive self):** Actually, the last three weeks have been some of the happiest days of my life, and it *was* real! In fact, it was terrific!

**Partner (as your negative self):** This relapse proves that you're worthless after all.

**You (as your positive self):** That's just ridiculous! I have tons of flaws and always will, but I have a lot of strengths too.

If you get stuck and can't convincingly smash one of your negative thoughts, do a role reversal. You can play the role of your negative self and your partner can play the role of your positive self. Keep doing role reversals with the same thought until you can both knock it out of the park.

Don't settle for a partial victory when you do this exercise. When you relapse, the thoughts will seem really powerful and persuasive. That's why you need to prepare for them ahead of time. If you're struggling with a relapse, you can listen to the recording you made. You'll probably find that it's extremely helpful.

And if you're still struggling, you can reach out to a therapist for help. There's no shame in that. I tell all my patients that I will never terminate them and that if they want, they can think of me as their shrink for the rest of their life. I explain that if they ever need a tune-up, they can just give me a call. I give lifetime guarantees, and the tune-ups are all free of charge! I also tell them that I really hope they *do* relapse because if they don't, I'll never see them again!

Does relapse prevention training work? I've had nearly 40,000 therapy sessions with individuals struggling with severe depression and anxiety. I've always done relapse prevention training prior to discharge. It only takes about thirty minutes at most. Over the years, very few of my patients have ever returned for a tune-up, and in almost every case, it was just one or two sessions and they were good to go again.

Well, my goodness, we're just about done. I'm sad, to be honest, because I have really loved writing this book for you. There have been tremendous and exciting developments in psychotherapy since I wrote *Feeling Good* so many years ago, and it has been my pleasure and an honor to share them with you.

In the next chapter, you're going to meet a most unusual man, Dr. Mark Noble from the University of Rochester. He's a Stanford-trained geneticist and molecular biologist with an illustrious research career. In fact, he's one of the early pioneers of stem cell research, and he's world famous. And he's also a really nice, funny, down-to-earth guy.

But why in the world would he be writing a chapter in this book? Well, you're about to find out, and it's pretty exciting!

# Research Update: Does Science Support TEAM-CBT?

# 30 | TEAM-CBT and the Art of Micro-Neurosurgery

## WHO IS DR. MARK NOBLE?

One of the important next steps in the development of TEAM-CBT is to understand how this therapy works at the level of brain functioning. This chapter of *Feeling Great* offers the first steps in this direction, provided by Dr. Mark Noble, a professor of genetics and neuroscience at the University of Rochester Medical Center.

Dr. Noble is considered one of the founders of modern stem cell biology, and his laboratory has made important contributions to our understanding of the development of the central nervous system, the adverse effects of cancer treatments on the brain, the development of safer and more effective treatments for cancer, as well as peripheral nerve and spinal cord injuries and more.

Dr. Noble contacted me because his laboratory was investigating the toxic side effects of some widely used antidepressants, and he wanted to learn more about drug-free treatments for depression and anxiety. After witnessing the remarkable recoveries occurring with TEAM-CBT, he became interested in understanding the neuroscience underlying such recovery. When his ideas were sufficiently developed, he presented them to our Tuesday training group at Stanford, which we recorded and published as *Feeling Good* podcast 100.

Dr. Noble then graciously agreed to write this chapter for *Feeling Great*. After working together on the following chapter, he also recorded a follow-up podcast (#167) that incorporates further thinking on the topic of how TEAM-CBT works at the level of brain function.

This chapter focuses on how the techniques of TEAM-CBT can rapidly modify highly specific networks of nerve cells in the brain, but many of the ideas will provide insights about how any effective treatment for depression and anxiety works. Moreover, he offers a possible explanation as to why the rapid emotional changes that we can achieve with TEAM-CBT not only make perfect sense but may even be the most appropriate brain-based definition of a successful therapy for depression, anxiety, and related problems.

## A BRAIN USER'S GUIDE TO FEELING GREAT

### by Dr. Mark Noble

Let's say you have a bacterial infection and you have a choice of three different therapies:

1. The first treatment can take years and is often not successful, but it has no side effects.

2. The second treatment is a pill that may make you feel somewhat better, somewhat worse, or could have no benefits at all. You may end up taking it for years, it could have a variety of unpleasant side effects, and it might be very difficult to stop taking it. Moreover, outcome studies have shown that it's not much more effective than a placebo.

3. The third choice often works rapidly and has no side effects.

You would definitely choose the third therapy. This is precisely the situation with TEAM-CBT:

1. Traditional talk therapies for depression or anxiety have no side effects but often continue for years.

2. Antidepressant medications can help some people, make others feel worse, and are often without benefit. Many people take them for years, and some people find it difficult to stop taking them. Outcome studies have shown that they are barely more effective than placebos.

3. In contrast, TEAM-CBT often works rapidly and has no side effects.

In fact, I've observed this rapid recovery many times on my trips to visit Dr. Burns's weekly training groups at Stanford and his famous Sunday hikes. In this book, you've read about many individuals who recovered rapidly as well—people with years of depression and anxiety who experienced a complete or near complete elimination of symptoms in a single extended therapy session.

This has been an amazing experience for me, but as a neuroscientist, I've had to ask myself three questions: (1) Is it real?, (2) Can it last?, and (3) How does it work?

I've concluded that the effects of TEAM-CBT are real and can last if the patient receives relapse prevention training following recovery. I've also concluded that these effects are strikingly consistent with our current understanding of how the brain works. I think that if we tried to design a therapy from scratch based on our most advanced understanding of how our brains work, we would probably come up with something that looks very much like TEAM-CBT.

# HOW DO OUR BRAINS WORK?

When I think about how the brain does its work, I like to think of the SNEFF model:

- **S = Structures.** Your brain is organized in *structures*, with different functions occurring in different regions of the brain.

- **N = Networks.** Information is stored and transmitted from one region to another in your brain by nerve cells, which also are called neurons. Neurons that work together are called *networks*.

- **E = Emotions.** If we are going to understand how TEAM-CBT works, then we need to understand why your *emotions* are so powerful and important to brain functioning.

- **F = Filters.** Your perceptions of the world are modulated by *filters*, which keep you from being overwhelmed by the enormous amount of information your brain is receiving every second of every day.

- **F = Frames.** Your thoughts are organized into *frames* that are critical in understanding how you organize your knowledge of the world.

Any biologically useful theory of cognitive and emotional change needs to begin with these five basic components of brain functioning.

## Structures

The brain has specialized structures that are devoted to particular tasks, including regions that specialize in the generation of emotions, the use of language, the ability to create and understand music, and so on.

Two regions thought to be important in depression and anxiety are the *amygdala* and the *prefrontal cortex*. The amygdala serves as part of an early warning system that gets activated by the possibility of danger. This "harm/alarm" system is essential to survival because responses to danger cannot be delayed until the last possible moment. If it's necessary to respond to a threat, then it is critical to have your body ready to go into fight, flight, or freeze mode before you are attacked.

You've probably seen a pet, like a cat, suddenly jump in terror at hearing a loud, unexpected sound. That's the work of the early warning system!

Activation of this early warning system occurs without conscious thought. You start breathing faster, your heart races, and chemicals that get your body ready to respond start pouring out. There is no time for logical reasoning—our responses need to be primed and ready to go. Conscious awareness of what is triggering the early warning system frequently occurs only *after* the system has already been turned on.

The early warning system prepares the body to respond to that threat. The amygdala also transmits the threat information to other parts of the brain so you can decide whether the danger is real and what, if anything, you need to do about it.

In terms of evolution, there is some value in erring on the side of going into an alarm state a little bit too easily and erring on the side of "better safe than sorry." After all, you're more likely to survive if you think there might be a tiger coming toward you and you turn out to be wrong than if there really is a tiger and you don't recognize the threat.

One job of the prefrontal cortex is to evaluate the alarm signal from the amygdala and judge whether or not action is necessary. Responding to every danger signal would not be an effective survival strategy because your brain would waste a lot of resources responding to things that really aren't threats.

You can think of the prefrontal cortex as part of a quality control system. It sends information to the amygdala that can say, "I agree with you, and we need to treat this potential threat seriously" or "I think you're overreacting, and we just need to calm down."

Many studies suggest that the early warning functions of the amygdala may be activated more easily in people with depression and anxiety, while the quality control system of the prefrontal cortex does not work as effectively. This could result from increased sensitivity of the amygdala, decreased feedback from the prefrontal cortex, or both.

Although additional brain structures are also important in understanding depression and anxiety, we can focus on the amygdala and prefrontal cortex to get a better idea of how to integrate the rapid effects of TEAM-CBT with current ideas about how the brain works.

## Networks

The human brain has an amazingly large number of nerve cells, and these cells have a lot of connections with each other. There are an estimated 100 billion nerve cells in the human brain, and each one can connect with hundreds or even thousands of other nerve cells.* That means there are as many as 100 trillion connections between the nerve cells in your brain.

Networks are groups of nerve cells that work together to transmit information from one region in the brain to another. They also send messages to the nerves that control your muscles, your heart, and your breathing, as well as the other organs in your body. Neuronal networks are also the physical units that underlie your thoughts, feelings, and behaviors, and they change whenever you learn something new, like the techniques of TEAM-CBT.

Whenever you learn, you are modifying groups of nerve cells that work in a coordinated manner. There are small networks that are very specific, and groups of small networks can work together to form larger networks. However, even the largest networks only involve a tiny fraction of the total number of nerve cells in the brain. Thus, when you are learning something new or modifying your thinking, you are changing the function of small and very precise networks of nerve cells.

How do you change the networks in your brain? Through FTWT and WTFT!

- **FTWT.** One of the most famous concepts in the science of learning is called what **F**ires **T**ogether **W**ires **T**ogether (FTWT). Nerve cells that

---

* This may actually be a low estimate, as some studies suggest that a single nerve cell can interact with as many as 10,000 other nerve cells. That would make the numbers we are considering up to ten times more amazing. The importance of these numbers for the treatment of depression and anxiety is particularly intriguing to consider because the number of neurotransmitters (which are the chemicals that nerve cells use to communicate with each other) that have been identified is in the range of 100. Thus, drugs that work on the level of neurotransmitters—which is how antidepressants, antianxiety agents, and other psychoactive drugs work—are going to affect very large numbers of nerve cells. In other words, changing neuronal function in networks by using effective learning paradigms is highly specific, like flipping a switch to control a particular light. Changing neuronal function with chemicals like antidepressants, in contrast, is like disrupting the electricity supply to an entire city because you want to turn on or off a single light somewhere in that city.

frequently interact with each other become functionally connected, and the more they fire together, the stronger the connections become. This is how new networks are formed and how existing networks become stronger.

- **WTFT.** In addition, nerve cells that are **W**ired **T**ogether tend to **F**ire **T**ogether (WTFT). WTFT explains why once you've learned something, it gets easier to repeat it every time you do it.

Let's say that you're a baby learning to put round blocks into round holes and square blocks into square holes. You start out with no idea about how to do this, but you go ahead and use nerve cells that control your hand and arm to move the block, and nerve cells in the visual parts of the brain to see the shape of the block and where the holes are. After some attempts, these different nerve cells start functioning together and create or strengthen the networks that connect these brain regions with each other. Moreover, as you repeat the exercise, these networks become stronger and stronger. Even better, you rapidly get to the point where you can just look at the shape of a new block and hole and have a good sense about whether or not they go together. In learning how to put blocks through the correct holes, you also distinguish between wrong ideas (such as "any block can fit into any hole") and correct ones (such as "the shape and size of the block and the hole need to match").

In learning, you've reached into your own brain and conducted micro-neurosurgery. In other words, you've modified specific networks in your brain so you can accomplish a new task. And you're doing this with a level of specificity that is completely out of reach of any other approach to modifying brain functioning.

The idea that you can change a small number of specific nerve cells in your brain may seem hard to believe—but that is precisely what you do every time you learn something new. And you've been doing this type of micro-neurosurgery to modify the networks in your brain ever since you were born!

### Emotions

Emotions can be so powerful that they can almost overwhelm our thoughts. That's because our emotions motivate us to do whatever it takes to increase the likelihood of survival. It makes no difference whether your interpretation of an event is wrong or right—your brain will create an emotional response appropriate to that interpretation. For example, if you're outside and hear a loud noise that sounds like a gunshot, you will instantly become afraid and fear for your life. This emotional reaction can occur so quickly and automatically that you're not even consciously aware of what caused the emotion.

Emotions also need to change when circumstances demand. If your brain's quality control systems identify a more accurate interpretation, then your emotions will change as well, and this can occur instantly and unconsciously as a natural function of the way your brain works. For example, if you realize that the loud noise you heard is actually a car backfiring, then your fear will dissipate. We've all had numerous experiences of how we began to feel differently when we suddenly realized that our thinking was off-base.

These normal workings of the brain provide an answer to the question of how TEAM-CBT can often achieve rapid recovery from depression and anxiety. The goal of TEAM-CBT is to modify the distorted negative thoughts that trigger your negative feelings. The very moment you stop believing a negative thought, like "I'm a loser" or "My problems are hopeless," your brain automatically switches to a new emotional state.

But there are times when negative emotions won't turn off so easily, as you probably know from personal experience. You may be so overwhelmingly convinced that your negative thoughts are valid that you can't easily dispute them. That's because your negative thoughts and feelings may sometimes seem to reinforce each other in a vicious cycle.

The genius of TEAM-CBT is that it provides many powerful methods based on the natural functions of the brain to weaken or eliminate these distorted thinking patterns. Even if you've been feeling emotionally overwhelmed for years or even decades, TEAM can help you change your negative thoughts and feelings, and this often can happen quickly.

## Filters

To understand why inaccurate interpretations can occur so frequently and why they can often be difficult to change, it's necessary next to consider the topics of filters and frames.

The information that we take in is heavily filtered. You can't possibly pay conscious attention—or even unconscious attention—to every noise, sight, and smell that comes your way. If you did, you'd be overwhelmed and paralyzed and wouldn't have any time or energy left for all the things you need to do.

Emotions help regulate what gets filtered out and what gets conscious attention. Have you ever noticed that when you're depressed, anxious, or angry, you're likely to focus on all the negatives and overlook the many positives that might capture your attention when you're feeling good? It seems as though the negative emotions focus your attention almost entirely on details and memories that are consistent with the way you feel.

In depression and anxiety, these information filters can cause you to interpret new information in a way that is consistent with your emotions even if that interpretation is wrong. The cognitive distortions are examples of this filtering process. All-or-nothing thinking, overgeneralization, mental filtering, discounting the positive, mind reading, fortune telling, magnification and minimization, should statements, labeling, and self-blame all occur when your brain filters information in negative ways, even when there's no valid reason to do so.

These filters can make a bad matter even worse. For example, if you're depressed and interpret neutral or even positive information in negative ways, this will make you more depressed. The increase in depression will make you continue to ignore positive information and interpret neutral information as negative. The result is a worsening spiral of negative filters and feelings.

TEAM-CBT uses many tools to break this cycle. One of the most effective ways is simply to identify the many cognitive distortions in your negative thoughts, a critical component of TEAM-CBT.

## Frames

If the goal of therapy is to change the *way* we think, then it is important to understand *how* we think. As you have learned, the connections between our thoughts are due to the connections between networks of nerve cells in our brains. However, there's not enough space in the brain to have a different set of networks for every event in our lives, so networks combine with each other, just like words combine in different ways to tell new stories. Frames are the neurologic equivalents of the stories we tell ourselves about what's happening. *They organize the way we think.*

For example, let's say that you're going to a Chinese restaurant for dinner. Thinking about this event rapidly brings to mind a large number of frames or thoughts that are related to this activity, such as:

- You will leave your home just prior to going to the restaurant. Your brain will activate a large number of related networks—and thoughts—that are needed for this activity, such as grabbing your coat from the hallway closet, opening the front door, locking it behind you, and so forth.

- As you drive to the restaurant, your brain will activate the networks that are relevant to driving, such as opening the car door, sitting in the driver's seat, fastening your seat belt, turning on the engine and the lights, putting the car in gear, and so forth.

- When you get to the restaurant, you will leave your car and walk to the front door. This involves more familiar networks and thoughts.

- Someone will greet you, take you to a table, and give you a menu. More networks.

Those are just some of the networks involved in going to a Chinese restaurant, and these networks are all carrying out familiar tasks. That's why these activities are so easy—you've done similar things before. And it's all automatic!

In addition, emotional frames also exist, and they may be included in the way you think about this experience. For example:

- Do you like Chinese food? Or did someone else choose this particular restaurant?

- Do you enjoy hanging out with the people you're dining with?

- Do you have social anxiety and struggle with things to say when you're out to dinner with people you don't know very well?

- Is there someone in the group who perhaps talks or drinks too much or promotes political views that are upsetting to you?

As you can see, your brain's framing of this simple outing brings together many different types of expectations, feelings, and memories. This means that many selective neuronal networks in your brain are working together.

At the same time, your brain filters out a massive amount of information, or networks, that are not relevant to going out to dinner. This protects you from drowning in a huge amount of distracting information. After all, only a tiny part of what is stored in your brain is relevant to going to a Chinese restaurant.

This filtering is invaluable but can have negative consequences as well. For example, let's say your brain automatically filters out positive memories and expectations about going out to dinner and instead selects negative memories, like feeling foolish or embarrassed in social situations, when you create your frame for this evening. Then you'll be more likely to feel anxious or even depressed about this experience.

Frames and networks can help us understand the concept of "fractal psychotherapy," which is one of the most important and revolutionary concepts in TEAM-CBT. This is the idea of focusing on a "fractal," or single moment, when you were feeling upset and recording exactly how you were thinking and feeling at that moment on the Daily Mood Journal. Dr. Burns has stated that all of your problems will be encapsulated in that one moment, so when you understand what was going on at that moment, you will understand the cause of *all* of your problems. And when you truly change how you were thinking and feeling at that specific moment, you will understand the solution to all of your problems.

Why is this, and how can it be? It's because of frames. Your feelings of depression, anxiety, inferiority, hopelessness, and anger are the expression of frames—familiar, related networks—that your brain is imposing on many, if not all, of your experiences. And when you change the way you're thinking and feeling at that one moment, you create new networks and frames that you can also use in many situations.

Therefore, while the focus in TEAM-CBT is highly specific and narrow, the impact on your life can be extensive.

However, creating and strengthening the new networks will require practice—psychotherapy homework—so the networks will FTWT. The practice makes the new frames stronger and stronger in just the same way that daily practice is necessary if you are taking tennis lessons. Just talking to the coach once a week won't get the job done!

## INTEGRATING TEAM-CBT WITH BRAIN FUNCTIONING

Now it's time to start solving the mystery of how to integrate TEAM-CBT with brain functioning so we can begin to understand why TEAM-CBT is so powerful. We won't try to solve everything in this short chapter, but I hope to point the way forward. All scientific explorations are steps on the road of knowledge. We can only move down that road if we begin the journey, so here's a first step!

## T = Testing

As you've learned in this book, TEAM-CBT places a huge emphasis on testing before and after every therapy session. This focus on repeated testing represents a sharp departure from conventional therapy where nothing is typically measured.

One example of the enormous value of the Brief Mood Survey is provided in the story about Lillya in chapter 17. Lillya was racked with anxiety and ambivalence about having a second child. But it was not having a child per se that gave her anxiety. Rather, Lillya's anxiety stemmed from her perception that her husband wasn't helping out enough with their daughter. She felt, like so many mothers, that it was up to her do everything. But because she was exceptionally nice, it had been hard, almost impossible, for her to recognize her anger, so her feelings were disguised as anxiety.

It may not have been possible to uncover the true cause of Lillya's anxiety had she not taken the Brief Mood Survey. Her relationship satisfaction scores on the survey were quite low, and that turned out to be the central clue to what was *really* going on. If the conversation had been guided only by Lillya's initial fears about having or not having a second child, the resulting discussion would have seemed sensible, but the emotional impact of the session would have been minimal at best. Once the "real" story was open for exploration, the therapy could progress.

Without the Brief Mood Survey, neither Lillya nor Dr. Burns could have known that the conversation was off track. He might have helped her challenge her distorted thoughts about having (or not having) a second child or might have tried to help her with this difficult decision. But those interventions would have failed because the most relevant brain circuits would not have been activated.

The information from the T = Testing helped Dr. Burns get the session on track and led to an intervention that provided almost instantaneous recovery—Lillya became more assertive, and new networks representing more effective ways to communicate with her husband were established.

But T = Testing may accomplish even more. By quantifying the intensity of your feelings immediately before and after every session, the Brief Mood Survey tells the patient and therapist right away if the micro-neurosurgery has been effective and whether there's a need for additional rewiring of the brain.

## E = Empathy

At each session, your therapist will attempt to establish a warm, empathic connection with you. This means skillfully listening to and accepting you as you are without trying to help, change, or rescue you. Although empathy is not sufficient to create change, it is absolutely essential for change to occur. Approaching TEAM-CBT from the perspective of brain functioning helps us understand why empathy is necessary but not enough.

Successful empathy means that you feel like you're in a safe space where no one is going to attack you. When you're in this safe space, you and your therapist can more easily pinpoint the specific problems you need to solve. You can let down your guard, open up, and share all your negative thoughts and feelings. Activating these networks is critical if you are going to modify them.

But if you're not feeling safe, then the brain's early warning system is activated, and that means that the filters and frames in your brain will tell you that you are in potential danger. Therefore, your brain and your attention will be focused on issues that seem important for your survival. This will make it difficult for you to move out of a high-alert, high-survival mode and to let down your guard so you can unburden yourself and tell your story.

Although empathy is crucial to the process of learning and change, empathy alone will not be enough to modify the networks that trigger depression and anxiety. In fact, if therapy is based entirely on endless complaining and venting, that could actually make the problem worse by further activating and strengthening the circuits that trigger your negative feelings. That's why the next two steps in TEAM-CBT are also necessary to set the stage for rapid therapeutic change.

## A = Assessment of Resistance

You probably know from personal experience that it's not easy to change the way you think and feel. You may not have a great deal of success until you reduce or eliminate your resistance to change. Melting away your resistance is one of the most important keys to psychological and emotional change, and it's equally important to the way the networks in your brain function.

In TEAM-CBT, this reduction in the patient's resistance is often carried out paradoxically by revealing what's incredibly positive and healthy about each of the patient's negative thoughts and feelings. For example, Dr. Burns once treated a woman named Christine who'd been raped and beaten for thirty years by her sadistic and narcissistic husband. Although she'd finally gotten divorced and moved away from him, she was still paralyzed by unbelievably intense feelings of depression, anxiety, shame, and anger. During her treatment by Dr. Burns in front of a live audience, her anxiety became so intense that she said she had to fight an overwhelming urge to run off the stage and hide.

Although Christine initially said she would gladly push the magic button to make all her symptoms disappear, she discovered something totally unexpected when she did positive reframing with Dr. Burns: All her negative thoughts and feelings were actually beneficial and revealed incredibly beautiful things about her and her core values.

For example, her intense, chronic anxiety resulted, in part, from this negative thought: "I can't trust men." This thought was not the result of a "mental disorder" that needed "treatment" with drugs or psychotherapy. It reflected an incredibly important form of self-protection! After all, she'd been in hell for three decades when she was married. And once she began to "see" the beauty and value of her anxiety, as well as the rest of her negative feelings, she began to feel way more relaxed and at peace.

In fact, Christine began experiencing a significant mood elevation before Dr. Burns even had a chance to introduce techniques to challenge her distorted thoughts. Her peacefulness resulted from a deeper form of empathy that allowed her brain to evaluate her negative thoughts and feelings from a more realistic and compassionate perspective, or "frame," which set up a strong foundation for challenging her distortions in the final phase of the session. That's because she no longer felt she had to get rid of her negative feelings. All she had to do was dial them down a bit!

During the A = Assessment of Resistance phase of TEAM, you learn to accept your thoughts and feelings with compassion. You pinpoint the tremendously positive aspects of your "negative" thoughts and feelings. Paradoxically, this process decreases your resistance to giving those feelings up!

## M = Methods

Once your therapist has reviewed your test scores, listened empathically while you tell your story, and melted away your resistance, it will be time for the M = Methods part of the session. This is where the most dramatic changes happen through micro-neurosurgery.

We've talked about the fact that TEAM is a type of "fractal psychother-apy" because you're asked to focus on *one* specific moment when you were upset in your Daily Mood Journal. That's because it is much easier to focus on one brief moment when you were upset. It takes a large, overwhelming problem and reframes it as a single moment in time.

Think about Christine. For decades, she'd been telling herself, "I'm defec-tive. That's why my husband beat me. He could see that I'm defective." This negative thought was actually a small network in Christine's brain that had fired over and over again, hundreds of thousands of times or even more.

But during the M = Methods phase, Dr. Burns asked her to examine these negative thoughts, or networks, from a variety of angles. First, he asked her if there were any cognitive distortions in the thought "I'm defective," and she was able to find many. For example, it was a huge overgeneralization because she was generalizing from the abuse she received to the idea that she was defective, that she had a defective "self," and that there was something profoundly broken or "wrong" about her.

Remember one of the important principles of brain functioning: If the brain has to choose between two views of a situation—for example, whether the sound you heard was a tiger or wasn't a tiger—the brain will choose the correct interpretation once it has some data to see what the truth is. So the simple act of identifying the distortions in any negative thought you've re-corded is an important step in your micro-neurosurgery! You're building new frames and networks.

Or to use an ancient religious metaphor—the truth shall make you free!

Once Christine identified the distortions, Dr. Burns asked her to look at some evidence that may not be entirely consistent with this harsh interpreta-tion. For example, could it be that her husband beat her not because she was "defective" but because he was sadistic and controlling and thought he could get away with it? In addition, could she really be "defective" if she was able to get a PhD in clinical psychology and develop a tremendous practice treating other abuse victims?

During this time, Dr. Burns was helping Christine's story shift from "I'm a terrible, defective human being" to "I stayed in the marriage to protect my sons, and that was incredibly courageous. And I have a lot to be proud of in spite of the horrible traumas I've had to endure and the many mistakes I've made along the way."

Because the brain can use the same neuronal networks for many purposes, when Christine learned how to challenge and defeat one negative thought, she could use those same positive networks to challenge the rest of her negative thoughts.

Now Christine could bring the many positive things about her life to conscious awareness without diminishing the fact that what she endured was awful. And why did she suddenly respond so rapidly and dramatically? It's because her resistance to change (her stuckness) was vastly diminished during A = Assessment of Resistance, so now a strong, positive, loving voice could suddenly emerge—in other words, new nerve networks were created, and they started firing together.

These new networks and interpretations made it easy to crush her negative thoughts. In fact, by the end of Christine's session, not only had her negative feelings disappeared completely, but she was in a state of incredible joy that has persisted to this very day.

The writing that you do while using the Daily Mood Journal also helps you focus your micro-neurosurgery on the precise networks that need to be changed, one at a time. We cannot keep more than a small number of items in consciousness. Without the Daily Mood Journal, your thoughts will simply spin around, from negative thought to negative thought, and you'll get demoralized and confused. In addition, writing is very good for focusing our attention because we use more regions of our brains in writing than talking. Thus, the writing further strengthens the new networks on the principles that neurons FTWT.

This rewiring of the circuits in your brain can only occur by focusing on negative thoughts and not by focusing on emotions. This is because statements about your feelings are inherently true, so if you try to challenge your feelings, then your efforts probably won't be effective. If someone says he or she feels angry, worthless, ashamed, or hopeless, then this is truly how that person feels at that moment. But the distorted thoughts that trigger these feelings can be fairly easily challenged. The negative thoughts are the neuronal networks we will target for modification.

The very moment that you stop believing a negative thought that triggers your distress, your emotions will suddenly begin to change. This is exactly what happened tens of millions of years ago when your ancestors heard an alarming sound, panicked, turned their heads, and saw that there was no tiger.

Rapid relief! And that's exactly what happened to Christine and what can happen for you too!

When TEAM-CBT works, it seems like magic. But there is no magic other than the magic of biology. This is the same awesome magic that enables wounds to heal, hearts to keep beating, the energy of sunlight to be converted by plants into the foodstuffs on which all forms of life ultimately depend, and every other wonder in our daily lives.

It is the magic of the world working properly. TEAM-CBT just enables the brain to do its job in evaluating the correctness of our interpretations. And when our interpretations change and we subsequently experience the magical feeling of rapid emotional change, this is simply a reflection of what our brains are designed to do. In the end, TEAM-CBT is just good medicine carried out at the highest orders of effectiveness.

### For More Information

If you want to learn more about some of the specific neuroscience topics discussed in this chapter, there are excellent books and wonderful lectures available on YouTube (or similar sites) by a variety of brilliant contributors to each of these topics. A good starting point for learning about frames is *Don't Think of an Elephant* by George Lakoff. The basis for our emotions has been explored by many authors, including Joseph LeDoux in *Anxious: The Modern Mind in the Age of Anxiety*. For a consideration of evolutionary aspects of our brain's functions, a great starting place is *Why Zebras Don't Get Ulcers* by Robert Sapolsky.

# 31 | What Causes Depression and Anxiety? What's the Best Way to Treat It?

In this closing chapter, I'll share my thoughts about a number of controversial topics. I won't be able to give you the ultimate truth on each topic—I can only share my own best thinking with you based on my research training, clinical experience, and critical reading of the research literature.

So if you come to different conclusions on any of these topics and decide that I'm way off base, that's totally okay! I'm not always right! I will provide references so you can always check them out for more information.

Here are the questions I'll focus on:

1. Do depression and anxiety result from a chemical imbalance in the brain?

2. What *does* cause depression? Is it our genes? A troubled childhood? Does depression result from poverty, social injustice, physical illness, or traumatic events? Does depression result from rejection or failure?

3. Do negative thoughts cause negative feelings? Or is it the other way around?

4. How effective are antidepressants? What does the research show?

5. How effective are the new experimental treatments for depression and anxiety that use party drugs, like marijuana, ketamine, and ecstasy, as well as psychedelic agents, like magic mushrooms or LSD?

6. Should benzodiazepines (the so-called "minor tranquilizers"), like Valium, Ativan, Xanax, and Klonopin, be used in the treatment of depression and anxiety?

7. How effective is psychotherapy for depression and anxiety? What's the most effective school of therapy?

8. How does psychotherapy actually work? What are the key ingredients of therapeutic success or failure?

9. How effective are some of the popular new treatments that are currently in vogue, like meditation, yoga, prayer, exercise, relaxation training, nutritional supplements, and more?

10. How effective is bibliotherapy (reading a self-help book)?

## 1. Do depression and anxiety result from a chemical imbalance in the brain?

For more than fifty years, psychiatrists have promoted the idea that depression and anxiety result from a chemical imbalance in the brain, and this idea is still popular today. But is this theory valid?

We know that the billions of nerves in the brain use chemical messengers (called neurotransmitters), like serotonin, norepinephrine, dopamine, GABA, and many others, to send messages to each other. So when a nerve cell fires, it releases a chemical messenger, like serotonin, into the tiny synaptic gap that separates it from the next nerve cell in the network. The serotonin diffuses across the synaptic gap and attaches itself to receptors on the next nerve cell, causing it to fire.

Early psychiatric researchers proposed that these chemical messengers may play a role in emotional problems like depression, anxiety, and even anger outbursts. Specifically, they proposed that depression results from a deficiency of serotonin in the brain and that mania, in turn, results from an excess of serotonin.

It was a simple and appealing theory that spawned a multibillion-dollar drug industry since pharmaceutical companies could develop and market drugs that increased levels of serotonin or stimulated the serotonin receptors in the brain. These "antidepressant" drugs would presumably compensate for the "chemical imbalance" in the brain and cure the depression. Just take a pill and you'll be happy!

Many people today still believe this theory, but is it true?

Toward the end of my psychiatric residency, I had a chance to test this theory. I did three years of basic research on the chemical imbalance theory during my postdoctoral fellowship at the University of Pennsylvania School of Medicine. I worked on the Depression Research Unit at the Veterans Hospital that was affiliated with Penn.

Just before I began working there, my colleagues had begun conducting an experiment with the depressed veterans on our research unit. Over a several week period, half of the veterans got daily milkshakes laced with massive amounts (20 grams) of L-tryptophan, whereas the other half did not. It was a "double-blind" experiment in that neither the patients nor the doctors knew which patients were receiving L-tryptophan and which were not.

What is L-tryptophan, and what was the goal of the study?

L-tryptophan is an essential amino acid that your body cannot manufacture. You have to get it in your diet. Certain foods, including eggs, poultry, and milk, contain significant amounts of L-tryptophan. Once L-tryptophan goes into your stomach, it crosses into the bloodstream and then diffuses into the brain, where it is converted into serotonin, the "happy chemical." That means half of the veterans in our study were experiencing massive increases in brain serotonin whereas the other half were not.

Our hypothesis was simple. If a deficiency in brain serotonin causes depression, then patients who received massive daily doses of L-tryptophan should have experienced antidepressant effects.

So what happened?

Sadly, there were no antidepressant effects of L-tryptophan. We found absolutely no differences in depression between the two groups. In other words, the huge boost in brain serotonin did not relieve depression. We published this finding in the top psychiatry journal in 1975 and concluded there was no convincing evidence for the chemical imbalance theory. *To this day, I am still not aware of any consistent or convincing evidence that depression, or any other psychiatric problem, results from any "chemical imbalance" in the brain.*

A press release from the University of Colorado described amazing genetic studies involving up to 440,000 individuals. The investigators analyzed highly studied genes claimed to be involved in boosting susceptibility to depression over the past twenty-five years. The investigators concluded that all the previously published studies were incorrect and that the genes involved in the synthesis or regulation of neurotransmitters in the human brain are no more associated with depression than genes chosen at random.[*]

---

[*] Border, R., Johnson, E. C., Evans, L. M., Smolen, A., Berley, N., Sullivan, P. F., & Keller, M. C. (2019). No support for historical candidate gene or candidate gene-by-interaction hypotheses for major depression across multiple large samples. *American Journal of Psychiatry, 176*(5), 376–387.

This doesn't mean there are no genetic causes of depression, just that the genes involved in the regulation of certain neurotransmitters in the brain are clearly *not* involved in susceptibility to depression. These incredible new findings underscore the conclusion that my colleagues and I reached in 1975: There is simply no convincing or consistent evidence for the chemical imbalance theory of depression.

## 2. What *does* cause depression?

If a chemical imbalance doesn't cause depression, then what *is* the cause? I think the most honest answer is that we just don't know.

There are lots of theories, including:

- Traumatic childhood experiences, like abuse, neglect, bullying, or intimidation
- Social pressures to be popular, perfect, or successful, which lead lots of people to conclude "I'm just not good enough"
- Environmental factors, like poverty, social injustice, and prejudice, or a lack of loving, supportive relationships
- Poor diet or nutritional factors
- Poor self-care, such as a lack of exercise, or alcohol or substance abuse
- Chronic stress and more

But in my opinion, none of these theories has much, if any, convincing experimental support either. It's great to explore all hypotheses, but it's equally important not to jump on a bandwagon simply because a certain theory sounds good. We just don't have any solid research that has convincingly pinpointed the psychological, biochemical, or genetic causes of depression or anxiety.

One day, we will know a great deal more about the causes of emotional problems. For now, I am simply grateful that psychotherapy is evolving rapidly and that we have a number of promising new treatment techniques, including the ones I've described in this book, to help individuals recover more rapidly so you can wake up and say, "It's great to be alive. I have so much to look forward to today!"

## 3. Do negative thoughts cause negative feelings? Or is it the other way around?

Is there any scientific evidence that negative thoughts cause negative feelings? Or is it perhaps the other way around? What if negative feelings come first, and they actually trigger negative thoughts?

This is a bit like the classical question of: What came first? The chicken or the egg? And this is a really important question because the whole basis of cognitive therapy is that feelings like depression and anxiety aren't the result of what happens to us but of the way we think about what's happening.

You've seen tons of examples of the causal impact of negative thoughts on feelings in this book. For example, in chapter 4 you saw that Karen's feelings of depression, anxiety, and shame did not result from the fact that her daughter was shot in the mouth but from the way she was thinking about this horrific event. And the very moment she changed the way she was thinking, there was a mind-blowing and almost instantaneous change in her feelings.

And in chapter 8, you saw that Marilyn's feelings of depression, guilt, and hopelessness didn't result from her sudden, unexpected diagnosis of stage 4 lung cancer but from the way she was thinking about it. She was telling herself she was a spiritual failure because she'd lost her belief in God and had begun to doubt the existence of life after death.

But is this theory true? Do our feelings *really* result from our thoughts, or is it the other way around?

Questions of circular causality can be exceedingly difficult to test in the laboratory. For example, it would be unethical to try to persuade experimental subjects that they were worthless losers and to then see if they got depressed. However, I did have a chance to answer the question of what comes first—your thoughts or your feelings—in a study I did on the inpatient unit of Stanford University Hospital several years ago.

I measured the intensity of the negative thoughts and feelings of more than 100 patients who were participating in daily cognitive therapy groups. I took measurements at the start and end of each group session to look for fluctuations in how the patients felt. Some experienced profound improvements by the end of the group, others did not change at all, and a few felt even worse.

I analyzed the data with non-recursive structural equation modeling. This is a sophisticated statistical method that allows you to tease apart the causal links between two variables that are correlated with each other. It's one way of answering the classic chicken versus the egg problem.

What did the study show?

First, there was a massive causal effect of patients' negative thoughts on their negative feelings. The study confirmed that when patients' thoughts became more negative, their feelings became more negative, and when their thoughts became more positive, their feelings brightened up. This was the first scientific confirmation, as far as I know, of the idea that you *feel* the way you *think*, a theory first proposed by Epictetus nearly 2,000 years ago.

However, the analyses suggested there was a powerful effect in the opposite direction as well: Negative feelings appeared to trigger more negative thoughts. When patients experienced negative emotions, it seemed to fire up those circuits in the brain that create negative thoughts like "I'm no good" or "I'm a hopeless case." If you've ever felt depressed, anxious, or angry, then I'm sure you've experienced this vicious cycle. Your negative thoughts trigger negative feelings, which in turn trigger more negative thoughts.

But there was some good news: Positive thoughts appeared to trigger positive feelings, which in turn led to more positive thoughts. Another cycle, but a really helpful one!

Now let's be fair. Did this study show what causes depression and anxiety?

Not really. The study shed light on how the brain creates negative and positive feelings, which has important implications for treatment. But the study didn't show why some people are more prone to having more negative thoughts and feelings.

You might think of it as the difference between physiology and pathology. For example, we now know an enormous amount about how the human body works, including the heart, lungs, kidneys, liver, and so forth. That's called physiology. You could say that my study shed a little bit of light on the physiology of thoughts and feelings—how the brain works.

But pathology is different. It's the study of the factors that lead to diseases, like pneumonia, cardiac failure, and so forth. And our understanding of the pathology of depression and anxiety is still very minimal. To put it in the simplest way possible, we still do not know *why* some individuals are more susceptible to negative thoughts and feelings, while others seem to be born with a far more positive outlook.

But although we don't yet know the causes of depression and anxiety, we do have pretty powerful techniques to help you change the way you think and feel so you can experience greater joy and better relationships with others. And I think that's fantastic news!

## 4. How effective are antidepressants? What does the research show?

The vast majority of studies on the efficacy of antidepressants have been conducted by drug companies who are trying to get permission from the US Food and Drug Administration to market these drugs as "antidepressants." Sadly, a reexamination of these findings seems to indicate four disturbing facts:

1. These drugs appear to have little or no clinical effectiveness above and beyond their placebo effects.*

2. The research strategies that drug companies use to test potential antidepressant medications are severely flawed.†

3. The popular SSRI antidepressants dramatically increase the likelihood of suicidal urges and completed suicides in children and adults.‡

4. Many people experience severe discontinuation effects when they try to taper off of the newer antidepressants.

Unfortunately, antidepressants don't appear much more effective than placebos. Of course, we all know someone who was treated with antidepressants who *did* improve or recover. But the best evidence indicates that this person would have likely recovered with a placebo as well.

---

* Jakobsen, J. C., Gluud, C., & Kirsch, I. (2019). Should antidepressants be used for major depressive disorder? *BMJ Evidence-Based Medicine.* Advanced online publication. http://dx.doi.org/10.1136/bmjebm-2019-111238.

Kirsch, I., & Sapirstein, G. (1998). Listening to Prozac but hearing placebo: A meta-analysis of antidepressant medication. *Prevention and Treatment, 1*(2), Article 2a.

Kirsch, I., Moore, T. J., Scoboria, A., & Nicholls, S. S. (2002). The emperor's new drugs: An analysis of antidepressant medication data submitted to the U.S. Food and Drug Administration. *Prevention and Treatment, 5*(1), Article 23.

Kirsch, I. (2011). *The emperor's new drugs: Exploding the antidepressant myth.* New York: Random House.

† Antonuccio, D. O., Burns, D., & Danton, W. G. (2002). Antidepressants: A triumph of marketing over science? *Prevention and Treatment, 5*(1), Article 25.

‡ Healy, D., & Aldred, G. (2005). Antidepressant drug use and the risk of suicide. *International Review of Psychiatry, 17*(3), 163–172.

Many people take offense at the idea that the improvement they or a loved one experienced when taking antidepressants was "just" a placebo effect. But a placebo response isn't a terrible thing since placebos can trigger improvement in roughly 35% to 40% of individuals with depression. And that improvement *is* absolutely real. However, the gold standard for any medical or psychological treatment is that it must outperform placebos to a statistically and clinically significant degree.

And here's another problem: The placebo effect means that a patient improves because he or she believes the drug will work. This leads to greater hope, which could be what causes the depression to improve. In addition, patients with increased hope begin to do things that are more rewarding, pleasurable, and satisfying—and this increased involvement in life also triggers improvement. The sad thing is these patients nearly always give the credit for their recovery to the medication rather than to themselves.

If you'd like to listen to a scholarly and informative online talk by Dr. Irving Kirsch on the placebo effect of antidepressants, you can find it on YouTube ("The Emperor's New Drugs: Exploding the Antidepressant Myth").

The lack of effectiveness is not the only problem with antidepressants. Many research studies have shown that the newer antidepressants can double the likelihood of suicide among children, teenagers, and adults. Some studies even suggest that the long-term use of antidepressants can lead to a worsening of depression.[*]

Moreover, many individuals have trouble getting off the new antidepressants because they experience what is known as "antidepressant discontinuation syndrome." This consists of potentially severe withdrawal symptoms, such as dizziness, shock-like sensations, nausea, crawling sensations in your skin, and an intensification of suicidal urges.[†] If you're interested, you can find an informative article on this topic in *The New York Times*.

---

[*] Hengartner, M. P., Angst, J., & Rössler, W. (2018). Antidepressant use prospectively relates to a poorer long-term outcome of depression: Results from a prospective community cohort study over 30 years. *Psychotherapy and Psychosomatics, 87,* 181–183.

[†] Fava, G. A., Gatti, A., Belaise, C., Guidi, J., & Offidani, E. (2015). Withdrawal symptoms after selective serotonin reuptake inhibitor discontinuation: A systematic review. *Psychotherapy and Psychosomatics, 84*(2), 72–81.

Harvey, B., & Slabbert, F. (2014). New insights on the antidepressant discontinuation syndrome. *Human Psychopharmacology, 29*(6), 503–516.

I'm not arguing that medications should never be used in the treatment of psychiatric problems. Sometimes medications can be helpful, even lifesaving. And for problems like schizophrenia or mania, they may be absolutely necessary.

I'm also not arguing that you should suddenly stop taking any medications your doctor has prescribed. You should never change medication without the supervision of your physician.

What I am saying is that we now have effective and sustainable drug-free treatments for depression and anxiety, like TEAM-CBT, which is extremely exciting and welcome news for individuals who prefer to be treated without medications.

One disclaimer: I am not providing medical advice in this book, just my own best understanding of the latest research. I'm not always right, and some experts will intensely disagree with the conclusions I've drawn.

But here's the bottom line: You should never discontinue or change the dose of any medication without the supervision of your doctor.

### 5. How effective are the new experimental treatments for depression and anxiety that use party drugs, like marijuana, ketamine, and ecstasy, as well as psychedelic agents, like magic mushrooms or LSD?

I am happy that psychiatry is finally beginning to move beyond the traditional use of antidepressants and antianxiety drugs, which have sadly not delivered, at least in my opinion. When I was a medical student at Stanford in the late 1960s, LSD was legal and freely available, so I tried it on half a dozen occasions. It was a pretty fantastic experience, and I was sad when it was made illegal and demonized by the government.

I always felt that LSD had way more potential for research, and possibly for treatment, because it actually *did* something! And what it did was mind-boggling, to say the least. So I am really pleased investigators are finally beginning to research the possible therapeutic value of LSD, psilocybin (magic mushrooms), and psychedelic agents.

At the same time, I'm a bit skeptical because I never experienced any kind of mood elevation from LSD, and there was also the very real possibility of a bad trip. And a bad trip can involve a massive intensification of negative thoughts, as well as paranoia. So while I loudly applaud this research, I'd hold off on getting too euphoric before all the facts are in. And at this point,

I would definitely not recommend that you try to treat your own depression or anxiety by taking these agents.

The party drugs are quite another cup of tea. Although I've never personally taken drugs like MDMA (also called ecstasy), these drugs can definitely make you incredibly high and can also increase loving feelings toward others. A colleague of mine has been involved in research using MDMA in the treatment of veterans with PTSD, but much more research is needed regarding its therapeutic potential and associated risks. After all, ecstasy is an intensely euphorigenic drug with an immense potential for abuse, and it can be lethal when abused.

For more information on MDMA-assisted psychotherapy, you can check out this link: https://maps.org/research/mdma. You can also check out my latest podcast with Dr. Fabrice Nye on this subject (Podcast 177).

Ketamine is another party drug that's received enormous clinical and media attention in the treatment of depression. Once again, I think we have to be cautious until there's more research. Although preliminary reports indicate immediate improvements in depression after a single treatment, the effects don't tend to last, and the treatment can be costly. In addition, the toxic effects of ongoing treatment have not yet been evaluated.

One topic that interests me greatly is the potential conflict of interest when drug companies get involved in the research and marketing of any of their products. For example, Janssen Pharmaceuticals has recently marketed a drug called Esketamine that is almost identical to ketamine. They are promoting this new version not because it is safer or more effective but because they can patent and market it for huge profits.

I recently got this eye-opening email about Esketamine from a brilliant and highly ethical colleague, Dr. Brandon Vance:

> *The economics and cultural issues around Esketamine are interesting... Janssen, the company that makes it, was clearly just looking for something to patent because of the recent data for ketamine on the rapid treatment of depression. They spent lots of money doing studies that were unnecessary, as the regular form of ketamine is perfectly fine... and probably just as effective or even more effective.*
>
> *Any physician can call a local compounding pharmacy and have them make a nasal spray of regular ketamine. Esketamine costs about $500–$800 per*

*treatment. In contrast, regular ketamine, if given nasally, costs about $4 per treatment.*

*While all the media around Esketamine has brought attention to the problem of depression and a different angle on biological treatments, it is also one clear example of greed, advertising, power, and incentive for financial gain over health and accessibility of health care—absurdities that drive unfair and unnecessary increases in health care costs.*

For more information on the possible hazards of ketamine, there is an excellent story on the NBC news and health website.

For now, I'd say let's keep an open mind and continue to encourage creative research on biological treatments. But for the moment, I still have my money on the truly powerful and promising new, drug-free treatments like TEAM-CBT and many others that are constantly emerging.

## 6. Should benzodiazepines (the so-called "minor tranquilizers"), like Valium, Ativan, Xanax, and Klonopin, be used in the treatment of depression and anxiety?

Benzodiazepines are potent antianxiety agents, and at first, they can work like a charm. If you've never taken one, and you're feeling anxious and having trouble getting to sleep, you can take the smallest dose of Xanax (.25 mg), and you'll fall asleep, sleep like a baby, and wake up feeling totally refreshed and wonderful, with no side effects at all. And you'll be convinced you've found your magic bullet.

And you have!

So what's wrong with that? It sounds terrific!

Here's the rub: All these agents can become intensely addictive if you take them for three weeks or more, and that's how they're usually prescribed—typically several pills per day—if you're struggling with some form of anxiety on an ongoing basis.

And then, when you try to discontinue them, you'll experience withdrawal effects, such as intense anxiety and insomnia, which are the exact same symptoms you took them for in the first place. So you and your doctor will wrongly conclude that you still need these drugs, and you're hooked.

Is it possible to get off of them? Yes, but it's not easy. I took Xanax for several months for insomnia during my residency before I realized that I, too, was hooked. The drug company had claimed it was entirely safe, but that was not true.

Drug company marketing can be very misleading, especially when a new medication is first released. And the problems with Xanax and all the benzodiazepines are real. So I stopped taking Xanax and just decided to bite the bullet and endure the anxiety and insomnia for several weeks until the withdrawal symptoms eventually wore off.

That's why I no longer take or prescribe these drugs for psychiatric problems. The addiction can actually prevent or greatly slow recovery for several reasons:

- They promote the idea that you need to control, suppress, or avoid anxiety. But this idea is the very cause of anxiety. The cure comes when you confront the thing you fear and surrender to the anxiety. As you'll recall, this is called exposure.
- The effects of benzodiazepines on memory can interfere with the exposure-based learning that's needed for effective treatment.
- They are addictive, not curative, and if you try to get off of them, you may experience an intense and debilitating worsening of your anxiety.

There are now many drug-free treatment methods for every type of anxiety, so I no longer see benzodiazepines as necessary or even useful. For more information on how to defeat every type of anxiety without drugs, check out my book, *When Panic Attacks*.

### 7. How effective is psychotherapy for depression and anxiety? What's the most effective school of therapy?

If drugs aren't the answer, then what *is* the best treatment for anxiety and depression?

When CBT was first developed by Drs. Albert Ellis and Aaron Beck, people were incredibly excited because it was the first form of psychotherapy shown to be as effective as antidepressant medications. This had never been shown before. That research, along with my book, *Feeling Good*, put CBT on the map in the United States and around the world.

When I wrote *Feeling Good*, there were only a dozen or so cognitive therapists in the world, and most psychiatrists and psychologists considered CBT a form of quackery. Now it's become the most extensively researched and practiced form of psychotherapy in history. Many studies have confirmed that CBT is as effective as antidepressants in the short term and somewhat more effective in the long term.

But is this news really as reassuring as we had thought in the early days?

Here's one big problem: As I discussed earlier, recent research has indicated that antidepressants are barely more effective than placebos. Although this finding is clearly shocking and controversial, my own research and reading of the literature suggests these new studies are valid. So the claim that any treatment compares favorably with antidepressants is not a very strong or exciting proof of effectiveness. In fact, you could argue that this is condemnation through faint praise.

In addition, outcome studies indicate that all forms of psychotherapy, including CBT, are also only slightly better than placebos in the treatment of depression. Fewer than 50% of patients recover, no matter what form of psychotherapy is used.

The British CoBalT trial, published in the research journal *Lancet*, is considered by many experts to be the most convincing study documenting the effectiveness of CBT. What did that study show?

In that study, 469 patients with chronic depression were randomly assigned to one of two treatment conditions for six months:

- Treatment as usual. These patients continued to receive a variety of antidepressants.
- Treatment as usual plus CBT.

How did the two groups do? Who won the battle?

In the treatment-as-usual group (antidepressants alone), only 22% of patients had improved significantly at the six-month evaluation. These results confirmed what I was experiencing in my private practice: The antidepressants I was prescribing usually did little or nothing to help my patients.

How about the patients who received CBT in addition to antidepressants? At the six-month evaluation, 46% of those patients had improved. That was way better than the patients who only received antidepressants, and it clearly showed that CBT *was* helpful. The findings at the three-year follow-up were similar.

However, if you look at this study with a more critical eye, you may not stand up and cheer. These findings were pretty disappointing since more than

50% of patients who were treated with antidepressants plus CBT did *not* improve significantly.

Before you get discouraged, let me say that negative findings in science can be disturbing but incredibly helpful if you just hang in there and think about what the findings might mean. Negative results are nearly always trying to tell us something important we've been missing.

Many published outcome studies have shown that therapy is not very effective in treating depression, no matter what school of therapy you're using. If we could find out why all the schools of psychotherapy are falling short, then perhaps we could correct the problem and develop new and way more effective treatment strategies. And that would be something to get pretty excited about.

## 8. How does psychotherapy work? What are the key ingredients of therapeutic success or failure?

Given that all the different treatments for depression typically come out about the same in outcome studies, with no clear "winner," I decided to focus my research on how psychotherapy actually works and not on what "brand" of therapy is best. My hope was that if I could pinpoint the actual ingredients of therapeutic success or failure, then I might be able to create a more effective approach based on what actually helps people, as opposed to the methods of a particular school of psychotherapy.

Here's what I've learned: The keys to therapeutic success are T = Testing, E = Empathy, A = Assessment of Resistance, and M = Methods. Sound familiar? Here's why these four dimensions will revolutionize psychotherapy.

### T = Testing

First, it's critically important to measure the severity of each patient's symptoms at the start and end of every therapy session. That's because clinicians' perceptions of how patients feel are frequently way off base.

In a study I conducted on roughly 160 patients admitted to Stanford University Hospital's inpatient service, expert interviewers had shockingly low accuracy when they estimated how depressed, suicidal, anxious, or angry patients felt—in fact, their accuracy was less than 10% in most cases.

This means a patient could be actively suicidal, but the therapist might believe the patient has no suicidal urges at all.*

Therapists in clinical practice tend to think they know their patients really well, but they usually aren't measuring anything to find out if their perceptions are correct. This is pretty mind-boggling when you think about it. You can't do good work, much less great work, when your perceptions of how your patients feel aren't accurate, and you don't even realize this.

But this is an easily solvable problem. As I've mentioned, I've developed brief, accurate scales that ask patients to indicate how they're feeling at the start and end of every therapy session. These scales ask about feelings of depression, suicidal urges, anxiety, anger, happiness, and relationship satisfaction.

My colleagues and I require every patient to complete these tests in the waiting room, just before the session begins, and once again right after the session is over, with no exceptions. This only takes a couple of minutes.

The scores inform therapists about what's really going on with their patients so the therapist can see, for the first time, exactly how effective or ineffective the session was. This information allows therapists to fine-tune the treatment on an ongoing basis.

You can see the latest version of my Brief Mood Survey on the next page, filled out by a man named Bradley whom I worked with yesterday. As you can see, Bradley's depression, anxiety, and anger scores fell by 77%, 90%, and 100%, respectively, by the end of the session. And his happiness score increased by a whopping 140%. That's terrific!

Clearly, this session was incredibly helpful, but there's still room for improvement, as Bradley still reported slightly low self-esteem and slightly decreased pleasure and satisfaction in life at the end of the session. In addition, I'd like to see a score closer to 20 on the happiness scale, which would mean he was experiencing feelings of joy. Most people want to feel completely free of depression and not just slightly less depressed, and these scales show me that we're not quite there yet. But we *are* on the right track, and that's something to be excited about!

---

* This was a secondary analysis of data published in this study: Burns, D., Westra, H., Trockel, M., & Fisher, A. (2012). Motivation and changes in depression. *Cognitive Therapy and Research*, *37*(2), 1–12.

## Brief Mood Survey[*]

**Instructions:** Use checks (✓) to indicate how you're feeling *right now.*

**Answer all items.**
How *depressed* do you feel right now?

| | Before Session | | | | | After Session | | | | |
|---|---|---|---|---|---|---|---|---|---|---|
| | 0—Not at all | 1—Somewhat | 2—Moderately | 3—A lot | 4—Extremely | 0—Not at all | 1—Somewhat | 2—Moderately | 3—A lot | 4—Extremely |
| 1. Sad or down in the dumps | | | ✓ | | | ✓ | | | | |
| 2. Discouraged or hopeless | | ✓ | | | | ✓ | | | | |
| 3. Low in self-esteem, inferior, worthless | | | | ✓ | | | ✓ | | | |
| 4. Unmotivated to do things | | | ✓ | | | ✓ | | | | |
| 5. Decreased pleasure or satisfaction in life | | ✓ | | | | | ✓ | | | |
| Total → | | | | **9** | | Total → | | | **2** | |

**Suicidal urges:** Do you sometimes:

| | Before Session | | | | | After Session | | | | |
|---|---|---|---|---|---|---|---|---|---|---|
| 1. Feel like you'd be better off dead? | ✓ | | | | | ✓ | | | | |
| 2. Have suicidal thoughts or fantasies? | ✓ | | | | | ✓ | | | | |
| 3. Have urges or plans to end your life? | ✓ | | | | | ✓ | | | | |
| Total → | | | | **0** | | Total → | | | **0** | |

How *anxious* do you feel right now?

| | Before Session | | | | | After Session | | | | |
|---|---|---|---|---|---|---|---|---|---|---|
| 1. Anxious | | | ✓ | | | ✓ | | | | |
| 2. Frightened | | ✓ | | | | ✓ | | | | |
| 3. Worrying about things | | | | ✓ | | | ✓ | | | |
| 4. Tense or on edge | | | ✓ | | | ✓ | | | | |
| 5. Nervous | | | ✓ | | | ✓ | | | | |
| Total → | | | | **10** | | Total → | | | **1** | |

How *angry* do you feel right now?

| | Before Session | | | | | After Session | | | | |
|---|---|---|---|---|---|---|---|---|---|---|
| 1. Frustrated | | | ✓ | | | ✓ | | | | |
| 2. Annoyed | | ✓ | | | | ✓ | | | | |
| 3. Resentful | | | | ✓ | | ✓ | | | | |
| 4. Angry | | | ✓ | | | ✓ | | | | |
| 5. Irritated | | ✓ | | | | ✓ | | | | |
| Total → | | | | **9** | | Total → | | | **0** | |

### Happiness Test*

**Instructions:** Use checks (✓) to indicate how you're feeling *right now.*

**Answer all items.**

| | Before Session | | | | | After Session | | | | |
|---|:-:|:-:|:-:|:-:|:-:|:-:|:-:|:-:|:-:|:-:|
| | 0—Not at all | 1—Somewhat | 2—Moderately | 3—A lot | 4—Extremely | 0—Not at all | 1—Somewhat | 2—Moderately | 3—A lot | 4—Extremely |
| 1. Happy and joyful | | ✓ | | | | | | | ✓ | |
| 2. Hopeful and optimistic | | ✓ | | | | | | | ✓ | |
| 3. Worthwhile, high self-esteem | ✓ | | | | | | | ✓ | | |
| 4. Motivated, productive | | ✓ | | | | | | | ✓ | |
| 5. Pleased and satisfied with life | | | ✓ | | | | | ✓ | | |
| | Total ➔ | | 5 | | | Total ➔ | | 13 | | |

### Relationship Satisfaction*

Put the name of an important relationship in your life:

*My wife*

Use checks (✓) to indicate how you feel about this relationship.

**Answer all items.**

| | Before Session | | | | | | | After Session | | | | | | |
|---|:-:|:-:|:-:|:-:|:-:|:-:|:-:|:-:|:-:|:-:|:-:|:-:|:-:|:-:|
| | 0—Very dissatisfied | 1—Moderately dissatisfied | 2—Somewhat dissatisfied | 3—Neutral | 4—Somewhat satisfied | 5—Moderately satisfied | 6—Very satisfied | 0—Very dissatisfied | 1—Moderately dissatisfied | 2—Somewhat dissatisfied | 3—Neutral | 4—Somewhat satisfied | 5—Moderately satisfied | 6—Very satisfied |
| 1. Communication and openness | | | | | | ✓ | | | | | | | | ✓ |
| 2. Resolving conflicts | | | | | | ✓ | | | | | | | ✓ | |
| 3. Degree of affection and caring | | | | | | | ✓ | | | | | | | ✓ |
| 4. Intimacy and closeness | | | | | | | ✓ | | | | | | | ✓ |
| 5. Overall satisfaction | | | | | | | ✓ | | | | | | | ✓ |
| | Total ➔ | | | 28 | | | | Total ➔ | | | 29 | | | |

How much psychotherapy homework have you done since your last session?

| None | A little | A moderate amount | A lot |
|:-:|:-:|:-:|:-:|
| | | ✓ | |

Without the information provided by the Brief Mood Survey, a therapist could never make such refined observations. The scores tell me exactly how my patients are feeling and where I'm at. The Brief Mood Survey is like having an emotional X-ray machine that precisely measures changes in symptoms.

One tremendously exciting implication of this new development is that we can now measure and benchmark the effectiveness of therapists. For example, I mentioned that the reductions in Bradley's depression, anxiety, and anger scores were 77%, 90%, and 100%, respectively, and the improvement in his feelings of happiness was 140%.

I call these numbers the recovery coefficients, and they are a precise measure of the therapist's effectiveness. To me, that's super cool and sort of amazing.

Wouldn't it be great if therapists had to publish these ratings online so prospective patients could find out exactly how skillful each therapist is before scheduling an appointment? You could select a therapist with proven skills in the treatment of your problem and avoid those who don't document their effectiveness. My son, Erik, and several colleagues are actually working on this right now.

Extreme therapist accountability is possible now. This is not some grandiose vision for the future but a possibility that already exists. But it will require courage on the part of therapists.

Sadly, many therapists fear these assessment instruments because they don't want to be held accountable. And some therapists, especially psychoanalysts, are intensely opposed to these instruments because they think it will somehow sabotage or even ruin the therapeutic relationship.

Isn't that totally weird? I don't get it, but I've heard that argument frequently.

My own point of view is the opposite. I think it is *impossible* to do consistently good therapy without using accurate assessment instruments at every therapy session. In fact, I predict that ten years from now, assessment instruments like the ones I've developed will no longer be optional but will be required of all therapists, just like doctors are required to take an X-ray if you've got a broken arm.

## E = Empathy

For decades, therapists have believed that empathy plays an important role in therapy. Although many studies have confirmed a positive correlation between patient assessments of therapist empathy and recovery from depression, it's been difficult to prove that empathy helps because correlations simply do not prove causality.

However, I was able to measure the causal effects of empathy on recovery from depression using sophisticated statistical modeling techniques and reported, for the first time, that therapist empathy does appear to have a modest causal effect on recovery from depression.*

That's why I've developed the Evaluation of Therapy Session form that patients complete at the end of each session. Patients rate therapists on empathy and helpfulness so therapists can find out immediately how they're doing and address empathy failures at the start of the next session.

If you look on the next page, you'll see how Bradley filled out this form at the end of our session. He gave me a perfect score on therapeutic empathy, which was great, but only 18 out of 20 on helpfulness. This tells me that although he found the techniques helpful, he needed more time to talk about his problems and express his feelings. The next time we work together, I'll focus on that. You'll also notice that he had a little trouble answering some of the survey questions honestly. This is also important, and I can ask him about that the next time we meet.

---

\* Burns, D. D., & Nolen-Hoeksema, S. (1992). Therapeutic empathy and recovery from depression in cognitive-behavioral therapy: A structural equation model. *Journal of Consulting and Clinical Psychology, 60*(3), 441–449.

## Evaluation of Therapy Session*

**Instructions:** Use checks (✓) to indicate how you felt about your most recent therapy session.

Answer all items.

### Therapeutic Empathy

| | 0—Not at all true | 1—Somewhat true | 2—Moderately true | 3—Very true | 4—Completely true |
|---|---|---|---|---|---|
| 1. My therapist seemed warm, supportive, and concerned. | | | | | ✓ |
| 2. My therapist seemed trustworthy. | | | | | ✓ |
| 3. My therapist treated me with respect. | | | | | ✓ |
| 4. My therapist did a good job of listening. | | | | | ✓ |
| 5. My therapist understood how I felt inside. | | | | | ✓ |

Total → 20

### Helpfulness of the Session

| | 0 | 1 | 2 | 3 | 4 |
|---|---|---|---|---|---|
| 1. I was able to express my feelings during the session. | | | | ✓ | |
| 2. I talked about the problems that are bothering me. | | | | ✓ | |
| 3. The techniques we used were helpful. | | | | | ✓ |
| 4. The approach my therapist used made sense. | | | | | ✓ |
| 5. I learned some new ways to deal with my problems. | | | | | ✓ |

Total → 18

### Satisfaction with the Session

| | 0 | 1 | 2 | 3 | 4 |
|---|---|---|---|---|---|
| 1. I believe the session was helpful to me. | | | | | ✓ |
| 2. Overall, I was satisfied with today's session. | | | | | ✓ |

Total → 8

### Your Commitment

| | 0 | 1 | 2 | 3 | 4 |
|---|---|---|---|---|---|
| 1. I plan to do therapy homework before the next session. | | | | | ✓ |
| 2. I intend to use what I learned in today's session. | | | | | ✓ |

Total → 8

### Negative Feelings During the Session

| | 0 | 1 | 2 | 3 | 4 |
|---|---|---|---|---|---|
| 1. At times, my therapist didn't seem to understand how I felt. | ✓ | | | | |
| 2. At times, I felt uncomfortable during the session. | | ✓ | | | |
| 3. I didn't always agree with my therapist. | ✓ | | | | |

Total → 1

### Difficulties with the Questions

| | 0 | 1 | 2 | 3 | 4 |
|---|---|---|---|---|---|
| 1. It was hard to answer some of these survey questions honestly. | | ✓ | | | |
| 2. Sometimes my survey answers didn't show how I really felt inside. | ✓ | | | | |
| 3. It would be too upsetting for me to criticize my therapist. | ✓ | | | | |

Total → 1

What did you like *the least* about the session? *I felt somewhat uncomfortable because I often find it difficult to openly discuss problems that I feel very ashamed of.*

What did you like *the best* about the session? *Dr. Burns opened my eyes to new and better ways of looking at things and showed me more effective ways to smash my negative thoughts. It was a master class!*

---

\* Copyright © 2001 by David D. Burns, MD. Revised 2004.

Many therapists don't believe they need to use these scales because they believe their perceptions of empathy and helpfulness are accurate. They think they can "sense" the quality of the therapeutic relationship. In addition, they believe patients won't be honest when they fill out the scales and will just say whatever the therapist wants to hear.

Research has not confirmed these beliefs. Remember, in my study at Stanford, I found that therapists' perceptions of their own accuracy and helpfulness were less than 10%, which was shocking but consistent with other published research.* In addition, the real problem is not that patients won't be honest but that they *will* be honest. That's why therapists receive so many failing grades on empathy and helpfulness. This is understandably upsetting to therapists, but the feedback provides tremendous opportunities for therapists who want to improve their empathy skills.

In fact, empathy failures need not be a bad thing—they can actually be a really *good* thing—if the therapist knows what's happening and talks it over with the patient in a nondefensive spirit of curiosity and respect. This can lead to the development of a far more meaningful therapeutic relationship. In fact, what feels like a therapeutic failure can often be the springboard to a therapeutic breakthrough.

That's happened to me twice in the past week alone. Two patients gave me horrifically low ratings on empathy and helpfulness—some of the worst scores I've received in thirty years! It was upsetting, but in both cases I'd sensed something was "off" and not clicking during the sessions. But I had no idea I was doing as terribly as the ratings indicated.

So I had to humble myself, bite the bullet, and encourage the patients to tell me how much I'd missed the boat. This was painful but led to incredible breakthroughs in our work and feelings of joy. I cannot emphasize the importance of this strongly enough.

## A = Assessment of Resistance

So far, we've talked about the immense value of measuring patients' symptoms at the start and end of each session, along with patients' assessment of

---

* Hatcher, R. L., Barends, A., Hansell, J., & Gutfreund, M. J. (1995). Patients' and therapists' shared and unique views of the therapeutic alliance: An investigation using confirmatory factory analysis in a nested design. *Journal of Consulting and Clinical Psychology, 63*(4), 636–643.

therapist empathy and helpfulness at the end of every session. My research has also highlighted the enormous importance of motivation and resistance in therapy.* Clinical failure nearly always results from the therapist's well-intentioned but misguided attempts to try to "help" the patient without reducing or eliminating the patient's resistance first.

This finding has now been replicated in numerous studies, including a recent study I did on the inpatient unit of Stanford Hospital.† A patient's motivation to do psychotherapy homework between sessions is the first and only variable I am aware of that's been shown to have significant causal effects on recovery from depression and anxiety. That's one of the reasons I created TEAM-CBT.

## M = Methods

The powerful cognitive therapy techniques I described in *Feeling Good* are still great—and I use them every day in my clinical work and teaching. I've listed fifty of these tools at the end of this book. Some of the tools are especially powerful for depression, while others are helpful for anxiety disorders, relationship problems, and habits and addictions.

Research and clinical experience confirm that you can't effectively treat everybody with just one tool, method, or school of therapy. That's why the methods in TEAM-CBT are drawn from more than fifteen different schools of therapy. And when you use the recovery circle, you can individualize the treatment and select the methods most likely to work for you.

And here's what's really cool. The new TEAM-CBT techniques that reduce resistance make those techniques even more effective. In fact, you may only need a few.

That's great news, and that's why I've written this book for you.

We'll need more research to find out how effective TEAM-CBT is in the hands of community therapists trained in TEAM-CBT. The first outcome

---

* Burns, D. D., & Nolen-Hoeksema, S. (1991). Coping styles, homework compliance, and the effectiveness of cognitive-behavioral therapy. *Journal of Consulting and Clinical Psychology, 59*(2), 305–311.

Burns, D. D., & Spangler, D. (2000). Does psychotherapy homework lead to changes in depression in cognitive-behavioral therapy? Or does clinical improvement lead to homework compliance? *Journal of Consulting and Clinical Psychology, 68*(1), 46–59.

† Burns, D., Westra, H., Trockel, M., & Fisher, A. (2012). Motivation and changes in depression. *Cognitive Therapy and Research, 37*(2), 1–12.

study is already in progress at the Feeling Good Institute in Mountain View, California (www.feelinggoodinstitute.com), and I'm excited to see what new insights will emerge!

### 9. How effective are some of the popular new treatments that are currently in vogue, like meditation, yoga, prayer, exercise, relaxation training, nutritional supplements, and more?

These nonspecific treatments can be helpful for some people and not helpful for others, so it's really a matter of personal choice. If you find these activities to be helpful, go for it. My daughter is a huge yoga and exercise enthusiast and says these disciplines are very beneficial for her fitness and outlook, which is great.

But in my therapy, I tend to focus on specific, as opposed to nonspecific, interventions. For example, in one of my recent *Feeling Good* podcasts, I described my work with an elderly man named Ezekiel who had felt like a "totally worthless human being" ever since childhood. His depression hadn't improved at all in spite of incredible success in life, as well as decades of psychotherapy.

At the time, aerobic exercise was the latest thing for improving your mood, presumably because it boosted brain endorphins. Of course, that claim is a bit suspicious to me since there's no way to actually measure levels of endorphins in the human brain. However, a lack of evidence does not seem to discourage people who want to believe something that sounds exciting. And I thought, well, maybe that's what Ezekiel needs.

I told Ezekiel he needed to start a vigorous exercise routine to boost his brain endorphins. I got the poor man jogging farther and farther until he was running twelve miles a day. I asked him how he felt at the start of his twelve-mile run the day before the session.

He said, "I felt like a totally worthless human being."

Then I asked how he felt at the end of the twelve-mile run. He said, "I felt like a totally exhausted worthless human being."

So much for boosting brain endorphins!

One day, I asked Ezekiel *why* he felt worthless. He confessed something that he'd been hiding from everyone, including all of his previous psychiatrists, for decades. He told me he had claustrophobia and was afraid of the dark ever since he was a child. He felt intensely ashamed because he thought these fears meant he was cowardly and not a real man.

You can now see why the nonspecific treatment—aerobic exercise—hadn't helped. He could have run from New York to Los Angeles and still would have felt worthless. And he could have done months or years of meditation or yoga, and taken all kinds of food supplements from health food stores, but it wouldn't have helped. Perhaps you can also see why decades of traditional talk therapy had not helped either.

In my experience, the most effective treatment, by far, always has to be specific, individualized, and aimed at each person's unique negative thoughts. There's nothing wrong with meditation, and exercise might also be great, but these nonspecific approaches were never going to help Ezekiel.

Once Ezekiel told me what the real problem was, I said I was pretty sure I had a solution, which he was eager to hear. I told him exposure was incredibly important in the treatment of phobias and that I wanted him to set his alarm clock for two in the morning, when it would be dark outside.

Then I told him to go down to his basement, where it was pitch-dark, and roll himself up in a carpet so he'd be trapped in a confined space. I told him to just lie there until he was cured. I also told him not to fight the anxiety—his job would be to make it as intense as possible until it eventually diminished and disappeared.

He said I was crazy and refused to schedule another therapy session!

I didn't hear from him for several weeks. But he finally called and scheduled another session. He said he'd gotten a second opinion from a psychiatrist and asked if Dr. Burns was totally nuts. Fortunately, the psychiatrist told him I was absolutely right and told Ezekiel to follow my advice. I don't know who that psychiatrist was, but I'll always be grateful for the assist.

Ezekiel told me he was absolutely terrified but had decided to do what I'd asked. He said that for the first fifteen minutes of the exposure, he had an overpowering urge to run out of the basement, but he kept his promise and hung in there. It turned out he was afraid that a big, fat ghost would suddenly appear, sit on his chest, and suffocate him.

After fifteen minutes, Ezekiel blurted out, "I'm tired of waiting. If you're going to sit on my chest, do it now and get it over with!" But no ghost appeared! And at that instant, his fear fell to zero and he started laughing like crazy. He was not only cured of his fears, but his depression vanished at the same time.

That's why I prefer specific, as opposed to nonspecific, treatment techniques. They usually work rapidly, and the impact can be pretty amazing. And that's probably because these specific approaches allow for a rewiring of specific networks in the brain, as described so elegantly by Dr. Noble in the previous chapter.

### 10. How effective is bibliotherapy (reading a self-help book)?

In the introduction, I mentioned that Dr. Forrest Scogin and his colleagues published many research studies examining the antidepressant effects of my first book, *Feeling Good.** They found that more than 60% of patients with depression who read my book improved so much that they no longer required treatment, and these effects continued two and three years later!

That was amazing, but there was still a theoretical problem. It was possible the effects of *Feeling Good* were just a placebo effect and weren't because of the information and techniques I suggested in the book. In other words, maybe *any* book would have the same effect.

To find out, the researchers did a new study, but they gave half of the patients a copy of *Feeling Good* and the other half a copy of Viktor Frankl's book, *Man's Search for Meaning*. Since the Frankl book was not a self-help book, this would allow them to find out if the improvement in mood in the earlier studies was simply a placebo effect.

---

* Ackerson, J., Scogin, F., Lyman, R. D., & Smith, N. (1998). Cognitive bibliotherapy for mild and moderate adolescent depressive symptomatology. *Journal of Consulting and Clinical Psychology, 66*, 685–690.

Floyd, M., Rohen, N., Shackelford, J. A., Hubbard, K. L., Parnell, M. B., Scogin, F., & Coates, A. (2006). Two-year follow-up of bibliotherapy and individual cognitive therapy for depressed older adults. *Behavior Modification, 30*(3), 281–294.

Floyd, M., Scogin, F., McKendree-Smith, N. L., Floyd, D. L., & Rokke, P. D. (2004). Cognitive therapy for depression: A comparison of individual psychotherapy and bibliotherapy for depressed older adults. *Behavior Modification, 28*, 297–318.

Scogin, F., Hamblin, D., & Beutler, L. (1987). Bibliotherapy for depressed older adults: A self-help alternative. *The Gerontologist, 27*, 383–387.

Scogin, F., Jamison, C., & Davis, N. (1990). A two-year follow-up of the effects of bibliotherapy for depressed older adults. *Journal of Consulting and Clinical Psychology, 58*, 665–667.

Scogin, F., Jamison, C., & Gochneaut, K. (1989). The comparative efficacy of cognitive and behavioral bibliotherapy for mildly and moderately depressed older adults. *Journal of Consulting and Clinical Psychology, 57*, 403–407.

Smith, N. M., Floyd, M. R., Jamison, C., & Scogin, F. (1997). Three-year follow-up of bibliotherapy for depression. *Journal of Consulting and Clinical Psychology, 65*(2), 324–327.

The results of their new study were equally striking. Once again, more than 60% of patients who read *Feeling Good* improved, whereas those who read the Frankl book did not. Additional studies have confirmed that *Feeling Good* is helpful for individuals of all ages, from teenagers to older adults.

Because bibliotherapy "treatment" has no side effects and is so inexpensive, some experts have even argued that *Feeling Good* bibliotherapy should be the first treatment for all individuals with depression and that more costly interventions should be reserved for those who do not quickly recover.

And subsequent surveys have indicated that *Feeling Good* is the top-rated and most frequently "prescribed" book for patients with depression by American and Canadian health professionals. *Feeling Good* has now been translated and published throughout the world. I am extremely indebted to Dr. Scogin for helping to make all this possible!

Given all that research on *Feeling Good*, why have I written *Feeling Great*? As I've mentioned, I've been intrigued by the people who did not recover from depression when given a copy of *Feeling Good*, as well as by those who do not seem to recover even after lengthy and costly treatments with psychotherapy and antidepressant medications. I've wondered why they get stuck and what we might be able to do to get them unstuck. And that, of course, brings us to this book, as well as the new TEAM-CBT.

# Section VI

*Additional Resources*

# 32 | Incredible Free Stuff for You!

If you are a therapist wanting to improve your therapy skills or someone look-ing for help with depression, anxiety, relationship conflicts, or habits and ad-dictions, my personal mission has been to provide you with the tools you need to change your life. This book is one example, but I have tons of additional resources for you as well, and most of them are *free*.

## RESOURCES FOR EVERYONE

### Feeling Good Podcasts

Check out my weekly *Feeling Good* podcasts with my first host, Dr. Fabrice Nye, and my new host, Dr. Rhonda Barovsky. By the time this book is released, downloads will exceed 2 million from people around the world. A recent survey indicated that 60% of our listeners are general citizens look-ing for self-help, and 40% are therapists who want to improve their therapy skills. However, nearly 100% of therapists who listen have indicated that they are also looking for self-help to speed up their own healing.

Some of the podcasts recorded so far feature real, live therapy sessions, as well as a wide range of topics like these:

- What's the secret of a meaningful life?
- Rapid trauma treatment
- Smashing shyness
- You feel the way you think!
- Changing the beliefs that defeat you
- Flexing—and challenging—the mindfulness muscle
- A quick cure for procrastinators
- Five simple ways to boost your happiness
- The five secrets of effective communication
- The ten worst errors therapists make—and how to stop making them

- David's top ten techniques
- And much more

You can find a list of all my podcasts on the Feeling Good website.

## My TED Talk

If you want a brief introduction to cognitive therapy with some inspiring examples of how it works, you may enjoy my TED Talk in Reno. You'll learn about the intense anxiety I struggled with after the birth of my son, Erik, when he was placed in the neonatal intensive care unit because of difficulties breathing.

This was a personal test of the idea that we are disturbed, not by events, but by our thoughts about them. Was my panic and despair due to the actual event or the way I was thinking about it?

You'll also learn about how I treated Katrina, an elderly immigrant from Latvia, during the early days of cognitive therapy. You might recall her story from chapter 19. Katrina had just been discharged from the intensive care unit of our hospital for a serious suicide attempt and was convinced she was worthless because she'd never accomplished anything meaningful during her life.

Did you ever feel that way?

If you want to take a listen, you can find my TED Talk on YouTube.

Me and my son, Erik. (*Source: Nancy Mueller*)

## Feeling Good Blogs

You'll find many free blogs on my website, such as "The Secrets of Self-Esteem," "Overcoming the Fear of Death," "The Dark Side of Clinical Practice," and more.

My entire website is now fully searchable so you can type in any topic of interest to you—like "relapse prevention training" or "suicide prevention"—and you'll immediately find many free resources, including podcasts and blogs that you can link to immediately.

## Facebook Videos

You can watch my free Facebook Live videos, such as "The Perfectionist's Script for Self-Defeat" or "Integrating TEAM-CBT with Your Religious Beliefs."

## Books

My books, like *Feeling Good: The New Mood Therapy* and *The Feeling Good Handbook*, have sold 6 million copies in the United States and many more abroad. These are the highest rated self-help books for individuals suffering from depression and anxiety.

Here's what one reader named Amy said:

*I just wanted to write a quick note to say thank you! Twenty years ago (when I was only 15!), I found your book,* Feeling Good, *at my local bookstore and brought it home with me.*

*I've carried it with me EVERYWHERE because it literally changed my life. And it continues to ground me and bring me comfort/relief whenever I have an anxiety or depression relapse.*

*Recently, I discovered your* Feeling Good *podcasts. What a thrill! I love to listen after a long day and learn about your new techniques, behind-the-scenes vignettes, and enjoy your humor and humility.*

*What a GIFT you have given so many people for so, so many years. Thank you, thank you!!*

If you're struggling with depression or anxiety, I hope you find my books helpful too. Feeling good feels wonderful—and you owe it to yourself to feel good!

## RESOURCES FOR MENTAL HEALTH PROFESSIONALS

### Unlimited Free Psychotherapy Training

I offer free weekly psychotherapy training and personal work for Northern California mental health professionals every Tuesday evening at Stanford. Participants can also join my Sunday hikes where we practice therapy techniques, do personal work, and provide additional mentoring to refine their therapy skills while hiking on breathtaking California trails.

Here's how one of my students, Alisha Beale, described her experience in the Tuesday psychotherapy class:

> *I can't even begin to describe how lucky I feel to have found David's training group. Once I became licensed, I began searching for training opportunities because I knew I still had a lot to learn, but I had no idea how much my life would improve by attending the TEAM training groups.*
>
> *Not only has my professional life improved dramatically, but the skills David teaches have improved my personal life as well. I am forever grateful to David for being so generous with his time, and there's no place I'd rather be than learning from him!*

You can find more information regarding my free Tuesday evening training group at Stanford in the resources section on my Feeling Good website.

### Workshops

More than 50,000 American and Canadian mental health professionals have attended my psychotherapy workshops over the past thirty years. I have been honored to receive many wonderful workshop testimonials, like this one from Nik Chertudi:

> *I attended your "Scared Stiff" conference in Salt Lake City yesterday. It was wonderful.*

*I've been a clinician for 15 years and never has any conference been superior to yours! In fact, I've attended this workshop three times over the years, and I'm always pushed to the next level of thinking and understanding!*

*Thank you for your dedication and your willingness to share your incredible skill and knowledge. YOU ARE MY HERO!! I look up to you and your work!*

*Thanks again for your wonderful conference!*

The following are some unsolicited, heartwarming comments I discovered on workshop evaluations:

- The live demonstration in the evening was freaking incredible!!!
- The live demonstration was dynamite! It was beautiful!!
- The entire process was fantastic!
- I liked all of it! I appreciated Dr. Burns's willingness to be vulnerable with his own flaws and fears.

# 33 | Fifty Ways to Untwist Your Thinking

## Table of Contents for this Chapter

| Methods | |
|---|---|
| 1. Fifty Ways to Untwist Your Thinking—Basic Tools for Patients and Therapists | 476 |
| **Lists and Charts** | |
| 2. Checklist of Negative and Positive Distortions | 494 |
| 3. The Role-Play Techniques | 496 |
| 4. Strategies for Defeating Dysfunctional Thoughts | 497 |
| **Overview of the Great Deaths** | |
| 5. The Four Great Deaths of the Therapist's Ego in TEAM-CBT | 498 |
| 6. The Four Great Deaths of the Patient's Ego in TEAM-CBT | 499 |

## Fifty Ways to Untwist Your Thinking:
## Basic Tools for Patients and Therapists*

### 1. Positive Reframing

Focus on the negative thoughts and feelings in your Daily Mood Journal, one by one, and ask yourself two questions: (1) What are some advantages, or benefits, of this negative thought or feeling? (2) What does this negative thought or feeling show about me and my core values that's beautiful, positive, or even awesome? List them on the Positive Reframing List.

### 2. Magic Dial

After you complete positive reframing, imagine that you have a magic dial that would allow you to dial down each negative feeling to some lower level so you could preserve the positives associated with that feeling. Record these in the "% Goal" column of your Daily Mood Journal.

In other words, ask yourself how strongly you might want to feel each negative feeling on a scale from 0 (not at all) to 100 (the worst).

### 3. Straightforward Technique

Try to substitute a more positive and realistic thought for each negative thought. Ask yourself, "Is this negative thought really true? Do I really believe it? Is there another way to look at the situation?"

## Compassion-Based Techniques

### 4. Double Standard Technique

Instead of putting yourself down, talk to yourself in the same compassionate way you might talk to a dear friend who was upset. Ask yourself, "Would I say such harsh things to a friend with a similar problem? If not, why not? What would I say to him or her?"

---

## Truth-Based Techniques

### 5. Examine the Evidence

Instead of assuming that your negative thought is true, examine the evidence for it. Ask yourself, "What are the facts? What do they show?"

### 6. Experimental Technique

Do an experiment to test the validity of your negative thought in much the same way a scientist would test a theory. Ask yourself, "How could I test this negative thought to find out if it's really true?" For example, if you believe you're on the verge of losing control during a panic attack, you can test this belief by trying to drive yourself crazy through willful effort. You can roll around on the floor, flail your arms and legs in the air, and speak gibberish. It can be a relief to discover that you *can't* go crazy, no matter how hard you try.

### 7. Survey Technique

Conduct a survey to find out if your thoughts are realistic. Ask yourself, "How do other people think and feel about this? Could I ask some friends and get some feedback?" For example, if you believe that social anxiety is rare or shameful, you could simply ask several friends if they've ever felt that way.

### 8. Reattribution

Instead of blaming yourself entirely for a problem, think about the many factors that contributed to it. Ask yourself, "What caused this problem? What did I contribute, and what did others contribute? What can I learn from the situation?"

## Logic-Based Techniques

### 9. Socratic Method

Ask yourself questions that will show the inconsistencies in your negative thoughts. For example, you might ask yourself, "When I say that I'm a failure at life, do I mean that I fail at some things some of the time or at all things all the time?"

If you say, "some things some of the time," then you can point out that this is true of all human beings. If you say, "all things all the time," then you can point out that this isn't true of anyone since no one fails at everything.

### 10. Thinking in Shades of Gray

Instead of thinking about your problems in black-and-white categories, you can evaluate them in shades of gray. When things don't work out as well as you'd hoped, you can think of the experience as a partial success or a learning opportunity. Pinpoint your specific errors instead of writing yourself off as a total failure.

## Semantic Techniques

### 11. Semantic Method

Substitute language that's less colorful and emotionally loaded. Instead of thinking, "I *shouldn't* have made that mistake," you can tell yourself, "*It would be preferable if* I hadn't made that mistake." This method is especially helpful for should statements and labeling.

### 12. Let's Define Terms

When you label yourself as "inferior," a "fool," or a "loser," ask yourself what those labels mean. What's the definition of a fool or loser? When you try to define these terms, you'll discover there's no such thing. Foolish behavior exists, but "fools" and "losers" do not.

### 13. Be Specific

Stick with reality and avoid making global judgments about yourself. For example, instead of thinking of yourself as defective or worthless, focus on your *specific* flaws, errors, or weaknesses, as well as your *specific* strengths.

### 14. Worst, Best, Average is a combination of be specific (#13) plus thinking in shades of gray (#10), which I described in chapter 21. It can be helpful for overgeneralization and labeling. Let's say you have a negative thought like "I'm a bad father" or "I'm a bad teacher." List five specific skills or characteristics of a "good father" or "good teacher," and then rate yourself in each specific area using a scale from 0 to 100 when you're at your worst, at your best, and on average.

You'll find that you're never at a 0 or 100 and that your ratings vary quite a bit from time to time. Then you can select a specific area where you'd like to improve, such as "doing fun things with my son" or "being patient and supportive when my students are confused," and make a plan to improve in that area.

## Quantitative Techniques

### 15. Self-Monitoring

Keep track of repetitious negative thoughts or anxiety-producing fantasies by counting them. You can keep an index card in your wallet or pocket and put a check mark on it each time you have a negative thought. Alternatively, you can wear a wrist counter, like the ones golfers use to keep track of their scores. Record the total number of negative thoughts each day on a calendar. Often, the upsetting thoughts will diminish or disappear within two to three weeks.

### 16. Negative Practice/Worry Breaks

Schedule time to intentionally worry or criticize yourself. For example, if you constantly beat up on yourself because of your shortcomings, you can schedule several five-minute periods each day to berate yourself and feel miserable. At those times, you can be as self-critical as you want and rip yourself to shreds with gusto. Use the rest of your time for positive, productive living.

If you catch yourself worrying or criticizing yourself between those scheduled times, remind yourself that you can worry or criticize yourself during your next worry break. Then you can return to what you were doing.

## Humor-Based Techniques

### 17. Paradoxical Magnification

Instead of trying to refute your negative thoughts, you can buy into them and exaggerate them. Try to make them as extreme as possible. For example, if you feel inferior, you could tell yourself, "Yes, it's true. In fact, I'm probably the most inferior person in California at this time." Paradoxically, this can sometimes provide objectivity and relief. Of course, if you're really upset, this technique may have the unintended effect of making you feel even worse. If so, try another method.

### 18. Shame-Attacking Exercises

If you suffer from shyness, you probably have intense fears of looking foolish in front of other people. Shame-attacking exercises are a specific and potent antidote to these kinds of fears. You intentionally do something foolish in public so you can get over this fear. For example, you could stand up and announce each stop on a bus or shout out the time in a crowded department store.

When you make a fool of yourself on purpose, you discover that the world doesn't come to an end after all and that people don't really look down on you. This discovery can be liberating.

## Role-Play Techniques

### 19. Externalization of Voices

This technique transforms intellectual understanding into emotional change at the gut level. It's the most powerful of all the CBT techniques, but it can be quite challenging and even a bit upsetting at first.

You and another person take turns playing the role of your negative thoughts and positive thoughts. The other person starts by playing the role of your negative thoughts. He or she will attack you by reading one of your negative thoughts to you while speaking in the second person ("you"). You start by playing the role of your positive thoughts, defending yourself and speaking in the first person ("I"). Use role reversals when you get stuck.

For example, if you have the thought "I'm a useless human being," the other person will say, "You're a useless human being." The other person doesn't just attack you by saying random, mean things—he or she only uses the negative thoughts from your Daily Mood Journal to attack you. He or she goes through each negative thought one at a time and translates them into the second person ("you").

When you defend yourself, you can use either the self-defense paradigm (arguing with the negative thought and pointing out that it's distorted and incorrect), the acceptance paradox, or both. Then you can ask, "Who won? The negative self or the positive self?"

The goal is for the positive voice to win "huge." If the positive voice does not win "huge," keep doing role reversals. For this technique, a "small win" or a "big win" is not enough. We're looking for "huge."

### 20. Feared Fantasy

Like the externalization of voices, this is a two-person technique. You and the other person act out your worst fears, such as being rejected by an exceptionally hostile critic because you aren't smart enough or good enough.

When you face your worst fear, you often gain liberation from it. Your worst fears don't usually turn out to be real monsters but figments of your imagination that you can defeat with a little logic, compassion, and common sense.

## Other Role-Play Methods

Many techniques are much more effective in a role-play format. These include cognitive techniques like the **double standard technique** (#4) and the **acceptance paradox** (#21); motivational techniques like the **devil's advocate** (#30); and exposure techniques like the **talk show host** (#43) and **flirting training** (#45). Interpersonal techniques, like the **five secrets of effective communication** (#49) and **one-minute drill** (#50), also work extremely well in a role-play format.

## Philosophical/Spiritual Techniques

### 21. Acceptance Paradox

Instead of defending against your own self-criticisms, you find truth in them and accept your shortcomings with tranquility. Tell yourself, "It's true that I have *many* inadequacies. In fact, there is very little, if anything, about me that couldn't be improved considerably."

## Visual Imaging Techniques

### 22. Time Projection

**Future Projection.** If you're depressed, you can take a mental trip into the future and imagine that you've recovered. The current self who feels worthless and defeated can have a conversation with the future self who feels joy and self-esteem. The outpouring of emotion will often have a cathartic effect.

**Past Projection.** You can also take a mental trip into your past and have a conversation with someone who hurt or abused you. This will give you the chance to express the thoughts and feelings that have been bottled up and eating away at you for many years.

### 23. Humorous Imaging

When you feel consumed with anxiety or anger, it can sometimes help to visualize something humorous. For example, a woman with depression obsessed about the fact that she'd gotten screwed in her divorce settlement.

She could barely make ends meet and became furious every time she fanta-
sized about her ex-husband cavorting with his new trophy wife on his yacht,
living in the lap of luxury. The constant feelings of anger and resentment
were making her miserable. She found that picturing him at a board meet-
ing in his underpants made her giggle. This was a useful antidote to the
feelings of rage that were plaguing her.

Of course, motivation is massively important with every technique. If she
had wanted to be angry with her ex, the technique would not have worked.
Whenever you're angry, some positive reframing can be really helpful. List
the many overwhelming benefits of being angry, as well as what your anger
shows about you that's positive and awesome.

Then ask yourself if you want to dial down your anger to some lower level
or if you'd prefer to continue feeling really ticked off!

### 24. Cognitive Hypnosis

You'll need a therapist who uses hypnosis if you want to try this technique,
and you'll have to be hypnotizable—which only includes about a third of
us. After inducing a trance, the hypnotist may suggest that you're standing
in a special library with two sets of shelves. The shelves on the left contain intensely negative books, like *The Book of Hopelessness* and *The Book of
Despair*, and the shelves on the right contain positive books, like *The Book
of Joy* and *The Book of Self-Esteem*.

When you take a book from the left shelf, you'll discover that it's about you.
It contains descriptions of all your negative thoughts, memories, and fears.
When you read from this book, you'll feel overwhelmed with feelings of
depression, anxiety, hopelessness, and shame. Your hypnotist will guide you
as you destroy this book. You can burn it, bury it, or shred it.

Then you'll find yourself in the library again, where you'll take a book from
the right shelf. Once again, you'll discover that it's all about you, but this
time, it's filled with positive messages of self-esteem, creativity, and optimism.
As you read from this book, you'll be flooded with feelings of inner peace.

### Other Visual Imaging Techniques

**Cognitive flooding** (#39), **image substitution** (#40), and **memory
rescripting** (#41) are also visual imaging techniques, but they're categorized as cognitive exposure techniques because they're extremely useful in
the treatment of anxiety.

## Uncovering Techniques

### 25. Individual Downward Arrow

Draw a downward arrow under a negative thought in your Daily Mood Journal and ask yourself, "Why would it be upsetting to me if this thought were true? What would it mean to me?" A new negative thought will come to mind. Write that new thought down under the arrow, and repeat this process several times. When you review the chain of negative thoughts, along with the list of common self-defeating beliefs, you can pinpoint the attitudes and beliefs that make you vulnerable to depression and anxiety, such as perfectionism, the achievement addiction, or the brushfire fallacy.

### 26. Interpersonal Downward Arrow

This technique is similar to the individual downward arrow, but it's geared toward relationship problems. Draw a downward arrow under a negative thought in your Daily Mood Journal and ask yourself, "If this thought were true, what would it tell me about the type of person he or she is? The type of person I am? The type of relationship we have?" A new negative thought will come to mind. Write it down under the arrow, and repeat this process several times. This technique will help you uncover the self-defeating beliefs that lead to problems in your relationships with other people, such as entitlement, truth, or submissiveness. For example, perhaps you believe you need to hide your feelings in order to please other people because you think that their needs are far more important than your own.

### 27. What-If Technique

This uncovering technique is another type of downward arrow technique, but it was developed specifically for anxiety. If you're struggling with anxiety, draw a downward arrow under a negative thought in your Daily Mood Journal and ask yourself, "What's the worst that could happen if that were true? What do I fear the most?"

A new negative thought or fantasy will come to mind. Write it down under the arrow and repeat this process several times. You'll generate additional thoughts that will lead to the fantasy that frightens you the most. Then you can ask yourself, "How likely is it that this will happen? And could I live with it if it did?"

You can also use cognitive flooding to imagine what you fear the most. Make yourself as anxious as possible for as long as possible. Over time, your anxiety will diminish and disappear.

## 28. Hidden Emotion Technique

This technique is based on the idea that when you're anxious, you may be avoiding a personal problem that you don't want to face. Bringing the problem to conscious awareness and expressing your feelings will often eliminate your anxiety. Ask yourself, "Am I focusing on my anxiety to avoid dealing with something upsetting? What's the real problem that's bothering me? Do I secretly resent my spouse or my job? Am I unhappy about being in school? How do I really feel?"

## Motivational Techniques

## 29. Straightforward and Paradoxical Cost-Benefit Analysis

When you do a **straightforward** cost-benefit analysis, you list the advantages and disadvantages of a negative thought ("I'm such a loser") or self-defeating belief ("I should be perfect"). You can also do a cost-benefit analysis for a negative feeling (like anger, guilt, inferiority, or anxiety), a habit (such as drinking, using drugs, overeating, or procrastinating), or a relationship problem (such as blaming your spouse for your marital problems).

Ask yourself, "What are the advantages and disadvantages of this belief, feeling, or habit? How will it help me, and how will it hurt me?" After you list all the advantages and disadvantages, balance them against each other on a 100-point scale so you can see whether the costs or benefits are greater.

When you do a **paradoxical** cost-benefit analysis, you list only the *advantages* of a negative thought, belief, feeling, habit, or relationship problem. Now ask yourself, "Given all these advantages, why should I change?" This will make you aware of the powerful forces that keep you stuck.

## 30. Devil's Advocate Technique

This is a role-play technique. First, you record the thoughts you have when tempted to give in to your habit or addiction. For example, if you struggle with overeating, you might be thinking:

1. Oh, that glazed donut looks *so good*.

2. I'll just have one little bite. That can't hurt!

3. I deserve it, I've had a hard day.

4. I can have a light dinner to make up for it.

Next, you identify the positive distortions in your tempting thoughts. The ten positive distortions are the mirror images of the ten negative distortions, and they're listed on the Checklist of Negative and Positive Distortions on page 494.

For example, when you say, "I'll just have one little bite," you are discounting a lot of data to the contrary. This distortion is called **discounting the negative**. It triggers the urge to give in to your addiction and is the exact opposite of discounting the positive, a distortion that triggers depression.

Next, you ask another person—it could be your therapist or a friend or family member—to play the role of the devil who tempts you to drink, overeat, procrastinate, or date the wrong person. Your job is to talk back to those thoughts in real time. Use role reversals when you get stuck.

For example, if you're struggling to stick with your diet, imagine that you're walking past your favorite bakery and you smell fresh donuts. The devil (played by your friend) might say, "Gee, why don't you go and get one of those warm, soft, glazed donuts? It would taste *so good.*"

You can fight back and say, "I don't need a donut, and I'll feel terrible if I give in. I'm determined to stick with my diet, and I'm looking forward to fitting into more attractive clothes."

The devil will try to break you down again and say, "You deserve it! You've had a hard day."

Then you can fight back again.

This method can be surprisingly challenging, especially if the devil verbalizes your tempting thoughts in a seductive and persuasive manner.

When you are playing the role of the devil, try your hardest to persuade the other person to give in to the temptation. If he or she cannot defeat you, *do not* try to help. Instead, say something like, "It seems like you can't convincingly defeat your tempting thoughts. Perhaps this is not something you really want to change. After all, you only live once, and a nice fresh glazed donut (or whatever tempts you) can be *so good!*"

## 31. Stimulus Control

If you're trying to break a bad habit, such as alcoholism or overeating, you can reduce temptation rather than struggle with it. For example, if you drink too much, you can get rid of all the alcoholic beverages in your house and avoid going to places where alcohol is served. Stimulus control is not a complete treatment for any addiction, but it can be an important part of a more comprehensive program.

## 32. Decision-Making Tool

If you're stuck on the horns of a dilemma, the decision-making tool can help you sort out your options and get unstuck. It won't tell you what you *should* do, but it will show you what the real issues are and how you feel about them.

To use this technique, list all the possible options you're deciding among, and then choose the best two. You can call them Option A and Option B. Then list all the advantages and disadvantages for both options. Once you've done that, you compare and contrast the advantages and disadvantages for each option to get a point total score for Option A and Option B. I'm developing an app that automatically walks you through the tool and automatically does all the calculations for you.

This app allows you to compare the total points for Option A and Option B. The option with the more positive number is more desirable.

- If one option is strongly positive and the other is strongly negative, your decision is a no-brainer.
- If both numbers are positive, this is a can't lose decision.
- If both numbers are negative, it's a can't win decision
- If both numbers are around zero, it's a fence sitter.

A variety of other interesting patterns may also emerge. Remember that when you use the decision- making tool, you don't have to feel trapped or locked in by the results. You can fill it out on several occasions until you feel comfortable with your decision.

## 33. Daily Activity Schedule

When you're depressed, everything seems overwhelming. Nothing seems worth doing, so you may give up on life. Creating a daily activity schedule can help you overcome do-nothingism. Record what you do each hour from the time you get up in the morning to the time you go to bed at night. Rate how satisfying each activity was on a scale from 0 (not at all satisfying) to 5 (the most satisfying). A review of the schedule will show you which activities boost your mood the most.

## 34. Pleasure-Predicting Sheet

Schedule a series of activities with the potential for pleasure, learning, or personal growth. Indicate who you plan to do each activity with. Include activities you can do by yourself (such as jogging), as well as with other people.

Predict how satisfying each activity will be on a scale from 0 (the least) to 100 (the most). After you complete each activity, record how satisfying it actually turned out to be on the same scale. Now compare your actual satisfaction ratings with your predictions. Many people with depression find that lots of activities turn out to be more rewarding than they predicted. This discovery can boost your motivation to become more actively involved in life again.

You can also compare the satisfaction you get from being alone to the satisfaction you feel from being with other people. This can help you test self-defeating beliefs such as, "If I'm alone, I'm bound to feel miserable."

## 35. Anti-Procrastination Sheet

Rather than telling yourself you have to do everything all at once, break down an overwhelming task into tiny steps that you can tackle one at a time. Create an anti-procrastination sheet by dividing a piece of paper into five columns. In the left-most column, list each step that you need to do in order to complete the task. In the next two columns, predict how difficult and how satisfying each step will be on a scale from 0 (not difficult/not satisfying) to 100 (very difficult/very satisfying). After completing each small step, record how difficult and how satisfying it turned out to be in the last two columns. Now compare your predictions with the outcome. Many people discover that each step is far easier and more rewarding than they expected.

## Other Anti-Procrastination Techniques

If you're struggling with procrastination, and you're telling yourself that you just can't seem to get started, what you really mean is "I don't want to get started." If you're feeling stuck, use the **Socratic method** (#9) to ask yourself a series of questions that will lead to the absurdity of your claim that you just "can't" get started on a task you've been avoiding. First, break the task down into tiny steps. What's the first thing you'd have to do? The second thing?

Next, ask yourself, "What do I mean when I claim that I can't do the first step? Or the second step?"

## Classical Exposure Techniques

### 36. Gradual Exposure and Flooding

When you use **gradual exposure**, you expose yourself to the thing you fear in small steps. For example, if you have an elevator phobia, you could get on an elevator, go up one floor, and get off. Once you're comfortable with that, you could ride the elevator for two floors and gradually increase the length of time you spend in the elevator. You can use gradual exposure for any phobia, such as a fear of heights, needles, or dogs, as well as other forms of anxiety, such as shyness or OCD.

You can also create a fear hierarchy, in which you make a list of the things that trigger your anxiety and rank them from least threatening (1) to most threatening (10). Every day, record the type and amount of exposure you perform on each item from your hierarchy, as well as how anxious you felt during the exposure, using a scale from 0 (not at all anxious) to 100 (the most anxious possible).

When you use **flooding**, you expose yourself to the thing you fear all at once. For example, if you have an elevator phobia, you can force yourself to get on an elevator and ride up and down, no matter how anxious you feel, until your fear disappears. Flooding is more frightening than gradual exposure, but it works more rapidly. In fact, I've treated a number of people with elevator phobias, and they all recovered in just a few minutes.

Both approaches have been used successfully in the treatment of nearly all forms of anxiety, so you can use the approach that appeals to you the most.

### 37. Response Prevention

Response prevention is an important key to the treatment of all forms of anxiety. It's often combined with exposure. For example, let's say you have a powerful urge to check the mailbox over and over again after you drop a letter in. Using response prevention, you would drop the letter in the mailbox and walk away without checking it as you usually do. Your anxiety will temporarily get worse, and you'll feel compelled to check it. But if you refuse to give in to this urge, your anxiety will eventually disappear.

## 38. Distraction

If you feel anxious, you can distract yourself from the upsetting thoughts by concentrating intensely on something else. For the best results, you can combine distraction with gradual exposure or flooding. For example, if you feel panicky during an airplane flight, you can work on a crossword puzzle or engage the passenger next to you in conversation.

## Cognitive Exposure Techniques

## 39. Cognitive Flooding

Cognitive flooding is useful when you can't expose yourself to the thing you fear in reality. For example, if you have a fear of flying, you can't expose yourself to an actual airplane crash in order to overcome your fears! However, you can confront this fear in your mind using cognitive flooding.

Visualize your worst fear, such as feeling trapped in a plane that's crashing toward the earth in a ball of flames while all the passengers scream in terror. Try to endure the anxiety for as long as you can. If you become panicky, don't fight it! Instead, try to make the panic even worse. Eventually, the anxiety will burn itself out because your body simply cannot create anxiety indefinitely.

## 40. Image Substitution

Substitute a more positive or peaceful image for a frightening one. For example, during an airplane flight, you can fantasize landing safely or relaxing on a beach instead of imagining the plane crashing in flames.

## 41. Memory Rescripting

If you've been a victim of sexual or physical abuse, you may experience flashbacks with vivid memories of the traumatic episode. These mental pictures can be likened to a horrifying internal movie that you play over and over again the same way every time. You can edit the frightening scenes in this movie in much the same way that you can change your negative thoughts.

For example, if your best buddy was killed by a hand grenade when you were fighting together in Vietnam, horrifying memories of his body being blown apart may haunt you. You can bring him back to life in your mind and tell him all the things you never got to say before he died. Then you can give him a proper burial and say goodbye.

Changing the images can create a sense of mastery and help you overcome the feelings of helplessness that resulted from being a victim. In addition, the intentional exposure will desensitize you, and the traumatic memories will lose their power to intimidate you.

## Other Cognitive Exposure Techniques

**Negative practice/worry breaks** (#16), the **feared fantasy** (#20) and the **acceptance paradox** (#21) are all forms of cognitive exposure.

## Interpersonal Exposure Techniques

### 42. Smile and Hello Practice

If you're shy, you can force yourself to smile and say hello to ten or twenty strangers each day. Use an index card to record how many people respond positively, neutrally, and negatively. You'll often discover that people are much friendlier than you expected. This discovery can help you overcome your fears of rejection or looking foolish.

### 43. Talk Show Host

You can learn how to make casual conversation with anyone by using the **five secrets of effective communication** (#49), especially the disarming technique, inquiry, and stroking. These are the same skills used by successful talk show hosts like David Letterman and Jay Leno. They appear charming, personable, and relaxed because they always keep the spotlight on the other person.

Instead of trying to impress people by talking about yourself, you can focus on them in a friendly way. Find truth in what they say. Express curiosity and admiration. Ask questions and encourage them to open up. You'll find that most people are somewhat bored and lonely, and they love to be the center of attention.

### 44. Self-Disclosure

Instead of shamefully hiding your feelings of shyness or nervousness in a social situation, you can disclose them openly. This technique requires a good sense of self-esteem to be effective. If it's done skillfully, it will allow you to form real relationships with people instead of trying to put on a show and pretend to be something that you're not. This technique is based on the rather unintuitive idea that shyness without shame is actually an asset because it makes you seem more human and personable.

## 45. Flirting Training

You learn to flirt in a playful, lighthearted way rather than interacting with others in such a formal, heavy manner. Paradoxically, when you lighten up and learn to stop taking people so seriously, they're more likely to find you attractive and may even start chasing you.

## 46. Rejection Practice

If you're shy and afraid of rejection, you can try to accumulate as many rejections as you can instead of trying so hard to find someone to love you. Although this takes tremendous courage, you'll discover that the world doesn't actually come to an end when you're rejected. Paradoxically, when you stop fearing rejection, you stop getting rejected.

## Other Interpersonal Exposure Techniques

**Shame-attacking exercises** (#18) are categorized as a humor-based technique, but they're also interpersonal exposure techniques. You can also use the **rejection feared fantasy,** which is a variation of the **feared fantasy** technique (#20). Let's say that you're intensely shy and afraid of rejection. You can enter an Alice-in-Wonderland nightmare world where your worst fears come true. A friend or therapist can play the role of the most rejecting, hostile person you can imagine. He or she will be far worse than any real human being would ever be and will try to rip you to shreds. If you respond with the acceptance paradox, you'll discover that you can easily handle anything the hostile critic throws at you without getting perturbed. Use role reversals if you get stuck.

## Interpersonal Techniques

## 47. Blame/Relationship Cost-Benefit Analysis

List the advantages and disadvantages of blaming the other person for the problems in your relationship. You'll discover that there are lots of advantages:

- You can feel morally superior.
- You won't have to examine your own role in the problem.

- You'll feel like truth is on your side.
- You can get back at the other person without feeling guilty.
- You can feel powerful.
- You can tell your friends what a loser the other person is, and they'll probably agree with you.

There may also be some disadvantages. You won't be able to resolve the problem or get close to the person you're mad at. The conflict will go on and on, and you'll feel consumed by feelings of frustration and anger. Your friends may get tired of your constant complaining. And there won't be any room for personal or spiritual growth.

Once you've listed all the advantages and disadvantages, balance them on a 100-point scale. Ask yourself whether the costs or the benefits of this mindset are greater. If you decide to keep blaming the other person, then the prognosis for the relationship will be extremely poor. Your willingness to stop blaming him or her and to examine your own role in the problem is the key to developing a more satisfying relationship.

## 48. Relationship Journal

The relationship journal can help you improve your relationships with family members, friends, and colleagues with these five steps:

**Step 1.** Write down one thing the other person said to you.

**Step 2.** Write down *exactly* what you said next.

**Step 3.** Analyze what you wrote down in Step 2. Was it an example of good or bad communication?

**Step 4.** Think about the consequences of what you wrote down in Step 2. How will the other person think and feel? What will he or she say next? Will your response make the situation better or worse?

**Step 5.** Generate a more effective response using the five secrets of effective communication.

## 49. Five Secrets of Effective Communication

The five secrets of effective communication can help you resolve virtually any relationship problem quickly. These techniques require considerable practice and must come from the heart or they'll backfire.

1. **The Disarming Technique.** Find some truth in what the other person is saying even if it seems totally unreasonable or unfair.

2. **Empathy.** Try to see the world through the other person's eyes. Paraphrase the other person's words (*thought empathy*) and acknowledge how the other person is probably feeling based on what he or she said (*feeling empathy*).

3. **Inquiry.** Ask gentle, probing questions to learn more about what the other person is thinking and feeling.

4. **"I Feel" Statements.** Express your own ideas and feelings in a direct, tactful manner. Use *I feel* statements (such as "I'm feeling upset") rather than *you* statements (such as "You're making me furious!")

5. **Stroking.** Convey an attitude of respect even if you feel angry with the other person. Find something genuinely positive to say even in the heat of battle.

## 50. One-Minute Drill

You and your partner take turns playing the roles of talker and listener. The talker spends 30 seconds expressing his or her feelings about a relationship problem. The listener paraphrases what the talker has said as accurately as possible. The talker rates the listener's accuracy from 0% to 100%. Once the listener receives a rating of 95% or better, you can do a role reversal.

This technique ensures nearly perfect communication. It quickly breaks the pattern of accusation, self-defense, and hostility, and it shifts the dialogue to a level of greater vulnerability and intimacy.

## Other Interpersonal Techniques

**Interpersonal Decision Making.** When you're at odds with someone, you have three choices: You can settle for the status quo, work to make the relationship better, or leave the person you're not getting along with. Most of the time, people know what they want, but sometimes it's confusing. You may ask yourself, "Should I get engaged or break up and look for someone more exciting?" or "Should I get divorced or try to make my marriage better?"

The **decision-making tool** (#32) can help you sort out your options when you're having a tough time making up your mind. A wide variety of patterns can emerge, and each one will lead to a unique solution.

## Checklist of Negative and Positive Distortions

This checklist contains definitions of the top ten cognitive distortions. The positive distortions are all exact mirror images of the negative distortions that trigger depression and anxiety. In contrast, the positive distortions trigger mania, addictions, narcissism, relationship conflicts, and violence.

Positive distortions are more difficult to challenge because they're rewarding and make you feel terrific. In contrast, negative distortions make you feel terrible, so you're usually much more motivated to challenge and crush them.

| Distortion | Negative Example | Positive Example |
|---|---|---|
| **1. All-or-Nothing Thinking.** You think about yourself or the world in black-or-white, all-or-nothing categories. Shades of gray do not exist. | When you fail, you tell yourself that you're a complete failure. | When you succeed, you tell yourself that you're a winner. |
| **2. Overgeneralization.** You think about a negative event as a never-ending pattern of defeat or a positive event as a never-ending pattern of success. | When you're rejected by someone you care about, you tell yourself that you're an unlovable loser who will be alone *forever*. | When you recover from depression and feel terrific, you tell yourself that all your problems are solved and that you'll be happy forever. This sets you up for a severe crash. |
| **3. Mental Filter.** You focus on something bad and filter out all the positives—or you focus on something positive and ignore all the negatives. | You obsess about some shortcoming and ignore your positive qualities. This is like a drop of ink that discolors the entire beaker of water. | You dwell on the successes you've had and overlook your failures or setbacks, causing you to develop an overly positive view of things. |
| **4. Discounting the Positives/ Discounting the Negatives.** You tell yourself that certain negative or positive facts don't count so as to maintain a universally negative or positive image of yourself or the situation. | When someone compliments you, you tell yourself that they're only saying that to make you feel good (*discounting the positive*). | When you feel tempted to eat something tasty, you tell yourself, "I'll only have one little bite" (*discounting the negative*). How often have you told yourself this, and how often has it been true? This is also called denial. |
| **5. Jumping to Conclusions.** You jump to conclusions that aren't warranted by the facts.<br>• **Mind Reading.** You assume you know what other people are thinking and feeling.<br>• **Fortune Telling.** You make negative or positive predictions about the future. | If you're shy, you may tell yourself that people will judge you if they find out how insecure you feel (*mind reading*). If you're depressed, you tell yourself that your problems can never be solved and that you'll be depressed forever (*fortune telling*). | You tell yourself that a relationship is going really well when the other person is actually annoyed with you (*mind reading*). Or you tell yourself, "I'll just have one drink" when, in reality, you practically *never* stop after just one drink (*fortune telling*). |

| | | |
|---|---|---|
| **6. Magnification and Minimization.** You blow things out of proportion or shrink their importance inappropriately. This is also called the "binocular trick" because things look much bigger or much smaller depending on what end of the binoculars you look through. | When you procrastinate, you think about *everything* you've been putting off and tell yourself how *overwhelming* it will all be (*magnification*). You may also tell yourself that your efforts today would only be a drop in the bucket, so you put it off (*minimization*). | When you're struggling with temptation, you tell yourself, "This ice cream will taste *so good!*" (*magnification*). Then you tell yourself, "One little bite won't hurt!" (*minimization*). But how often do you stop after one little bite? |
| **7. Emotional Reasoning.** You reason from how you feel. This can be very misleading because your feelings result entirely from your thoughts and not from external reality. | You tell yourself, "I *feel* like a loser, so I must really *be* one." Or "I *feel* hopeless, so I must *be* hopeless." | You tell yourself, "I *feel* lucky! I just *know* I'm going to hit the jackpot!" So you buy another lottery ticket or put a bunch more dollars in the slot machine. |
| **8. Should Statements.** You make yourself miserable with *should*s, *must*s, or *ought to*s. Self-directed shoulds cause feelings of guilt, shame, depression, and worthlessness. Other-directed shoulds trigger feelings of anger and frustration toward others. World-directed shoulds cause feelings of anger and frustration toward the world. | You tell yourself, "I *shouldn't* have screwed up and made such a stupid mistake" (*self-directed should*). Or "That jerk *shouldn't* cut in front of me in traffic. I'll show him!" (*other-directed should*). Or "The train *shouldn't* be late when I'm in such a hurry!" (*world-directed should*). | You tell yourself, "I've had a hard day. I *deserve* a drink" (*self-directed should*). Or you tell yourself other people *should* treat you the way you want them to (*other-directed should*). Or you tell yourself that good things *should* happen because you're a good person who works really hard (*world-directed should*). |
| **9. Labeling.** You label yourself or others so you see your entire self (or someone else) as totally defective or superior. | You label yourself or someone you're not getting along with as a "loser" or "self-centered jerk." | You think of yourself as a "winner" because you won or did something that worked out really well. |
| **10. Blame.** You use all your energy finding fault with yourself (*self-blame*) or others (*other-blame*). | You criticize yourself mercilessly for every error and shortcoming instead of using your energy to find creative solutions to your problems (*self-blame*). | You tell yourself that the other person is to blame for the problems in your relationship, so you feel like an innocent victim and overlook your own role in the problem (*other-blame*). |

## The Role-Play Techniques

| Technique | Patient's Name | Therapist's Name | Role Reversals? |
|---|---|---|---|
| Double Standard Technique | His or her real name | The name of an imaginary dear friend of the same gender as the patient but not someone the patient knows | No |
| Externalization of Voices | His or her real name | Same name as the patient | Yes |
| Feared Fantasy | His or her real name | The name of some judgmental or critical person the patient is afraid of | Yes |
| Devil's Advocate | His or her real name | The seductive devil who tempts the patient to give in to a habit or addiction | No |
| Forced Empathy | Some person the patient is not getting along with | A trusted friend of the person the patient is not getting along with | No |

## Strategies for Defeating Dysfunctional Thoughts

| Strategy | Healing Method | Negative Thought | Example of How to Defeat the Negative Thought |
|---|---|---|---|
| **Self-Defense Paradigm** | **Victory.** You defeat or crush the negative thought by arguing with it and insisting that it's *not* true. | A patient who suddenly relapses several weeks after recovery will often think, "This shows that the therapy didn't work and that I really am a hopeless case." | "That's ridiculous. I had a fight with my spouse last night, so it's not surprising that I'd be feeling upset. The therapy was very effective, and this would be a good time to pull out the tools I learned and get to work." |
| **Acceptance Paradox** | **Surrender.** You defeat the negative thought by buying into it and insisting that it *is* true, but you do this with a sense of humor or inner peace. | During a moment of insecurity, a therapist may think, "I'm not as good as I should be." | "As a matter of fact, I have tons of flaws and a great deal to learn. Even when I'm 85 years old, there will still be tons of room for learning and improving, and that's kind of exciting." |
| **Be Specific** | **Reality.** You defeat overgeneralization or labeling by focusing on specific flaws instead of labeling your entire self as defective. | You might think, "I'm a loser" or "I'm a failure as a parent." | You ask, "What are some specific things I've failed at or errors that I've made?" or "What are the things I do as a parent that aren't so good?" |
| **Positive Reframing** | **Melting Resistance.** You show the advantages of your negative thoughts and feelings, as well as what they show about you that's positive and awesome. | You have thoughts like, "I'm a loser" or "I'm defective." | This thought shows that you: <br>• Have high standards. <br>• Are realistic since you do have many flaws. <br>• Are accountable since you're not blaming everyone else. <br>• Are humble. <br>In addition, your high standards may motivate you to work hard and not settle for mediocrity. |
| **Experimental Method** | **Truth.** You conduct an experiment to test the validity of a negative thought. | A shy patient might think, "I'm the *only one* who feels this way. There must be something wrong with me!" | The patient could ask several friends if they've ever felt shy, anxious, or uncomfortable in social situations. |
| **Double Standard Technique** | **Compassion.** You treat yourself kindly and talk to yourself in a compassionate and realistic way, the same way you'd talk to a dear friend or family member whom you loved. | A woman diagnosed with terminal cancer told herself, "I'm letting my family down." | The therapist would ask the patient if she'd talk that way to a dear friend with the same problem. If not, what would she say? And would she be willing to talk to herself in the same compassionate way? |

## The Four Great Deaths of the Therapist's Ego in TEAM-CBT

| Phase of TEAM | Type of Great Death | Explanation |
|---|---|---|
| T = Testing | The Confident, Effective Self | When you test before and after every session, you may discover that:<br><br>• The patient's symptoms did not improve.<br><br>• Your interventions were not helpful.<br><br>• You got a failing grade on the empathy and helpfulness scales.<br><br>• The patient's ratings on the scales are valid.<br><br>• Your perceptions of how the patient was feeling, and what the patient thought about you, were not correct and that you are not particularly sensitive to how other people feel.<br><br>These disturbing failures are highly desirable because they can lead to radical modifications in how you work with patients. |
| E = Empathy | The Compassionate, Understanding Self | When you look at your scores on the empathy scale, you will probably see that you received a failing grade, especially if you're using the rating scale for the first time. This can be a blow to your ego, especially if you (wrongly) believed that you had good empathy skills.<br><br>You can use the five secrets of effective communication (especially the disarming technique) to acknowledge the painful truth in the patient's criticisms. This is a sharp departure from conventional therapy, where the patient's criticisms are thought of as an expression of his or her pathology (e.g., "transference").<br><br>For example, if the patient insists that you are incompetent and don't care how he or she feels inside, the patient is telling you something that is true. It is not just a distorted perception of the therapeutic relationship. It is something that is actually happening.<br><br>When you genuinely find the truth in the accusation, your ego will die, but you will suddenly feel much closer to the patient, and this can lead to a therapeutic breakthrough. You have to experience this to understand it. Angry, challenging patients are, in a sense, trying to kill you. The question is this: Are you willing to die for your patients? |
| A = Assessment of Resistance | The Helping, Rescuing Self | You give up trying to help the patient change. Instead, you become the voice of the patient's resistance and argue for the status quo. You may also have to issue the gentle ultimatum and sit with open hands if the patient refuses to do what is necessary for change, like psychotherapy homework or using exposure to treat anxiety.<br><br>However, many therapists are unwilling to do this because they won't tolerate the death of their "helping" self. They may believe that they know what is best for their patients and that helping and being "nice" will win the day! Therapist narcissism and codependency can sometimes get in the way. |
| M = Methods | The Powerful, Skillful Self | When you put a negative thought in the middle of a recovery circle, the goal is not success but, rather, to fail as fast as you can. That's because the faster you fail, the quicker you'll get to the technique that changes your patient's life. But this means the death of the self that "knows" the best way to help patients with a certain problem or diagnosis. |

# The Four Great Deaths of the Patient's Ego in TEAM-CBT

| Target | Type of Great Death | Explanation |
|---|---|---|
| Depression | The Special Self | Recovery requires the death of your "special" self or your efforts to become special or worthwhile. You accept the fact that you are not, in fact, special, superior, or especially worthwhile and that you are actually quite flawed, defective, and, for the most part, "average."<br><br>In addition, you will have to accept and grasp that you feel incredibly happy and fulfilled without the things you think you think you "need," like love, approval, and success. In addition, if you are really lucky, you will discover that you do not need "unconditional self-esteem" or even a "self." |
| Anxiety | The Fearful Self | Recovery from any form of anxiety requires you to confront and surrender to the monster you fear the most. It could be the fear of public speaking, heights, germs, or going crazy—anything at all.<br><br>When you try to avoid the monster or control your anxiety—as we do most of the time—it gets worse. That makes sense. No one wants to die or get eaten alive!<br><br>In contrast, when you confront the monster and surrender to the intense anxiety, you will discover that the monster has no teeth and that your fears have been based on a bit of a cosmic joke. At that moment, you will experience enlightenment. You will experience nirvana as your fearful self "dies." |
| Relationship Problems | The Blaming/ Blameless Self | You discover that you are, in fact, causing the very relationship problems you've been complaining about, possibly for years or even decades. For me, this is the most painful death.<br><br>This great death can feel intensely shocking, humiliating, and shameful. However, the moment your ego dies, you and the person you're at odds with will suddenly find a far more loving and meaningful relationship.<br><br>In addition, you will comprehend that you and the other person are "one" and that you have been creating your own interpersonal reality—for better or worse—at every minute of every day. This can be empowering because if you have been creating the problems, you can also create far more loving relationships. |
| Habits and Addictions | The Entitled, Pleasure-Seeking Self | Recovery requires the death of your entitled, pleasure-seeking ego. This seems like the loss of your main—or only—source of happiness, joy, pleasure, or satisfaction in life, such as eating, drinking, using drugs, procrastinating, and so forth.<br><br>Of course, some people are also addicted to love, approval, or success. There are many things we think we "need" for happiness and fulfillment, and these "needs" can be the source of a great deal of suffering.<br><br>In this Great Death, you discover that you never really needed those things you were so *sure* that you "needed." |

# About the Author

David D. Burns, M.D., is a renowned psychiatrist, award-winning researcher, and author of the phenomenally successful *Feeling Good: The New Mood Therapy*, which has sold 5 million copies worldwide. More than 50,000 American and Canadian mental health professionals have attended his popular training programs, and his weekly *Feeling Good* podcast has surpassed 2 million downloads.

Dr. Burns graduated magna cum laude from Amherst College, received his M.D. from Stanford University School of Medicine, and completed his psychiatry residency at the University of Pennsylvania School of Medicine. He has served as Acting Chief of Psychiatry at the Presbyterian / University of Pennsylvania Medical Center (1988) and Visiting Scholar at the Harvard Medical School (1998), and is certified by the National Board of Psychiatry and Neurology.

Dr. Burns is currently Adjunct Clinical Professor Emeritus of Psychiatry and Behavioral Sciences at the Stanford University School of Medicine, where he is involved in research and teaching. He has received numerous awards, including the A. E. Bennett Award for his research on brain chemistry, the Distinguished Contribution to Psychology through the Media Award, and the Outstanding Contributions Award from the National Association of Cognitive-Behavioral Therapists. He has been named Teacher of the Year three times from the class of graduating residents at Stanford University School of Medicine, and feels especially proud of this award.

In addition to his academic research, Dr. Burns has written a number of popular books on mood and relationship problems. Articles about Dr. Burns have been featured in more than 100 popular consumer magazines, including *The New York Times* and *Reader's Digest*, and he has been interviewed on more than 1,000 radio and television shows.

In 1995, Dr. Burns and his family returned to California from Philadelphia. When he is not crunching statistics for his research, he can be found teaching his famous Tuesday evening psychotherapy training group for Stanford students and community clinicians, or giving workshops for mental health professionals throughout the United States and Canada.

# Index

% After column, Daily Mood Journal, 33, 86, 89–90, 116, 153, 222–223, 420

% Belief column, Daily Mood Journal, 115, 152, 420

% Goal column, Daily Mood Journal, 31, 79, 98, 133, 148–149, 199, 476

% Now column, Daily Mood Journal, 24, 60, 62, 143–144, 159, 174, 176

100% cure, 47

200% cure, 47

## A

A = Assessment of Resistance, 81, 436–437, 461–462

acceptance paradox, 481, 490, 497
   magnification and minimization, 298
   should statements, 323–325

accountability of therapists, 458
   Evaluation of Therapy Session survey, 460–461

achievement
   less worthwhile human being, 379–380
   more worthwhile human being, 365–369, 370

addictions
   death of entitled, pleasure-seeking self, 404–406, 499
   free bonus chapter downloads, 405
   magnification and minimization, 295
   medications for psychiatric problems, 452
   relapse prevention. *See* relapse prevention training
   stuckness/resistance, 38, 55–56
   Temptations Test, 7–8, 411

agoraphobia, 43, 269. *See also* anxiety

alcoholism. *See* addictions

alexithymia, 175

Alia ("am I unlovable?"), 383, 385–387

Alicia (depression and sexual abuse), 52–54

all-or-nothing thinking, 16, 22, 24–25, 67, 83–84, 110–111, 135, 150, 209–215, 343, 361, 377, 385, 419, 494
   "all" side, 414
   Daily Mood Journal, 68
   exercises, 210–211, 215
   negative, 209–210
   positive, 209–211
   positive reframing, 211–212
   thinking in shades of gray, 212–215, 314

allowing your "helpful self " to die, 264

American Psychiatric Association, 4, 26

anger
   magnification and minimization, 294
   subconscious, 283, 285

Anger and Relationship Satisfaction Scales, 5–7, 410

angry, blaming self, 397–404, 499

Annie (OCD), 271–272

antianxiety agents, 451–452

antidepressants, 447–449
   chemical imbalance, 305
   effectiveness vs. CBT, 453
   neuronal function, 429
   reduction in symptom severity, 123

anti-procrastination sheet, 487

anxiety
   100% cure, 47
   200% cure, 47
   antianxiety agents, 451–452
   chemical imbalance, 27
   cognitive flooding, 48–49
   Depression and Anxiety Scales, 3–5, 409
   effectiveness of psychotherapy, 452–454
   exposure, 46–50, 272–274
   fortune telling, 269–292
   gentle ultimatum, 240
   hidden emotion technique, 283–292
   illusion of, 202
   magical thinking, 45–46, 58, 271
   magnification and minimization, 294
   outcome resistance and process resistance, 270–272
   overcoming, 46–47
   overcoming resistance with positive reframing, 279–282
   people who struggle with depression, 270
   phobias, 5
   positive reframing, 188
   Recovery International, 412
   self-defeating beliefs, 274–279
   shame, 158
   shyness, 5
   stuckness/resistance, 38, 43–50
   treatment, 46–50
   types of, 43, 269–270

*Anxious: The Modern Mind in the Age of Anxiety* (LeDoux), 440

AON. *See* all-or-nothing thinking

approval addiction, 278

apps
 decision-making tool, 486
 Feeling Great, 169

Ariella (overgeneralization), 217–223, 225

assertiveness, 287–288, 292, 400, 402

assessment of resistance (TEAM-CBT), 81,
 436–437, 461–462

Ativan, 451

**B**

Barovsky, Rhonda, 469

be specific, 221, 386, 478, 497
 emotional reasoning, 310–311

Beale, Alisha, 472

Beck, Aaron, xii, 176, 185, 305, 452

belief
 % Belief column, Daily Mood Journal, 115,
 152, 420
 self-defeating, 274–279

Ben (rejection by Richard), 170–171, 174,
 179–180, 375–378

Bennie (suicidal depression and intermittent
 explosive disorder), 247–255

benzodiazepines ("minor tranquilizers"), 451

Berna (sexual abuse), 311–314

bibliotherapy, 465–466

Biyu (depression), 39–42

black holes, 21–22, 120, 260, 343, 351

blame (self-blame and other-blame), 21, 26,
 335–353, 378, 385, 419, 495
 blame beacon, 337
 cost-benefit analysis, 346–349
 death of angry, blaming self, 397–404, 499
 exercises, 339, 341, 344, 349
 forced empathy, 350–352
 positive reframing, 339–341
 reattribution, 104, 343–346
 relationship problems, 52–54
 resistance, 353
 self-blame, 67, 83, 135, 145, 151, 278
 semantic technique, 341–343

blame cost-benefit analysis, 491–492

blog, 471

blowing things out of proportion. *See* magnification
 and minimization

bonus chapter downloads, 405

books, 471–472

brain functioning, 425–440
 chemical imbalance, 442–444
 Daily Mood Journal, 439
 emotions, 430–431

filters, 431–432

frames, 432–434

FTWT (Fires Together Wires Together), 429–430

integrating with TEAM-CBT, 434–440

nerve cells, 429

networks, 429–430

SNEFF model, 427–434

structures, 427–429

WTFT (Wired Together Fire Together), 430

Brief Mood Survey, 3–10, 142, 236, 262, 409–412,
 435–458

British CoBalT trial, 453–454

brushfire fallacy, 278, 294

Buddha/Buddhism, 38–39, 102, 372
 Great Death, 364
 oneness, 404
 self, 391

Burns, Erik, 458, 470

**C**

cancer. *See* Marilyn (stage 4 lung cancer)

case studies
 "failure" as a father. *See* Mark ("failure" as a
 father)
 afraid of germs. *See* Sara (afraid of germs)
 fear of being judged. *See* Melanie (fear of being
 judged)
 mother. *See* Karen ("bad mom")
 stage 4 lung cancer. *See* Marilyn (stage 4 lung
 cancer)

catastrophizing. *See* magnification and minimization

cause of depression, 444

CBT. *See* cognitive behavioral therapy (CBT);
 TEAM-CBT

changing thinking changes feelings, 70, 141, 154,
 445–447

Checklist of Cognitive Distortions, 65, 144, 173

"chemical imbalance" theory of depression, 27, 305,
 442–444

Chertudi, Nik, 472

Choi, Sunny, 397

Christine (sexual and physical abuse), 436–439

chronic worrying, 43. *See also* anxiety

claustrophobia, 463–465

CliffsNotes of *Feeling Great*, 15–34
 cognitive "click", 32–34
 cognitive distortions, 15–26
 positive reframing, 26–31

cognitive behavioral therapy (CBT), xii
 British CoBalT trial, 453–454
 effectiveness of, 452–454
 TEAM-CBT. *See* TEAM-CBT

cognitive "click", 32–34

cognitive content specificity, 176–178
cognitive distortions, 15–26, 494–495
    all-or-nothing thinking. *See* all-or-nothing
        thinking
    blame. *See* blame (self-blame and other-blame)
    cheat sheet, 105–109
    Checklist of Cognitive Distortions, 65, 144, 173
    Daily Mood Journal, 181
    discounting the negative, 228, 485, 494
    discounting the positive. *See* discounting the
        positive
    emotional reasoning. *See* emotional reasoning
    exercises, 360–362, 376–378, 384–385, 418–419
    filtering, 431–432
    identifying, 281
    jumping to conclusions. *See* jumping to
        conclusions
    labeling. *See* labeling
    magnification and minimization. *See*
        magnification and minimization
    Maria (postpartum depression), 24–26
    Mark ("failure" as a father), 134–136
    mental filtering. *See* mental filtering
    overgeneralization. *See* overgeneralization
    self-blame and other-blame. *See* blame
        (self-blame and other-blame)
    should statements. *See* should statements
    top ten distortions, 494–495
Cognitive Distortions Quiz, 66–68, 82–84, 109–111,
    134–136, 149–150, 360–362, 376–378,
    384–385, 418–419
cognitive exposure techniques, 489–490
cognitive flooding, 48–49, 300–302, 482, 489
cognitive hypnosis, 482
cognitive therapy, 305
communication
    EAR Checklist, 287, 292, 400
    five secrets of effective communication, 138–139,
        287–288, 292, 386, 400, 402, 490, 492
compassion-based techniques, 476
compulsive gamblers, overgeneralization, 218
cost-benefit analysis, 484, 491–492
    blame, 346–349
    exercises, 349
    paradoxical, 250–255
    straightforward, 255–258
cotherapists, 59
counting the positives, 229–230
cravings, Temptations Test, 7–8, 411
critical thinking about TEAM-CBT, 139
criticism, finding truth in, 54
crushing negative thoughts, 70, 91, 111, 119, 138,
    202, 204, 225, 314
    brain functioning, 439

Christine (sexual and physical abuse), 439
cognitive distortions. *See* cognitive distortions
conditions for emotional change, 69–70
Fifty Ways to Untwist Your Thinking, 91, 100,
    104, 111, 203–204, 258, 475–493
Karen ("bad mom"). *See* Karen ("bad mom")
Keeshawn (magnification and minimization),
    298–299
Marilyn (stage 4 lung cancer). *See* Marilyn
    (stage 4 lung cancer)
Mark ("failure" as a father). *See* Mark ("failure"
    as a father)
Megan (self-blame), 341–343
Melanie (fear of being judged). *See* Melanie
    (fear of being judged)
recovery circle. *See* recovery circle
relapse prevention, 416
starting out with motivational technique, 353

**D**

Dahmer, Jeffrey, 382
daily activity schedule, 486–487
Daily Mood Journal, 42, 59–60, 169
    % After column, 33, 86, 89–90, 116, 153,
        222–223, 420
    % Belief column, 115, 152, 420
    % Goal column, 31, 79, 98, 133, 148–149,
        199, 476
    % Now column, 24, 60, 62, 143–144, 159,
        174, 176
    brain functioning, 439
    Checklist of Cognitive Distortions, 65, 144, 173
    circling/rating emotions, 174–175
    defeat of negative thoughts, 87–90
    electronic version (Feeling Great app), 169
    identifying cognitive distortions, 181
    magic button, 182
    magic dial, 198–199
    Maria (postpartum depression), 23–24
    Mark ("failure" as a father), 128, 133, 140
    Melanie (fear of being judged), 115–118
    miracle cure question, 181–182
    necessary/sufficient conditions for emotional
        distress, 201–202
    negative emotions, 60
    negative thoughts, 62, 63, 68, 176–181
    positive reframing, 182–198
    recovery circle, 203–205
    upsetting event, 23, 60, 92, 93, 117, 128, 140,
        143, 158–159, 169–172, 178, 434
decision-making tool, 486, 493
    app, 486
depression

cause of, 444

"chemical imbalance" theory, 27, 305, 442–444

effectiveness of psychotherapy, 452–454

fortune telling. *See* hopelessness

illusion of, 202

people who struggle with anxiety, 270

Recovery International, 412

self-defeating beliefs, 275

Depression and Anxiety Scales, 3–5, 409

devil's advocate, 481, 484–485, 496

*Diagnostic and Statistical Manual of Mental Disorders* (DSM-5), 4, 26–27, 77, 198

dieting, 55–56

disarming technique, 54, 386, 493

Law of Opposites, 54

discounting the negative, 228, 485, 494

counting the positives, 229–230

discounting the positive, 17, 25, 67, 83, 110, 135–137, 150, 227, 230–234, 377, 385, 419, 494

double standard technique, 230–234

exercise, 233

distraction, 489

Don ("bad father"), 328–329

*Don't Think of an Elephant* (Lakoff), 440

double standard technique, 476, 481, 496–497

emotional reasoning, 314

Mark ("failure" as a father), 137–138

Melanie (fear of being judged), 114–115

mental filtering and discounting the positive, 230–233

role-play, 114–115

should statements, 322–323

downward arrow technique, 276–278

exercise, 277–279

individual, 483

interpersonal, 483

DP. *See* discounting the positive

drug addiction. *See* addictions

DSM-5 (*Diagnostic and Statistical Manual of Mental Disorders*), 4, 26–27, 77, 198


**E**

E = Empathy, 81, 436, 458–461, 496

five secrets of effective communication, 287–288, 292, 400, 402

EAR (empathy, assertiveness, and respect), 287–288, 292, 400, 402

EAR Checklist, 287, 292, 400

Edison, Thomas, 247, 369

ego. *See* Great Deaths

Ellis, Albert, xii, 48, 362, 452

emotional change, conditions for, 69–70, 115

emotional distress, conditions for, 63, 69, 201–203

emotional reasoning, 19, 22, 67, 83, 111, 135, 151, 303–314, 344, 378, 385, 419, 495

be specific, 310–311

double standard technique, 314

examine the evidence, 305, 306, 308–309

identifying, 281

let's define terms, 314

negative, 307

positive, 307–308

positive framing, 311–312

survey technique/experimental technique, 313–314

thinking in shades of gray, 314

emotions

alexithymia, 175

brain functioning, 430–431

hidden emotion technique, 283–292

rating, 174–175

empathy, 71, 81, 94, 436, 458–461, 493

five secrets of effective communication, 287–288, 292, 400, 402

thought and feeling empathy, 386

forced empathy, 350–353, 496

*The Enchiridion* (Epictetus), 61

endorphins, 463

entitled, pleasure-seeking self, 404–406, 499

Epictetus, 61, 446

Esketamine, 450–451

Evaluation of Therapy Session, 459–461

examine the evidence, 258–261

emotional reasoning, 305, 306, 308–309

exercise, 308–309

magnification and minimization, 298

Mark ("failure" as a father), 137

exercise, 56, 463–464

exercises

all-or-nothing thinking, 210–211, 215

blame, 339, 341, 344, 349

cognitive distortions, 360–362, 376–378, 384–385, 418–419

cost-benefit analysis, 349

Daily Mood Journal, 171–173

doing psychotherapy homework, 42–43

downward arrow technique, 277–279

examine the evidence, 308–309

exposure, 272–273

hidden emotion technique, 284, 290–292

importance of, 171, 174

labeling, 329–333

less worthwhile human being, 376–381

let's define terms, 259–260

magnification and minimization, 299

Melanie's recovery circle, 102–112

mental filtering and discounting the positive, 233
mind reading, 246
more worthwhile human being, 366–371
necessary/sufficient conditions for emotional distress, 201–202
negative thoughts, 179–181
outcome resistance and process resistance, 271
overgeneralization, 218–220, 224–225
positive reframing, 130–131, 161–162, 263, 279, 296, 319, 339
Positive Reframing Chart, 96–97
Positive Reframing Table, 145–146
Positive Reframing Tool, 184–186, 196–197
reattribution, 344
relationships, 290–292
self-defeating beliefs, 277–279
semantic technique, 341
shame-attacking, 282, 346
should statements, 318–319, 326
Your Recovery Circles, 205
experimental method/technique, 477, 497
emotional reasoning, 313–314
exposure, 89, 272–273
anxiety treatment, 46–50
classical exposure, 488–489
cognitive exposure, 489–490
cognitive flooding, 489
distraction, 489
exercise, 272–273
flirting training, 491
flooding, 488
gradual exposure, 488
image substitution, 489
magnification and minimization, 300–301
memory rescripting, 489–490
myths about, 273–274
rejection feared fantasy, 491
rejection practice, 491
response prevention, 488
self-disclosure, 490–491
shame-attacking exercises, 491
shyness, 345–346
smile and hello practice, 490
talk show host, 490
externalization of voices, 264–266, 420–422, 480, 496
Ezekiel (claustrophobia and fear of the dark), 463–465

**F**

Facebook Live videos, 471
failure
be specific, 386
flaws, 383–389
joyful failure, 12–13
more worthwhile human being, 369
fathers
Don ("bad father"), 328–329
Mark ("failure" as a father). *See* Mark ("failure" as a father)
fear. *See also* anxiety
facing, 46–50, 89
of being judged. *See* Melanie (fear of being judged)
of change, 163–165
of dark, 463–465
of disapproval, 294
of flying, 269
of judgement. *See* Melanie (fear of being judged)
of rejection, 278
types of, 269–270
feared fantasy, 242–245, 480, 481, 490–491, 496
more worthwhile human being, 372–374
fearful self, 396–397, 499
*Feeling Good: The New Mood Therapy* (Burns), xi–xiii, 10, 15, 48, 317, 413, 422, 452, 462, 465–466
cognitive distortions list, 65
Nadine, 335
podcasts, 35
website, 35
*Feeling Good* blogs, 471
*The Feeling Good Handbook* (Burns), 471
Feeling Good Institute, 463
*Feeling Good* podcast, 35, 127, 141, 469–470
Dr. Mark Noble, 425
Lee (marital problem), 403
Marilyn (stage 4 lung cancer), 154–155
Rameesh (negative thoughts), 181
Sara (afraid of germs), 167
*Feeling Good Together*, 347
Feeling Great app, 169
*Feeling Great* CliffsNotes, 15–34
cognitive "click", 32–34
cognitive distortions, 15–26
positive reframing, 26–31
feelings
% increase in positive feelings during session, 123
% reduction in negative feelings during session, 122
alexithymia, 175
Anger and Relationship Satisfaction Scales, 410
cognitive content specificity, 176–178
depression and anxiety scales, 409
emotional reasoning. *See* emotional reasoning
Happiness Test, 9–10, 411
hidden emotion technique, 283–292
"I feel" statements, 386

magic dial. *See* magic dial
negative emotions, 60–61, 64–65
feelings cause thoughts, 445–447
positive reframing. *See* positive reframing
rating emotions, 174–175
thoughts create feelings, 70, 141, 154, 445–447
Fifty Ways to Untwist Your Thinking, 91, 100, 104,
   111, 203–204, 258, 475–493
filters, brain functioning, 431–432
Fires Together Wires Together (FTWT), 429–430
first Great Death: special self, 391–396, 499
five secrets of effective communication, 287–288,
      292, 386, 400, 402, 481, 490, 492–493
   Mark ("failure" as a father), 138–139
flaws, 383–389
   be specific, 386
   specific flaws, 389
flirting training, 481, 491
flooding, 488
   cognitive flooding, 489
   flooding flowsheet, 301–302
forced empathy, 350–352, 496
fortune telling, 17, 25, 67, 83–85, 110, 135,
      235, 494. *See also* jumping to conclusions
   identifying, 281
   mind reading, 343
fortune telling: anxiety, 269–292
   exposure, 272–274
   hidden emotion technique, 283–292
   magical thinking, 271, 272
   outcome resistance and process resistance,
      270–272
   overcoming resistance with positive reframing,
      279–282
   self-defeating beliefs, 274–279
   shame-attacking exercises, 282
fortune telling: hopelessness (depression), 247–267
   Bennie (suicidal depression and intermittent
      explosive disorder), 247–255
   examine the evidence, 258–261
   externalization of voices, 264–266
   let's define terms, 258–261
   paradoxical cost-benefit analysis, 250–255
   positive reframing, 261–264
   straightforward cost-benefit analysis, 255–258
four Great Deaths. *See* Great Deaths
fourth Great Death: entitled, pleasure-seeking self,
      404–406, 499
fractal psychotherapy, 434
frames, brain functioning, 432–434
Fran (anxiety), 43–45
Frank (depression), ix–xi
Frankl, Viktor, 465–466
Freud, 35

resistance to change, xiii, 198
FT. *See* fortune telling
FTWT (Fires Together Wires Together), 429–430
future projection, 481

**G**

Gabriella (ovarian cancer), 230–233
gamblers, overgeneralization, 218
generalization. *See* overgeneralization
generalized anxiety, 270
genes, 443–444
gentle ultimatum, 240
germ phobia. *See* Sara (afraid of germs)
goal of TEAM-CBT, 431
Goal column, Daily Mood Journal, 199, 476
gradual exposure, 488
Grateful Dead, 406
Great Deaths, 364, 391, 498–499
   angry, blaming self, 397–404, 499
   entitled, pleasure-seeking self, 404–406, 499
   fearful self, 396–397, 499
   patient's ego, 401, 499
   special self, 391–396, 499
   therapist's ego, 498
Great Rebirth, 406
guilt, positive reframing, 73–77, 184–185, 189

**H**

habits
   death of entitled, pleasure-seeking self,
      404–406, 499
   free bonus chapter downloads, 405
   magnification and minimization, 295
   relapse prevention. *See* relapse prevention training
   stuckness/resistance, 38, 55, 56
   Temptations Test, 7, 8, 411
Happiness Test, 9–10, 411, 457
helping others, more worthwhile human being,
   371–374
hidden emotion technique, 283–289, 484
   exercise, 284
   figuring out hidden problems or feelings,
      290–292
hidden shoulds, 20, 22, 67, 111, 277, 316–318,
      344, 378, 419. *See also* should statements
   identifying, 281
high-level solution, 362–363
high-speed treatment, 121–126
   % increase in positive feelings, 123
   % reduction in negative feelings, 122
   reasons for success of TEAM-CBT, 123–125
Hitler, 381

homework, 42–43
  doing psychotherapy homework, 42
  homework survey, 457
  motivation, 462
hopelessness, 247–267
  Bennie (suicidal depression and intermittent
    explosive disorder), 247–255
  examine the evidence, 258–261
  externalization of voices, 264–266
  let's define terms, 258–261
  paradoxical cost-benefit analysis, 250–255
  positive reframing, 185–186, 190, 261–264
  straightforward cost-benefit analysis, 255–258
Hughes, Howard, 157
humor, 152
  humor-based techniques, 479
  humorous imaging, 481–482
hypnosis
  cognitive hypnosis, 482
  reverse hypnosis, 47
hypochondriasis, 43, 241–242, 269. See also anxiety
  magical thinking, 45, 58

**I**

"I feel" statements, 386, 493
identity, 357. See also self
image substitution, 482, 489
individual downward arrow, 483
inquiry, 239–240, 386, 493
intermittent explosive disorder. See Bennie
  (suicidal depression and intermittent
  explosive disorder)
interpersonal decision making, 493
interpersonal downward arrow, 483
interpersonal techniques, 490–493

**J**

JC. See jumping to conclusions
Jesus, 372
journals
  Relapse Prevention Journal, 417, 420
  relationship journal, 286–288, 291, 398, 492
  Daily Mood Journal. See Daily Mood Journal
joyful failure, 12–13
Julia (special needs child), 315, 317–322
jumping to conclusions, 17, 18, 25, 67, 83, 110,
    135, 151, 235, 377, 378, 385, 419, 494
  fortune telling, 17, 25, 67, 83–85, 110, 135,
    235, 494. See also fortune telling
  mind reading, 18, 22, 67, 83, 88–89, 235–246,
    494. See also mind reading

**K**

Karen ("bad mom"), 59
  cause of negative feelings, 61, 64
  cause of negative thoughts, 63
  cognitive distortions, 66–68, 81–85
  Daily Mood Journal, 60, 62–63, 79, 86–88
  exposure, 89
  fortune telling, 84–85
  listening respectfully/empathizing, 71
  magic button, 72
  magic dial, 78–80
  mind reading, 88–89
  Mood Journal, 90
  necessary/sufficient conditions for emotional
    change, 70
  positive reframing, 73–77
  recovery, 89–90
Katrina (suicide attempt), 305–308, 470
Keeshawn (magnification and minimization), 293–301
  acceptance paradox, 298
  examine the evidence, 298
  exposure/cognitive flooding, 300–301
  positive reframing, 295–298
Keisha (hopelessness)
  externalization of voices, 264–266
  positive reframing, 261–264
Klonopin, 451
Krumm, Angela, 91, 94, 99, 110–111, 114, 119

**L**

labeling, 20, 26, 67, 84, 111, 135, 151, 327–333,
    328–329, 344, 378, 385, 419, 495
  exercises, 329–330, 333
  negative, 327
  positive, 327
  worst, best, average technique, 327, 329–333, 478
Lakoff, George, 440
Lam, Richard, 351–352
Law of Opposites, 54
laws of the universe should, 317
LeDoux, Joseph, 440
Lee (relationship problem), 398–403
legal shoulds, 317
less worthwhile human being, 375–382
  achievement, 379–380
let's define terms, 258–261, 478
  emotional reasoning, 314
Levitt, Jill, 12, 59, 71, 72, 78, 81, 84, 85, 88, 89,
    127, 129, 133, 138, 229, 351, 352
Lillya (anxious about second child), 283–290, 435
listening respectfully, 71, 94
logic-based techniques, 477–478
losing weight, 55–56

low-level solution, 362
LSD, 449
L-tryptophan, 443
Lucretia ("double trauma"), 236–237
Luther (shame and perceived perfectionism), 396–397

# M

M = Methods, 81, 437–440, 462–463
MAG. *See* magnification and minimization
magic button, 182
    Berna (sexual abuse), 312
    Biyu (depression), 39–40
    downside to pressing, 198
    Fran (anxiety), 44
    habits and addiction stuckness, 55
    Karen ("bad mom"), 72
    Maria (postpartum depression), 28
    Mark ("failure" as a father), 129
    Melanie (fear of being judged), 95
    outcome resistance and process resistance, 270–272
    relationships, 51
    Sara (afraid of germs), 160
magic dial, 101, 198–199, 476
    Karen ("bad mom"), 78–80
    Maria (postpartum depression), 30–31
    Marilyn (stage 4 lung cancer), 148
    Mark ("failure" as a father), 133
    Melanie (fear of being judged), 98
    subconscious mind, 79–80
magic mushrooms, 449
magical thinking, 43, 45–46, 271
Magical Thinking Quiz, 45
    answers, 58
magnification and minimization, 18, 25, 83, 110,
    135, 151, 293–302, 343, 378
    acceptance paradox, 298
    anger, 294
    anxiety disorders, 294
    examine the evidence, 298
    exercises, 299
    exposure/cognitive flooding, 300–302
    fear of disapproval, 294
    flooding flowsheet, 301–302
    habits and addictions, 295
    OCD, 300
    panic attacks, 295
    perfectionism, 295
    positive reframing, 295–299
    procrastination, 295
    reattribution/self-monitoring, 300
*Man's Search for Meaning* (Frankl), 465–466
Maria (postpartum depression), 23
    cognitive "click", 32–34

cognitive distortions, 24–26
Daily Mood Journal, 23–24
magic button, 28
magic dial, 30–31
positive reframing, 26–31
Marilyn (stage 4 lung cancer), 141–155
    before-session Brief Mood Survey, 142
    challenging negative thoughts, 152–153
    cognitive distortions, 144, 149–152
    Daily Mood Journal, 141–145, 148–149,
        152–153
    magic dial, 148
    podcast episodes, 154–155
    positive feelings survey, 142
    positive reframing, 146–148
    tune-up session, 154
Mark ("failure" as a father), 127–140
    cognitive distortions, 134–136
    Daily Mood Journal, 128, 133, 140
    double standard technique, 137–138
    examine the evidence, 137
    five secrets of effective communication, 138–139
    magic button, 129
    magic dial, 133
    positive reframing, 130–132
    recovery circle, 136
    resistance, 129, 133
    two-year follow-up, 138–139
    video links, 139
May, Matthew, 141, 145, 152, 395
MDMA, 450
medications
    addiction, 452
    antidepressants. *See* antidepressants
    benzodiazepines ("minor tranquilizers"), 451
    experimental treatments/psychedelics, 449–451
meditation, 463
Megan (self-blame), 337–343
Melanie (fear of being judged), 91–92
    cognitive distortions, 105–111
    Cognitive Distortions Quiz, 109–111
    Daily Mood Journal, 93, 98, 115–118
    double standard technique, 114–115
    hiding of awards, 94
    listening respectfully/empathizing, 94
    magic button, 95
    magic dial, 98
    Melanie's escape, 102–120
    necessary/sufficient conditions for emotional
        change, 115
    overgeneralization, 108–110
    positive reframing, 95–97
    rapid recovery, 119–120
    recovery circle, 99–113

resistance, 99
straightforward technique, 101
video of session, 120
Melinda (depression), 36
memory rescripting, 482, 489–490
mental filtering, 17, 22, 25, 67, 83, 110, 135–137,
150, 227–234, 377, 385, 419, 494
counting the positives, 229–230
discounting the negative, 228, 485
discounting the positive, 227
double standard technique, 230–233
exercise, 233
negative, 227
positive, 227–228
methods (TEAM-CBT), 81, 437–440, 462–463.
See also techniques
MF. See mental filtering
microneurosurgery. See brain functioning
Milton H. Erickson Foundation, 394
MIN. See minimization
mind reading, 18, 22, 67, 83, 88–89, 235–246,
343, 494. See also jumping to conclusions
exercise, 246
feared fantasy, 242–245
identifying, 281
inquiry, 239–240
negative, 236–239
positive, 236–239
self-disclosure, 239–243
minimization, 18–19, 25, 67, 83, 110, 135, 151,
293–302, 495. See also magnification and
minimization
miracle cure question, 181–182. See also magic
button
mood
Brief Mood Survey, 3–10, 142, 236, 262,
409–412, 435–458
Daily Mood Journal. See Daily Mood Journal
Depression and Anxiety Scales, 3–5, 409
doing psychotherapy homework, 42
Happiness Test, 9–10, 411
Temptations Test, 7–8, 411
Willingness Test, 11–12
moral shoulds, 317
more worthwhile human being, 365–374
failure, 369
feared fantasy, 372–374
helping others, 371–374
success, 365–368, 370
Moses, 372
Mother Teresa, 372
mothers
Julia (special needs child), 315, 317–322
Karen ("bad mom"). See Karen ("bad mom")

motivation
importance of, with techniques, 482
optimism, 247
homework, 462
positive labeling, 327
resistance. See resistance; stuckness
motivational techniques, 107, 484–488
starting out with, 353
MR. See mind reading
Muhammad, 372

N

Nadine (self-blame), 335–337
Nathaniel (shyness), 343–346
necessary conditions for emotional change, 69–70, 115
necessary conditions for emotional distress, 63, 69,
201–203
negative emotional reasoning, 307
negative feelings/emotions
% increase in positive feelings, 123
% reduction during session, 122
causes of, 64–65
cause of negative thoughts, 445–447
cognitive content specificity, 176–178
magic dial, 78–80
mood journal, 60–61
positive reframing. See positive reframing
negative labeling, 327. See also labeling
negative mind reading, 236–239. See also mind
reading
negative overgeneralization, 217–218
negative practice/worry breaks, 479, 490
negative thoughts
all-or-nothing thinking, 209–210
cause of negative feelings, 445–447
cause of, 63
cognitive content specificity, 176–178
cognitive distortions. See cognitive distortions
conditions for emotional change, 69–70
crushing, 70, 91, 111, 119, 138, 202, 204, 225,
298, 299, 314, 341–343, 353, 416, 439
Daily Mood Journal, 176–181
defeat of, 89–90
examine the evidence, 309
magic dial, 78–80
mood journal, 62–63
positive reframing. See positive reframing, 132
nerve cells, brain functioning, 429–430
networks, brain functioning, 429–430
The New Mood Therapy (Burns), 471
Noble, Mark, xiv, 422, 425
nutritional supplements, 463
Nye, Fabrice, 469

# O

OB. *See* other-blame
Obie the cat, 391–396
obsessive-compulsive disorder (OCD), 43, 47,
   157–158, 269. *See also* anxiety
   magical thinking, 45, 58, 271–272
   magnification, 300
   Sara. *See* Sara (afraid of germs)
OG. *See* overgeneralization
one-minute drill, 481, 493
oneness, 404
other-blame, 21, 26, 335–353, 495. *See also* blame
   (self-blame and other-blame)
   cost-benefit analysis, 346–349
   exercises, 339, 341, 344, 349
   forced empathy, 350–352
   positive reframing, 339–341
   reattribution, 343–346
   relationship problems, 52–54
   semantic technique, 341–343
other-directed shoulds, 19, 316. *See also* should
   statements
outcome resistance, 36–37, 270–272
   overcoming with positive reframing, 279–282
overeating, 55. *See also* addictions
overgeneralization, 16, 25, 67, 84, 108–110,
   135–136, 150, 217–225, 343, 361, 375–378,
   385–386, 419, 438, 494. *See also* labeling
   be specific, 221, 386
   Daily Mood Journal, 68
   exercises, 218–219, 224–225
   negative, 217–218
   positive, 217–218
   positive reframing, 219–221
   semantic technique, 223–224
   survey technique, 222
   worst, best, average technique, 327, 329–333, 478

# P

panic attacks, 43, 269. *See also* anxiety
   magnification and minimization, 295
paradoxical cost-benefit analysis, 250–255, 484
paradoxical magnification, 479
past projection, 481
patients
   Alia ("am I unlovable?"), 383, 385–387
   Annie (OCD), 271–272
   Ariella (overgeneralization), 217–223, 225
   Ben (rejection by Richard), 170–171, 174,
      179–180, 375–378
   Bennie (suicidal depression and intermittent
      explosive disorder), 247–255

   Berna (sexual abuse), 311–314
   Christine (sexual and physical abuse), 436–439
   Ezekiel (claustrophobia and fear of the dark),
      463–465
   Gabriella (ovarian cancer), 230–233
   Karen. *See* Karen ("bad mom")
   Katrina (suicide attempt), 305–308, 470
   Keeshawn (magnification and minimization),
      293–301
   Keisha (hopelessness), 261–266
   Lee (relationship problem), 398–403
   Lillya (anxious about second child), 283–290, 435
   Lucretia ("double trauma"), 236–237
   Marilyn. *See* Marilyn (stage 4 lung cancer)
   Mark. *See* Mark ("failure" as a father)
   Megan (self-blame), 337–343
   Melanie. *See* Melanie (fear of being judged)
   Nadine (self-blame), 335–337
   Nathaniel (shyness), 343–346
   Robert (shyness), 240–241
   Roberto (shyness and public speaking anxiety),
      276–282
   Rose (suicide attempt), 237–238
   Sara. *See* Sara (afraid of germs)
   Saul (all-or-nothing thinking), 209–213
Pedro (depression and OCD), 47–48
perceived perfectionism, 278, 396
perfectionism, 278
   magnification and minimization, 295
performance anxiety, 43, 270. *See also* anxiety
   magical thinking, 45, 58
perspective, 363–364
philosophical/spiritual techniques, 481
phobias, 43, 269. *See also* anxiety
   anxiety, 5
   germ phobia. *See* Sara (afraid of germs)
   magical thinking, 45, 58
pivot question, 162–163
pleasing others, 278
pleasure-predicting sheet, 487
pleasure-seeking self, 404–406, 499
podcast, 35, 127, 141, 469–470
   Dr. Mark Noble, 425
   Lee (marital problem), 403
   Marilyn (stage 4 lung cancer), 154–155
   Rameesh (negative thoughts), 181
   Sara (afraid of germs), 167
positive emotional reasoning, 307–308. *See also*
   emotional reasoning
positive framing, 311–312
positive labeling, 327. *See also* labeling
positive mind reading, 236–239. *See also* mind
   reading

positive overgeneralization, 217–218
positive reframing, 26–31, 100, 182–198,
    476, 497
    all-or-nothing thinking, 211–212
    blame, 339–341
    exercises, 279, 296, 319, 339
    fortune telling, 261–264
    Karen ("bad mom"), 73–77
    magnification and minimization, 295–299
    Maria (postpartum depression), 26–31
    Marilyn (stage 4 lung cancer), 146–148
    Mark ("failure" as a father), 130–132
    Melanie (fear of being judged), 95–97
    negative feelings, 183–190
    negative thoughts, 191–195
    overcoming outcome and process resistance,
        279–282
    overgeneralization, 219–221
    Sara (afraid of germs), 160–162
    should statements, 319–320
    thinking in shades of gray, 212–215
Positive Reframing Chart, 96–97
Positive Reframing Map for Negative Feelings,
    187–190
Positive Reframing Map for Negative Thoughts,
    192–195
Positive Reframing Tool, 183–184, 196–198
positive thoughts
    100% beliefs, 115
    all-or-nothing thinking, 209–211
postpartum depression. See Maria (postpartum
    depression)
post-traumatic stress disorder (PTSD), 43, 269.
    See also anxiety
    magical thinking, 45, 58
    memory rescripting, 489–490
prayer, 463
process resistance, 36–37, 270–272
    overcoming with positive reframing, 279–282
procrastination
    anti-procrastination sheet, 487
    magnification and minimization, 295
psilocybin, 449
psychedelic agents, 449
psychotherapy
    cognitive behavioral therapy. See cognitive
        behavioral therapy (CBT); TEAM-CBT
    effectiveness of, 452–454
    homework, 42–43
    training, 472
PTSD (post-traumatic stress disorder), 43, 269.
    See also anxiety
    magical thinking, 45, 58
    memory rescripting, 489–490

public speaking anxiety, 43, 269, 277–278,
    280–282. See also anxiety
    downward arrow technique, 277–278
    overcoming resistance with positive reframing,
        279–282
    self-defeating beliefs, 276–279
    shame-attacking exercises, 282

**Q**

quizzes. See also exercises; tests
    Cognitive Distortions Quiz, 66–68, 82–84,
        109–111, 134–136, 149–150, 360–362,
        376–378, 384–385, 418–419
    Magical Thinking Quiz, 45, 58

**R**

Rader, Dennis, 372
Rameesh (negative thoughts), 180–181
rapid recovery, 426, 439–440
    % increase in positive feelings, 123
    % reduction in negative feelings, 122
    high-speed treatment, 121–126
    Melanie (fear of being judged), 119–120
    reasons for success of TEAM-CBT, 123–125
rating emotions, 174–175
reasoning
    emotional reasoning. See emotional reasoning
    positive reframing. See positive reframing
reattribution, 104, 477
    blame, 343–346
    exercises, 344
    magnification and minimization, 300
recovery circle, 203–205
    exercise, 204–205
    Mark ("failure" as a father), 136
    Melanie (fear of being judged), 99–113
Recovery International, 412
referral suggestions, 412
reframing. See positive reframing
rejection
    Ben (rejection by Richard), 170, 171, 174,
        179–180
    positive reframing, 189
    rejection practice, 346, 491
    rejection feared fantasy, 491
Relapse Prevention Journal, 417, 420
relapse prevention training, 120, 154, 260,
    413–422, 427
    cognitive distortions, 418–419
    externalization of voices
        technique, 420–422
    feelings assessment, 409–412

step 1, 414–415
step 2, 415
step 3, 415–416
relationship cost-benefit analysis, 491–492
relationship journal, 286–288, 291, 398–399, 492
    EAR Checklist, 287, 292, 400
Relationship Satisfaction Scale, 5–7, 410, 457
relationships
    Alia ("am I unlovable?"), 383, 385–387
    Ben (rejection by Richard), 170–171, 174,
        179–180, 375–378
    blame, 52–54
    exercise, 290–292
    five secrets of effective communication,
        287–288, 292, 386, 400, 402
    hidden emotion technique, 283–289
    Lee (marital problem), 398–403
    Lillya (anxious about second child),
        283–290, 435
    oneness, 404
    overgeneralization, 217–223, 225
    stuckness/resistance, 38, 50–54
    survey, 457
relaxation training, 463
resistance, xiii, 35. *See also* stuckness
    assessment of, 81, 436–437, 461–462
    blame, 353
    examine the evidence/let's define terms, 258–261
    externalization of voices, 264–266
    magic dial, 31
    magical thinking, 43
    Marilyn (stage 4 lung cancer), 148
    Mark ("failure" as a father), 129, 133
    Melanie (fear of being judged), 99
    outcome resistance, 36–37, 270–272
    overcoming with positive reframing, 279–282
    paradoxical cost-benefit analysis, 250–255
    positive reframing, 261–264, 295
    process resistance, 36–37, 270–272
    Sara (afraid of germs), 163–165
    straightforward cost-benefit analysis, 255–258
    subconscious, 31, 35, 43, 80, 95, 99, 130,
        163, 264
    taking role of subconscious resistance, 163,
        264, 283
Resistance Table, 38
resources
    books, 471–472
    Facebook Live videos, 471
    *Feeling Good* blogs, 471
    *Feeling Good* podcasts. *See Feeling Good* podcast
    free psychotherapy training, 472
    TED Talk, 470
    workshops, 472–473

respect, five secrets of effective communication,
    287–288, 292, 400, 402
response prevention, 488
reverse hypnosis, 47
Robert (shyness), 240–241
Roberto (shyness and public speaking anxiety),
    276–282
role-play, 480, 496
    Melanie (fear of being judged), 114–115
Rose (suicide attempt), 237–238
Rumi, 406
runner's high, 56, 463

## S

Sapolsky, Robert, 440
Sara (afraid of germs), 157–167
    Daily Mood Journal, 158–159
    follow-up email, 166–167
    magic button, 160
    OCD, 157–158
    pivot question, 162–163
    positive reframing, 160–162
    resistance/fear of change, 163–165
SB. *See* self-blame
scales. *See also* testing (TEAM-CBT)
    Anger, 5–7, 410
    Anxiety, 3–5, 409
    Relationship Satisfaction, 5–7, 410, 457
    comparing before and after scores, 411–412
    Depression, 3–5, 409
    Evaluation of Therapy Session, 460–461
    Happiness Test, 9–10, 411
    Willingness Test, 11–12
Scared Stiff conference, 472
Scogin, Forrest, xii, 413, 465
second Great Death: fearful self, 396–397, 499
self, 357–364
    blaming self, 397–404, 499
    pleasure-seeking self, 404–406, 499
    fearful self, 396–397, 499
    flaws and failures, 383–389
    Great Death, 364
    less worthwhile human being, 375–382
    more worthwhile human being, 365–374
    overgeneralization, 375–376
    special self, 391–396, 499
self-acceptance, 222
self-blame, 21, 26, 67, 83, 145, 151, 278, 335–353,
    378, 385, 419, 495. *See also* blame
    (self-blame and other-blame)
    cost-benefit analysis, 346–349
    exercises, 339, 341, 344, 349
    forced empathy, 350–352

positive reframing, 339–341
reattribution, 104, 343–346
resistance, 353
semantic technique, 341–343
self-defeating beliefs, 274–279
downward arrow technique, 276–278
exercise, 277–279
what-if technique, 276
self-defense paradigm, 497
should statements, 323–325
self-directed shoulds, 19, 316, 318. *See also* should statements
self-disclosure, 239–243, 345, 490–491
self-doubt, 359–362
self-esteem, 249, 358–359
self-help books, 465–466
self-love, 222
self-monitoring, 479
magnification and minimization, 300
semantic method/technique, 223–224, 478
blame, 341–343
exercises, 341
should statements, 320–321
semantic techniques, 478–479
serial killers
Dennis Rader, 372
Jeffrey Dahmer, 382
serotonin, 442–443
sexual abuse, 52–54
memory rescripting, 489–490
SH. *See* should statements
shame, 158, 270, 396–397
Melanie (fear of being judged). *See* Melanie (fear of being judged)
shame-attacking, 282, 346, 397, 479–480, 491
should statements, 19–20, 22, 26, 67, 83, 111, 135, 151, 179, 277, 315–326, 344, 378, 385, 419, 495
double standard technique, 322–323
exercises, 318–319, 326
hidden shoulds, 20, 22, 67, 111, 277, 281, 316–318, 344, 378, 419
identifying, 281
laws of the universe shoulds, 317
legal shoulds, 317
moral shoulds, 317
other-directed shoulds, 19, 316
positive reframing, 319–320
self-defense paradigm/acceptance paradox, 323–325
self-directed shoulds, 19, 316, 318
semantic method, 320–321
Socratic method, 322
world-directed shoulds, 19, 316

shy bladder syndrome, 241, 269
shyness, 43, 269. *See also* anxiety
anxiety, 5
downward arrow technique, 277–278
exposure, 345–346
magical thinking, 45, 58
overcoming resistance with positive reframing, 279–282
reattribution, 343–346
self-defeating beliefs, 276–279
shame-attacking exercises, 282, 479–480
skepticism about TEAM-CBT, 139
smile and hello practice, 345, 490
SNEFF model, 427–434
emotions, 430–431
filters, 431–432
frames, 432–434
networks, 429–430
structures, 427–429
Socratic method, 328–329, 477, 487
should statements, 322
special self, 391–396, 499
spotlight fallacy, 278
SSRI antidepressants, 447
stimulus control, 485–486
straightforward cost-benefit analysis, 255–258, 484
straightforward technique, 101, 476
stroking, 386, 493
structures, brain functioning, 427–429
stuckness, 35–58
anxiety, 43–50
assessment of resistance, 436–437, 461–462
depression, 38–43
examine the evidence/let's define terms, 258–261
externalization of voices, 264–266
Magical Thinking Quiz, 45, 58
Marilyn (stage 4 lung cancer), 148
Mark ("failure" as a father), 129, 133
Melanie (fear of being judged), 99
outcome resistance, 36–37, 270–272
overcoming, 56–58
paradoxical cost-benefit analysis, 250–255
positive reframing, 261–264, 279–282, 295
process resistance, 36–37, 270–272
relationships, 50–54
Resistance Table, 38
straightforward cost-benefit analysis, 255–258
subconscious
anger, 283, 285
magic dial, 31, 79–80
resistance, 31, 35, 43, 80, 95, 99, 130, 163, 264
taking role of subconscious resistance, 163, 264, 283

success
  less worthwhile human being, 379–380
  more worthwhile human being, 365–368, 370
suffering, 38
sufficient conditions
  emotional change, 6–70, 115
  emotional distress, 63, 69, 201–203
suicidal depression
  Bennie. See Bennie (suicidal depression and
    intermittent explosive disorder)
  Katrina, 305–308, 470
  Rose, 237–238
Sunday hikes, 214, 315, 328, 396, 426, 472
Superman, 279
supplements, 463
survey technique, 222, 346, 477
  emotional reasoning, 313–314
surveys
  Evaluation of Therapy Session, 460–461
  homework survey, 457

**T**

talk show host, 345, 481, 490
TEAM-CBT, xiii–xv, 81
  A = Assessment of Resistance, 81, 436–437,
    461–462
  brain functioning. See brain functioning
  cotherapist, 59
  critical thinking and skepticism about, 139
  E = Empathy, 81, 436, 458–461
  four great deaths of therapist's ego, 498
  goal of, 431
  high-speed treatment, 121–126
  M = Methods, 81, 437–440, 462–463
  pivot question, 162–163
  positive reframing, 73–77
  reasons for rapid recovery, 123–125
  T = Testing, 81, 89, 175–176, 435, 454–458.
    See also testing (TEAM-CBT)
techniques. See also methods
  anti-procrastination, 487–488
  compassion-based, 476
  exposure, 488–490
  humor-based, 479
  interpersonal, 490–493
  logic-based, 477–478
  motivational, 484–488
  philosophical/spiritual, 481
  role-play, 480, 496
  semantic, 478–479
  strategies for defeating dysfunctional
    thoughts, 497
  truth-based, 477

  uncovering, 483
  visual imaging, 481–482
TED Talk, 470
Temptations Test, 7–8, 411
Ten Commandments, 317
Ten Days to Self-Esteem (Burns), 358
test anxiety, 43, 270
testing (TEAM-CBT), 81, 89, 175–176, 435,
  454–458
  Brief Mood Survey, 3–10, 142, 236, 262,
    409–412, 435–458
  Cognitive Distortions Quiz, 66–68, 82–84,
    109–111, 134–136, 149–150, 360–362,
    376–378, 384–385, 418–419
  doing psychotherapy homework, 42–43
  Happiness, 9–10, 411
  Magical Thinking Quiz, 45, 58
  mood (depression and anxiety), 3–5, 409
  positive feelings survey, 142
  relationships, 5–7, 410, 457
  temptations (cravings and urges to use),
    7–8, 411
  value of, 236–238
  Willingness, 11–12
therapists
  accountability, 458
  Evaluation of Therapy Session survey, 460–461
  four great deaths of therapist's ego, 498
  thinking. See thoughts
  thinking in shades of gray, 478
  emotional reasoning, 314
  third Great Death: angry, blaming self,
    397–404, 499
  thought and feeling empathy, 386
  thoughts
    100% beliefs, 115
    changing thinking changes feelings, 70, 141,
      154, 445–447
    cognitive "click", 32–34
    cognitive content specificity, 176–178
    cognitive distortions. See cognitive distortions
    conditions for emotional change, 69–70
    crushing negative thoughts. See crushing
      negative thoughts
    Daily Mood Journal, 176–181
    discounting the positive. See discounting the
      positive
    jumping to conclusions. See jumping to
      conclusions
    mental filtering. See mental filtering
    negative thoughts, 62–63
    positive reframing. See positive reframing
    shades of gray, 212–215
    strategies for defeating dysfunctional thoughts, 497

time projection, 481
tranquilizers, 451
treatments
    in-vogue treatments, 463–465
    medications. *See* medications
truth-based techniques, 477
*The Twilight Zone*, 163–164

## U

uncovering techniques, 483
unstuck, getting, 56–58
upsetting event, 23, 60, 169–172, 178
    Ben (rejection by Richard), 170
    choosing, 169–171
    fractal psychotherapy, 434
    Karen ("bad mom"), 60
    Maria (postpartum depression), 23
    Mark ("failure" as a father),
        128, 140
    Melanie (fear of being judged), 92–93,
        117, 143
    Sara (afraid of germs), 158–159
urges to use, Temptations Test,
    7–8, 411

## V

Valium, 451
value
    less worthwhile human being, 375–382
    more worthwhile human being, 365–374
Vance, Brandon, 406

videos
    Facebook Live, 471
    Mark ("failure" as a father), 139
    Melanie (fear of being judged), 120
    Sara (afraid of germs), 165
    TED Talk, 470
    trauma victim at four-day intensive, 122
visual imaging techniques, 481–482

## W

what-if technique, 276, 483
*When Panic Attacks* (Burns), 290, 452
*Why Zebras Don't Get Ulcers* (Sapolsky), 440
Willingness Test, 11–12
Wired Together Fire Together (WTFT), 430
workshops, 472–473
world-directed shoulds, 19–20, 316. *See also* should
    statements
worry breaks, 479
worrying, 43. *See also* anxiety
worst, best, average technique, 327, 329–333, 478
    exercises, 330, 333
worthwhile human being
    less worthwhile, 375–382
    more worthwhile, 365–374
WTFT (Wired Together Fire Together), 430

## X–Y–Z

Xanax, 451
yoga, 463
Zeig, Jeffrey, 394